TIBET

LEZLEE BROWN HALPER
STEFAN HALPER

Tibet

An Unfinished Story

OXFORD
UNIVERSITY PRESS

OXFORD

UNIVERSITY PRESS

Oxford University Press, Inc., publishes works that further
Oxford University's objective of excellence
in research, scholarship, and education.

Oxford New York

Auckland   Cape Town   Dar es Salaam   Hong Kong   Karachi
Kuala Lumpur   Madrid   Melbourne   Mexico City   Nairobi
New Delhi   Shanghai   Taipei   Toronto

With offices in

Argentina   Austria   Brazil   Chile   Czech Republic   France   Greece
Guatemala   Hungary   Italy   Japan   Poland   Portugal   Singapore
South Korea   Switzerland   Thailand   Turkey   Ukraine   Vietnam

Copyright © 2014 by Oxford University Press

Published by Oxford University Press, Inc
198 Madison Avenue, New York, New York 10016

Published in the United Kingdom in 2014 by C. Hurst & Co. (Publishers) Ltd.

www.oup.com

Library of Congress Cataloging-in-Publication Data
Halper, Lezlee Brown and Halper, Stefan
Tibet
ISBN 978-0-19-936-836-5 (hardback)

1 3 5 7 9 8 6 4 2

Printed in India
on Acid-Free Paper

For Avril and James Mayall, mentors, companions, and dear friends on our long journey from Cambridge to India, China, Tibet and beyond …

As the People's Liberation Army massed on Tibet's borders, members of the Tibetan National Assembly telegraphed Mao Tse-tung:

Tibet is a sacred place of Buddhism, which does not allow armed forces from foreign countries. This type of bullying activity shall not happen. Tibetan and secular people are very frightened and feel uneasy. We hope you order all border troops not to exercise force towards Tibetan soldiers, and immediately withdraw to their original locations. We pray and look forward to your prompt telegraph reply.[1]

Of course, there was no reply.

[1] 'Telegram to Mao Zedong from the Tibetan National Assembly,' 30 September 1950, Document no. 10500018–06(1), Ministry of Foreign Affairs of the People's Republic of China.

CONTENTS

CONTENTS

PART II

LIST OF ILLUSTRATIONS

(Between pages 202–203)

1. President Roosevelt and Prime Minister Churchill fishing at Shangri-La, the Presidential retreat in the Catoctin Mountains in 1942. © Popperfoto/Getty Images
2. President Roosevelt's letter to the 14th Dalai Lama, Tenzin Gyatso. © Popperfoto/Getty Images
3. The 14th Dalai Lama at the age of nine. © Popperfoto/Getty Images
4. Lowell Thomas letter to Secretary of State, Dean Acheson following his difficult trip to Lhasa in 1949. © Heinrich Harrer, VMZ 400.07.04.002 © Ethnographic Museum of the University of Zurich
5. Tibetan army, 1950. © Heinrich Harrer, VMZ 400.07.04.002 © Ethnographic Museum of the University of Zurich
6. George Patterson, a Scottish missionary arriving in India in March, 1950. He brought news of the PLA's coming invasion of Tibet. © Heinrich Harrer. VMZ 400.06.242 © Ethnographic Museum of the University of Zurich
7. The 284 mile route of the Dalai Lama from Lhasa to Yatung in December 1950. © Heinrich Harrer. VMZ 400.06.242 © Ethnographic Museum of the University of Zurich
8. Khampa tribesmen protecting the Dalai Lama on his journey from Lhasa to Yatung in December 1950. © Heinrich Harrer. VMZ 400.06.242 © Ethnographic Museum of the University of Zurich
9. The Dalai Lama in his sedan chair making the trip from Lhasa to Yatung in December 1950. The chair was so heavy that different teams of servants could only carry him for a few hundred yards at a time. © Heinrich Harrer. VMZ 400.08.01.176 © Ethnographic Museum of the University of Zurich
10. A Top Secret unsigned letter from the American government to the Dalai Lama © ITAR-TASS/Alamy
11. Prime Minister Nehru greeted by huge crowds in Moscow in 1955. The banner in Hindi and Russian says, "Greetings to Prime Minister Nehru! Welcome!". © ITAR-TASS/Alamy

DRAMATIS PERSONAE

Dean Acheson: US Secretary of State under President Truman, 1949–53.

Gompo Tashi Andrugtsang: leader of the resistance effort known as Four Rivers, Six Ranges (Chushi Gangdrug).

Girja Bajpai: Secretary-General of the Indian Ministry of External Affairs, 1947–52.

Frank Bessac: former OSS officer and anthropologist, fled with Douglas Mackiernan from Urumqi in 1949.

Helena Petrovna Blavatsky: co-founded the Theosophical Society of New York in 1875 and was interested in spiritualism and the occult.

George Bogle: sent to Tibet in 1774 by Warren Hastings, the Governor General of India.

Muhammad Ali Bogra: Pakistani Prime Minister, 1953–55.

Chester Bowles: US Ambassador to India, 1950–52.

Edmund Candler: the *Daily Mail* Correspondent, who accompanied Younghusband in 1903–04.

General Chang Ching-wu: appointed as the Commissioner and Administrator of Civil and Military Affairs of Tibet, 1951.

Chou En-lai: Premier, People's Republic of China, 1949–76.

Lord Curzon: Viceroy of India in 1899–1905.

Surkhang Depon: a member of the Tibetan trade delegation to the United States in 1948.

Brooke Dolan and Ilya Tolstoy: OSS officers sent on the first covert mission to Tibet in 1943–44. In 1931 and 1934–1935 Brooke Dolan headed up German expeditions to Tibet to 'explore the roots of the aryan race'.

DRAMATIS PERSONAE

Aghvan Dorjiev: Mongol Buddhist monk, studied in Lhasa in the 1880s and became a friend to the 13ᵗʰ Dalai Lama.

Allen Dulles: Director of the Central Intelligence Agency, 1953–61.

John Foster Dulles: US Secretary of State under President Eisenhower from 1953–1959.

Robert Ford: a British radio operator posted in Tibet from 1945–49.

Qiao Guanhua: vice-minister in the PRC Foreign Ministry, 1950.

Henrich Harrer: German explorer, former prisoner of war and friend of the Dalai Lama.

Chen Jiakang: the Director-General of Asian Affairs in the PRC Foreign Ministry, 1950.

Ngabo Ngawang Jigme: Governor of Kham.

The Kashag: the governing body of Tibet.

The Khampas: Tibetan tribesmen.

Sir Zafrulla Khan: Foreign Minister of Pakistan, 1947–54.

Panchen Lama: the second most authoritative figure in Tibetan Buddhism.

Dzasa Liushar: the Tibetan Foreign Secretary.

Henry Luce: publisher of *Time*, *Life* and *Fortune Magazines*.

Frank Ludlow: head of the British mission in Lhasa, 1942–43.

Bob Lynn and Bill Gibson: CIA operations officers at the American consulate in Calcutta.

Douglas Mackiernan: Vice-Consul in Urumqi; CIA officer.

General George Marshall: President Truman's Secretary of State, 1947–48.

K.P.S. Menon: First Indian Foreign Secretary and Ambassador to China at the time of India's independence.

V.K. Menon: Indian High Commissioner to the UK, Indian Representative to the United Nations; Indian Minister of Defence.

B.N. Mullik: the head of India's Intelligence Bureau.

Jawaharlal Nehru: Indian Prime Minister 1947–64.

Thubten Jigme Norbu: the Dalai Lama's brother.

Ambassador Vijayalakshmi Pandit (Madame Pandit): Prime Minister Nehru's sister and Ambassador to the United States, 1949–1951.

DRAMATIS PERSONAE

Topgyay Pangdatshang: Khampa leader.

K.M. Panikkar: Indian Ambassador to China, 1949–52.

Sardar Vallabhbhai Patel: India's first Deputy Prime Minister.

George Patterson: Scottish missionary and Tibetologist.

Thupten Woyden Phala: Lord Chamberlain to the Dalai Lama.

Hugh Richardson: British diplomat, last head of the British mission in Lhasa from 1946–1950.

Reting Rimpoche: from the Reting Monastery appointed regent after the 13th Dalai Lama died in 1933.

Taktra Rimpoche: a senior, well respected lama who took Reting Rimpoche's place in 1941.

Yapshi Sey: brother-in-law of the Dalai Lama.

Tsepon Shakabpa: Tibet's Finance Minister and head of the Tibetan trade delegation that came to the United States in 1948.

Philip Sprouse: Director of the Office of Chinese Affairs, 1949–50.

Chiang Kai-shek: general, statesman, president of China (1928–31; 1943–49) and of the Republic of China (Taiwan) (1950–75).

Lowell Thomas: American broadcaster.

Gyalo Thondup: the Dalai Lama's brother.

Samuel Turner: continued Bogle's trade discussions in in Tibet in 1783.

Lieutenant Colonel Sir Francis Edward Younghusband: led an expedition into Tibet in 1903–04.

Vasili Zvansov: a White Russian refugee who fled with Douglas Mackiernan from Urumqi in 1949.

ACKNOWLEDGMENTS

Tibet: An Unfinished Story was a ten year project undertaken in Cambridge. In the course of thinking and writing about Tibet, we visited Lhasa and the surrounding area on several occasions; in Washington we spoke with many of those who had helped fashion latter twentieth century US policy toward Tibet; in Beijing we held extended discussions on numerous occasions between 1996 and 2008 with government, academic, religious, and other organizations; and we gained great insight into Indian views from discussions in Delhi, Sikkim, and Dharamsala—the site of the Tibetan government-in-exile.

The late George Patterson, a Christian missionary in Tibet and friend of the Dalai Lama, was particularly inspiring. We were guided and encouraged by the late Jim Lilley, US ambassador to China, Taiwan, and Korea; Brent Scowcroft, White House National Security Advisor 1975–7 and 1989–93; Robert (Bud) McFarlane, White House National Security Advisor 1983–5; and the late Peter Rodman, of the National Security Council and State Department.

Our thanks to Michael Dwyer and the staff at Hurst Publishers, whose enthusiasm and support made it possible to bring the manuscript to publication. We are deeply grateful to Brenda Stones for her excellent editing and preparation of the manuscript.

Our colleagues and friends at Cambridge have provided suggestions, insights, editorial assistance—and endless encouragement. Our thanks to Dr Philip Towle, Department of Politics and International Studies; Mrs Anne Lonsdale, former University Pro-Vice-Chancellor and President of New Hall College, Cambridge; Professor Christopher Hill, Head of the Department of Politics and International Studies; Professor Tarak Barkawi, of the London School of Economics; Professor George Joffe, Department of Politics and International Studies; Dr Arthur Williamson, Department of Politics and International Studies, Sir Richard Dearlove, Master of Pembroke College, Cambridge; Professor Christopher Andrew, Life Fellow and former President, Corpus Christi College, Cambridge; Professor Jonathan Haslam, Corpus Christi College, Cambridge; Dr Karina Urbach, Clare College, Cambridge; Professor Eamon Duffy and Mrs Jennifer Duffy, both of Magdalene College, Cam-

ACKNOWLEDGMENTS

bridge; Dr Tristram Riley-Smith; Dr Barbara Bodenhorn and Dr Hildegard Diemberger of the Department of Social Anthropology, University of Cambridge.

Great support was forthcoming from friends in the United States, the UK, and in India. Special thanks are due to Mackie and Rabbit Christenson, Rosi and Jim Stark, Beth Mendelson, Ben Tyree, Doug Bandow, Gwilym Parry, Al and Audrey Regnery, Kris Srinevassen and Sherrad Javoli.

We thank the Master Lord Rowan Williams and the Fellows of Magdalene College, Cambridge for their stimulating conversation and probing questions. This book would not have been the same without the benefit of Magdalene's High Table.

Finally, friends and family became, over time, part of the 'Tibet story.' With this in mind, we are grateful to our family, including Elizabeth Halper, Marin Halper, Deb Loeser, Faryl Hausman, Ron McCloskey, Lawrence and Karen Hausman, and Finigan and O'Malley Halper for their insight and encouragement.

Lezlee Brown Halper
Stefan Halper
Great Falls, Virginia.

NOTE ON TRANSCRIPTION

We have chosen to use the Wade–Giles system for Chinese names, the system that was used until Pinyin was introduced in the 1950s. We use the spelling Chiang Kai-shek instead of Jiang Jieshi; Formosa instead of Taiwan, when referring to events before 1949; Kuomintang instead of Guomindang; Mao Tse-tung instead of Mao Zedong; and Chou En-lai instead of Zhou Enlai. For place names, we use the Chinese Postal Map system of romanization, for example Sinkiang, Chungking, Nanking; but Peking only for the historical period, and Beijing from the PRC onwards.

PROLOGUE

In the treacherous days following the attack on Pearl Harbor, America awoke to the realities of war. Relentless and aggressive German U-boat attacks along the east coast forced the Secret Service to conclude that the presidential yacht, a favorite source of respite, would have to be set aside until the war's end and be replaced by a retreat away from Washington's wartime tensions and humid summers. Roosevelt's home at Warm Springs, Georgia, was thought too far, as was the Roosevelt family home at Hyde Park, NY.

The National Park Service was asked to find a suitable location not more than two hours from Washington. On 22 April 1942, Park Service and White House officials toured Camp Hi-Catoctin in Maryland's Catoctin Mountains.[1] It was a modest place with a few cabins and a swimming pool. At 1,800 feet it had spectacular mountain and river views and was 10 degrees cooler than Washington. The President visited a week later and, making reference to *Lost Horizon*, James Hilton's famed 1933 novel, remarked 'This is Shangri-La.'[2] He gave final approval on 30 April saying he was 'very much pleased with the area,' especially the cool mountain air.[3]

Roosevelt was clearly influenced by *Lost Horizon*. Five years earlier, on 5 October 1937, when seeking to counter rising 'non-interventionist' sentiment in the country, the President spoke in Chicago proposing a quarantine of aggressor nations, including Japan which was then in Manchuria, Italy which had troops in Ethiopia, and Hitler's Germany which six months later would absorb Austria. It was Friar Perrault in *Lost Horizon* that Roosevelt quoted that day.[4] Drawing on the Friar's vision, he said:

Perhaps we foresee a time when men, exultant in the technique of homicide, will rage so hotly over the world that every precious thing will be in danger, every book and picture and harmony, every treasure garnered through two millenniums, the small, the delicate, the defenseless—all will be lost or wrecked or utterly destroyed.[5]

Having heard the speech on the radio, Hilton wrote to the President the same day to say 'it was a great honor to have been linked with your tireless campaign for the peace and democracy of the world...'[6]

Roosevelt wrote back thanking Hilton for sending 'the delightful' copy of *Lost Horizon*. He said he had enjoyed reading it and wished 'even more people could read it throughout the world.'[7] Roosevelt continued: 'It gave me just the questions I needed when I was preparing my Chicago speech.'[8]

A half century later, Bill Roosevelt, the President's grandson, speaking to the authors, recalled trout fishing with his grandfather in the cool streams running into the Monocacy River from Shangri-La.[9] For Bill and his grandfather, Shangri-La was a place of renewal and discovery ... his own Tibet, remote, obscure, and faraway.

FDR made his first official visit to the newly refurbished retreat on the weekend of 18–20 July 1942. The war, of course, could not be kept away from the Catoctin retreat: while there in August, FDR was plunged into the planning for the battle of Guadalcanal in the Pacific; in November, he was briefed on the invasion of North Africa; and in July 1943 while there he learned of Mussolini's resignation. There was also a succession of visitors, from the head of the Office of Strategic Services (OSS), William Donovan, to Princess Juliana of the Netherlands to Winston Churchill, in May 1943.[10]

Roosevelt's visit in July 1942 holds special relevance for this volume. While he was enjoying Shangri-La that July, the first covert American foray into Tibet was unfolding.[11]

At the request of Bill Donovan and Secretary of State Cordell Hull, Roosevelt wrote to the Dalai Lama on 3 July to ask that he receive two OSS officers, Brooke Dolan and Ilya Tolstoy, whose stated mission was to survey new supply routes following the closure of the Burma Road. Requesting Roosevelt's approval, Hull told the President: 'The letter is addressed to the Dalai Lama in his capacity of religious leader of Tibet, rather than his capacity of secular leader of Tibet, thus avoiding any possible offense to the Chinese government which includes Tibet in the territory of the Republic of China.'[12] Roosevelt's letter to the fourteenth Dalai Lama, while foreshadowing the complexities of future US–China–Tibet relations, expressed for the moment America's friendship and interest in Tibet.[13]

The President's enjoyment of Hilton's magnificent, imaginary *Lost Horizon*, the story of a remote, spiritual kingdom informed by renewal and ageless wisdom, was a notion that would frame Tibet in the Western mind for decades to come.

But at that moment, standing at the center of a world wrought by war, Roosevelt had authored the first official American exchange with Tibet.

He had touched upon the story of two Tibets: one the Tibet of myth, fable, and aspiration, shrouded in an inspirational fantasy, embodied by the Dalai Lama and the famed city of Lhasa; the other the harsh story of Cold War perfidy, a Tibet seduced and eventually abandoned by its friends, buffeted by treacherous political currents and now a part of China. Neither story can be secreted away; both stories have yet to end.

INTRODUCTION

The peripheries of imperial powers are often unstable in the wake of epic events. After World War II former colonies, including India, Pakistan, and Burma, and mountain autocracies in the region, such as Nepal and Bhutan, rose to become independent nations. Tibet did not. Why?

With the end of World War II an isolated and naïve Tibet, unschooled in political–military realities, was caught in a Cold War process over which it had little control.

Unable to decipher the nuanced diplomacy between its two giant neighbors, India and China, or to rely upon Britain debilitated by war, or upon Washington constrained by Cold War realities, Lhasa succumbed to China's invasion in 1950. The hardened People's Liberation Army (PLA) sought nothing less than to deconstruct traditional Tibet, unseat the Dalai Lama, and 'absorb' the vast region—twice the size of France—into the People's Republic.

In the course of a few years Chinese soldiers destroyed hundreds of monasteries and religious sites, imprisoned thousands of Buddhist monks and nuns, criminalized the display of the Dalai Lama's likeness, installed China-friendly curricula in schools, and assumed control of municipal governments across the great expanse of what is called today the Tibet Autonomous Region.

Declassified documents tell the story of Mao's collusion with Stalin to subdue Tibet quickly before its unique character brought sympathy and assistance from the West. Today events make clear that Mao's and Stalin's concerns were not unfounded.

Tibet's enduring myth occupies a special place in the mind of the West and provides it with a unique 'soft power' that invites a harsh judgment of China's civil society and has much to do with how China is seen in the world today. Global abhorrence at Beijing's policies in Tibet and its attempts to vilify the Dalai Lama have compromised China's attempts to gain the stature it needs for global leadership.

The Tibetan myth, and China's dramatic inability to suppress it, has sustained the Tibetan story across the globe. Animated by the remarkable tales of nineteenth-century British adventurers and military expeditions to the Himalayas, and more recently framed by James Hilton's 1933 novel *Lost Horizon*, the idea of Tibet today remains shrouded in the Himalayan fastness, and is for some an inspirational fantasy. For others it provides a morality play about the failure of force to subdue the human spirit. Like the Himalayan mist, the story drifts across 'The Great Wall' defying Beijing's formidable censors.

Anthropologist Christiaan Klieger makes the point that 'the Shangri-La paradigm of Tibet is one of the longest enduring myths in the West.'[1] It is rooted in stories of 'gold-digging ants' dating from 500 BC.[2] Tibet remained a mythic topic during the Middle Ages when the region, explored by clerics seeking to spread Christianity, was thought a refuge of Hieronymus Bosch-like monsters and hideous phantasmagoria. Later, in the eighteenth century, the British came for commerce and then in service of the 'Great Game'. It was this imperial enterprise and the romantic and determined British Army Major Francis Younghusband who, with his fellow officers, later illuminated the drawing rooms of *fin de siècle* London, fashioning the concept and the myth of modern Tibet.

By the mid-nineteenth century 'imagined Tibet' had become a fascination for writers, researchers, explorers, and well-to-do elites embarked upon spiritual odysseys, and as such was seen as a quasi-mystical land of peace, rationality, and self-discovery—although, in fact, only three Europeans actually visited Tibet in the whole of the century. By the mid-twentieth century its imagery became a commodity to be used for every conceivable purpose: just as Franklin Roosevelt named his presidential retreat Shangri-La, so Nazi Reichsführer Heinrich Himmler dispatched eight SS officers to Tibet in 1938 to find the roots of the Aryan race.

Today Tibet stands apart for a variety of reasons, including its contested territory, its government-in-exile, and the remarkable stature of its spiritual leader, the Dalai Lama. In contrast to the Iranian imams, for example, the Dalai Lama exercises great global influence, a reflection of his moral authority, which is rooted in a message of peace. His role as spiritual leader of the Tibetan people remains separate from the Tibet government-in-exile. The acceptance of his message in Tibet and many parts of the West, and the spiritual quality of Tibetan society, is particularly offensive to the Communist Party, which believes that his presence denies their appeal and stands as a rebuke to China's claims. Indeed, China's determination to diminish the Dalai Lama as spiritual leader and global icon, and the methods employed to do so, stand in sharp contrast to the Dalai Lama's message of compromise. The irony for Beijing is that the contrasting values evident in its vigorous assault have enhanced and accelerated Tibet's 'soft power.'

Yet despite the attraction of its myth, Tibet's twentieth-century journey through the world of realpolitik has been less edifying. Here Lhasa proved unable to negotiate the treacherous currents of 'Big Power' politics and Chinese nationalism, where Tibet is thought to be an inextricable part of sovereign China.

It is not a happy story. When Britain granted Indian independence in 1947, Nehru assumed responsibility for Tibet. He proved a difficult interlocutor and an 'uncertain trumpet' on the vital question of Tibet's status and India–China border questions. In 1950 the People's Liberation Army invaded to settle these questions which had vexed the region for centuries. But the subjugation has gone poorly: both in Tibet, where as of this writing over 115 monks have immolated themselves in the past twelve months in protest of Chinese rule; and in global opinion, where China's harsh and excessive methods have helped to keep the story of Tibet alive.

This volume thus presents the story of two Tibets: one, the Tibet of discovery and aspiration; the other, a Tibet buffeted by powerful Cold War currents and treachery, denied the independence gained by others, including Mongolia and Ukraine for example. Four questions present themselves. Firstly, what role did Britain, India, Russia, China, and the US play in all of this? Secondly, is it possible that, in one of history's great ironies, conservative anti-communists forming the China Lobby in Washington prevented the Truman and Eisenhower administrations from assisting Tibetan independence? Thirdly, how is it that China, so adroit in avoiding diplomatic reversals, now draws the derision of the global public for its policies in Tibet, even while it makes so little progress there? And finally, why does Tibet and its story hold such a unique fascination for so many in the vast sweep of global affairs today?

Our story begins in 500 BC.

PART I

1

EARLY BEGINNINGS:
THE WESTERN IMAGINATION

Mythical Tibet has long been an integral part of the story of the West. Back in the fifth century BC, the Greek historian and scholar Herodotus wrote of a high plateau in a mountainous region where there were gold-digging ants; this marked the beginning of the many myths and mysteries that, taken together, are known as the 'Tibet story.'[1] With the travels of Alexander the Great in the fourth century BC, and later, through the dawn of the Middle Ages, myths about Central Asia became common.

In the early part of the fourteenth century, twenty years after Marco Polo travelled to the East, Odoric of Pordenone, a Franciscan friar from northern Italy, traveled to China, India, and Tibet. Hoping to spread Catholicism, Friar Odoric's observations, combined with a liberal dose of fantasy, further fueled visions of the region's mystical qualities. After traveling to what he called the kingdom of Tibet, he wrote 'there is more plenty of bread and wine than in any other part of the whole world.'[2] Odoric continued to fuel the other-worldliness of Tibet, writing in his diary that he saw a woman who had two teeth as long as a boar's tusk.[3] The friar witnessed a sky burial, and told of Tibetans eating the flesh of the deceased's head and making a drinking cup out of the skull.[4] He wrote: 'Many other vile and abominable things doth the said nation commit, which I meane not to write, because men neither can nor will beleeue, except they should haue the sight of them.'[5]

Missionary expeditions continued to Tibet throughout the seventeenth and eighteenth centuries, but it wasn't until 1774 that the first non-secular mission arrived, marking a turning point in European perceptions of Tibet. Peter Bishop, writing on the myth of Shangri-La, said: 'the encounter between Britain and Tibet in the last quarter of the eighteenth century marked the beginning of something new: the sustained creation of Tibet as an important imaginal landscape for Western cultures.'[6]

TIBET: AN UNFINISHED STORY

British travelers of the eighteenth century

In 1774, a young Scot named George Bogle was sent to Tibet by Warren Hastings, the governor general of India. Bogle was among the first British travelers to the region, and his vivid account of Tibet laid the foundations for later depictions of Shangri-La.

Aware of gold and other valuable minerals there, the East India Company wanted to expand its influence to the north, beyond India, and Governor General Hastings was eager to make contact with the third Panchen Lama, traditionally the second most authoritative figure in Tibetan Buddhism, who resided at Shigatse in western Tibet.[7] The Panchen Lama held great influence in this period, not only in Tibet but also at the Manchu court in Peking, where the British hoped to open diplomatic relations.

Born in Scotland in 1746, Bogle obtained a position with the East India Company in Calcutta. By 1774 he had climbed the ranks to hold three posts simultaneously.[8] It has been written that 'the genius of Warren Hastings is shown in nothing more than in his rare insight in the selection of subordinates,' a point apparently confirmed by his selection of Bogle as the first British envoy to Bhutan and Tibet.[9]

A decisive and organized man, Hastings instructed Bogle to open 'a mutual and equal communication of trade, observe what goods might be manufactured and traded with other countries, and inquire about the people, the form of their government, and the mode of collecting their revenue.'[10] Hastings wanted Bogle to bring back any 'curiosities, whether natural productions, manufactures, paintings, or what else may be acceptable to persons of taste in England.'[11] He also wanted seeds for planting, and specifically asked for rhubarb, ginseng, and walnuts. Hastings remarked that the 'religion and hierarchy' in Tibet is even a curiosity.[12] He had heard that the Dalai Lama was so superior 'that his excrements are sold as charms at a great price.'[13]

In best anthropological fashion, Hastings specifically instructed the Scotsman to:

Keep a diary, inserting whatever passes before your observation which shall be characteristic of the people, the country, the climate, or the road, their manners, customs buildings, cookery … carrying with you a pencil and pocket-book for the purpose of minuting short notes of every facto or remark as it occurs, and putting them in order at your leisure while they are fresh in your memory.[14]

Bogle was also asked to obtain insight into the Tibetan practice of polyandry. Hastings wrote: 'I wish to know if this practice obtains in all the ranks of society, and whether those husbands who all have intercourse with one woman have not likewise other women that are their wives, with whom likewise they hold an intercourse in common.'[15]

Of course, even the intensely thorough Hastings failed to prepare Bogle for the truly arresting moments ahead. For as Bogle descended to the small town of Phari, he saw a group of monks laboring to carry a body up the mountainside to perform a sky burial. Bogle, to his horror, saw 'eagles, hawks, ravens, and other carnivorous birds were soaring about in expectation of their prey.'[16]

Eventually Bogle reached the Tashilhunpo Monastery, home to the Panchen Lama in western Tibet. In keeping with his instructions he started a diary, and little escaped his vivid curiosity. His recordings included descriptions of Tibetan customs, mannerisms, religious rites, flora and fauna, and of course the dramatic mountain terrain—all of which helped to fashion the images that formed the myth and later the romance of Tibet in the twentieth century.

Bogle wrote: 'Crowds of people assembled to look at us ... just as people go to look at the lions in the Tower.'[17] He continued: 'These exhibitions were very irksome at first, but I have grown to be accustomed to them.'[18] He added that the Tibetans 'in general are downright and good humored' and 'fond of laughing, dancing, singing and taking snuff.'[19] His room at the monastery of the Panchen Lama was regularly filled with Tibetans, 'from morning til night.'[20] He was the first European they had ever seen. Shortly after his arrival, the Panchen Lama gave Bogle Tibetan clothing: heavier and more suitable for the climate, and which had the added advantage of making him less of a spectacle.

Bogle was pleased with his transformation and recorded in his journal that: 'In this I equipped myself, glad to abandon my European habit, which was both uncomfortable and exposed me to abundance of troublesome curiosity which the Tibetans possess in a degree inferior to no other people.'[21]

Bogle found the Panchen Lama to be intelligent and curious, and the two developed a mutual friendship.[22] Their discussions were wide-ranging, from science to religion to trade and culture. During his stay with the Panchen Lama, Bogle was content; his mind was 'free from care and anxiety.'[23]

When it was time to say goodbye, Bogle, with a heavy heart, expressed his feelings in a poignant letter to his sister Bess:[24]

When I look at the time I have spent among these Hills it appears like a fairy dream. The novelty of the Scenes and the People I have met with, and the novelty of the Life I have led, seems a perfect Illusion. Although my Days have been spent without Business or Amusement, they have passed on without Care or Uneasiness, and I may set this down as the most peaceful period of my Life. It is now almost over, and I am about to return to the Hurry and bustle of Calcutta.[25]

Bogle's farewell note to the Panchen Lama was quoted more than a century later by Sir Francis Younghusband, the British commander who later opened Lhasa to the West. Bogle wrote:

Farewell, ye honest and simple People! May ye long enjoy that Happiness which is denied to more polished nations; and while they are engaged in the endless pursuits of Avarice and Ambition, defended by your barren mountains, may ye continue to live in peace and contentment, and know no wants but those of nature.[26]

Bogle's enchantment with this untouched land spoke to future writers, most notably James Hilton, who nearly two centuries later would draw upon these qualities in fashioning the mythical Shangri-La.

His observations, carefully noted in his journals and diaries, became a point of departure for European knowledge of Tibet. It is through these notes, published over a hundred years after the trip, that readers got a first-hand glimpse of Tibet. Scholar Peter Bishop observed in his book *The Myth of Shangri-La* that 'Bogle's travels to Tibet ... [introduced] ... most of the themes that were to fascinate Europeans ... funerals, dogs, diplomacy, bureaucracy, religion, polyandry, national character, dirt, landscape views, and lamaistic power.'[27]

Upon returning to Calcutta, Bogle recommended to Warren Hastings that the East India Company establish trade relations with the Tibetans. Eager to maintain his Tibetan contacts, Hastings appointed Samuel Turner in 1783 to continue trade discussions. Turner, like Bogle, was struck by the immense mountains which later captured the Western imagination and became an integral part of Tibet's 'other-worldly' character. He wrote:

After dinner our tents were struck, and we advanced on our way over the summit of Soomoonang. Here a long row of little inscribed flags, fixed in rude heaps of stones, were fluttering in the wind. They mark the boundaries of Tibet and Bootan; and are supposed, at the same time, to operate as a charm over the Dewtas, or genii loci, who are paramount here. No mountain is thought to be wholly exempt from their influence; but they are peculiarly given to range in the most elevated regions; where, drenched with dews, and worried by tempestuous weather, they are supposed to deal around them, in ill humour, their most baneful spells, to harass and annoy the traveler.[28]

And Turner also saw the sky burial site on the plains before Phari as he made his way into Tibet. He described what he saw in his journal:

We descended, by an easy declivity, towards the plain of Phari; and as we proceeded, the first object viewed upon it, from the road, was a low hill, rising abruptly from a dead flat, and crowned with a square stone building, dedicated, as I was told, to funeral ceremonies. According to the custom of Tibet, which, in this respect, is in direct opposition to the practice of almost all other nations, instead of that pious attention which is shewn to the remains of the dead, in the preservation of their bodies from pollution, by depositing them in the ground, they are here exposed, after their decease, like the Persees of India, in the open air, and left to be devoured by ravens, kites, and other carnivorous birds. In the more populous parts, dogs also come in for a share of the prey, and regularly attend the consummation of the last obsequies.[29]

Tibetan spirituality, encompassed by prayer flags, the Himalayas, and sky burials, all later became emblematic of Shangri-La. Bishop later wrote that while Tibet was 'by no means the sacred landscape it later became in Western fantasies, the moment of entry for Bogle and Turner was replete with vivid symbolism.'[30] While neither Bogle nor Turner were able to bring back a tangible trade agreement for the British, 'Turner brought back something else which was to prove far more durable than material goods: an idea, a fantasy, a tale of the marvelous.'[31]

After Hastings resigned in 1784 (he was impeached for corruption but later vindicated), formal communications between the British and Tibet became uneven, until Sir Francis Younghusband's expedition in 1904 made them a priority again.[32]

Into the nineteenth century

Meanwhile, informal links remained. In 1811 a British adventurer, Thomas Manning, reached Lhasa and stayed for four months. Manning had 'no recognized position or official position'—he traveled in the guise of a medical practitioner.[33] Manning was an 'avowed Sinophile,' not particularly interested in traveling to Tibet but rather using the journey as a way to reach Peking.[34]

Manning's very detailed diary was first printed in 1876 and recounted an arduous trip. His daily notations reveal that he was neither as seduced by nor as enamored of his physical surroundings as were his predecessors, Bogle and Turner. He chronicled the misery of his accommodations: the dirt, grease, and smoke of the rooms; in one place the smoke was so thick he could barely see.[35] The cold and the filth forced him to sleep in his clothes. On one particularly bad night, in a room so tiny he could barely move about, he wrote that 'the smoke was so thick that the slightest exertion made me breath quick and almost suffocated me, where all was dirt and dust, was so painful to think of, so I often lay in my clothes…'[36] With his hands and face stained from smoke, he eventually slept without a fire in freezing temperatures.[37]

Adding further misery were hoards of biting insects and noisy rats; a good night's sleep was elusive.[38] Rounding out the journey was his 'good-for-nothing horse': Manning found the animal to be vicious and uncontrollable, and prone to running off.[39] (He reports being bitten and kicked when he tried to lengthen the stirrups.)[40]

While Manning's journey could have been more pleasant, he was greatly impressed with the young Dalai Lama. He arrived at the Potala Palace on 17 December 1811 and was blessed by the ninth Dalai Lama, who was at the time just nine years old.[41] Manning wrote that the young Lama had the 'unaffected manners of a well-educated princely child' and, commenting on the meeting, said: 'I was extremely affected by this interview with the Lama [and] could have wept through strangeness of sensation.'[42]

By the time Manning arrived in Lhasa, the city had become important as a commercial center, the distillation of real and symbolic Tibetan power, and as the remote and fabled redoubt of the Dalai Lama.[43] Armed with this new awareness, the British became obsessed with Lhasa—a passion that would span the next two hundred years. But it wasn't just the British who were obsessed by Lhasa; it was the Tibetans as well. While the British saw Lhasa as critical to their interests in the region, the Tibetans strove to maintain Lhasa's isolation in order to preserve their religious integrity. Yet, myth, rumor, and conversation in the drawing rooms of Europe now pushed Lhasa along to 'take its place alongside Mecca and the source of the Nile as one of the fabled places.'[44]

It would be some thirty-five years before other Europeans would reach the capital. Manning and two missionaries were the only Europeans to see Lhasa in the whole of the nineteenth century.

The latter nineteenth century—forming the Tibetan ideal

In 1846 the French Lazarist missionaries Évariste Régis Huc and Joseph Gabet, disguised as lamas, succeeded in entering Lhasa. Unfortunately they were refused permission to stay. The tale of their journey was successfully published in Paris in 1851, and editions were subsequently published in German and French.

By the latter part of the nineteenth century, an idealized Tibet—a land shrouded in myth and spirituality, hidden among the high Himalayan peaks—had begun to form.

Indeed Tibet was now in the minds of many. Tibet had come into Whitehall's sphere by the late 1870s: in concrete terms the British wanted to open Tibet and establish a trade route linking India with China and Central Asia. But while the British were focused on trade routes, for others Tibet had become the place where every kind of fantasy could be projected and played out by travelers, writers, and just about anyone with an imagination. Just as occult writer Madame Helena Petrovna Blavatsky insisted that the Mahatmas she had met in Tibet had telepathic powers and left their bodies to travel, the British announced that they had obtained permission from the Chinese to send an exploratory mission to Tibet. Thus, as the century drew to a close, Tibet provided a canvas reflecting both its compelling story and the real world of Britain's geopolitical and commercial ambitions.

Helena Petrovna Blavatsky's writing fanned the already glowing embers of Tibet's mystery, rendering the Himalayan redoubt even more exotic. She co-founded the Theosophical Society of New York in 1875, and was interested in spirituality, the occult, and Asian and Egyptian religions; she and her partner Henry Steel Olcott removed any doubt about the direction of their lives, naming their Manhattan apartment 'The Lamasery.'[45]

Blavatsky claimed to have lived in Tibet, where she had met spiritual masters with whom she was in regular contact through telepathy, visions, and dreams.[46] Although her 'travels' to Tibet were later proven bogus, indeed part of her own fantasy, her diva-like status, her social circle, and her writing added a dimension—perhaps an unwanted one—to Tibet's growing cachet. It has been suggested that Blavatsky's relationship with 'these spiritual masters' capitalized on and compounded Tibet's mystery, and at the same time enhanced Blavatsky's own presentation.[47] Blavatsky's writing, particularly *The Secret Doctrine*, became a favorite work for later writers on Tibet; her use of the word 'Shambhala' is thought to have inspired James Hilton's use of 'Shangri-La' in *Lost Horizon*.

Rudyard Kipling, also popular at the time, was quite another matter. He formed visions of India and Tibet's mysteries for a generation of English-speaking children at the turn of the century. As the nineteenth century came to a close, Kipling's widely-read novel *Kim*, set in British India about an Irish orphan and his friend, a Tibetan lama, became widely popular—a classic for British children on India. *Kim* was heavily advertised after Colonel Francis Younghusband's mission to Tibet as a 'most important novel … which gives a most concise idea of the relationship between Tibet and India.'[48] In 1905 the *New York Times Saturday Review* called the novel 'A great book, the masterpiece of its author … one of the few novels that have enriched both literature and life.'[49] Set against the background of the Great Game, the book brings to life imperial India while exploring a unique and reassuringly naïve British–Tibetan friendship between Kim and his beloved Lama who he called 'Tesho'.

The twentieth century

As the twentieth century unfolded, Tibetan exploration began in earnest with official and semi-official expeditions to the Tibetan region and Central Asia by Russia, France, Britain, Sweden, and the United States.[50] Lhasa was the prize: the city that had not been discovered, the blank space on maps of the world. 'Tibet was not just *any* place; it wasn't just one among many within scope of Western imagination, [it was] *the* place.'[51]

It was for the *fin de siècle* what Tahiti and China had been for the eighteenth century, what the Arctic was for the early-to-mid-nineteenth century and the source of the Nile for the late nineteenth century. The acclaim given to explorers of Tibet and Central Asia was exception; it was as if Tibet touched some fundamental surface of the era's imagination.[52]

If George Bogle was the beginning of the British experience in Tibet, then Sir Francis Younghusband—in service to Victorian England and her imperial ambitions—was the end.[53] For the British, as Younghusband noted, the mission in Tibet was the culmination of a journey that spanned 137 years.[54] For Younghusband, what began as part of the Great Game, became a life-changing spiritual quest that remained with him until he died.[55]

13

2

SIR FRANCIS YOUNGHUSBAND

SOLDIER, VISIONARY, ROMANTIC

By the time Colonel Francis Younghusband readied his men, Tibet had captured the imagination of British society from London to Oxbridge: it was the expedition of choice for well-to-do young men, writers, and adventurers. Perceval Landon combined these attributes and was something of an expert on the continuing quests to Lhasa.[1] Landon joined Colonel Francis Younghusband on his expedition to Lhasa in 1903–4 as 'Special correspondent for the *Times* of London.'

The problem facing the British at the *fin de siècle* in dealing with Tibet was how to overcome Lhasa's refusal to permit British entry. Edmund Candler, the *Daily Mail* correspondent who also accompanied Younghusband, spoke for many in Whitehall. To describe the dilemma facing the British, Candler used the analogy of a 'big boy at school who submits to the attacks of a precocious youngster rather than incur the imputation of a bully.' He wrote: 'At last the situation becomes intolerable, and the big boy, bully if you will, turns on the youth and administers the deserved thrashing. There is naturally a good deal of remonstrance from spectators who have not observed the by-play which led to the encounter.'[2]

The confrontation tested not only British and Tibetan determination, but it was now seen by London as part of the Great Game—a test of wills between the British Empire and the Russians. In December of 1893, following a series of indecisive engagements along the Sikkim border, the British signed a trade agreement with the Chinese which allowed them to establish a trade mart at Yatung in Tibet, just across the border with Sikkim, which had by then become a British protectorate.

Unfortunately the Tibetans were not consulted about a British trade establishment within their borders and rejected China's presumption of authority to conclude treaties on their behalf. Lhasa further asserted that Sikkim was subject to Tibetan rule and pointedly repudiated the British–Chinese agreement.[3]

This was the situation when Lord Curzon assumed the post of Viceroy of India in 1899; and it was the beginning of a long and protracted battle of wills that culminated with the Younghusband expedition in 1904. Curzon actively pursued the opening of a trade route from India to Tibet. He also brought to the office an ongoing concern about Russian ambitions, having written some ten years earlier in his book *Russia in Central Asia in 1889 and the Anglo-Russian Question*:

Whatever be Russia's designs upon India, whether they be serious and inimical or fictional or imaginary or fantastic, I hold that the first duty of English statesmen is to render any hostile intentions, to see that our own position is secure, and our frontier impregnable, and so to guard what is without doubt the noblest trophy of British genius, and the most splendid appendage of the Imperial Crown.[4]

Curzon wrote to the thirteenth Dalai Lama on several occasions in the hope of establishing relations, but his letters were returned unopened. Moreover, it became clear that the Chinese could not compel the Tibetans to acquiesce to British demands. Curzon said in parliament on 13 April 1904: 'We regard the so-called suzerainty of China over Tibet as a constitutional fiction, a political affectation.'[5]

When the Viceroy discovered that a Mongol Buddhist monk (known as a Buriat Lama), Agvan Dorjiev, had befriended the Dalai Lama in Lhasa, Curzon's longstanding suspicions about Russian designs were reawakened. Recalling that Dorjiev had been the Dalai Lama's ambassador to St Petersburg, and aware that Russian 'explorers' were in Tibet and possibly reporting their findings to Moscow, Curzon now concluded that Russia was actively seeking to extend its influence into Tibet.[6] Confronted with the prospect that the Czar might indeed have imperial aspirations in Tibet, which of course bounded 'the jewel of the British Empire' to its south, Curzon wasted no time in assembling men for a mission to Lhasa. Curzon was determined 'to come to an understanding with these turbulent children,' wrote Landon, the London *Times* correspondent.[7]

In June 1903, under the leadership of Colonel Francis Younghusband, the expedition was prepared. Younghusband was an officer in the Indian Political Service with extensive experience in Asia. A minor legend, he had travelled the remote valleys of the Wakhan Corridor in Afghanistan to the east and across the Gobi Desert. Moreover, his excitement at leading the mission was evident in a personal letter to his father. Younghusband wrote that he was going to Tibet in charge of a very 'important mission,' and a few weeks later told his father that 'this is really magnificent business that I have dropped in for.'[8] Both Younghusband and Curzon saw the mission in epic terms, hoping the expedition would be seen to have the significance of Sir John Malcolm's mission to Persia in 1799 or Sir Alexander Burnes' mission to Kabul in 1837.[9]

In the letter to his father of 21 May 1903, Younghusband plainly stated his objectives: 'I have to put our trade relations with Tibet upon a proper footing; and I have to settle the boundary between us. What has brought matters to this head is that the Russians have concluded, or tried to conclude, a secret treaty with Tibet...'[10] Yet Tibet remained more than boundaries, trade routes, and the Russian threat; Tibet was, as Perceval Landon pointed out, 'the last country to be discovered by the civilized world' and it had a cachet, a mystery.[11]

Younghusband had read extensively about the travels of George Bogle and of Turner. He remembered well Bogle's poignant farewell speech to his Tibetan hosts, and also that the first British traveler to Tibet had had 'warm-hearted and affectionate feelings' for the Tibetans.[12] But the romance of Tibet did little to ease the unusual hardships—the altitude, the terrible cold, and the rough terrain—confronting Younghusband when he and his men left Sikkim in July 1903.

At Khamba Jong, just over the border, they remained encamped for four months, forbidden by the Tibetans to proceed further. The Tibetans refused negotiations, and indeed all contact, shutting themselves up in their fort. The only man who could speak Tibetan, Captain Fredrick O'Connor, summed up their position thus:

We cannot accept letters; we cannot write letters; we cannot let you into our zone; we cannot let you travel; we cannot discuss matters because this is not the proper place; go back to Giogong and send away all your soldiers and we will come to an agreement.[13]

The force now consisted of a large army of Sikhs, Gurkhas, the Royal Artillery, the No. 7 Mountain Battery, a Maxim gun detachment of the Norfolk Regiment, field hospitals, telegraph, postal, survey detachments, along with thousands of camp followers, porters, yaks and mules and other animals.[14] In November, as Younghusband's escort was increased, they began their trek further inland, determined to reach Lhasa by force if necessary.[15]

They arrived at Phari Jong in December and then proceeded to Tuna at an elevation of 15,300 feet, where they would spend the winter. Tuna, an isolated hamlet on the Tibetan plateau, was host to Asia's coldest winds, with temperatures often 25 degrees Fahrenheit below zero. It was said that 'a more miserable place to winter than Tuna cannot be imagined.'[16] Often, that winter, the ink in Candler's pen was frozen and his hand too numb to write.[17] The men found their breath frozen outside their mouths after awakening in the morning, a cup of tea would be frozen in a minute's time, the cup froze on the saucer if one wasn't quick enough, and the rifle oil was constantly freezing over.[18] One soldier had the poor judgment to put his teeth into a tumbler of water, only to find them frozen solid in the morning, the dentures looking like a 'quail in aspic.'[19]

Throughout his stay at Tuna, Younghusband received Tibetan envoys with messages imploring the British to go no further. As negotiations had come to a standstill, it became clear to Younghusband that his entry into Lhasa would not be a peaceful one.[20] The Tibetans underscored this point by building a stone wall across the road to Guru, the only route to Lhasa…and making camp on the other side.

Younghusband concluded that he had no choice but to move forward, so dispatched squads of Gurkhas and Sikhs to remove the Tibetans who in effect were surrounding his forces. Younghusband sent Captain O'Connor to announce to the Tibetans at the wall that they would be disarmed.[21] But a tugging match ensued. When a Tibetan 'threw' himself on one of the Sepoys, shots were fired and a melee broke out.[22] The Tibetans, with swords and black-powder muzzle-loading rifles, were no match for Britain's modernized forces.[23] Sadly, the Tibetans proceeded with the belief that the Dalai Lama's blessing would protect them from British arms. In the course of the ensuing battle some 600–700 Tibetans were killed. Candler, was one of the British wounded; his hand was later amputated. As his wounds were being treated on the battlefield, he saw to his astonishment that amidst the gunfire the Tibetans were just walking away. He wrote:

Why, in the name of all their *Bodhisats* and *Munis*, did they not run? There was cover behind a bend in the hill a few hundred yards distant, and they were exposed to a devastating hail of bullets from the Maxims and rifles, that seemed to mow down every third or fourth man. Yet they walked![24]

It was, certainly in the telling, a slaughter. The Tibetans, in their first true confrontation with a modern military power, were eviscerated; their charms and prayers and mantras had failed them.[25]

In April 1904, with snow still on the ground, Younghusband's army began finally to move towards the town of Gyantse. The men remained there until mid-July and then began the journey to Lhasa.

Contrary to Curzon's suspicions, there were no Russians to be seen when Younghusband finally arrived in Lhasa on 2 August 1904. The expedition's officers proceeded to negotiate a treaty with the Regent, Ganden Tri Rinpoche (Younghusband called him the Ti Rimpoche), who had been left in charge as the thirteenth Dalai Lama had fled to safety in Mongolia.[26]

In the end, the Younghusband mission not only opened up the trade route between British India and Tibet, but it reminded the Manchu of their limited influence in Tibet, which in time led them to impose greater control over Tibetan institutions, including the government and the monasteries.

The treaty signed by Younghusband and the Tibetan lamas in Lhasa enabled the British to establish trade marts in Gyantse, Yatung, and Gartok. But the mission was not without controversy; not all at Whitehall were pleased with results. In his own words, Younghusband was acutely aware that some in the House of Commons called his mission 'a folly and a waste of money,' an 'ignoble little raid.' They said it was 'wicked' to enter Lhasa forcibly, and had in the end 'lowered' British prestige.[27]

Certainly the Younghusband expedition provided the British and Western publics—who were hungry for stories, anecdotes, insights, and photographs about this closed kingdom—with much new material. For Francis Younghusband, who was later knighted, the expedition had profoundly impacted the direction of his spiritual life.

It was not widely known that while in Tibet Younghusband had pursued a spiritual journey that began years earlier. Captain Frederick O'Connor observed in his expedition memoir that even in the frigid temperatures of the winter on the Tuna plateau, with fierce winds and blizzards, Younghusband 'could be seen every morning after breakfast clad in his thick Jaeger coat with a book under his arm, making his way to a little heap of rocks near-by, where he ensconced himself in a sheltered corner and studied his favorite philosophic or religious works.'[28]

Younghusband, like George Bogle and later Rudyard Kipling's Kim, became connected to his lama, the Ti Rimpoche, finding him humorous and benevolent.[29] The Ti Rimpoche gave Younghusband a gift of the 'image of Buddha' that he said had brought peace for the High Lama; he hoped that the Colonel would look at the image and 'think kindly of Tibet.'[30] Younghusband was touched and wrote: 'he was full of kindliness, and at that moment more nearly approached Kipling's lama in *Kim* than any other Tibetan I met.'[31] Younghusband felt himself a part of something bigger. Realizing his own spiritual quest, he wrote that 'he felt like taking a part in a religious ceremony'; he was glad to part with the lama 'as friends, man with man.'[32]

When the men returned to camp to prepare to leave Lhasa, Younghusband went off into the mountains alone and wrote that he 'gave myself up to all the emotions of this eventful time.'[33] And it is here in the mountains that he had an epiphany which, it appeared, changed his life:

My task was over and every anxiety was passed. The scenery was in sympathy with my feelings; the unclouded sky a heavenly blue; the mountains softly merging into violet; and, as I now looked towards the mysterious purpley haze in which the sacred city was once more wrapped, I no longer had cause to dread the hatred it might hide. From it came only the echo of the Lama's words of peace. And with all the warmth still on me of that impressive farewell message, and bathed in the insinuating influences of the dreamy autumn evening, I was insensibly suffused with an almost intoxicating sense of elation and good-will. This exhilaration of the moment grew and grew till it thrilled through me with overpowering intensity. Never again could I think evil, or ever again be at enmity with any man. All nature and all humanity were bathed in a rosy glowing radiancy; and life for the future seemed naught but buoyancy and light. Such experiences are only too rare, and they but too soon become blurred in the actualities of daily intercourse and practical existence. Yet it is these few fleeting moments which are reality. In these only we see real life. The rest is ephemeral, the unsubstantial. And that single hour on leaving Lhasa was worth all the rest of a lifetime.

George Seaver, in his biography of Younghusband, wrote:

[Younghusband's] experience of life up to the forties had been intensive, and his adventures—geographical, military, political—had been unique. Interpenetrating and irradiating them all had been his deep religious faith, and now, as the crown and culmination of them all, came that spiritual experience on the mountainside overlooking Lhasa, compared with which all else was but as dust in the balance.[34]

When Younghusband returned to England he lectured on spirituality and talked about his experience in Tibet. He called his epiphany the 'greatest experience in life'; 'in those moments we really live.'[35] 'These experiences,' he told rapt audiences, 'are only too rare—[yet] it is in those fleeting moments that God is made real to us.'[36] When Sir Francis died, his daughter had an engraved relief map of Lhasa made on his tombstone. She placed the gift from his Tibetan lama, the Buddha, on the lid of his coffin.[37]

It seems likely that James Hilton's Shangri-La (discussed below) was influenced by Francis Younghusband's journey to Tibet, his diaries, and his later spirituality. The vivid account of his journey and epiphany were detailed in his book *India and Tibet*, published in 1910. Younghusband's obituary of 2 August 1942 in the *New York Times* observed that Younghusand resembled Hilton's hero. The *Times* said: 'If, as James Hilton strongly suggested in *Lost Horizon*, Shangri-La is somewhere in Tibet rather than merely somewhere—anywhere—suitable for a point of origin for bombing raids on Japan, then Sir Francis probably came closer than anyone else to being Hugh Conway.'[38] Regardless of how one sees the connection, Younghusband's expedition and the elegant account of his personal journey clearly influenced the writers of the time and helped to frame perceptions going forward.

3

BRITISH AND NAZI VERSIONS
OF TIBET

After the Younghusband excursion, the British had a permanent presence in Tibet, providing the world with a window into this mysterious land. As the twentieth century unfolded, a distinctive image of Tibet was constructed that would inform Western intellectual and spiritual life in the century ahead.[1]

Yet this 'constructed image' did not proceed unchallenged—and the Younghusband mission provides a good example. Just as the British had consciously crafted an image of Tibet that found steady acceptance in the West, so the Chinese communists and the Kuomintang challenged that portrayal of Tibet. In the retelling, Chinese communist sources in particular contend that resistance to the British—the Younghusband mission in particular—arose because the Tibetans were loyal to the Qing dynasty in Peking, not because they sought to curtail the British entry into Tibet. Presenting Younghusband as a marauder and a bandit, his mission is seen as an episode in the 'Century of Humiliation' in which British intentions were not simply to open trade marts but to annex Tibet—and eventually China.[2]

Still, despite this contest of narratives, the Tibet story has remained a largely British creation. The Younghusband expedition to Lhasa had 'unveiled the last mystery of the East.'[3] Candler correctly noted that there were 'no more forbidden cities which men have not mapped and photographed.'[4] But writing in 1905, he was incorrect when he said:

[F]rom now on there are no real mysteries, no unknown land of dreams, where they may still be genii and mahatmas and bottle-imps, that kind of literature will be tolerated no longer. Children will be skeptical and matter-or-fact and disillusioned, and there will be no sale for fairy-stories any more.[5]

Writing over a hundred years ago, Candler could not have imagined that Tibet would still capture the world's imagination for centuries to come. Once the forbidden land was penetrated and British military planners were more comfortable with what was thought a strategically important region, it was the public's turn to absorb all things Tibetan, as historian Alex McKay described:[6] 'After 1910, the British began to describe Tibetan government and society as decent, virtuous, and of value to the world at large—generally the sort of image that we might have expected if the Tibetans had hired a modern American public relations firm!'[7]

Thus, images of Tibet were fashioned and told by the British officers who were stationed there. Many of these men had the same education and were from families with a tradition of 'imperial service.'[8] They had a collective mentality and, as McKay noted, their first duty was to the government of India and its policies.[9] To that end, their views were positive, their reports did not address the inherent problems of a class system in which many were serfs, but rather portrayed Tibet and the Tibetan people on the whole as a happy contented people. A Western predisposition to clothe Tibet in mystery made it that much easier for the British to present Tibet as a Shangri-La.

The British sought to control the images, perceptions and news flow that came out of Tibet. And for the most part, they were successful. Visitors, for example, were required to have a permit from the political officer in Sikkim; and while many did journey to the India–Tibet border town of Yatung, travel into the Tibetan heartland was much more difficult.[10] The Tibetans, of course, had no problem with this policy. Wishing to keep Tibet closed to the outside world, they viewed all strangers with suspicion.

The 'unified voice' of the British officers became a 'powerful weapon' and also the 'dominant one because it deliberately suppressed alternative perspectives.'[11] Over time they published books about their time in Tibet but, with a public audience in mind, portraying Tibet as an exotic land accented by sky burials, oracles in trances, and the sheer splendor of the Himalayas.

Tibetan imagery as a political instrument

Above all, the British wanted a compliant, friendly, and cohesive buffer state at their border, so constructing a carefully crafted image of their Tibetan neighbor was important. While Whitehall did not recognize Tibet as an independent and sovereign nation in the modern nation-state model, it advised the Tibetans to adopt their own flag, currency, and stamps.

In large part to benefit India, the British supported Tibetan modernization and infrastructure development. They believed that 'national unity was essential to a strong Tibet' and sought to include this notion in what they termed 'the core image' of Tibet.[12] By the time Hugh Richardson, the last British head of mission, left Lhasa in 1949, the Tibetans enjoyed an undisputed positive image in Britain, where a unified, evolving Tibet, positively disposed towards British India, was thought an advantage to London. A (cheerleading) Richardson wrote:

Western visitors so diverse in personality and objective as the Jesuit Fathers Francisco d'Azvedo in the seventeenth century and Ippolito Desideri in the eighteenth, the British emissaries George Bogle and Samuel Turner also in the eighteenth century, the India Civil Servant Sir Charles Bell and the mountaineer and explorer Heinrich Harrer in the twentieth century, all agree in describing the Tibetans as kind, gentle, honest open and cheerful.[13]

The British may take some credit for transforming Tibet's mystical and spiritual imagery into a narrative that has provided the mountain kingdom with a powerful weapon. Historian Alex McKay correctly points out that Tibet's 'mystical image was, and indeed is, a weapon against which China has no effective response.'[14]

James Hilton's Lost Horizon

As British images of Tibet melded into a wider Western view in the early twentieth century, James Hilton brought out the book *Lost Horizon* in 1933. It was followed in 1937 by a movie directed by the legendary Frank Capra. Inspired, it seems, by Helena Blavatsky's Shambhala writings and by Joseph Rock, an Austrian ethnologist and botanist, whose *National Geographic* magazine articles described his travels in China and Tibet, Hilton described a place devoted to the pursuit of wisdom and meditation while 'conserving the frail elegancies of a dying age': 'one can live forever in a place called Shangri-La.'[15] According to Bishop:

Hilton's 1933 vision of Shangri-La joined Blavatsky's mahatmas and Kipling's lama in *Kim* as one of the greatest mythologizing books about Tibet. It was for twentieth-century Tibet what the other two were for *fin-de-siècle* Tibet. It gathered the threads of fantasy, shaped them and articulated them.[16]

Hilton had seen the ravages of World War I and the economic depression of the late 1920s and 30s, and Shangri-La was his refuge from the modern world. After the book came out, many called him an 'escapist'; and although he strongly objected to this label, he told a *New York Times* reporter that 'the idea for *Lost Horizon* was germinated out of anxiety over the European situation and a desire to stage a conception of the world as far removed from this sort of thing as possible.'[17]

In *Lost Horizon*, the main character, Hugh Conway, is a rather disillusioned consular officer in His Majesty's Service, fatigued by war. Conway, who was consul in Baskul (near Peshawar), and three others—a woman missionary, Roberta Brinklow; a US citizen, Henry Barnard; and Vice-Consul Captain Charles Mallinson—are the last to be evacuated from the war-torn city. They all board a small aircraft expecting to land at Peshawar, but a few days later, after a crash-landing in the High Himalaya, begin a new life in Shangri-La.

Hilton adroitly combined several of Tibet's most arresting images—gold-digging ants, the mysterious High Himalaya, the telepathic powers of the lamas, the promise of eternal youth—in his brilliant depiction of a place called Shangri-La. His book became an international best-seller almost immediately,[18] casting Tibet as Shangri-La in the Western mind, and rendering the name a part of the vernacular.

In the novel, after the initial shock, Hugh Conway was infused with the tranquility of his surroundings, through imagery most likely drawn from Younghusband's experience after his epiphany. Conway felt a deep sensation, 'half mystical, half visual of having reached at last some place that was an end…a finality.'[19] In *Lost Horizon*, the novel unfolds in a place where one may pursue one's thoughts and interests without interference, and without physically aging. The group is told that the inhabitants have found happiness by, among other things, avoiding excess.[20]

Conway is blissfully happy rising each morning to see the soft 'lapis blue of the sky' through his window and the splendor of the snow-covered mountain wall: he 'would not have chosen to be elsewhere on earth—either in Peshawar or Piccadilly.'[21] It was not only the stunning beauty of Shangri-La which drew Conway into a state of supreme contentment: it was also the lamasery's extensive library—books in English, French, German, Russian, and Chinese, the music room, the art collection, space for contemplation, all designed to foster individual intellectual pursuits.

During his regular solitary evening stroll, Conway experienced 'an extraordinary sense of physical and mental settlement. It was perfectly true; he just rather liked being at Shangri-La. Its atmosphere soothed, while its mystery stimulated, and the total sensation was agreeable.'[22] Conway establishes an intimate rapport with the High Lama, cultivating and focusing their lengthy discussions. This, of course, follows the relationship that Bogle, Kim, and Younghusband had established with their lamas. And Conway, like Younghusband, was often overcome with a 'deep spiritual emotion.'[23] While he played Mozart in the music room or sat reading in the library, he felt 'as if Shangri-La were indeed a living essence, distilled from the magic of the ages and miraculously preserved against time and death.'[24] Conway had never in his life been more content or happier than in Shangri-La.

With the novel in wide popular circulation, 'Tibet assumed a new and expanded dimension; it is seen as the cure for an ever-ailing Western civilization, a tonic to restore its spirit.'[25]

Shangri-La expands

With Tibet's image increasingly framed by *Lost Horizon* in social exchange and the mainstream media, a number of books, including comic books, followed. In 1956 Lobsang Rampa, who purported to be a Tibetan lama, published his autobiography, *The Third Eye*. A widely read and popular book, it explored some of the more bizarre and other-worldly aspects of the Tibet phenomenon, selling over half a million copies in the first two years.[26] He maintained that he was able to read people's auras; he cultivated clairvoyant abilities and could 'astral travel'—leaving his earthly body attached by a silver cord.[27]

Of course, it was all a bit much. And indeed, it was discovered just two years after publication that Rampa was in fact the son of an English plumber, named Cyril Henry Hoskin who claimed to have been possessed by a Tibetan lama who had taken over his body. Hoskin who legally changed his name to Rampa, continued the series to write eighteen more books before his death in 1981. The books were best-sellers and are still reprinted and read in several languages today. Hoskin's writing at least gave the Tibet issue a significant profile.[28]

With the Tibet story now uniquely combining the nation's history, the mysteries of Buddhism in the remote Himalayas, and the fantasies of Blavatsky and Hoskin it gained a further place in the mind of the West. A flow of Tibet books appeared, including Lionel Davidson's *The Rose of Tibet*, Junius Podrug's *Frost of Heaven*, and of course George Remi's *Tintin in Tibet*, continuing to the present. Hoskin was not the first to have borrowed from the Theosophists or from the now expanding circle of fantasists and spiritualists, to construct psycho-ethnic theories about the journey of humankind into new realms.

The Nazis

Among the most bizarre aspects of the Tibet story was the attempt by Reichsführer-SS Heinrich Himmler to locate the roots of the Aryan race in Tibet. Nazi theorists dutifully assembled bits and pieces of the Tibetan myth and, together with Blavatsky's claims, endeavored to produce a coherent racial theory.[29] Demonstrated in work largely attributed to Karl Haushofer (1869–1946), a German general, geographer and geopolitician, the Nazis believed that the Tibetans and certain other Pacific-rim peoples, who tended not to marry outside of their ethnic group, held—through their racial purity—the key to unlocking a transcendent energy that revitalized the magical powers they thought were dormant in pure Aryan blood.

Fictional accounts about early German contact with Tibet had grown through the 1920s; meanwhile Haushofer was introduced to Himmler, who was, among other things, considered an authority on racial matters in the Reich. This folded nicely, according to historian Christopher Hale, into his role as a 'patron of science.'[30] 'He believed most conventional wisdom was bogus and that his unique power and perspective in the new Germany provided an opportunity to promulgate new thinking.'[31] He had founded the *Ahnenerbe* or Ancestral Heritage Society in 1935 'to pursue issues of interest to the German people' that were not necessarily accepted or pursued by 'official science.'[32]

While Haushofer's theories were intriguing, they were only some of several ideas drawing Himmler to Tibet. Beyond finding the roots of 'the Aryan race,' Himmler thought Tibet might hold the key to a better understanding of Asian mysticism. He further believed that the right research team in Tibet might be able to advance an alternative pseudo-scientific theory of relativity, developed by Hans Horbigers and called 'Glacial Cosmogony.' The latter was important to Himmler because it was a way to mute the success of Albert Einstein, whose 'Theory of Relativity' then confirmed the Jewish dominance of theoretical physics.

Three separate multi-disciplinary expeditions were assembled that ultimately reached Tibet. The first two (1931 and 1934–5) were headed by the American Brooke Dolan (he would later travel to Tibet with Tolstoy as part of the first American covert expedition to Lhasa) and the German Ernst Schäfer. Schäfer, an accomplished hunter, had a great interest in exploration, especially Tibet, and was interested in zoology; Dolan, a Princeton dropout from a wealthy Philadelphia family, also had an interest in zoology.[33] The two men met in Hanover where Dolan was organizing an international expedition of anthropologists and zoologists to explore Asia; he was backed by the Academy of Natural Sciences in Philadelphia.[34] Both men were 'obsessed' with hunting down the famous giant panda, their 'holy grail'—they considered it their sacred duty to find this 'white bear,' as it was called locally.[35] The expedition made its way from Chengdu in China onwards to Tachienlu and upwards into the dense thickness of the forest of the Wuyaoling Mountains. On 13 May, near the Tibet–China border, their 'determination and ruthless tactics' paid off.[36] Schäfer shot and killed a giant panda; he was photographed afterwards with the panda under his arm and a bird dangling in his hand.[37]

The third exploration to Tibet in 1939 was called the 'German Tibet Expedition,' headed by Ernst Schäfer under the patronage of the Reichsführer-SS Himmler and connected to the *Ahnenerbe*. The mission was known to be Himmler's 'pet project,' a seemingly odd diversion for the director of the Reich's police and security, including the Gestapo apparatus.[38] To ensure the requisite status, the *Ahnenerbe* was located within Himmler's office; its eight academics held SS ranks and wore SS uniforms.[39]

The expedition had a very difficult time getting permission from the British and of course from the reclusive Tibetan government to travel to Lhasa. Hugh Richardson, the British trade agent/Head of Mission in Lhasa, and Sir Basil Gould, the British political officer in Gangtok were both adamantly opposed to a German expedition sponsored by Himmler, the Reichsführer, crossing into Tibet.[40]

Along the way Schäfer was able to film and shoot the 'mysterious bharal' or blue sheep, wolves, wild asses and the 'black mountain ghost,' a sacred goat that was not to be harmed, killed or spoken about; these were just a few of the animals they were able to send back to the museums of the Reich.[41]

After great difficulty, they finally crossed into Tibet at Yatung on Christmas Eve 1938. Over the next few months the members of Himmler's expedition paid courtesy calls on Tibetan ministers and others, distributed Nazi flags and propaganda, and filmed and took photographs of the region. They spent over two months in Lhasa collecting information on culture, religion, agriculture, and literature and received many valuable ethnographic artifacts, including a copy of the '108-volume *Kangyur*, one of the holiest of all Tibetan religious texts.'[42] The group collected three breeds of Tibetan dogs, including a Tibetan mastiff, and the skins of wolves, badgers and other animals. In the end they recorded the measurements of '376 people, mainly Tibetans but also from other ethnic groups, took over two thousand photographs, made casts of the heads, faces, hands and ears of seventeen people' and 'took facial casts of 17 heads.'[43] In addition they collected enormous numbers of seeds, plants, and butterflies, and took 'eighteen thousand metres of 16mm black and white film and coloured film and forty thousand photographs.'[44]

Clearly the group's mission lacked focus, and determining its objectives today remains difficult, if not impossible. Yet the preponderance of information seems to indicate that 'the principal goal of the Schäfer expedition was gathering geophysical, zoological and botanical, ethnological and anthropological material—hence racial studies—data.'[45]

The myth grows

If Tibet held the key to the roots of the Aryan race for the Nazis, for the British it was first about the Great Game, then about frontiers, and then it became a spiritual quest. Curzon's 1906 lecture traced this evolution when he described the British fascination with boundaries, the romance of frontiers, and the manhood fostered by them—like the American West.[46]

Yet, as the twentieth century proceeded, the imagery surrounding Younghusband, Madame Blavatsky, James Hilton, and then Himmler, together with the myth of Shangri-La, filtered through the literature to become a topic of fascination across Europe and America. Where people spoke of adventure and coming of age, the Tibet story assumed a life of its own, becoming a platform for drama, a space separate from everyday events in the West, and a metaphor for discovery.

Jamyang Norbu captures this in his chapter 'Behind the Lost Horizon: De-mystifying Tibet':

The West, whatever its failings, is real; Tibet, however wonderful, is a dream; whether of a long-lost golden age or millenarian fantasy, it is still merely a dream. It is this dreamlike, 'Shangri-La' quality of Tibet, most observed in the medieval flavour of its society and culture and in its strange, esoteric religion, that Westerners find most attractive. From tourists to academics, this is the feature of Tibet that is focused on, to the exclusion of other aspects of Tibetan life or culture, no matter how important they may be to the Tibetans themselves.[47]

And it is this juxtaposition of myth to everyday circumstances that has made Tibet's journey so uniquely complex and difficult. It is the failure to close the gap between the mythologized dream of Tibet referred to by Norbu and the geopolitical reality surrounding Tibet that has freighted the link between Tibet's aspirations and its supporters in the West and has permanently constrained effective policy-making.

We turn now from the centuries-old tales of Tibet's other-worldliness and more recent imagery fashioned by the British, the Theosophists, and the Nazis to Tibet's entry upon the world stage, and its attempt to join the family of nations. Not surprisingly, it is to America that the Dalai Lama turns.

4

STILWELL, THE BURMA HUMP AND THE OSS

The summer of 1942 saw the Allies reeling before the German advance through Europe to the North Sea and the Atlantic coast, and the Japanese thrust into Southeast Asia. General Stilwell had arrived in India after Japan's January 1942 invasion of Burma. Confronted with the challenge of maintaining the supply route to General Chiang Kai-shek's Nationalist forces, he concluded that the DC-3s flying the 'Burma hump' couldn't carry the needed munitions and equipment often or quickly enough.[1] Moreover, the route over the High Himalaya was unreliable due to weather. A land route was essential, and Tibet was at the center of the equation. Little did Stilwell know that he would soon find himself enmeshed in what would become one of the twentieth century's most complex diplomatic conundrums—one with rich historical precedents, sovereign claims and counter-claims extending back over several centuries.

Tensions were already high between China and Tibet over the terms and conditions of road access when Stilwell tabled his proposals. The Chinese Nationalists demanded that the Tibetans allow military equipment and other goods bound for China to transit Tibet. Not wanting any excuse for a Chinese presence in Tibetan territory, the Tibetans refused. They feared that should arrangements go awry, the Chinese army and their 'new' equipment and men might acquire a permanent home on Tibetan roads.[2] As the impasse threatened to invoke a wider dispute, the Chinese appealed to the United States and Britain to help persuade Lhasa. Amidst fears that the Chinese might take military action, Secretary of State Hull requested on 3 July 1942 that the American ambassador in Peking, Clarence E. Gauss, 'discreetly' inquire into the situation.[3]

Meanwhile, the dispute brought to the surface the question that had bedeviled China–Tibet relations for centuries and which continues today. Hull, noting the words 'independence' and 'autonomy' in prior US State Department and White House memoranda on Tibet, wrote that 'it is not clear whether these words are used interchangeably or not.'[4] In fact, George Patterson, a Scottish missionary and Tibet-ologist, later explained to the American government, and subsequently to the authors, that since the Tibetans had been self-ruling in every respect there was no Tibetan word for 'independence.'[5]

Hull had hoped to avoid any misunderstanding surrounding the US position on Tibetan independence and did not wish to offend the Chinese who claimed suzer-ainty over the region. But misunderstandings around the word 'independence' arose in the modern era (with Tibet's first trade mission to the United States in 1948 during the Truman administration) and would continue to plague both Tibetans and American diplomats over the next three decades.

In view of the deteriorating allied position that summer, General Stilwell and allied commanders were determined that hostilities between Tibet and China be avoided at all costs. The British made it clear that they were prepared to 'speak plainly' to the Tibetans.'[6] Using a classic 'carrot and stick' approach set against the backdrop of Tibet's desire for independence, the British agreed to help the Chinese and exert pressure on the Tibetans, if the Chinese 'respect[ed] Tibetan autonomy and refrain[ed] from interfering in Tibet's internal administration.'[7] British officials in Delhi obtained the help of Frank Ludlow, the head of the British mission in Lhasa, in an effort to force the Tibetans to acquiesce under the threat 'that Britain might withdraw its acceptance of Tibet's autonomy.'[8] This was one of Tibet's earliest expo-sures to the 'cut and thrust' of international politics. For while the Tibetans had for centuries enjoyed varying degrees of autonomy and taken responsibility for conduct-ing their own foreign policy after the fall of the Manchu dynasty in 1911, the game of international politics was, for them, *terra incognita*.

1942 was a notable year for Tibet for another reason, however. As mentioned in the prologue, the OSS requested that the State Department seek permission for Ilya Tolstoy, the grandson of the Russian novelist, and Brooke Dolan to enter the rooftop kingdom.[9] The ostensible purpose: to survey a possible supply route from India to China via Tibet to replace the Burma Road that had two months earlier fallen to the Japanese.

Lhasa initially refused the Chinese request to admit Tolstoy and Dolan. Permission for the pair to enter through India was only arranged with the government of India's intervention after much 'backing and forthing' between various diplomatic offices in Peking, Delhi, Lhasa, London, and Washington. Impatient to begin their mission, Tolstoy and Dolan had departed the United States without travel permits, arriving at General Stilwell's Imperial Hotel headquarters in Delhi, carrying only a letter of introduction from President Roosevelt, and waited there for permission to proceed.[10]

Throughout the sweltering Indian summer, the Americans pressed the British for assistance on this matter, and finally, with some reluctance, Frank Ludlow, who headed the British Mission to Lhasa, again used his stick and played on Tibetan fears. Ludlow was a great friend of the Tibetans and highly respected by the Dalai Lama and his government. Speaking with the Tibetan Foreign Minister Surkhang Szasa, he underscored that the Tolstoy/Dolan visit was 'no ordinary' visit and that it would be of great advantage to Tibet's future to let the two Americans proceed.[11] His advice carried weight and the Tibetans reluctantly granted the permits.

Declassified British cables provide a rich picture of this Byzantine process and of their own musings as to what might be afoot. On the one hand, the British were feeling quite pleased about the whole affair, and particularly the implied confirmation of their influence and status. This was evidenced by handwritten marginalia on Ludlow's February 1943 report. There, H. A. F. Rumbold of the India Office in Delhi scribbled:

The fact that Tibetans refused permission for Americans to visit Lhasa when they were approached on the subject through the Chinese Govt, but agreed to the present visit by Tolstoy and Brooke Dolan when approached through us should be a useful corrective to any stories which the Chinese Govt may be retailing to the State Department about Tibet being part of China.[12]

Still, the British were puzzled by the American determination to gain access to Tibet and by their extraordinary secrecy. Ludlow wondered why they had not gone through regular channels.[13] He remarked to his superiors in Delhi that it appeared that the Americans' chief preoccupation was to obtain permission to proceed to China; noting a certain duplicity in the matter, he told Delhi that he would not be associated with their request.[14] In the end it was Tolstoy who persuaded the Tibetans to permit the small party to transit to China. Ludlow concluded that this was hardly an uncomplicated outcome. He wrote:

Now the Tibetan Government are hoping that the United States will support Tibet in her efforts to maintain her freedom and independence. Consequently they were anxious, very anxious indeed, that the President's envoy should have no cause for complaint. But if Tibet had not been fearful of the future, and alarmed at Chinese activities on her eastern borders, Tolstoy and Dolan would never have been permitted to proceed eastwards. They would have been requested very politely, to retrace their footsteps to India.[15]

The government in Lhasa, now a small player in the great power game, had acted to serve its longer-term interests: the Americans might indeed be helpful, should relations with the Chinese further deteriorate.

What is most significant about this episode is that not only did Ludlow pinpoint Tibet's specific expectations regarding Washington but, through instinct, he stumbled upon what would be an ongoing clandestine channel in the US–Tibet relationship.

The Tolstoy/Dolan mission

What was the real purpose of the trip to Lhasa? While many of the files relating to the expedition remain classified, available documents answer some of the British questions about the pair. Tolstoy and Dolan were indeed operating under instructions from Donovan and General Stilwell to proceed to OSS Headquarters in Chungking. In a five-page document in the Personnel File, marked 'Secret—Far East Theatre,' the Tolstoy/Dolan mission is recorded as 'Project FE 2'; the project was one of a number of operations the Americans executed in the Far East between 1942 and 1943.[16] The stated purpose of their trip was a 'reconnaissance mission via India to Tibet ... observing the attitudes of people of Tibet; to secure allies and discover enemies; locate strategic targets and survey the territory as a possible field for future activities.'[17] Clearly, as the British suspected, the pair were not there to examine the prospects for new roads.

A description of the Tolstoy/Dolan mission may also be found in a declassified document entitled 'Psychological Warfare Undertakings.'[18] Apparently the Tolstoy/Dolan mission fell into a category of missions that were to 'conduct, in close cooperation with the Chinese, psychological warfare activities designed to harass the enemy in China and elsewhere in the Far East, including morale and physical subversion and black propaganda.'[19] With specific reference to Tolstoy/Dolan, Donovan's note to Secretary of State Cordell Hull stated that the project was 'most secret' and 'the mission is of strategic importance and we hope it will prove of long term value.'[20]

Journey into Tibet

Tolstoy and Dolan's remarkable visit was America's first official covert foray into Tibet. Their uncertain status, combined with the official military formalities of the time, brought more than a few awkward moments. On arrival at Lhasa, there was such consternation over where and when the American flag should be flown that the British in the end erected a separate flagpole. Then there was the matter of clothing. An official in the Foreign Office in Delhi posed the question to Ludlow in Lhasa: 'As they are US Army officers it is presumed that [it] is desirable for them to travel to Lhasa as such and not as civilians, or should they wear mufti instead of uniform?'[21] But all of this soon passed.

The American pair made much of the lavish Tibetan hospitality.[22] A thrilled Tolstoy was granted an audience with the Dalai Lama to present the President's gifts: a gold watch and silver-framed picture of Roosevelt. The ever-observant Ludlow noted that not only was the Dalai Lama 'greatly impressed' with Captain Tolstoy, he 'positively beamed on him throughout the private audience' and then 'quaintly' enquired about the President's health.[23]

Tolstoy and Dolan quickly became aware of the importance Tibetans accorded to giving and receiving gifts.[24] They kept meticulous notes and compiled an extremely detailed report on the gifts they received and the protocols associated with the process. Commenting on the exchange of silk scarves when arriving at new places, Dolan noted that more modest officials gave 'small strips of plain cheesecloth.'[25] The Tibetans too were impressed with Dolan's knowledge of their culture and ability to speak their language.[26]

The Tibetans were pleased by the US initiative. In response to Roosevelt's open and friendly letter of introduction, the Tibetan Foreign Office responded with gifts and a note saying: 'this is the first time that friendly relations were established between Tibet and the USA.'[27]

By contrast, the pair had not endeared themselves to the British. Ludlow found Tolstoy secretive and wrote that he seemed to be a man 'that trusted nobody,' not even his companion Dolan.[28] Washington also had its complaints about Tolstoy, who seemed to have offended other officers working in the CBI theatre.[29] In a 'Top Secret' declassified memorandum to General Donovan, Colonel John G. Coughlin, a senior OSS officer, wrote that Tolstoy's mission had been 'very embarrassing to OSS in this theatre' and that he had 'annoyed General Stilwell with his secret plans and the Tolstoy way.'[30]

Washington and many of the officers working in the CBI theatre were upset by Tolstoy's offer to the Tibetans of radio equipment and his enthusiastic suggestion that they attend a World Peace Conference to be held in 1944; he had, in a moment of excess, overstepped the bounds of his position.[31]

In the end a road was not built and the dispute over the transport of goods through Tibet fell by the wayside. The Chinese abandoned their plans to build the road, realizing it would take too long and have little impact on the war effort. It was not until the summer of 1949 that the United States would once again receive 'on the ground intelligence' about the closed kingdom.

These early US–Tibet encounters show that official Washington remained cognizant of China's claims to Tibet. The secretary of state reflected the delicacy of the US position in a memorandum to Donovan at the OSS when he said: 'Tibet is, as you know, regarded by the Chinese as a dependency of China, and the Government of the United States has never taken action in contravention or disregard of the Chinese view.'[32] While the Tibetans took these events to be the beginning of an important new friendship, when seen through Washington's gimlet eye, they foreshadowed a coldly realistic Cold War policy.

It was not until a few years later, during the Truman administration, that Washington found itself dealing in earnest with the complexities of Tibet's entrance onto the global stage and its struggle for independence amidst the onset of the Cold War. Truman and his policies are important. They provide a glimpse of how Tibet was perceived by Washington, now positioning to confront the Soviet Union in a conflict that would extend over half a century. And it is within the Truman administration that we find the decision-makers and the policies that influenced Eisenhower and Tibet's way forward in the 1950s, ending with the Dalai Lama's flight from his homeland to India in 1959.

5

TRUMAN 1945–1948

In the first three months of his presidency, Harry Truman was confronted with larger, more difficult, and more far-reaching decisions than almost any president before him.[1] With Japan's surrender in 1945, he had been plunged into what was, to him, the unfamiliar world of foreign affairs and faced nothing less than the challenge of structuring a new global order. Soviet ambitions were of particular concern—perhaps more than he let on.[2] The new president had been alarmed by a top secret OSS report given to Roosevelt on 2 April 1945, ten days before his death. The report ominously warned that after the war the United States would face a danger that rivaled the rise of Japan and Nazi Germany.[3] It predicted: 'Russia will emerge from the present conflict as by far the strongest nation in Europe and Asia—strong enough, if the United States should stand aside, to dominate Europe and at the same time to establish her hegemony over Asia.'[4] Furthermore, the OSS believed that Russia could, in the 'easily foreseeable future,' outrank the US in her military potential.[5] So vivid was the Soviet threat for Truman at the time that in his memoirs he wrote: 'In spite of the turmoil and pressure of critical events during the years I was President, the one purpose that dominated me in everything I thought and did was to prevent a third world war.'[6]

As vice president, Truman had not been included in Roosevelt's inner circle and was clearly at a disadvantage when he suddenly assumed the presidency. In a poignant letter to his wife Bess, Truman wrote, 'He never did talk to me confidentially about the war, or about foreign affairs or what he had in mind for peace after the war.'[7] He had been separated from the White House policy process in several important foreign and domestic areas and was unaware, for example, that the United States was just months away from developing a nuclear weapon.

On the night of his swearing in, just hours after the announcement that Roosevelt had died, Henry Stimson, the secretary of war, approached Truman quietly after the others had left the cabinet room. Stimson asked Truman for a moment to discuss a matter of utmost urgency; he said it 'concerned a new explosive of unbelievable power.'[8]

Some nine months later, the dimensions and implications of the Soviet challenge were brought home when, on 9 February 1946, Washington was stunned by a speech delivered by Premier Joseph Stalin who declared that 'capitalism and communism were incompatible and that another war was inevitable.'[9] Armageddon, it appeared, was now on the table. The Soviet threat had arrived in primary colors. Washington struggled to achieve a measure of strategic clarity in the face of fading imperial systems, the aspiring new powers, and challenges that extended from Western Europe to South Asia and the Far East.

This new reality was memorialized by Churchill at Fulton Missouri in 1946. In remarks that would define the next half century, he said: 'From Stettin in the Baltic to Trieste in the Adriatic, *an iron curtain* has descended across the Continent.' A year later, Harry Truman extended this Anglo-American vision in his Truman Doctrine speech.

To implement these ideals, in July of 1947 the US Congress passed the National Security Act, dramatically altering the administrative structure of US national security policy. The legislation authorized a new National Security Council, the Central Intelligence Agency, a new Department of Defense, and separated the Air Force from the Army. Six months later the era of covert activity began with the passage of NSC 4A, a top-secret addendum that launched a range of peacetime covert action operations.[10] Among them was authorization for the Director of the Central Intelligence Agency to conduct psychological warfare—an arena that would receive great emphasis in the decade ahead. Tibet, which was to assume a growing role in Washington's global anti-communist effort and would provide the platform for future US special operations, was directly impacted by these developments.[11] And it was within this context that the US weighed the question of Tibet's aspiration to sovereignty.

It would soon become clear that Tibet's path forward was freighted with complications and divided intentions, involving the Chinese Nationalists, the politics of Joe McCarthy, and the 'Red Scare.' In one of history's great ironies, anti-communist supporters of the failing Chinese nationalist cause would prevent the US government from supporting Tibetan independence, due to objections by Nationalist China. Moreover, it must be remembered that opinion within the administration was itself deeply divided: Washington was, among other things, drawn by a long tradition in which states have been generally reluctant to support secession; Lincoln, it must be remembered, had regarded it as anarchy.

The Truman Doctrine: clarion call or uncertain trumpet

In March 1947 the president delivered the Truman Doctrine address to Congress, and indeed to listeners around the world, establishing the principles and parameters of US Cold War foreign policy. His affirmation that America stood in support of 'free peoples resisting attempted subjugation by armed minorities or by outside pressure' proved to have uneven application, however, with Tibet eventually providing a disturbing example.[12]

Meanwhile, a small delegation of Tibetans, traveling by horseback, made its way along a 300-mile snow-packed track to attend the first Asian Relations Conference in India. The nearly month-long journey included crossing four treacherous Himalayan passes, ranging in altitude from 14,000 to more than 16,000 feet, where one misstep meant instant death. Hosted by Prime Minister Jawaharlal Nehru, then leading a provisional government preparing for Indian independence, the conference, organized by the Indian Council of World Affairs, drew leaders from several Asian independence movements and represented the first attempt at Asian unity.[13]

The Dalai Lama's envoys, resplendent in their saffron robes, arrived and raised the Tibetan flag to represent their nation at what was thought to be a landmark event in Asia's post-war recovery. It was a poignant moment. It was the first attempt by the Buddhist nation to break its self-imposed isolation, assert its independence, and stand with others in the region. The newly minted members of the Tibetan Foreign Office attended, along with the Nationalist Chinese and nearly thirty other nations.

As Nehru and Mahatma Gandhi met with the delegation to establish a framework for economic and political relations between Delhi and Lhasa, Nehru got a taste of what lay ahead as tensions between Tibet and China erupted. When the conference convened, Nationalist China officially protested at the seating of the Tibet delegation, on the basis that Tibet was a part of China and should therefore not be recognized. Much pomp and drama yielded nothing. The Tibetans were seated. But Nehru took note, instructing his ambassador in Beijing, KPS Menon, to advise the Chinese that the conference would address cultural and economic issues and avoid political matters.[14] Careful note was also taken in Washington, where Nationalist China exerted political pressure through the China Lobby, a powerful group that included members of Congress, the Catholic Church, and business leaders.

The chilly international environment was not all that impeded Tibet's effort to present itself as a modernizing nation and gain acceptance in foreign capitals. Not unlike China, India, and others in the region shedding their colonial links, Tibet suffered instability in this period—but from very different causes.

Lhasa was wrestling with a difficult succession. Selecting the next Dalai Lama nearly brought the kingdom to civil war. Tensions dated back to the death of the thirteenth Dalai Lama in 1933, when the search for his reincarnation began. In the interim a young abbot, Reting Rimpoche from the Reting Monastery, had been appointed regent. Although Reting was able to establish and consolidate power, it was not without generating animosity. His adventurous personal life invited doubts about his ability to govern effectively. Reting was fun-loving and enjoyed the company of attractive women, which compromised his authority among Tibetan elites; he was responsible for administering the vows of monkhood, including the vow of celibacy, to the young Dalai Lama.[15] If the vows were given by a monk who did not adhere to celibacy himself, then the oath taken would be considered meaningless.[16]

Under pressure, Reting agreed to resign with the intention of regaining his position at a later time. Taktra Rimpoche, a senior, well-respected lama who advocated formal separation from China, took his place in early 1941. In 1944 Reting returned to Lhasa intending to regain his position as regent, but Taktra refused to step down. Tensions increased over the next few years as the larger monasteries supported different candidates to be regent.[17]

Chinese meddling and intrigue did not help. In 1944 the Chinese attempted to interfere with the selection of the Panchen Lama, the second most authoritative figure in Tibetan Buddhism. Of course Tibet rejected China's interventions, but the process created confusion and raised questions about Lhasa's ability to manage its own governance. Unfortunately, by the time the Tibetan delegation arrived at the Asian conference in March of 1947, events in Lhasa were lurching toward chaos and civil war.

In February 1947 events came to a head when Reting and his supporters failed in an unsuccessful attempt to murder Taktra. Two months later a hand grenade concealed in a parcel addressed to him blew off his doorman's hand.[18] On 14–15 April ex-regent Reting and several of his officials were arrested and charged with attempted assassination. He was murdered in prison a month later.[19]

All this was deeply disruptive and compromised attempts to present a viable, modern Tibetan state. Tibet's social structure and politics were theocratic in nature; it was a hierarchical system, with religion and government joined at the top in the person of the Dalai Lama. Amidst the political confusion, multiple factions, some based in the Kashag, others in the monasteries, sought to enhance their power.[20] Moreover, major decisions were routinely made in conjunction with the powerful State Oracle, an important institution in Tibet, which ensured that spirituality, revelation, and prophesy played a compelling role in matters of state.[21]

Unfortunately dissent among the regents, the Oracle, the Kashag, and the powerful monasteries in 1947–9 prevented Tibet from taking the steps that might have secured its independence in what is seen, retrospectively, as a unique geopolitical moment. Chiang's Nationalists were in retreat and the communists had not yet gained control of the mainland. Had Tibet been able to present a united front to Mao and the PLA and fielded even a minimally viable force, its potential and thus its options might have been assessed differently in global councils, and its future might have taken a different course. But that was not to be.

Still, the public square virtually rang with commitments to freedom and self-determination. Truman speaking to Congress, and Jawaharlal Nehru speaking at the Asian conference, celebrated liberty, the freedoms of speech, assembly, and belief, and the self-determination of peoples. Nehru told his audiences that 'Peace can only come when nations are free and also when human beings everywhere have freedom and security and opportunity...'[22]

It was a time of profound change and widely divergent expectations as one nation after another, like caterpillars shedding their cocoons, severed their colonial relations with the European powers. Both Nehru and Truman now faced the challenge of rising Maoism but, reflecting distinct geopolitical challenges, national characters, and their own personalities, they would proceed very differently.

The center of gravity had, meanwhile, shifted for Tibet. While the 'Tibet story' would remain an inspiration, animating social and literary circles from Paris to San Francisco, Tibet's prospective sovereignty was now clearly in play. A small piece on an ever more treacherous Cold War chessboard, Tibet's capacity and aspirations would be tested in the crucible of China's determination, India's fear, Britain's declining South Asian interests, and America's Cold War objectives.

6

THE IRON TRIANGLE

THE CHINA LOBBY, THE RED SCARE,
AND THE CATHOLIC CHURCH

It should be said that Tibet's independence was not a US foreign policy priority in the years following World War II. Still, it was reflected in the American discourse in several ways: the Tibet story inspired fascination with the remote, mystical kingdom and sympathy for its people in their quest for independence; second, although not specifically named, Tibet's situation was addressed by the Truman Doctrine and thus had standing in the hierarchy of US policy goals; and third, Tibet, as Secretary of State Dean Acheson pointed out in 1949, offered an opportunity to 'harass' the communist Chinese forces.[1] Further, it was thought that Tibet could provide a platform for covert operations that would make it more difficult for the communists to consolidate power.

After the CIA briefed Truman and Acheson in November 1949, the latter expressed the administration's intention: On the one hand, to 'oppose the Communist regime, needle it, and if an opportunity appeared to attempt to overthrow it';[2] and on the other to attempt to 'detach' the Chinese from their 'subservience to Moscow.'[3]

Still, if President Truman's promise to 'support free peoples who are resisting attempted subjugation … by outside pressure' was thought by Lhasa to guarantee Tibet's future as an independent, sovereign nation, it was a misplaced hope.[4] The Dalai Lama reflected this when he said that '… Tibetans, I think unrealistically, expected too much from America. We thought that if there was ever any Communist invasion or attempt to invade Tibet, America would help.'[5]

While Truman's statement combined principle and geopolitical interest, given the political dissent at home and the rising Cold War, his doctrine is more notable in retrospect for underscoring the gap between national ideals and real world politics

41

and diplomacy. The Truman administration was thus a mighty but constrained voice, stirring souls around the world who sought the promised freedoms of a post-colonial world. Meanwhile, it was mired in Washington's granular, often vicious politics and, quite separately, in a new 'Great Game' in Asia.

In February of 1948, General George Marshall, Truman's secretary of state, presented a report to the Senate and House Foreign Relations Committees outlining the conundrum that China posed for the administration.[6] Having served as Truman's liaison in China, Marshall arrived with a deep knowledge of the Chinese civil war. He described the Nationalist government, known as the Kuomintang (KMT), as 'impotent,' the situation 'practically unsolvable,' and the prevailing conditions characterized by 'disorder,' 'corruption,' and 'inefficiency.'[7] Marshall cut through the policy complexities, and said: 'We cannot afford to entirely withdraw our support of the Chiang Kai-shek government and … neither can we afford to be drawn in on an unending drain upon our resources.'[8] His views were widely shared and further detailed by Central Intelligence Agency Director Rear Admiral R. H. Hillenkoetter, who outlined the strength and capabilities of the Chinese communist armies in a memorandum to Truman.

As Truman's second term unfolded, it became clear that corruption and dissent within the Nationalist ranks had deeply compromised 'Generalissimo' Chiang Kai-shek's war effort. Continuing reports of Nationalist losses were alarming for both geopolitical and domestic reasons, as public anxiety about the 'Red Menace' had by then become a tangible and debilitating element in the American political discourse.

Fear of communism and communist subversion in Washington shifted the political center of gravity to the right. The administration and some in Congress—not to mention powerful voices in American business and the media—believed that America's post-war economic recovery was threatened by deteriorating conditions in Europe and Asia and by communist sympathizers from within. Fear of internal subversion and that democracy was in retreat around the globe had ushered in a shrill political climate. It was accented by the Soviet atomic bomb test in August 1949, Senator Joe McCarthy's House Un-American Activities Committee hearings, and the Rosenberg spy case. Emotion now informed politics. The administration had little choice but to confront directly the rising menace of communism in both Europe and Asia.

The China Lobby

Growing concerns about Chinese communism were sustained by the belief that the 'Red Chinese'—regimented, alien, godless, and doctrinaire—were even more virulent than the Soviets. Mao's harsh Leninism was frightening, and thereby generated broad and influential support for Nationalist China.

Drawing strength from these emotions, the China Lobby emerged in the late 1940s and continued to gain voice in the early 1950s to become a powerful advocate for the Chinese Nationalists. It comprised influential figures from industry, labor, publishing, the military, academia and religion; some were paid lobbyists, but most were not.[9] Their objective was to ensure that China did not come under communist control.

They were divided into two categories: first, 'an inner core' that supported and pursued the interests of Nationalist leader Chiang Kai-shek and the KMT in the US and abroad; and second, a 'kaleidoscopic array of affiliates', mainly in the US, whose sympathies were aligned with the Chiang regime.[10] The common denominator was their determination 'to secure the backing and support of the United States for the government of Chiang Kai-shek'.[11] Historian Nancy Bernkopf Tucker wrote of the group:

Whatever their reasons—selfless or self-seeking—members of the China Lobby dedicated their efforts to preserving the authority of Chiang Kai-shek. They sought not merely to arouse sympathy for an innocent victim of foreign aggression, but to commit the United States to a long-term program of military and economic assistance.[12]

Two individuals stand out in this loosely organized lobbying effort: Henry R. (Hank) Luce and Arthur Kohlberg. Luce, the publisher of *Time*, *Life*, and *Fortune* magazines, used his vast media empire to reach out to different constituencies to advance the Lobby's view of world affairs. And Kohlberg, a wealthy businessman and philanthropist, worked the inner parts of the Lobby—he was called 'Mr Inside,' the 'architect' of the group.[13]

Henry Luce: delivering the Red Scare

Henry Luce has been described as the 'most influential private citizen in America during his lifetime.'[14] As the publisher of *Time*, *Life*, and *Fortune* magazines as well as the producer of various film and radio documentaries, Luce was able to reach more than 'one-quarter' of the 'reading public' each week.[15] He crafted and delivered the anti-communist zeitgeist—the adhesive that bound culture, politics and passion together to support the Nationalists regardless of the price which (in the end) included Tibet's independence. He and his media empire impacted millions of Americans and three presidencies. Even the fourteenth Dalai Lama, when he was just a young boy in Lhasa, read *Life* magazine—which was how he became aware of the communist victory in China.[16]

Luce was born in China to missionary parents and, as historian Robert Herzstein has noted, two factors shaped his world-view: 'one was Protestant Christianity; and the other was a fervent faith in America's God-ordained global mission in Asia.'[17] He was a major figure in the China Lobby, a relentless campaigner for more involvement with China, and was fully connected not only with the private sector but also with many in government. Luce's Christian faith colored his world-view, strengthening his resolve to tell Americans, and the world, about the evils of godless communism.

Faith was his constant companion; few people knew, for example, the real reason he insisted on riding the elevator alone for thirty-six floors each morning to his penthouse. There were rumors over the years among his employees: some thought he was shy, others thought it was his ego or worse, perhaps 'Jim Crowism'—not wanting to ride with other races.[18] But it was actually quite simple: Harry, as he liked to be called, prayed to God every day, in silence, as his long-time elevator operator took him to his immense penthouse suite. The ritual was repeated at the day's end when he rode back down to the Madison Avenue rush hour.

Americans saw the world on the glossy pages of *Time* and *Life* magazines as Luce wanted it to be: illuminated with photographs and human-interest stories in *Life*, and crisp analysis in *Time*. The first managing editor of *Life* magazine, John Shaw Billings, commented that Luce was 'obsessed with the subject of foreign policy and his direct influence on it.'[19] He was single-minded in his fight against communism and determined to advance American hegemony in world affairs; he believed he was 'molding the destiny of the US in the world.'[20]

Behind the power of his media empire Luce was backed by a pantheon of the 'great and the good' including his wife, Clare Booth Luce, later a congresswoman and US ambassador to Rome, and his editor, C. D. Jackson, later a key aide to President Eisenhower. Luce was an intimate friend of Eisenhower and his secretary of state, John Foster Dulles.[21]

Luce first met Chiang Kai-shek in the spring of 1941 at Chungking when a *Time* magazine correspondent suggested that he visit the wartime capital to see events first-hand. Luce returned to America to become an ardent advocate for the Nationalists, 'propagandizing' their virtues in a way some saw as a kind of 'blind loyalty' to Chiang Kai-shek.[22] Historian W. A. Swanberg wrote that Chiang 'was the most important man in Luce's life—his pride, joy, worry and disaster.'[23] For Luce, the Generalissimo was the 'Christian Chiang, the America-oriented Chiang, and the Communist-hating Chiang.'[24] As historian Barbara Tuchman wrote, 'Once one had committed to his perfection, any suggestion of blemish was regarded as inadmissible.'[25]

Luce may have been the most ardent American exceptionalist of his era, taking it upon himself to tell Americans they were different, they had a purpose: they must fight until 'all men are free.'[26] He was fixated with China and believed that if the United States failed China it would 'fail totally,' and urged the Roosevelt administration to shift its emphasis from Europe to Asia.[27]

The Church

Through his wife Clare Booth Luce, a converted Catholic and great supporter of the Generalissimo, the Church became an integral part of Luce's life. Claire had become committed to the Nationalist cause after they toured China together, and as a Republican congresswoman she was an outspoken critic of the communists.[28] Among her closest friends was Cardinal Francis Spellman of New York, also an ardent anti-communist, who saw his mission of spreading the Gospel as an antidote to communism. The Cardinal was a virtual fixture on the pages of *Time* and *Life* in stories that contrasted communism with the goodness of Christianity.[29]

It was a common devotion to Christian values that bound Luce to John Foster Dulles, whose religion, in turn, informed his political views as Eisenhower's secretary of state.[30] And just as their Christianity informed policy, so Luce's editors were instructed to make Dulles 'look as pure as the driven snow.'[31] According to *Life's* Managing Editor, John Shaw Billings, Luce liked to say that Dulles was 'like old brandy ... you had to swish it around for a time to savor its full bouquet and flavor.'[32]

Generals Stilwell and Marshall: 'Villains of the Piece'

Luce used his magazines to warn the American public that if Chiang lost the civil war, China would fall to Mao and become a vassal to Moscow. Just as he attacked General Joseph Stilwell, he vilified General George C. Marshall after his failure in 1946 to broker a peace between Chiang Kai-shek and the communists. He had no faith in the career Foreign Service, arguing in the 6 January 1947 issue of *Life* that the 'career men at the State department are cautious and wooden ... our Chinese policy has been one of mere temporizing and is now demonstrably bankrupt.'[33] In his 13 January 1947 commentary, Luce called Marshall's plan for a coalition government 'stupidity' and reiterated his support for a $500 million loan to support the Nationalists, pointing to the strength of Christianity in China.[34] Devastated by Chiang's eventual retreat and the defeat that seemed all but inevitable, he blamed Marshall for a 'miserable failure.'[35]

In December 1949, two months after Mao's People's Republic of China (PRC) declared victory, Chiang Kai-shek fled the mainland to live on Formosa until his death. There was plenty of blame to go around. On 5 January 1950, President Truman addressed the question of continued US support for the Nationalists, stating the United States would not become involved in a civil conflict in China. He said that the US 'will not provide military aid or advice to Chinese forces on Formosa' and 'has no desire to obtain special rights or privileges or to establish military bases on Formosa at this time.'[36] Acheson quietly defined the moment, saying that the administration would 'let the dust settle' before deciding upon next steps.

The China Lobby was apoplectic. With the communists ensconced on the mainland, they insisted that Formosa be protected at all costs. In a frosty encounter, Senator William Knowland (R-CA), known as the 'Senator from Formosa,' and Senate Foreign Relations Committee Member Alexander Smith (R-NJ) met with Acheson on the morning of 5 January 1950, the same day as Truman's statement on Formosa.[37] The secretary remained firm and succinctly outlined the administration's stance, reiterating the position of the joint chiefs of staff: Formosa was 'not of vital importance' to the security of the United States.[38] Acheson told them the US would not go to war over the island, infuriating the senators. Senator Smith asked why the administration had not taken the advice of both General MacArthur and Admiral Radford who, like Ambassador Stuart (the former US ambassador to China), believed that under no circumstance should the US let 'Formosa fall into Communist hands.'[39] Senator

Knowland added that 'there was a high state of morale among the armed services as well as the Formosans and that if we would give a proper measure of both military and economic aid the situation could be saved.'[40] Acheson responded:

[T]hat inasmuch as Formosa was not of vital importance from a strategic standpoint, the United States had much more to lose than to gain if we were to take any military action, or adopt a policy of military assistance that would lead to military involvement designed to hold Formosa, and that distasteful as the possibility was, that the island might well be occupied by the Communists at some time in the future, we must concede the possibility and not compromise our entire position in the Far East by doing deeds that would give the lie to our words.[41]

Acheson's defense of the administration fell on deaf ears. Senator Knowland said he felt it 'his conscientious duty' to tell the American people that the administration was pursuing 'a fatal policy' of 'grave danger' that 'we would live to rue and regret.'[42] With that, Acheson noted that 'courteous but restrained goodbyes were offered.'[43]

The administration remained firm: it was not moved by pressure, neither from Luce's publications nor from Congress; it would not send troops to help the Nationalists nor would it increase the amount of financial aid.[44]

A week later, on 12 January, Acheson gave his now famous 'perimeter speech' at the Press Club in Washington where Japan, Okinawa, the Philippines, and the Aleutians were included in the US defense perimeter, but Formosa and South Korea were not. The backlash from the China Lobby was brutal and Senator Knowland, who had left Acheson's office in a huff the previous week, now called for his resignation. Acheson, writing in his memoirs years later, noted that some in Washington believed that he 'had given the green light' for the attack on South Korea.[45]

Luce would not forgive Truman or his administration for 'the loss of China,' continuing his attacks even after the president left office.

Arthur Kohlberg

Henry Luce, though pivotal in drawing together the 'Asia-Firsters,' Christian evangelicals, anti-communists and what we now call 'exceptionalists,' was only one part of the fraught environment known as the 'Red Scare.' The man working the inside levers was Arthur Kohlberg. Kohlberg was 'disarming and affable, but beneath the smooth exterior lurked a zealous ideological crusader...'[46] Kohlberg used his vast fortune to lobby for anti-communist causes. He financed both the China Lobby and Wisconsin Republican Senator Joe McCarthy.[47]

Allied with J. Edgar Hoover, the crusading director of the FBI, Kohlberg was responsible for compiling the infamous 'Red Channel,' the book that blacklisted individuals in television and radio.[48] His methods were questionable; he played on the dark side. Kohlberg was a 'master at planting innuendo and casting doubt on the loyalties of his targets.'[49] He would 'make a charge of pro-Communist activity; if it did not stick, make another one, repeat it, document it, and spread it around. Something would find its mark.'[50]

In 1946 Kohlberg told Chiang: 'I have been very busy in our campaign to attempt to re-educate America about China, for unfortunately America has been completely confused by the barrage of Communist propaganda that has poured out over us for the past three years.'[51] The Generalissimo's wife, Madame Chiang, joined him in this, working behind the scenes, rallying 'support among Republican Party, military and church leaders' and 'taking the battle from the Great Wall to Capitol Hill.'[52] She lobbied members of Congress and the American public with the help of an American public relations firm, and $200,000 of her husband's money, earning the epithet 'Madamissimo.'[53]

For his part, Chiang Kai-shek instructed his representatives, including his very able ambassador to Washington, V. K. Wellington Koo, to work with two Kohlberg creations: the American China Policy Association (ACPA), a vehicle to challenge communism and anyone who criticized the KMT; and a magazine called *Plain Talk*, which focused its attacks on those in the State Department it considered to be communist sympathizers.[54] Among its targets were John Service, John Carter Vincent, John Paton Davies, Owen Lattimore, and O. Edmund Clubb.

Sadly, several of these Foreign Service officers had worked in China during WWII, and later in the State Department. They were Mandarin speakers, sound analysts and were very knowledgeable about Chinese life and customs. There is no evidence that they advocated Tibetan independence. The China Lobby accused them of treason because they were deeply critical of Chiang Kai-shek and also because some were said to favor Mao's agrarian reform.

In 1946 the Truman administration initiated a series of investigations into individuals who were considered security risks, and on 21 March 1947 Truman issued Executive Order 9835, establishing a Loyalty Program and a Loyalty Security Board. Among the effects of this controversial process was the expulsion from government of many of the Department's 'old China hands,' leaving Washington less informed and mispositioned on the grave and mounting challenge in Asia, which would extend beyond China to Korea and Vietnam.

Senator Joseph McCarthy

Kohlberg, through the China Lobby and with the help of Senator Joe McCarthy, built on the public's fear that unbridled communism directly threatened the American way of life. The Kohlberg–McCarthy axis provided an unending stream of 'dirt'—fodder for the Senator's media machine. Historian Ellen Schrecker wrote that Kohlberg 'hit pay dirt with McCarthy.'[55] 'It was a *deus ex machina*, a devastatingly effective partnership which created a rising, irrational fear of Communists while sharply limiting the scope of US foreign policy options and approaches to complex problems.'[56]

Kohlberg's modus operandi fit perfectly with the junior senator from Wisconsin, who was known to fight 'dog patch style'—anything went—'gouging, biting, scratching, kicking, and head butting' so that his enemies were 'pelted and pummeled' until they relented.[57]

Detractors had been unaware that the FBI supplied McCarthy with information from communist apostates Elizabeth Bentley and Whittaker Chambers that revealed important breaches in US national security, including the names of US government employees subsidized by the Soviets, and other evidence that Julius Rosenberg was, in fact, guilty of espionage, that the 'Manhattan Project' was penetrated by Soviet agents, and that the US Communist Party took money and direction from the Kremlin.

In recent years M. Stanton Evans' *Blacklisted by History: The Untold Story of Senator Joe McCarthy and his Fight Against America's Enemies* and liberal *Washington Post* writer Nicholas Hoffman have asked if McCarthy was 'right about the left'—or at least more right than wrong.[58] Revisionist writers have made the case that McCarthy was generally correct about the cases he cited—that most individuals were, in fact, members of the Communist Party.

The question is, however, did the grand collection of liberals, New Dealers, government servants, Hollywood directors, writers, and left-leaning filmstars constitute what McCarthy called on the floor of the Senate 'a great conspiracy'?

How can we account for our present situation unless we believe that men high in this Government are concerting to deliver us to disaster? This must be the product of a great conspiracy, a conspiracy on a scale so immense as to dwarf any previous such venture in the history of man. A conspiracy of infamy so black that, when it is finally exposed, its principals shall be forever deserving of the maledictions of all honest men.[59]

McCarthy's overblown rhetoric harmed the cause of those legitimately concerned with Soviet espionage. He and Kohlberg conflated the hard evidence of communist infiltration and secret influence in government with paranoid fantasy. The effect was to embolden those who would dismiss the administration's attempts to root out communist infiltration as the hot pursuit of a mirage.

While few could be confident of the facts in these charges and counter-charges, much has become clear in the past half-century through intercepted intelligence from the Venona Project, defectors, and newly opened archives. Were Kohlberg and McCarthy correct? No, they were not. There is, however, unpleasant as it may be for many historians, a seed of truth in what they said.

In 1953 McCarthy became chairman of the Permanent Subcommittee on Investigations. From there he opened hearings on the State Department, the Voice of America, the US overseas libraries, the Government Printing Office, and the Army Signal Corps in 1953—which was his last investigation. He was censured by the Senate at the end of that year and the McCarthy period came to a close. He died three years later, many believed from alcoholism. And, for the most part, McCarthyism died with him.

It was against this toxic backdrop—a political environment laced with paranoia, vitriol, and fear—that decisions were taken that affected Tibet for decades. Many

China experts had been purged from the State Department. Congress and its deliberative process were convulsed, yielding little in the end except recrimination. Debate in the public square was truncated and suppressed until quite late in the game when, in 1954, Edward R. Murrow of CBS challenged McCarthy and the culture of fear that McCarthy had ushered in.

Of signal importance to the nation's future engagements in Asia, Washington mistakenly concluded that it confronted a monolithic communist threat. This meant, for example, that opportunities to exploit differences between the PRC and the USSR, such as the Sino-Soviet split in 1965, were missed. Likewise, Washington misinterpreted the nationalist insurgency in Vietnam, believing instead that it was directed from Moscow and Beijing.

Tibet policy was affected in several ways. Luce and Kohlberg, through the China Lobby and the Catholic Church, had advanced a policy that welded the US to the Nationalist cause. Many in Congress and the business community embraced the China Lobby/Nationalist China view on the question of Tibetan independence. Like Beijing today, they believed that any support for an independent Tibet would create precedents and encourage separatists in other contested areas, including Sinkiang, Mongolia, and Formosa, that could in effect split China, much as the European powers had in the nineteenth century. Tibetan independence, the Nationalists feared, would not only deprive China of valuable resources, but would stimulate instability on its periphery, something that China has feared throughout its history.

Washington's ability to extend recognition to Tibet was thus curtailed: had Washington openly supported Tibetan independence, the Nationalists believed the resulting loss of popular support in China would weaken any chance, however remote, of resisting Mao's communists; and Washington needed Nationalist cooperation against the communists.

That said, the China Lobby and the Red Scare it cultivated created an unambiguous anti-communist political environment in Washington which provided the context—some might say 'an iron spine'—for the US covert program directed against the Chinese communist occupation of Tibet (as will be discussed in Part Two).

But we turn first to India and Nehru's visit to Washington, where both the US and Indian interlocutors, limited by historical and cultural constraints, and now Nehru's personal ambition as the voice for non-alignment seemed more intent on detailing their differences than finding common ground on strategic matters—a missed opportunity that had profound implications for Tibet.

7

TRUMAN AND INDIA

The Nationalists were an important factor in US–Tibet policy and in Tibet's broader attempt to achieve independence, but they were not the only factor—and perhaps not even the most critical factor. By 1949, a smooth and productive relationship between Tibet and India began to seem as unlikely as it was crucial. India was the key to regional stability, and an important point of reference for a group of South Asian states including Nepal, Bhutan, and Burma, who were increasingly vulnerable to Chinese pressure and communist takeover. India, intent on smooth relations with China, was now the uncertain arbiter of Tibet's future, having assumed the rights and obligations of Britain's regional relations after the latter's handover in 1947.

America's relations with India throughout the twentieth century had been uneven, at best, and were more properly described as dysfunctional. Not only was Washington half a world away, but limited personal relationships, cultural differences, and differing political priorities and objectives, particularly with regard to the Korean War and Cold War tensions, had confirmed the relationship as one of 'problem management.' British imperial prerogatives had meant that the US had few assets in South Asia. Moreover, the US relationship with independent India, difficult from the outset, would become more so as Jawaharlal Nehru, determined to meet the communist bloc on his own terms, ascended the prime ministership. Given these circumstances, it is not difficult to see why Washington could exert only limited influence on Indian–Tibetan relations or China's territorial ambitions, including Tibet's status.

American interaction with India from the beginning of the twentieth century had taken a different path from the US relationship with China. Indeed, in the minds of most Americans, India, like China and Tibet, was a far-off place, an exotic land. But most of what Americans read in the early part of the twentieth century led them to see India and its people in negative stereotypes.[1]

More than any other book in its time, Katherine Mayo's *Mother India* profoundly influenced early American perceptions about the continent.[2] It was a 'scathing indictment of Hinduism' and depicted India as 'a place of destructive superstition and sexual perversity.'[3] She described India's 'inertia, helplessness, lack of initiative and staying power ... a strident polemic convincing many Americans that India did not deserve their attention.'[4]

Indians were, of course, outraged by Mayo's book and responded with their own disparaging views of America. The Indian nationalist press featured 'lurid depictions of sexual misconduct and corruption' in the US and the lynching of blacks in the South.[5] Taken together, such imagery allowed little common ground and instead distorted the relationship from well before Indian independence in 1947 through the decades that followed.

In 1947, as India prepared to claim her independence, Washington's attention was focused elsewhere. Historian H. W. Brands described Washington's posture toward India in the 1947–50 period as laissez-faire, writing that 'the Truman administration was quite happy to leave the security of South Asia to the British for the moment, desiring to carefully avoid stepping on British toes in that part of the world.'[6]

Still, caught in a mounting post-war food crisis, India looked to the United States for economic assistance, and when aid was not readily forthcoming became critical of a wealthy and aloof Uncle Sam; and of course Indian communists were happy to fuel the growing animosity.[7] George R. Merrell, the interim American chargé d'affaires in Delhi, forwarded an article from the communist paper *The People's Age* to the secretary of state in June 1946.[8] It was entitled '100 Million Indians Threatened with Starvation Death by Anglo-American Food Politics.'[9] Merrell wrote: 'The article in question not only represents an effort on the part of Indian Communists to exploit the food crisis, but is also indicative of the attitude of the Indian press in general on the subject of the United States and food.'[10] The article stated that no grain had reached India and alleged that President Truman remarked: 'The world is a bitch with too big a litter. We have to decide which of the puppies to drown.'[11]

Merrell summed up the anti-American sentiment during this period in a confidential memorandum to Secretary of State James Byrnes:

In the first place, it has become obvious that during the early part of our participation in the recent war, our Government—through various official channels—'oversold' itself to Indians. Rightly or wrongly many of them gained the impression that the United States was going to 'liberate' them from British rule. When this hope was not realized, Indians were bitterly disappointed and in many cases not only decided to question the United States' 'sincerity' as a democratic nation, but began to class the United States with Britain as an imperialistic power.[12]

India faced crises on both the political and economic fronts at the time of independence. From colonial India, two new dominions had been created in August 1947: India and Pakistan. And almost immediately the two nations began to fight over Kashmir.

Kashmir was predominately Muslim but ruled by a Hindu Maharajah who refused to ally with either Pakistan or India after partition. The princely state encompassed some 85,000 square miles and had a population of nearly four million, about three-fourths of whom were Muslims.[13] As the violence in the region escalated and amidst brutal carnage and mounting deaths, the Indian Secretary General Bajpai requested US military transport to assist with fleeing refugees.[14] Truman expressed sympathy. He stipulated, however, that American airplanes could only be provided if the request was made jointly with the government of Pakistan.[15]

Remaining neutral and uninvolved in the region's politics was awkward for the world's most powerful nation. In a late December 1947 meeting at the State Department's Bureau of South Asian Affairs, US Ambassador Henry F. Grady offered blunt advice when asked how best to handle the India–Pakistan situation: 'Encourage cooperation [and] stay out of Commonwealth questions.'[16] He continued:

[W]e must be very careful. Indians are very jealous of everything we do for Pakistan. I am constantly questioned on this point in India. If we made a loan to Pakistan, India would resent it unless we gave the same to India. This applies to all matters right down the line.[17]

Washington, ever mindful of Britain's sensitivities, looked to London for guidance on its new relationship with India. Whitehall, however, was leery of US involvement with the former 'jewel of the Empire,' and kept its cards close. While meeting with administration officials in Washington, Ambassador Grady spoke candidly about how Britain viewed Washington's evolving relationship with India:

The British have been friendly, but have made no attempt to consult with us on common problems or to ask our advice. Neither Shone nor Mountbatten thinks of us in any way as partners. They have over three hundred people working on trade relations. I have expressed more sympathy for British trade than the British have for American trade. On more than one occasion, Mountbatten has warned Nehru against dollar imperialism.[18]

'Mr Foreign Service'

When newly appointed Ambassador Loy Henderson arrived in New Delhi in July of 1948, he was confronted with both the growing tension between Hindu India and Muslim Pakistan over Kashmir—a disputed territory administered by two states, India and Pakistan—and the difficult task of quieting India's growing criticism of the United States. Tibet, at that point, was not on the agenda.

Henderson was a consummate diplomat, a straight-talker, an elegant political–military analyst, and an ardent anti-communist. He had led the first diplomatic mission to Moscow in 1934, warning a year later that the Kremlin would make a pact with Nazi Germany. Later he would guide the US through the complex South Asian diplomacy surrounding Tibet as assistant secretary of state for South Asia and ambassador to Iran and Iraq. But for now his task was to represent US interests to a skeptical, newly independent nation and to help Washington develop a formal—and workable—regional policy.

In the fall of 1948 Henderson attended a London dinner party hosted by Ernest Bevin, the British foreign secretary. Henderson told the group (which included Sir

Archibald Nye, the newly appointed high commissioner to India) that he looked forward to continued Anglo-American cooperation and that he 'had every reason to believe Washington and London would be able to coordinate their actions in the future as they had in the past.'[19] Bevin, sitting next to Henderson, patted him on the arm and said 'I like to hear that, Loy.'[20] He added that India is 'a country where we must keep together—although you must let us be in the shop window.'[21] Mildly surprised, Henderson replied, 'The United States realizes the importance of keeping the United Kingdom in the shop window, but you must keep us informed.'[22]

Matters assumed a less convivial tone in an after-dinner chat with Bevin and Sir Archibald. Bevin described a recent British Commonwealth conference in London, where Nehru's vitriol towards the United States was in 'full cry.'[23] 'Nehru,' he said, 'threatened to withdraw from the Commonwealth if the United Kingdom's relations with the United States continued to be closer than those with India.'[24] Bevin and other representatives present had some difficulty in quieting Nehru while insisting that India must remain in the Commonwealth.[25] To that end, he told Henderson, we wanted to 'assuage Nehru's feelings.'[26] Would Henderson mind, Bevin wondered, 'if Sir Archie, after his arrival in India, did not show any particular friendliness toward Henderson and the American Embassy, and if from time to time he could be publicly critical of the United States?'[27] Henderson replied, 'I would mind very much.' The publicly acknowledged alliance between the former colonial power and the new superpower was too important, he felt, to sacrifice for Nehru's pique. He conceded only that the two embassies might 'exercise a certain amount of restraint in our social relationships.'[28]

The next day brought a new round of etiquette disasters and fraught discourse. Henderson paid a courtesy call on the Indian high commissioner, V. K. Menon, though the courtesy seemed to go unnoticed. The high commissioner stood up from behind his desk when Henderson entered, but refused to come forward in greeting and shook hands only reluctantly.[29] His first remark to the new ambassador dripped with sarcasm: 'Well, this is interesting; you are the first American ambassador who has ever darkened my threshold.'[30] Throughout the meeting Henderson tried in vain to keep the conversation friendly, but his remarks were met with 'cold silence or sarcastic rejoinder.'[31]

To be fair, Menon was already notorious as the 'undiplomatic diplomat,' and his treatment of Henderson kept to that script. Menon's own biographer described him as 'a phenomenon that inspires few, infuriates many, and embarrasses all.'[32] But Henderson knew that Menon was also one of Nehru's closest personal friends, and the unpleasant encounter foreshadowed the difficulties he would later encounter.[33]

Tricky relations with Nehru

It was not until a year later that Henderson's colleagues in Washington began to view India in geostrategic terms. In June 1949 the National Security Council issued the first comprehensive position paper on South Asia.[34] Concerned with Nationalist

China's probable fall to the communists, diplomatic and strategic planners now began to focus on the importance of South Asia. The administration believed it necessary 'to increase our interest in and possible future dependence on South Asia, particularly India and Pakistan.'[35]

Both Henderson and the NSC's 1949 South Asian Policy white paper had asserted that a stable South Asia could 'exert a strong influence on the Middle East, Central Asia and the Far East.'[36] Moreover, India and Pakistan had several good harbors along the coast that were relatively safe from air or naval attacks by the Soviets.[37] In their contribution to the 19 April version of the white paper, the joint chiefs of staff underscored their interest in the 'South Asian countries, especially Pakistan, close to the USSR.' The JCS wrote: 'The Karachi–Lahore area in Pakistan may, under certain conditions, become of strategic importance. In spite of logistic difficulties, the JCS believed this area might be required as a base for air operations against central USSR and as a staging area for forces engaged in the defense or recapture of Middle East oil areas.'[38]

Intent on establishing a good relationship with the Indians, President Truman extended an invitation for Prime Minister Nehru to make an official visit to Washington. In preparation for what they knew would be a strained affair, the administration looked to Henderson to provide insights on the Indian leader. And clearly Henderson had a lot to say.

Nehru's continuing outbursts over American suggestions that he consider compromises related to Kashmir, often directed at Henderson, had come to flavor the ambassador's view of the prime minister. Henderson endured one particularly nasty encounter in August 1949. Knowing that Nehru was 'morbidly sensitive to criticism,' Henderson was not totally unprepared for what he called in his memo to Acheson, 'the Prime Minister's tirade.'[39] In the face of this, Henderson 'said nothing, remained calm and just looked Nehru straight in the face.'[40] Nehru, ranting about American 'misperceptions' over Kashmir, said:

He was tired of receiving moralistic advice from US. India did not need advice from US or any other country as to its foreign or internal policies. His own record and that of Indian foreign relations was one of integrity and honesty, which did not warrant admonitions… So far as Kashmir was concerned he would not give an inch. He would hold his ground even if Kashmir and the whole world would go to pieces.[41]

After the tantrum, Nehru calmed down and 'turned on his well-known charm.'[42] Later, upon making his exit, Girja Bajpai, the minister of external affairs, approached Henderson seeking to place Nehru's comments in context. He said his government had been 'disturbed' by reports that Washington believed India 'was not acting in good faith' over Kashmir.[43] Henderson responded bluntly, saying that 'Kashmir was a running sore' and that in an effort to promote stable US–Indian relations, the issue had to be resolved.[44]

Henderson took it all in his stride. He remained quite hopeful of forging a good US–India relationship. He underscored this in his memo to Secretary of State Acheson, writing that Nehru's visit could have 'tremendous importance to the future of our relations with India.' 'If everything clicks,' he wrote in a lengthy, personal letter to Acheson, 'Nehru will depart from the United States with really friendly feelings towards us.'[45] 'On the other hand,' Henderson wrote, 'he may leave the United States, in spite of everything which we try to do, with his present feelings of distrust and vague dislike still stronger than they seem to be at the present time.'[46] In Henderson's opinion Nehru was a 'vain, sensitive, emotional, and complicated person.'[47]

Henderson believed Nehru's attitudes derived from his 'schooldays' in England where he 'consorted with and cultivated a group of rather supercilious upper-middle-class young men who fancied themselves rather precious.' He thought the prime minister was at his best 'when playing the role of a critic and making appeals to persons and groups who are his intellectual and social inferiors.'[48] 'Nehru,' Henderson continued, 'still has some of the attitudes of a social climber' who 'has not been able [to] completely eradicate the pseudo-snobbish influences of those early days.' He liked, whenever possible, 'to assume the role of defender of the workers, peasants, and underdogs…'[49] From these early days, Henderson wrote, Nehru developed attitudes about the Americans that had been hardened by 'a group of Britishers who have gone out of their way to prejudice him against things American.'[50] He continued:

There is no doubt that people like the Mountbattens have had some success in strengthening his convictions that Americans in general are a vulgar, pushy lot, lacking in fine feeling and that American materialistic culture dominated by the dollar is a serious threat to the development of a higher type of world civilization.[51]

Summing up the underlying tension in the US–UK relationship that Henry Grady, the former ambassador, had also witnessed, Henderson wrote:

It is to our advantage that close friendly relations continue between Great Britain and India. It is unfortunate, however, that in so many circles in the UK there is still a belief that the development of closer relations between India and the United States will in some way or other result in a deterioration of the relations between Great Britain and India. There is no doubt that such a belief exists and this affects the actions of those who share it.[52]

Clearly, the administration had, in the course of the summer, been working to form a view of Nehru and determine how best to approach his forthcoming visit. While Henderson had, at various points, provided Washington with a rather acerbic measure of the man, it was his 18 June letter to Acheson that provided the context for the administration's view of Nehru and how to manage his visit to Washington. Henderson made a number of points. Offering perspective on a figure that had stirred not a little controversy, Henderson said 'it would be unfair if I did not add that in spite of his vanity and petty snobberies, he is a man of a warm heart, of genuine idealism, of shrewd discernment, and of considerable intellectual capacity.'[53] He went on to say that he thought Nehru a 'natural leader' and an 'expert politician' and admonished that 'if the United States could capture his imagination instead of getting on his English-strung nerves or stirring his jealousy, his visit would be more than worthwhile.'[54]

Overall, Henderson's letter to Acheson was very detailed, containing suggestions on whom Nehru might like to see, what events would please him, and how the State Department should arrange the trip. Henderson recommended 'a number of small affairs be arranged at which every fellow guest has been chosen with care.' 'Nehru should of course be the center of attention.'[55]

Henderson's letter was exactly what an ambassador's letter should have been: it was insightful and provided Washington with superb background on a leader they knew very little about. Henderson even commented on Nehru's preference in women, saying 'Nehru is fond of the company of beautiful well-gowned women, provided they possess good manners, pleasant voices, and a certain amount of intelligence.' There should not be too many stag affairs for him, and in selecting fellow guests the personality of the wives should not be overlooked.[56]

Nehru also was concerned that he be well-prepared for his upcoming trip to the United States. The prime minister shared his apprehensions with his sister, Vijaya Lakshmi Pandit, to whom he was very close and who was now ambassador in Washington.[57] He sought her advice on 'How should I address people? In what mood shall I approach America? How should I deal with the government there and businessmen and others?'[58] He continued, 'I want to be friendly with the Americans but always making it clear what we stand for. I want to make no commitments which come in the way of our basic policy.'[59] Separately, he told his sister that the economic situation in India was so 'very distressing and disturbing' that he planned to limit his purchases to 'save dollars.'[60]

Nehru was also concerned about his government's relationship with the administration. He perceived the US State Department as being unhelpful and unfriendly to India—a complaint he had voiced for years. In his words, 'they were not functioning in a manner satisfactory to us.'[61] The issue at the core of this was, of course, Kashmir, where Nehru believed the Department was 'definitely and constantly hostile to us.'[62]

Nehru shared Henderson's analysis of the US–UK relationship and believed that there was an 'inherent conflict' between the two countries. He would have to be mindful of this in his discussion in America. He explained in detail to his sister that he had 'seen evidence of this in many ways.'[63] He wrote:

If we deal with the USA in regard to the sale of certain atomic energy material, they frankly tell us that they do not want us to sell them to the UK, although the UK happens to be their close friend and ally. In England of course there is not too much friendship in evidence for the USA, partly because they feel themselves dependent on America and do not like it.[64]

Nehru's visit to Washington

US relations with India, on the cusp of Nehru's first visit to Washington, were uneven at best and did not improve as the deepening Cold War provided a chilling backdrop for Nehru's neutrality.

Beyond the granite façade of the immense Second Empire executive building which housed the Navy, War and State Departments, Pennsylvania Avenue blistered in the summer heat of 1949. The record-breaking temperatures matched the politics on Capitol Hill where the House Un-American Activities Committee, a permanent investigative sub-committee formed in 1945 to ferret out communist sympathizers, had charged Alger Hiss, a friend of Dean Acheson at Harvard Law School, with espionage. By late 1948 and throughout 1949 the entire nation had been riveted by the 'Red Scare' at home, just as they tracked the advance of communism across Greece and Italy.[65] But as the summer wore on, a barely contained anti-communist hysteria spilled over on 29 August with the detonation of a Soviet atomic bomb. And then just over a month later, on 1 October 1949, Mao's communists declared victory on the mainland, proclaiming the People's Republic of China (PRC).

From that point the China Lobby's shrill cry of 'Who lost China?' was everywhere: on magazine covers and newspaper front pages from coast to coast.[66] The 19 December 1949 *Life* magazine's editorial underscored Henry Luce's position on the new PRC: 'Any recognition *which signifies approval* of this regime will be a surrender to and approval of an enemy of the US and all that it stands for.'[67] Moreover, *Life* maintained it was time for Dean Acheson 'to come to grips with one or two tough problems, such as Communism in Asia.'[68] The 'Red Scare,' accented by political 'show trials,' informed the political discourse. That, in turn, provided the context for aggressive anti-communist policies in the Far East. Included in these policies was the notion that Washington would explore all possibilities to support those nations or groups that might help to contain China.

While this might have meant common ground for US and Indian interests, considering that India faced a seasoned People's Liberation Army across its northern border, these were outweighed by poor personal chemistry, a wrenching clash of cultures, and conflicting geopolitical goals. Nehru, as the exponent of 'neutralism' as it was then known, was thought by many in Washington to be 'fiddling while Rome burned.' Not only was his 'utopian' agenda thought profoundly unrealistic, but in Washington's Manichean world he was regarded as clearly immoral for refusing to confront and condemn the violent communist seizure of China and the human rights and other violations that followed.

Thus, despite Henderson's Herculean efforts, the political and security dialogue was strained, and in the end there was little scope for agreement on regional goals. And to the point of our discussion, Indian political and diplomatic equities did not support either Tibetan independence or a US role in assisting Tibetan independence.

A dyspeptic stay in the nation's capital

It was eleven days after Mao founded the People's Republic of China that Indian Prime Minister Jawaharlal Nehru touched down at the National Airport in Washington aboard President Truman's airplane—arriving to a nineteen-gun military salute. His entourage included his daughter Indira Gandhi, his sister Ambassador Pandit, Sir Girja Bajpai, secretary general of the Ministry of External Affairs, Sir Chintaman Deshmukh, Indian ambassador-at-large for Financial Matters, and a private secretary.

Truman greeted Nehru on the tarmac and was joined by Secretary of State Dean Acheson, Secretary of Defense Louis Johnson, and Secretary of Agriculture Charles Brannan.

Despite the obvious pomp and circumstance, and the painstaking care on the part of his hosts, Nehru arrived in the United States in a 'prickly mood' which, for want of a more specific reason, was attributed to his general annoyance over what he termed 'American intervention in the Kashmir dispute.'[69] The *New York Times* celebrated this historic visit with a front-page photograph of Truman and Nehru shaking hands. The headline read: 'Nehru, Greeted by Truman, Predicts Firm US India Tie.'[70] *Life* magazine began their coverage with: 'Everybody from the President to a taxi driver takes part in grand welcome for India's premier.'[71] They called the welcome 'unmatched in the history of American hospitality … Congressmen polished up their best oratory skills and one them even murmured poetic phrases from Tennyson and Elizabeth Barrett Browning.' But the article also told its readers that officials in Washington had heard that 'Nehru disliked Americans.'[72]

Life went on to say that the 'State Department acted as though they were walking on eggs and did considerable worrying over attempts to match his cultivated Cambridge accent instead of acting like plain homespun Americans.'[73] A smiling Nehru graced the cover of *Time* magazine which, reflecting Henry Luce's Cold War paradigm, called him the 'Anchor for Asia.' *Time* told its readers that 'In Washington's view, the problem was to persuade Jawaharlal Nehru that there was only one aggressive power with global designs—the Communists—and everybody else was in the same non-Communist boat.'[74]

Now that the communists had seized power in China, Nehru was the great Asian hope and, despite his difficult personality and disdain for contemporary American culture, Washington went all out to court the leader and his country.

But Nehru's neutralism, later called non-alignment, placed further strain on the relationship.[75] In his first 'All India' radio broadcast on 7 September 1949, he said: 'We propose, as far as possible, to keep away from the power politics of groups, aligned against one another, which have led in the past to world wars … We believe that peace and freedom are indivisible…'[76] Yet regardless of how Nehru's neutralism was couched, it was an affront to the administration, now locked in what it believed was an apocalyptic confrontation with communism, and this placed an impossible burden on those in Congress who advocated closer relations with India.

Despite the best intentions, the visit was, in the words of historian Robert McMahon, 'one of the most curious and least successful state visits in recent history.'[77] Former Undersecretary of State and UN Ambassador George McGhee wrote in his 1994 memoir that 'Nehru came to America with an apparent chip on his shoulder toward American high officials, who he appeared to believe could not possibly understand someone with his background.'[78] Nehru succeeded in making himself so unpopular with Americans generally that it would later prove difficult to muster support for helping to meet India's urgent need for wheat.

Ambassador McGee observed that in meetings Truman, Acheson, and Nehru often 'talked past each other.'[79] The policy differences revolved around Nehru's view that although there were areas where India disagreed with Moscow, Beijing, and Washington, he believed that confrontation would be unproductive and, instead, leaned 'towards recognizing China's Communist government.'[80] He underscored this point on 13 October while speaking with Secretary Acheson at the State Department, saying that India's shared border with China placed it in a different position regarding recognition of the new government.[81] Not surprisingly, in view of the 'Red Scare' enveloping Washington, this was poorly received.

A subsequent meeting that afternoon between Acheson, Ambassador Jessup, and George Kennan and the Indian delegation, including Nehru and his sister Madame Pandit, the Indian ambassador of India, ended with a chill. The Indians sat silently 'and made almost no contribution to the discussion beyond asking questions.'[82] In the wake of Britain's early recognition of Beijing, which many in Washington regarded as, at best, a mistake by London or, at worst, a betrayal, Nehru found himself entangled in an extremely sensitive issue.

After a state dinner at Anderson House, a nineteenth-century mansion on Massachusetts Avenue, Acheson took Nehru to his home in Georgetown for a more intimate talk in a further effort to develop a rapport. Acheson had hoped that 'uninhibited by a cloud of witnesses, we might establish a personal relationship.'[83] But Nehru 'would not relax' and Acheson remarked that the prime minister spoke in the same manner as Gladstone spoke to Queen Victoria, 'as though I were a public meeting.'[84] Nehru discussed stockpiling wheat and his point of view on the Kashmir solution, among other issues. It had been a long day for the secretary of state and by one o'clock in the morning, after nearly three hours of discussion, Acheson, in his own words, was 'becoming confused.'[85] Acheson's personal chat with Nehru made a 'deep impression on him.'[86] He wrote in his memoirs that 'I was convinced that Nehru and I were not destined to have a pleasant personal relationship ... he was one of the most difficult men with whom I have ever had to deal.'[87]

In New York, at a meeting with US–UN delegation members a few days later, Nehru played down events in China, and said that 'the situation in China did not represent a real danger to India in the sense of external aggression...'[88] He lectured the group on how the US should approach communism. Nehru believed it necessary that the US change its way of dealing with communism and assume a more 'indirect' and 'psychological' approach to Russia. He said, 'a sort of mental jujitsu would be more productive.'[89] On a personal level, Nehru found several of his hosts and their events ostentatious and crass.[90] He 'loathed the "gauche and commercial approach" of the US and was more disgusted than impressed by it.'[91] Frank Moraes, the editor of the *Times of India*, wrote in his biography of Nehru that a businessman at an event to encourage investment in India turned to Nehru and remarked: 'Do you realize, Mr Prime Minister, that you are eating dinner tonight with at least $20,000,000?'[92] Madame Pandit saw her brother 'literally shrinking into himself': '[H]is embarrassment and annoyance were acute.'[93] The meeting had originally been intended to discuss financial assistance, but Nehru was so upset that he refused to discuss the issue. Madame Pandit wrote: 'It is important to remember that though we all need money, our approach to it differs.'[94]

A few days later Nehru was feted at a dinner that the press called the 'epoch-making gesture of American hospitality which Kings might envy.'[95] Hosted by the US secretary of defense at the exclusive Greenbrier Hotel in White Sulphur Springs, West Virginia, Nehru 'disapproved' of the 'lavish and ostentatious' affair 'where the waiters were dressed in costumes of Civil War days,' and 'the menu was long and exotic.'[96] Nehru's sister wrote in her memoirs that these two functions 'could not have been more wrong had they been carefully planned to upset him.'[97]

Madame Ambassador, it appeared, was more accustomed to American etiquette blunders. She was unperturbed when the wife of a Senator excitedly told her at the Indian Embassy party for her brother that she had 'shaken hands with your tall, handsome new ambassador.'[98] 'He does look cute,' she continued, 'in his turban and with his long beard!'[99] Of course Madame Pandit was the Indian ambassador; the man in question was a Sikh security guard stationed at the entrance.

Nehru's unsuccessful visit to the United States underscored the tenuous nature of US–India relations and served to highlight the ideological differences and misperceptions that plagued the two countries. As for the American role in the visit, historian Robert McMahon wrote that 'for all the talk in Washington of India's centrality in the muddled Asian picture, the administration had made no hard decisions before Nehru's arrival.'[100] 'In that regard,' he continued, 'the lack of clarity among American planners is stunning.'[101] There was no discussion of how India could contribute to the stability of the region following the likely Nationalist collapse. Given the zeal with which the administration was trying to thwart the further spread of international communism, this is truly surprising. Moreover, there was no concrete discussion of the economic aid, particularly wheat, which India desperately needed.

There were several reasons for this. Firstly, Nehru himself was so diffident and seemingly uncomfortable, if not hostile, during his visit that the conditions for an understanding which might include economic assistance were not present. Secondly, Nehru's insistence that he meet communism on his own moral and philosophical grounds meant that Washington and Delhi lacked a common platform to address challenges to regional stability, including Chinese territorial claims—and of course the matter of Tibet's status.

Determined that the Americans not regard India as 'a beggar,' Nehru informed both Senate and House members that he would not 'seek any material advantage in exchange for any part of our hard-won freedom.'[102] In New York two days later, on 15 October, he reiterated his position:

I have not come to the USA to ask for or expect any gift from America. We are too proud and cultured a people to seek favors from others. It is not my intention to ask for this or that kind of help. We may have difficulties before us, but we shall make good in spite of everything. India will stand on her own feet.[103]

In the end, true to himself, Nehru neither asked for nor received aid from the United States. He pointedly 'left the business talks to others,' maintaining that he had mentioned economic and technical assistance only 'rather casually.'[104] He told his chief ministers that the trip 'represents the ending of the period of Asia's subservience, in world affairs, as well as in matters relative to Europe and America.'[105]

Indian resentment and criticism continued unabated after Nehru's return to India, which worried Washington officials. Everything did not, as Henderson had hoped, 'click.' Indeed, relations between the two nations declined even further. But as difficult as US–India relations seemed now, they would be further tested by the summer of 1950 as the realities of the Korean War and China's invasion of Tibet unfolded.

8

TIBETAN INDEPENDENCE

RESTING UPON A THREE-LEGGED STOOL

India as the dominant power in South Asia may be considered one leg of the three-legged stool upon which rested Tibet's prospective independence. The second leg was the United States, the self-described beacon of liberty and 'superpower' dedicated to the proposition of 'self-determination and freedom for all peoples.' For an untutored Tibet, these words had vital, even literal, meaning. Thus, it was not surprising that Tibet turned to Washington for help toward independence and recognition. It was an opaque, if not deceptive process, framed as we have seen by the troubled US–India relationship. The third leg of the stool was China, convulsed by revolution, haunted by its memory of nineteenth-century humiliation, vulnerable and determined not to permit 'splittists'—whether Formosans, Tibetans, or Uyghurs in Sinkiang—to separate from Beijing's rule.

But it was India that held the key to Tibet's future in many ways. During the first few years of India's independence, 1946–50, Nehru sought cordial relations with both Tibet and China. In his first radio address as vice president of the interim government, broadcast on 7 September 1946, Nehru described China, then under the Nationalists, as a 'mighty country with a mighty past, our neighbor [that] has been our friend through the ages and this friendship will endure and grow.'[1] Yet with independence and the inheritance of British obligations and rights for Tibet, India soon found that its interests conflicted with Chinese claims.[2]

India's independence in effect placed Nehru in the position of balancing the claims and objectives of two nations with competing interests. The Chinese had made it clear over time that they objected to any Indian gesture suggesting an independent Tibet. This was understood in Delhi. Well before India's official independence, Nehru signaled to China that he did 'not wish to do anything which might offend

63

Chinese susceptibilities or raise any question of status [and] desire[d] to avoid saying anything regarding Tibetans which may involve controversy.'[3]

Meanwhile, looking outward with hopes to join the global community at the end of 1947, Lhasa sent a trade delegation to Delhi as their first stop on a trip that would take them to Washington. The delegation brought a number of issues for discussion with the Indian government. Among them was a request for US dollars to finance their trip to the United States and to purchase machinery for use in agriculture and in their wool factories.[4] But it was more than financial assistance and trade support that the Tibetans wanted. In a private meeting with Nehru they asked the Indian prime minister to 'bear witness to Tibet's independent and sovereign status.'[5] The Chinese, who had received information about the Tibetan agenda, again made their position clear to the Indians. In a note to K. P. S. Menon, the head of India's Ministry of External Affairs and Commonwealth Relations, President Chiang's ambassador to India, Dr Lo Chio-Luen, asked that New Delhi 'discourage and refuse' discussions with the delegation bearing on Tibetan 'sovereignty and [the] administrative integrity of China.'[6] Menon obliged and in a quick response assured the Nationalists that India had 'no intention to discuss issues which would embarrass China in any way.'[7] The die was cast.

Relations between India and Tibet had not begun well: the Tibetans had refused to acknowledge that the Indian government was now Britain's successor. The Tibetans were hopeful that Nehru would recognize them as an independent nation. When the trade delegation arrived in Delhi at the end of 1947 and requested the release of funds for their trip and to purchase gold, Nehru refused, making it clear to the delegation that their government would have to negotiate a treaty with the Indians first. Nehru released just enough money to cover their trip expenses. The Tibetan Kashag reached an agreement with India in June 1948.[8]

The Tibetan trade delegation: 'babes in the wood'[9]

The Tibetan trade mission enjoyed only modest success. The hope had been to affirm Tibet's status as an independent nation and to begin the process of recognition in capitals around the world. There was no agreement on Tibet's independent national status, but it was generally accepted that while the mission demonstrated that Tibet 'had some sort of international identity independent of China, the nature of that identity was far from clear.'[10] In the end the visit alarmed China's Nationalist government and provoked the US to review its relationship with Tibet in the unforgiving light of its Chinese ties.

Thus, the trade mission, while a significant episode in Tibet's halting journey, was not an entirely positive one. It began in June 1947 when the Tibetan Foreign Affairs Bureau wrote to the US ambassador requesting that he notify the State Department of the Tibetan delegation's proposed visit to Washington. The objective of the mission was to buy gold and silver for use by the Tibetan government to back their currency and to establish trade relations with the United States. The Treasury Department indicated its willingness to sell the Tibetans gold provided the State Department affirmed this would not impair relations with the Nationalists. It was the Treasury's policy 'to sell gold to foreign governments and central banks' and in this case they were 'willing to consider Tibet a foreign government.'[11] The US embassy in India favorably advised the State Department about the impending Tibetan visit.

In a detailed report to Washington regarding the Tibetan mission, Counselor Donovan wrote that 'Tibet's position, as a vast island in Asia, cannot be safely ignored and is an area which in the future might prove extremely useful for military operations.'[12] Donovan felt that the Tibetans should be treated with the 'utmost courtesy' and that the Chinese embassy should not be permitted to interfere; 'our Government should not throw away its unique opportunity to strengthen the friendly feelings which the Tibetans have exhibited.'[13]

The flurry of cable traffic between Washington, Delhi, and the Foreign Office in London over the next year highlights the many unresolved issues surrounding Tibet. Questions included: should their Tibetan passport be accepted; what type of visa should they receive; was the visit to be considered official or unofficial; and, perhaps most importantly, how to appease the objections of the Chinese Nationalists. The KMT made it plain to Washington that they believed the mission was designed to show Tibetan independence, and thus they found it unacceptable.[14]

En route to the United States in February 1948, the Tibetans stopped in Nanking for meetings at the US embassy. The embassy reported to the State Department China Desk that the delegation discussed potential future commercial relations between Nationalist China and Tibet. During the course of their visit, Tsepon Shakabpa, the head of the delegation, was asked about conditions in Tibet, to which he replied:

[T]he country is prosperous and free of inflation. Everyone in Tibet has enough to eat, enough to wear and a house to live in. There is no labor trouble over wages and working hours and everyone is happy.[15]

Referring to living costs, Shakabpa said 'a good sized chicken costs about US$0.20. And meat, well, if a family needs some pork all they do is go out to the market, pay some money and come home with a whole hog.'[16] Shakabpa's comments prompted the ambassador to add, 'from his description one has an impression that Tibet truly qualifies as the Shangri-La of James Hilton's novel, *Lost Horizon*.'[17]

Later that year, in July as the Tibetan mission arrived in Washington, the Chinese foreign minister made his displeasure clear at the US embassy in Nanking where he stated the mission was not 'authorized by the Chinese government.'[18] He wrote: 'the intention of the Mission to act as independently as possible and, by any means available, to acquire recognition of its separation from China will create serious political embarrassment for [the] Nationalist Government...'[19] The minister was adamant 'that no American agencies have dealings with [the] Mission except when [accompanied] by the Chinese Embassy.'[20] The KMT position was reiterated when the Chinese minister in Washington, Dr Tan Shao-hwa, called on officials at the State Department.

Secretary Marshall, who had been under attack by Luce and others over his out-spokenness about the Nationalist corruption, was exasperated with Chiang; this was clearly apparent in his response to Nanking two days later, which reflected the complexities of the impending Tibetan visit both in terms of protocol and also in terms of the relations between Chiang's China and Tibet. Marshall wrote that while:

USGOVT [has] no intention of acting in a manner to call into question China's de jure sovereignty over Tibet [and] DEPT does not desire [to] offend sensibilities of either China or Tibet, but is of opinion that Tibetans could rightly be affronted if not received by President.[21]

Marshall made pointed reference to the question of China's sovereignty in the same cable: 'ChiGovt should appreciate that the fact that it exerts no de facto authority over Tibet is root cause of situation.'[22]

Marshall conveyed his concerns regarding the Tibetan visit, which highlighted the difficulties the administration faced brought on by the China Lobby. It was only his professionalism that prevented him from lashing out at the Nationalists and their Washington supporters. While the Luce media machine and others supported the Generalissimo, Marshall believed that if the American public were to learn that the Chinese Nationalist government forbade the Tibetans to visit the President, this would work to Chiang's disadvantage, for America stood fast in its commitment to promote 'self-determination for all peoples and nations.'[23] 'The President,' Marshall wrote in his memo, 'has expressed personal interest in greeting the Tibetans.'[24] In closing, the secretary wrote that 'USGOVT does not wish to add a mite to Chinese current preoccupation, but we are confronted with practical problem which discourtesy will not solve.'[25] Marshall was angry.

Eventually the Tibetan delegation arrived in the United States, using their own passports; they had managed to travel to Hong Kong (via Delhi) where they obtained US visas. This incensed George Yeh, China's vice minister of Foreign Affairs, who lodged a protest with the American embassy in Nanking asking why the American consul general in Hong Kong had issued the visas and reiterating that the Tibetan delegation had 'no authority to deal with other nations as an independent country.'[26] At the same time a protest was made to the State Department in Washington by the counselor of the Chinese embassy, T. L. Tsui, who spoke with the director of the State Department's Office of Chinese Affairs, Phillip Sprouse.[27] Again, the Chinese asked why the American consul general in Hong Kong had issued American visas on their Tibetan passports, and if the US had changed policy towards Tibet.[28]

With this as background, the Tibetan trade mission arrived in Washington on 19 July 1948. The Department of Commerce, who hosted the visit, informed the Chinese embassy that, contrary to their preference, an official embassy escort for the Tibetans would not be necessary. The reason given was that since the delegation was in Washington on an 'unofficial basis,' that is as 'businessmen on a purely commercial basis,' there was no need of embassy assistance.[29]

The Tibetan mission had specifically requested to see President Truman, however, and though the Nationalists knew that Truman wished to see the Tibetans, Nanking insisted that a meeting could not be held unless an embassy officer was present.[30] The impasse deepened following a lengthy meeting at the State Department on 2 August 1948, concerning protocol requirements, at which the Tibetans insisted there be no chaperone.

At that point the Tibetans were told that unless Ambassador Koo of the Chinese embassy in Washington accompanied them it would be 'very difficult if not impossible' to see the president. Mr Freeman of the State Department's Office of Chinese Affairs further explained that unless the ambassador was present it would embarrass the Chinese government which had '*de jure* sovereignty' over Tibet and was, moreover, the 'recognized diplomatic representative of their country.'[31] Indeed the Chinese were worried that the Tibetans would discuss political matters in the meeting with the President.[32] Thus, both the Chinese and Tibetan positions were etched in stone.

Ambassador Stuart in Nanking wrote to Secretary Marshall two days after the Washington meeting and said the Chiang government is 'so sensitive on [the] question [of] Chinese sovereignty that any action which by any stretch of the imagination could be construed as a reflection on that sovereignty is repugnant.' Stewart's memorandum goes on to say that the Yuan (Chinese legislative body) 'has openly and strongly been attacking the British Foreign Office with charges that it has not shown sufficient firmness in protecting Chinese interests in Tibet.'[33]

In the end, the Tibetans did not meet with President Truman, but neither did any official from the Chinese embassy accompany them to, or have knowledge of, their meeting with the secretary of state. On 6 August, Secretary Marshall, Mr Walton Butterworth, the director for Far Eastern Affairs, and Mr Fulton Freeman, director of the Office of Chinese Affairs, met with the four members of the Tibetan delegation and their translator at the State Department.[34]

Marshall was friendly and courteous to the Tibetans, recalling that he had met members of another Tibetan delegation in the summer of 1946.[35] The secretary was presented with pictures of the Dalai Lama and a traditional white Tibetan scarf. Through their interpreter the members of the mission told him that the main purpose of their trip abroad was to 'improve trade relations between Tibet and the United States.'[36] From Washington the delegation traveled to New York, where they met General Dwight Eisenhower, then president of Columbia University.

On their return to Lhasa from the United States in early January 1949, the delegation met with Nehru for a discussion that again centered on trade and economic issues. And although the Tibetans were disappointed with the meeting, the very charming Indian prime minister told them that the 'Government of India entertained the most cordial feelings of friendship for Tibet, her Government and people and that it would be his constant endeavor to foster relations of friendship.'[37] By the end of the year, however, India had decided that maintaining its friendship with China under the new People's Republic of China (PRC) took precedence.

In retrospect, the trip had its ironies. Though the Tibetans had, in a small way, exerted some measure of independence—they managed to arrive in the US on their own passports and to purchase $425,000 worth of gold from the US Treasury—the trip had also sparked, according to one US official, the 'strongest assertion of China's control over Tibet since 1911.'[38] For its part, the Department's seventh-floor executive suite nursed its resentment over Nationalist interference on whom the Tibetans should meet and who should accompany them—events that would not be soon forgotten. And, of course, it was of some consolation that Chinese officials, including Wellington Koo, were completely unaware that the Tibetans had held discussions with Secretary Marshall privately. Still, while the Tibetans learned a good deal about the niceties of diplomatic exchange and apparently precipitated a review in Washington of US–Tibet policy, the mission made little tangible progress in establishing a path to independence.

9

THE MATTER OF TIBET'S STATUS

Following the delegation's visit, Washington took a closer look at Tibet in geopolitical terms. The CIA, in conjunction with intelligence staffs at the Departments of State, Navy, and the Air Force produced a comprehensive background report for the President.[1] Analysts focused on what options might be available to the United States, should Washington choose to influence events, given Tibet's location, the Soviet interest in Tibet, and the likely communist victory on the mainland.

The report noted Tibetan distrust of the Soviets because of their religious suppression of lamaism in Outer Mongolia. There had been disturbing reports that year of visits to Tibetan monasteries by Soviet intelligence officers posing as lamas, which appeared to underscore Moscow's growing interest in the region.[2] Although the White House and foreign policy experts did not believe that the Soviets had an immediate interest in Tibet itself, administration analysts believed that should Russia 'gain influence over the Tibetan hierarchy, it could extend its influence among the peoples of western China and northern India' who accepted the Dalai Lama as their spiritual leader.[3] All of this—Soviet intentions, the geopolitical implications, the difficulty in establishing Tibet's status, and the interest expressed by the joint chiefs of staff in Tibet as a staging platform—led Washington to begin a full review of Tibet policy in 1949.

It was, in effect, initiated in January of that year by Ambassador Loy Henderson in Delhi, who cabled Secretary of State Acheson calling for a full review of US–Tibet policy, including Tibet's status 'in light of the changing conditions in Asia.'[4] Henderson quite sensibly suggested that 'If the Communists succeed in extending their control over all of China, the United States might wish to reconsider the extent to which it insists upon emphasizing the suzerainty of China over Tibet...'[5]

The confusion surrounding Tibet's status was subsequently addressed in April 1949 in a detailed report prepared by Ruth E. Bacon of the State Department's Office of Far Eastern Affairs (FEA). Looking at this and other issues, Bacon wrote:

'[I]t is to be noted in the files there are references to China's 'sovereignty' or 'suzerainty' over Tibet. It is, of course, known the two terms are not synonymous. It is difficult, however, to draw a precise line of demarcation between them.'[6]

The report went to Philip Sprouse, the director of the Office of Chinese Affairs.[7] It made the point that some documents and some officials used the word 'sovereignty,' others used 'suzerainty,' and the terms '*de jure*' and '*de facto*' were used interchangeably.

In an attempt to render these semantic usages a non-issue, the report suggested that Washington could avoid a possible controversy over 'sovereignty' versus 'suzerainty' by referring in future to Chinese 'de jure authority over Tibet or some similarly comprehensive term.'[8]

The report flirts with inconsistency when it separates its position on how best to describe Tibet's status—to avoid controversy—from its geopolitical argument that Tibet was 'one of the few remaining non-Communist bastions in Continental Asia,' and if the Communists gained control it would 'assume both ideological and strategic importance.'[9] Moreover, the Dalai Lama had influence in countries such as Nepal, Bhutan, and Mongolia, where Buddhism was practiced. It would thus be very much in America's interest for Tibet to be a 'friend.'[10]

Cognizant that the Nationalists were headed for defeat, Bacon's report addressed the form that US–Tibet policy might take if the communists took over all of China.[11] She wrote that under those circumstances it 'would be preferable and more advantageous to treat Tibet as independent.'[12] Left unaddressed at the time was the question that would later become a reality, namely what Tibet policy should be if an 'émigré National Government should continue to exist.'[13]

Significantly, the report stated that 'The Chinese Government cannot now assert—and currently there appears little likelihood that it ever again will be able to assert—effective de facto authority in Tibet.'[14] Ambassador Stuart in Beijing, in a telegram to Secretary of State Dean Acheson, supported this view, writing: 'Authority [of] Canton Government over Tibet non-existent ... and we agree any move with implications recognition autonomous status of Tibet should be made before relations established with Chinese Communist government.'[15]

Ambassador Stuart went on to say:

For the present we should avoid giving the impression of any alteration in our position toward Chinese authority over Tibet such as, for example, steps which would clearly indicate that we regard Tibet as independent, etc. We have recently given renewed assurances to China of our recognition of China's de jure sovereignty or suzerainty over Tibet. Any decided change in our policy might give China cause for complaint [and] might stimulate Soviet efforts at infiltration into Tibet and might not in itself be sufficient to hold Tibet to our side.[16]

While it was clear that the State Department did not want to 'give offence' to the Nationalists and wished to keep the policy 'as flexible as possible,' it was also clear that the Department hoped to preserve its strategic options while keeping the upper hand in dealing with Chiang Kai-shek's government. Accordingly, Bacon maintained that while the administration should avoid the confusion of 'suzerainty' and 'sovereignty' it was also best to inform 'China of our proposed moves in connection with Tibet, rather than asking China's consent for them.'[17]

With the Chinese communists on the cusp of victory, Tibet's status was also on Nehru's mind during the summer of 1949. Hugh Richardson, the head of the Indian mission in Lhasa, wrote to G. S. Bajpai, the Indian secretary general of the Ministry of External Relations, to express his concerns over what would happen to Tibet when the communists came to power.[18] 'The Tibetans,' Richardson wrote, 'looked to India for guidance.' Richardson wanted to know if the Indian government would consider supplying arms and material to help Tibet.[19] Not surprisingly, Nehru's response to Richardson's inquiries was similar to the US position. Nehru wrote to Bajpai: 'we should be very careful in taking any measures which might be considered a challenge to the Chinese Communist Government or which might mean an invasion of Tibetan sovereignty.'[20] Nehru added:

Whatever may be the ultimate fate of Tibet in relation to China, I think there is practically no chance of any military danger to India arising from any possible change in Tibet. Geographically, [to help would be] very difficult and practically it would be a foolish adventure.[21]

Nehru did not want to provoke a communist invasion and was determined not to disturb 'the balance [he] was trying to create in India.'[22]

After the Chinese communist victory in October 1949, the complexity of India's relations with the new People's Republic of China (PRC) and Tibet became increasingly apparent. Following Nehru's return from the US, he held a press conference on 16 November 1949. He was queried as to whether India would recognize the PRC, and how and this would impact Tibet. To the first question he responded that he would consult with K. M. Panikkar, the Indian ambassador to China; and to the second question, his answer was ambiguous.[23] Nehru acknowledged that the British had recognized 'a certain autonomy of Tibet' and that now there 'were direct relations between Tibet and India.'[24] He further acknowledged that China had a 'vague kind of suzerainty' over Tibet. 'All these things,' Nehru rambled on, 'were never clearly defined as to what the position was, matters remained vague and they have remained vague in that way.'[25]

Nehru then contacted the UK high commissioner in Delhi for advice. The UK government's view on how Delhi should view Tibet was consistent with what they had told Washington. The British maintained that it would be best if India adhered to:

[the] pre-independence Indian policy of recognizing Chinese suzerainty but supporting Tibetan autonomy, and particularly that GOI should not take any steps which could be considered open defiance to Chinese Communists such as recognition [of] independence [for] Tibet or sending brigade troops to Lhasa.[26]

On 12 December the US chargé d'affaires in London wrote to Acheson regarding the position of the Foreign Office. The British, while expressing 'their interest in

Tibet maintaining its autonomy,' made it clear that now this was 'almost exclusively of concern to India.'[27]

In November 1949, one month after the communists came into power, the Tibetans approached the Indian government for help. At the same time, Surkhang Depon, a member of the Tibetan trade delegation, arrived on the doorstep of the American embassy with a formal request in hand. Tibet's Foreign Bureau asked Washington for 'extensive aid in regards [to] civil and military requirements' and expressed the hope for an early and favorable reply.[28] They not only sought aid to resist the Chinese communists but also support for membership of the United Nations and to send a delegation to the United States.

In December 1949, as the last Nationalists exited the mainland, Secretary of State Acheson instructed Ambassador Henderson in Delhi to inform the Tibetan representative that the US was sympathetic to their request, but that if they sent a delegation to the United States it could 'serve to precipitate [a] Chinese Communist action to control Tibet.'[29] Acheson was 'convinced the Tibetan effort [to] obtain UN membership at this time would be unsuccessful.'[30] He believed that they would be opposed by the USSR and by the Chinese.[31] Acheson suggested that Ambassador Henderson:

[P]oint out informally and on a personal basis that Tibet now appears [to] enjoy de facto freedom [from] Chinese control and that any obvious move [at] this time [in] completing separation from China in form as well as substance would probably hasten Chinese Commie efforts thereby jeopardizing present status.[32]

Thus the administration experienced a range of pressures and balanced several interests as it considered the matter of recognizing Tibet. Among them was the China Lobby, which remained opposed to recognition even as the Nationalists fled to Taiwan, arguing such would violate China's sovereignty. They were followed by the geostrategists who feared that recognition would 'hasten a Communist Chinese invasion'; and of course India had expressed its own reservations.

Throughout 1949 and 1950 the issue of Tibet's legal status was discussed both in Washington and at Whitehall. In December 1950, two months after the People's Liberation Army invaded Tibet, the British government requested Washington's position on Tibet.[33] The response was both lengthy and detailed.[34] The State Department's Office of the Legal Advisor took the position that Tibet could not be classified as:

[A] fully sovereign and independent member of the family of nations … this is not to say that Tibet is not a state within the meaning of international law, for complete independence is not a prerequisite of international personality.[35]

The legal advisor, Mr Snow, wrote that in his opinion Tibet had *de jure* independence regarding its foreign relations and *de facto* and *de jure* independence regarding its internal affairs.[36] Snow said:

[I]f this Government is satisfied that Tibet possesses the machinery of a state, administers the government with the consent of the people and is able to fulfill its international obligations, the only legal bar to recognition of Tibet on our part might be Article I, Paragraph I of the

Nine Power Treaty of 1922 in which the contracting powers agreed to the administrative integrity of China.[37]

Snow added that 'the embarrassing factor here is that US government officials in Washington assured the Chinese Nationalists orally that the United States recognized Chinese sovereignty over Tibet.'[38] What might be thought even more embarrassing, however, was a seeming throwaway line at the end of his extended analysis: 'As a matter of fact, this Office believes that China does not have and has not had sovereignty over Tibet.'[39]

Referring to the Nine Power Treaty mentioned above, the legal advisor went on to note that: 'It is not believed that there is anything in the treaty structure relating to Tibet which would preclude the United States from recognizing Tibetan independence'.[40] But again the issue of the Nationalists was on Snow's mind as he wrote: 'If it should be decided to recognize Tibet, it must be borne in mind that the Chinese Nationalists will undoubtedly claim that this is an unfriendly act.'[41]

While the report was favorable towards the Tibetans, preserving the relationship with the Chinese Nationalists in the near term had assumed greater political importance. The Nationalists were, after all, the force on the ground opposing the communists and in whom the US had invested much money and credibility. Moreover, the Nationalists were not without power in Washington thanks to the China Lobby, or without sympathy among the American people thanks to Henry Luce. The perceived challenge for US policy-makers was thus to 'respect China's territorial integrity' while maintaining 'a friendly attitude toward Tibet in ways short of giving China cause for offence.'[42]

If the Office of the Legal Advisor seemed to find no reason why Tibet could not be seen as sovereign, Washington's vote-counters in the UN reported that an official attempt to gain recognition would not succeed. It therefore came down to the practical point that the US relationship with the Generalissimo remained the priority so long as the Nationalists were a going concern—or did it?

The golden hour

Between the end of 1948 until the beginning of the Korean War Washington's policy began to change, giving way to a reappraisal, as Washington resigned itself to a Nationalist defeat on the mainland. This was the time when the administration could have engaged more fully with Lhasa, but Acheson hesitated, in what seems a tragic error, fearing the Soviets might be spurred to invade Tibet.

Yet if a window of opportunity existed, it was in this brief period, because with the start of the Korean War and the near simultaneous communist invasion of Tibet, the geopolitics of the region changed dramatically. Now Taiwan had emerged as a platform for attacks on the mainland while the Nationalist government, now resident there, continued to claim sovereignty over all of China. Thus Washington continued to believe that its policy options regarding Tibetan recognition and independence were still limited by prior understandings—but not for long. As the communist grip on the mainland became a reality, both the Tibetans and the Nationalists on Taiwan would become important parts of the US covert effort against the People's Republic of China.

10

LOWELL THOMAS IN TIBET

The summer of 1949 saw the People's Liberation Army swarm over the mainland, moving ever further to the south-west and Tibet while driving the Nationalists inexorably toward their island sanctuary on Taiwan; the approaching apocalypse, refined and focused with each passing day, was an unfolding nightmare for Lhasa. That summer a comet had appeared in the night skies. Amidst much consternation, the monks warned that this was a bad omen, nearly as bad as an earthquake.[1] Heinrich Harrer, a German explorer, former prisoner of war, and friend of the Dalai Lama, would later say that '[Tibetans] were reminded that in 1910, before the Manchu invaded, a comet was seen streaking through the sky and monsters were born...'[2]

As the PLA installed the Communist Party in Beijing and the 'Red Scare' roiled dinner tables across America, Lhasa and the plight of the Tibetan people were briefly brought to light by the legendary broadcaster Lowell Thomas who travelled there in September 1949. Yet Tibet was far away and didn't necessarily come to mind even when the 'great and the good' spoke of 'self-determination' and America's commitment to the freedom of peoples around the world. The intelligence services, however, had begun to stir—as we shall see in the tragic story of Doug Mackiernan. But first a few words about Lowell Thomas whose broadcast journalism brought the Tibet story to the American public in the early 1950s.

After expelling all Chinese visitors from Lhasa in the summer of 1949, the Tibetans were leery about giving permission for foreigners to visit. The one exception is found that fall when newscaster Lowell Thomas and his son obtained an invitation. It was mainly through the efforts of Ambassador Henderson, with help from Tsepon Shakabpa, who had headed the Tibetan trade delegation to the United States, that the trip was arranged.[3]

While it may not have been 'a miracle,' as the hyperbolic Thomas claimed in his memoir, that he and his son were allowed into Tibet, it was certainly true that his request had reached Lhasa at 'a crucial moment.'[4] Officials in Lhasa were hopeful that this well-known broadcaster would make plain to his global audience that Mao had set his sights on Tibet.

Thomas and his son Lowell Thomas Jr arrived in Lhasa in September, staying little more than a week. They met with the young Dalai Lama, were feted with receptions and interviewed Tibetan officials who expressed their grave concern about how to preserve Tibetan independence if the communists took over. They asked Thomas what he thought the Americans would do if this were to happen.[5] But Thomas could offer nothing concrete.

On his way back to India later that month, Lowell Sr suffered a very serious injury. The Thomases, who were travelling on horseback and in a yak-skin boat with a small caravan of pack animals and Tibetan guides, left Lhasa in late September knowing the Himalayan snows would come early. The group reached the summit of the Kara-La mountain and had begun their descent. After stopping for a break Thomas went to mount his horse but neglected to have someone hold his horse's bridle; the horse was young and spirited, and bolted.[6] Thomas was sent 'flying out over the edge of the trail.'[7] He felt the 'agonizing sensation of bones breaking in his hip' and then crashed onto the sharp rocks below.[8] He struggled to remain conscious as his breathing became labored by the thin air at 17,000 feet.[9] Nightfall was almost upon them as he went into shock; there were no pain medicines available and the next village was four miles away. The next day Lowell Jr managed to find a telephone in the village and contact an Indian military medic in Gyantse, more than 30 miles away. The Tibetans carried Lowell Sr on a stretcher to Gyantse; he later learned that his hip and his leg were broken in eight places.[10] After securing a truck, they drove three days to reach an Indian border post, but with no planes or helicopters to rescue them, they had to travel another 200 miles to the larger Indian town of Gangtok. Loy Henderson and Prime Minister Nehru sent a military team and Air Force plane to meet them in Gangtok where they were flown to Calcutta and then to the States. It was a long recovery for the elder Thomas, but he relayed to the world the plight of the Tibetan people through press conferences, articles in the *New York Times*, and Lowell Jr did the same in a later account of his travels.[11]

After his trip, Thomas sent a letter to Dean Acheson and met with Pentagon officials in November to apprise them of his findings.[12] Thomas also met with Acheson, who was at the time suffering with a broken leg. He notes in his memoirs that the two men must have made an interesting pair. Thomas was still on crutches when he met Acheson, who was propped up on cushions on the floor of his office with his leg in a cast.[13] Thomas then went on to see President Truman, and they talked for an hour. Interestingly, while they were both conversant with the Tibetan myth and heard the practical analysis offered by Thomas as reflected in his letter, neither the president nor his secretary of state offered any promise of help to the people of Tibet.[14]

Former Ambassador to China James Lilley had been President George H. W. Bush's CIA Beijing station chief in 1975 when Bush was US representative in China. Mr Lilley confirmed to the authors that Thomas was in fact working with the 'US government to help the Tibetans.'[15] In September 1997 Lilley travelled to Lhasa with former President George W. H. Bush, Lowell Thomas, and James A. Baker III, among others. The group was taken to the Tibetan Revolutionary Museum in Lhasa by their Chinese hosts, where they were shown photographs of the Dalai Lama's government allegedly mistreating Tibetans. Lilley wrote: 'There were graphic photographs of people being tortured and expositions of children who had their kneecaps broken and had been stuffed into jars.'[16] There was an 'imperialist' section in the museum, and here Thomas was identified as an 'imperialist agent' and shown in a picture with 'members of the royal court' in 1949, allegedly passing money to them. The former president asked Lilley to check with Thomas to see if he really did work with the US government to help the Tibetans. When Lilley asked Thomas, he wasn't surprised at the answer. Thomas said with great vehemence, 'You're damn right I did, I supported the Tibetans. And I'd do it again.'[17]

11

MAJOR DOUGLAS MACKIERNAN

A TRAGIC INCIDENT

While Lowell Thomas and his son were in Tibet that September, a separate covert operation reporting to the War Department in Washington was unfolding in Tibet. It was the second time (Tolstoy and Dolan being the first) that Tibet had become involved with the US intelligence services.

This unfortunate story illustrates how poor communications in a remote, unstable border area caused Major Douglas Mackiernan's death. The episode raised questions just as Lhasa was trying to establish trade and diplomatic relations in post-war Asia and hoping to solidify relations with the United States. That said, Mackiernan's mission was a considerable success; at Tihwa (now Urumchi), the capital of China's north-west province of Sinkiang, vital information was gathered on the Soviet nuclear program. Later, in Lhasa, Frank Bessac (CIA officer and companion of Mackiernan's) was an eye-witness to the city's distress as it braced itself for the impending PLA invasion.

Douglas Mackiernan was a research scientist; he had studied physics at the Massachusetts Institute of Technology and had an interest in meteorology and radio technology.[1] Beginning in 1944, during World War II, Mackiernan operated a vital weather station for the United States in Tihwa. In this remote part of the world, he decoded Russian radio weather broadcasts that proved vital for US bombers striking Japan.[2] The tiny American consulate he occupied at Tihwa was a strategic listening post bordering on the Eastern Turkestan Republics (ETR), Kazakhstan, and Tajikistan—and on Mongolia, Afghanistan, Tibet, Pakistan, and India. Home to generations of Turkic peoples, including Kazakhs, central Asian nomads, and Muslim Uyghurs, it was a hotbed of activity and a contested region between Russia, China, and the Uyghurs.[3]

79

With the end of the war the Tihwa station closed and Major Mackiernan quietly returned to America in October 1945. He went to work for the US government's Strategic Services Unit (SSU) in the War Department in 1947, which later became part of the Central Intelligence Agency (CIA).[4] In June of that year he assumed the post of vice consul at the US consulate in Tihwa as cover for his CIA responsibilities. The British, who had their own listening post in Tihwa, noted Mackiernan's return.[5] They held the American contingent at arm's length—much the same as they had Tolstoy and Dolan in Lhasa two years earlier. They reported to London that the Americans carried a 'wireless,' which they claimed was needed in the event of 'serious trouble,' meaning an upsurge in tribal violence in the region.[6] The British were unimpressed with this explanation, but having no other, referred to them *sotto voce* as a 'corrupt bunch.'[7]

The Americans were, indeed, focused on things other than tribal violence. The region was rich in strategic mineral reserves and the US was concerned that the Russians were mining uranium needed to create a nuclear bomb.[8] Mackiernan's task, under his vice consular title, was to observe Soviet activities in the region and report back to Washington on Russian mining progress in Eastern Turkestan.[9] Mackiernan traveled the area extensively, sometimes on his Arabian–Kazakh cross horse, to try to determine if the Russians were conducting atomic research. Said to have cut a dashing figure, he would regularly ride to a remote spot in the desert brush where he had buried a container with his research notations and papers in the sand.[10] The CIA recently divulged that he cultivated a number of assets, including Osman Bator, a nomad Kazakh chieftain and resistance fighter who in later years became a source for the American government.[11]

By July of 1949, as a communist takeover seemed imminent, Washington began to consider closing its consulates in Canton, Chungking, Kunming, and Tihwa. The Department felt that Tihwa had the most strategic value: it was by now providing a flow of critical intelligence on Soviet uranium mining and also on inter-ethnic and tribal matters. Washington hoped to maintain personnel there as long as possible.[12] Yet, on 29 July, the secretary of state cabled John Hall Paxton, the consul at Tihwa, saying: 'After careful consideration all factors Dept has decided close Consulate Tihwa.'[13] Acheson was worried about the safety of the consulate staff and asked Paxton for his recommendations for disposing of US government property, as he did not think the consulate would be 'reopened in the foreseeable future.'[14]

A few weeks later, in August 1949, the consul general left Tihwa with sixteen others, including his wife Vincoe. After a treacherous ten-week journey that included crossing mountain passes at nearly 19,000 feet, traversing a 400-foot glacier and suffering nausea, frostbite, and insomnia, they finally crossed into India where they were flown to Delhi.[15]

As the PLA proceeded to take over the northern and western parts of China in 1949, Frank Bessac, a former OSS, now CIA officer and anthropologist, made his way across the Gobi desert to Tihwa, the capital of Sinkiang, and to the US consulate where he met Douglas Mackiernan. In a story that has become the stuff of myth,

Mackiernan, the only American left, was surprised when his future travelling companion, Frank Bessac, walked in the door; he invited Bessac to lunch a few days later. Bessac had studied Chinese at Cornell University, later joined the US Army and then the OSS. He was fluent in Mandarin, was awarded a Fulbright Scholarship to study Mongolian tribes in the Gobi desert, and later became a professor of anthropology at the University of Montana.

After days in the Gobi desert, Bessac was starved for a good meal—and was not disappointed. He and Mackiernan dined on a beautifully set table with American 'china', knives, forks, soup spoons, and napkins, and were served by a blond Russian boy who was appropriately dressed with a white towel draped over his arm; it was a delightful occasion.[16] The next day the two sat down in Mackiernan's office for a smoke—Mackiernan smoked a pipe and Bessac cigarettes. Mackiernan, without any preamble, spoke the word 'Oregon' and waited for Bessac's reaction.[17] True to his training, Bessac did not show his surprise but knew that this was the code word signifying that Mackiernan worked for the agency. Bessac, after a studied pause, simply said 'D.'[18] With that response, Mackiernan got up and shook Bessac's hands and said, 'Well, I am glad you replied, buddy. You had me worried for a minute.'[19]

On 24 August Mackiernan cabled Acheson to advise him that he would destroy 'all archives, cryptographic material and motion picture films.'[20] The men then destroyed hundreds of top secret documents and began the long walk out of China.

That September, as the Chinese again assumed control of Tihwa and the region, Major Mackiernan left the consulate with Bessac and Vasili Zvansov, a White Russian refugee whom Mackiernan had hired as a houseman and groom. White Russians had been loyal to the czar during the Russian revolution and remained strong anti-communists, though Zvansov had deserted the Russian army in 1941. Two other Russians, Stephani Yanuishkin and Leonid Shutov, were included in the small party. Their destination was Lhasa, 1,200 miles away.

Mackiernan's grim demise

After purchasing horses and provisions from Osman Bător, the Kazakh resistance fighter, Mackiernan and his party began the trek across the formidable landscape on 27 September 1949, almost a month after the Russians had exploded their first nuclear bomb at Semipalatinsk, on the steppes of Kazakhstan. For the first two weeks they remained close to Lake Barkol, a mountainous area in the north-eastern part of Sinkiang province. Before them was the vast Taklamakan desert; for locals, the word Taklamakan meant 'place of no return.' They would travel south-south-west to reach Tibet.

They rode on horseback, equipped with maps, a compass, and a barometer. The terrain was both unfamiliar and unforgiving: no roads, few paths, and shifting sands. On his last meeting with Osman, Mackiernan tore a $5 bill in half; each man put his thumbprint on a half and gave it to the other in a gesture of friendship and in anticipation of their eventual reunion.[21] Both men would eventually meet horrible deaths:

Osman was captured and executed by the Chinese communists; Mackiernan would be shot at the Tibetan border, becoming the first CIA officer to die in the line of duty.

* * *

Mackiernan and Bessac kept a detailed log of their journey from Tihwa to Tibet. Classified 'Top Secret' by the US government, the log was declassified in August 1997. They traveled for days in very harsh conditions, seeing only the skeletons of men, horses, and camels along the path.[22] The walk was a slog; they sank nearly knee-high into the desert sands. Each day brought new privations—hunger and exhaustion—and at one point they found themselves without water for three days.[23]

The small party traveled at night for fear of interception by the newly installed communist authorities. Occasionally they would come upon Kazakhs who offered shelter in their yurts and a dinner of mutton and tea; many of them had never seen a foreigner before.[24] They bartered to replace camels, tents, and supplies and acquired Kazakh clothing. They ate the meat from the animals they could kill—antelope, wild ass, or yak—and cooked on a fire made from dried yak dung. As the temperatures fell below freezing, they took shelter from November 1949 until March 1950 in a large Kazakh camp in the mountains bordering Tibet, in what Bessac wrote was the largest yurt he had ever seen.[25]

On 20 March they resumed the trek to Tibet, ascending the mountains with fifteen camels and two horses. They had little to eat and the altitude made it impossible to boil water; the food they killed was never fully cooked.[26] They were tired and ill; Bessac developed a rare protein poisoning from the meat and felt himself to be continually starving. The fillings in his mouth fell out and his teeth ached. The pain was almost unbearable.[27] The animals suffered even worse privation; the horses died but, rancid as the meat was, the camels ate it—and survived.[28]

On 29 April the party set up camp in a valley near a stream that ran into a small lake. With binoculars they saw black yak-hair Tibetan tents pitched on the mountainside. Higher up, Tibetan border guards could be seen.[29] Mackiernan and Bessac slowly made their way in front of the rest of their party towards the tents. The Tibetans had seen them, and as they approached a grinning young girl came forward and stuck out her tongue—the Tibetan form of greeting—and tried to make conversation.[30] Mackiernan waved a white flag and the girl eventually returned to the other Tibetans at the top of the hill. A short time later, they saw in the far distance six Tibetan men on horseback who were slowly descending towards them.[31] In the meantime, it was decided that Bessac offer a cloth friendship gift to a group of men who were watching from a rock formation. As he neared them they pointed their guns at him so he stopped about 50 yards in front of them, all the time waving the white flag. Bessac believed he had convinced them he was friendly and then turned to walk back to Mackiernan and the others. At that moment he heard shots fired near his tent a little distance away, where he heard Mackiernan shout out 'Don't shoot.' After the shooting stopped, the Tibetans tied Bessac's hands and he was walked toward three objects on the ground. In his report he wrote: 'I went to the three objects. They were men all right—very dead. Mac was lying on his back with his legs crossed. He looked not uncomfortable and was smiling, perhaps slightly ironically.'[32] Mackiernan, dressed in the clothing of a traditional Tibetan enemy, had been thought by the border guards to be a marauder. In the tense spring of 1950, Tibetan border guards had standing orders to 'shoot all foreigners who attempted to enter.' Mackiernan died on his birthday.

A star was placed on the wall of the Central Intelligence Agency in Mackiernan's memory. With it all, it seems Mackiernan's activities were not as covert as the Americans would have liked; the Chinese, like the British, carefully monitored the events unfolding at the American consular office in Tihwa. Archival documents from the Chinese Foreign Ministry in Beijing made available to the authors include a detailed seven-page report on Mackiernan's activities that began with his hasty departure from the consulate with Frank Bessac and the White Russians; each of their names were noted.[33] The PLA at Tihwa reported that Mackiernan left the keys to the US consulate, a letter, and various documents at the British consulate; and that on reaching the border, Mackiernan 'did not undergo any diplomatic process that foreigners do when leaving the border.'[34] In a report that reads like a spy novel, the PLA listed what they called the US consul's 'conspiracy activities.'[35] Mackiernan was reported to have been in daily contact with 'US spy agencies with their radios' and talked about the coming 'third World War.'[36] In addition, the PLA wrote that the group discussed 'issues to harm various ethnic nationalities in China and the interest of the Chinese people.'[37] The PLA asked Beijing if this information 'could be publicly announced through the New China News Agency to reveal the conspiracy activities by the American imperialists in Sinkiang?'[38]

Following the 29 April catastrophe at the border crossing, the guards took Bessac and Vasili Zvansov, who was injured, to a military outpost by camel, six days away. As Bessac was bundled onto a camel he spied 'three round balls' packed on the camel in front of him—the heads of Mackiernan and the two White Russians.[39]

On 4 May official Tibetan couriers carrying red flags approached their party. After talking with the border guards they began shouting at them; one of the couriers came toward Bessac and identified himself. In his hand he held official Tibetan entry permits for Bessac and Mackiernan—tragically, it was five days too late. The State Department had sent a message to the Dalai Lama seeking permission for the group to enter Tibet from China, but it had not reached the Tibetan border guards in time. One of the Tibetan officials offered Bessac his gun and then pointed it at the border guards; Bessac declined to shoot them.[40] In Lhasa, the Dalai Lama met with Bessac twice and personally offered his apologies; apologies were also sent to Washington. The border guards were tried in a military court and were given stiff sentences which including having their nose or ears cut off. Bessac asked that this not be done and they all received lashes—which he watched.[41]

Though it was a tragic episode, there was a modest silver lining. US and Tibetan authorities learned more about each other. They cooperated at a working level, arranging safe passage for the party, medical care, and meetings for Bessac with the Tibetan authorities, including the Dalai Lama.

Lhasa through the looking glass

Frank Bessac proceeded to Lhasa where he stayed from 7 June to 22 July 1950, observing the city and its inhabitants on the cusp of the Chinese invasion. His anthropological training informed his observations, which provided the most telling insights Washington had into Tibetan society at the time. Through their travels and contacts with the Tibetans, both the Thomases in 1949 and Frank Bessac in 1950 offered unique perceptions of Tibet. Bessac's reporting on the Tibetan military was without precedent. His writings, together with reports from Nepalese officials, were vitally important to Washington's understanding of Chinese initiatives in Tibet, and Lhasa's preparations for the PLA onslaught.

By the time Bessac landed in Lhasa in the summer of 1950, Beijing had begun daily propaganda broadcasts with radio announcements in Tibetan on Mondays, Wednesdays, and Fridays. The theme usually centered on the promise that Tibetans would be 'liberated' and would be 'reunited with the Motherland.'[42] The Chinese made their intentions clear: 'we have two objectives before us: the liberation of Tibet and Formosa, and we are determined to achieve both at any cost.'[43] The broadcasts were also designed to intimidate: 'we have heard that the Tibetan government is mustering forces to fight us: Chiang-Kai-shek did that and failed. What chances have the poor Tibetan troops against us?'[44]

Beijing would neither accept Tibetan autonomy nor accept any form of independence. This was underscored with the message:

Our people of the province of Tibet need not be apprehensive because we are coming. We are not coming to put you into further trouble but to liberate you from the shackles of the capitalists. You have nothing to lose but your chains and may, therefore, rest assured that the end of your privation is within sight.[45]

Concerned that the Chinese messages would have an impact on the Tibetan people, the government approached the Indian mission in Lhasa to 'arrange retaliatory broadcasts from All India Radio to combat the propaganda from Peking [*sic*], but without any result.'[46]

As indicated above, opinion among Tibetan officials was deeply divided in the early spring of 1950. There was no consensus on whether to fight or negotiate with the communists. Eventually, when it became plain that the National Assembly could not reach a decision, the state oracle was consulted and instructions were issued to resist and fight.[47]

When Bessac arrived at Lhasa in June he reported that the Tibetans had been united by the decision to resist.[48] They were training and preparing to field an army to defend against the expected PLA attack.[49] That June Bessac provided perhaps the most detailed military analysis of Tibetan readiness Washington had received. The

Tibetan army, Bessac guessed, was now around 25,000 strong, although officials in Lhasa claimed it was 100,000.[50] Bessac commented that the condition of the common Tibetan soldier had recently improved as 'he now receives cloth, food and regular pay, but he receives only about three months training at the most. His morale is possibly better than the ordinary Chinese soldier.'[51] Lack of training was a major issue, and Bessac noted that the highest officers of the army often came from noble families and were generally inefficient, untrained, lacking in enthusiasm, and without experience.[52]

The Tibetans, Bessac observed, did not take the Chinese seriously: 'they still look down upon the Chinese.'[53] Tibetans saw 'the Chinese Communist Army as an organization akin to the armies of Szechuan warlords … and reasoned that 'due to improvements in the Tibetan Army, the Chinese can be easily defeated.'[54] These attitudes were most prevalent among the abbots of the Drepung and Sera monasteries. He added that this did not reflect a reluctance to help; it was 'merely an expression of their lack of worldly knowledge.'[55] Bessac confirmed what Washington already knew: that the Tibetans were terribly naive. Bessac believed that if they had sufficient time, the Tibetans could develop a force that might block the Chinese invasion temporarily. But he felt that to 'hold the Chinese at bay' for a longer time, the Tibetans would require US air support.[56] He wrote:

But even if we cannot send air support I believe it worth our while to send other military aid. No one knows when the world war will commence. If war commences before the Chinese conquer Tibet we will be in a position, at [a] low cost to create much discomfort to the Chinese and Russians in their border regions.[57]

12

'THE BEARDED KHAMPA'

TIBET'S PAUL REVERE

While the Chinese quietly observed Mackiernan, their plans for invasion were being monitored through a most unlikely network consisting of the Khampas, a fiercely independent tribal people in eastern Tibet, a Tibetan-speaking Scottish missionary named George Patterson—and eventually the CIA. When the State Department learned that Mackiernan was dead and Bessac injured but still alive in Lhasa, Patterson, who had links to the Americans, the British, and the Dalai Lama's family, assumed an important role.

The American embassy in New Delhi was familiar with Patterson—known as the 'Bearded Khampa'; he had arrived on the scene in March 1950 in a disheveled state a month before Mackiernan was killed. Patterson, who had lived amongst the Khampa tribesmen in Kham, eastern Tibet, was asked by the US government to assist in bringing Bessac and his companion out of Lhasa.[1]

For our purposes, Patterson's story extends back to 1947, when he arrived in Shanghai with a group of Brethren missionaries fresh from the Missionary School of Medicine in London. He went from there to Kangting in western China near the Tibetan/China border, eager to join a recently established Tibetan language school for young missionaries.[2] Kangting, at 9,000 feet, was nestled in a valley overlooked by snow-capped mountains. It was the trading gateway to Tibet—the last stop on the southern Silk Route that began in Kalimpong, India. It was in this remote fastness that Patterson began a relationship with the Tibetan Khampas that would last throughout his life.[3]

The Khampa tribesmen formed a large part of Kangting's population.[4] Here, Patterson gave his first gospel sermon in Tibetan to a group of armed warriors clad in lambskins in the small town's church.[5] Patterson told us in an interview that he had been studying Tibetan for only a few months, and had such great difficulty with the sermon and choice of words that his audience was greatly amused.[6] After the sermon, Patterson was approached by Topgyay Pangdatshang, a 'revered' Khampa leader, who offered to 'teach him' Tibetan.[7] While widely respected by other tribesmen, the Pangdatshang brothers had had a troubled relationship with Lhasa.

With the 1933 death of the thirteenth Dalai Lama, a power struggle brought a period of political turmoil. The tribesmen of the eastern provinces of Kham and Amdo organized a revolt in an attempt to seize additional powers and eventual independence from the central government in Lhasa; the two Pangdatshang brothers led the uprising. But Tibetans loyal to Lhasa, including many monks and aristocrats, betrayed them, forcing them to abort the plan. Now, more than a decade after their exile to India, they were back in their homeland again organizing their followers, collecting arms and planning another rebellion. Their goal was independence, but they also wanted to overthrow the feudal government in Lhasa, and to this end obtained arms for their cause by convincing the KMT that they would fight against the Japanese.[8]

Patterson says his meeting with Topgyay Pangdatshang changed his life; he became a part of the Pangdatshang extended family. In Khampa homes and camps the Scottish missionary was treated as a family confidant—a valued addition to the many conversations ranging from politics to military operations against the government in Lhasa and the Chinese.[9]

By the summer of 1949, as communist forces moved into Kangting, many of the Khampas relocated further into eastern Tibet for protection. Patterson and his Brethren friend Geoffrey Bull were reluctant to leave Tibet and instead accepted Topgyay Pangdatshang's invitation to accompany the clan to Batang, in the deep interior of eastern Tibet. The journey took a month; Patterson crossed thirteen passes over 15,000 feet in temperatures that fell below zero. The region, heavily forested, with steep valleys, high mountain peaks and rushing rivers, was a natural refuge.

Patterson's accommodations along the route were modest at best, but the Pangdatshangs, as tribal leaders, were feted and entertained along the way with gifts of food and other pleasures as tribesmen came to show their respect.[10] For a month Patterson and his companion Geoffrey Bull, the only foreigners amongst hundreds of Khampas, made their way across the frozen reaches of eastern Tibet toward shelter at the main Pangdatshang encampment.[11]

Life in Tibet was harsh, often treacherous; the intense cold brought illness, disease, and a quick death. The cold caused Tibetans to go for months, even years, without washing. A cut from a sword could quickly become gangrenous, which was not helped by primitive Tibetan healing methods. While monks often provided treatment, performing rituals that used 'urine and feces in their pills and poultices,' Patterson's medical training set him apart.[12] His ability to treat life-threatening injuries and illnesses successfully earned him the gratitude of the Khampas and a unique status: he was known throughout the Khampa territory as an 'Angel of Mercy'—a miracle worker.

'THE BEARDED KHAMPA': TIBET'S PAUL REVERE

Communist attempts to enlist the Khampas

In January 1950, more than three years after Patterson's arrival in Kham, a messenger on horseback delivered an official letter from the communists to the Pangdatshangs. The Chinese had learned of the Khampa plans to revolt against the government in Lhasa and offered support.[13] The Chinese proposal was to supply the Khampas with arms, ammunition, and financial aid, and in return obtain an agreement from the Khampas not to oppose their 'liberation' of Tibet.[14] Because they sought to overthrow the feudal government in Lhasa, the Khampas were seen as 'factional revolutionaries.'[15] The implication was that if they accepted an arrangement 'to liberate Tibet' they would be welcomed as partners in the larger endeavor: namely to 'liberate the rest of Asia.'[16] Patterson recalled that when the Pangdatshang brothers received the letter they were surprised and knew immediately they could not cooperate.[17]

The 1935 Khampa revolt had left bad blood; the Lhasa government remained suspicious of the tribesmen in eastern Tibet. Thus, it would be of no use to warn Lhasa of the imminent Chinese invasion because the warning would likely be dismissed as a ploy, and in any event time was short. After much discussion among the Khampa tribesmen, Topgyay and Rapga Pangdatshang decided their only option was to take the information to India. Even in summer weather conditions, this would be a very difficult journey as the trail was seldom used and few Tibetans had ever completed this passage to India.[18] But now, despite being in the dead of winter, at 17,000 feet on frozen terrain, the journey seemed absolutely necessary.

In the end it was decided that Khampa leaders would try to hold off the Chinese until outside help arrived, while their friend, the 'Bearded Khampa,' took a message to India to alert the world to the impending invasion. The Pangdatshang brothers requested official travel documents from Lhasa for Patterson's journey so that he could use the Tibetan travel system known as *ulag*: this meant that at each stop Patterson would be provided with food and new animals.[19]

While arrangements were being made for Patterson's trek, the prospect of invasion became ever more vivid. The drumbeat of propaganda directed at Lhasa and the Tibetan people was now relentless. As Patterson departed that January, Beijing had become hyperbolic, objecting to a proposed Tibetan 'goodwill mission' to the United States and the United Kingdom. The broadcasts announced that 'Tibet is the territory of the Chinese People's Republic' and a mission to a foreign country is 'traitorous and a threat to the motherland.'[20]

The winter crossing into India

That January, as Mackiernan and his party made a miserable and frigid transit from China to Tibet, Patterson said goodbye to his Khampa family and to Geoffrey Bull. Along with his servant Loshay, a Khampa soldier named Tsering Dorje who had travelled this dangerous route before, and Geoffrey's servant Bajay, the four of them began the unprecedented winter trip by horseback across Tibet's eastern plateau.[21]

With limited provisions to make travelling easier, Patterson pulled down his hood, sheltering his face in his fur-lined coat, and rode out to face nature's elements.[22] In the massive ice fields covered with knee-deep snow, there was no way to tell where land ended and crevasses began as they crossed the icy passes at 17,000 feet, battling freezing winds and below-zero temperatures. Without footing, Patterson and the horses continually slid, sometimes nearly tumbling into the abyss. As protection, they formed a human chain by holding the reins of one horse and the tail of the horse in front. Yaks were of some help. The party relied upon their instincts to guide them to a safe path. When the yaks could not find a trail, a man would stretch out with another holding his feet to prevent a possible fall and drive a pick or sword into the ground to mark a path.[23] Their goggles, normally used to protect the eyes from the wind and snow, were of no use as the ice formed on them or they cracked from the cold. Patterson's beard and face remained frozen for most of the trip; sleep was almost impossible. To avoid the danger of snow blindness the men rubbed charcoal around their eyes and pulled their hair forward over their eyes to block the wind and the winter sun. Ascending one mountain summit, Patterson recalled 'we labored like men possessed, and by coaxing, beating, pulling, and yelling—managed eventually to get one yak to the summit where we left it to lie panting while we returned for the others.'[24] After weeks of travelling Patterson felt utter desolation; he told us in an interview that he was losing his will to live.

About four weeks later, on 20 February 1950, Patterson arrived at the Indian garrison in Walong. Noticing it was 2 p.m., he realized it was the first time in weeks that he knew the time. The commanding officer was astonished that Patterson had come all the way from Tibet—especially in winter.[25] The famous botanist and explorer Francis Kingdon-Ward, also at Walong, was equally shocked at Patterson's trek through the Himalayas. When his wife saw Patterson she said, 'John the Baptist, I presume?'[26] Patterson roared with laughter.

The commanding officer telegraphed Indian officials in Sadiya, the main town in north-east India, for permission for Patterson to continue on through India. After receiving his permit, Patterson and his companions traveled for a week to Sadiya, where he arranged a flight to Calcutta. On 8 March Patterson and his servant Loshay were soon back amidst the bustle of rickshaws, buses, animals, and street hawkers—both bewildering and intoxicating for Patterson after the years of solitude in China and Tibet. They found a place to stay, while there, with friends of Geoff Bull.

After nearly two months of travel, Patterson had to find someone who would listen to him and believe his story. A few days later, on 14 March, seven weeks after leaving the Khampas, Patterson wrote: 'What seemed natural, if somewhat dramatic, in the mountains of Tibet now appeared more than slightly ridiculous as I walked towards the British High Commission through the anonymous thousands of pedestrians in this strange city.'[27] Passing through the imposing gates of the building, he found people inside speaking in hushed tones, doors closed softly.[28]

Patterson received

With an unkempt beard and long hair, his light skin turned weathered and brown and wearing Tibetan style clothing, George Patterson cut a startling figure. A uniformed Indian guard delivered him to two skeptical security guards, to whom he relayed the message that China intended to invade Tibet and then Nepal, Sikkim, Bhutan, and India.[29] They stared at him in astonishment, and after some consultation and a phone call Patterson was ushered into the office of David Anderson, the British consul general. Anderson (though bewildered) heard him out. They spent some time going over details and looking at maps, and though Anderson had only the word of this bedraggled stranger—who, in turn, had it from a few warrior tribesmen in eastern Tibet—he relayed the message to London. While Anderson didn't hold out hope that much could be done, he told Patterson, 'strictly *entre nous*,' that he would introduce him to some Indian political and security officials, and then arrange a dinner.[30] Anderson also said that others would be there (including some Americans) and suggested that Patterson not 'enquire too closely what they do when you meet them.'[31] It was in this way that Patterson first came into contact with the Central Intelligence Agency, whose officers were in Calcutta monitoring Chinese movements in the region.

A few nights later Patterson attended Anderson's dinner, which turned out to be a lively affair. The British and Americans, including William Gibson, a CIA officer under cover as vice consul, took Patterson's measure. They bombarded him with questions about Tibet—his knowledge and experiences in the country. The conversation ranged from Tibetan politics to 'Buddhist tantric practices'; among other things, they asked Patterson's reaction, as a Christian, to Buddhism.[32] The next day Patterson departed for Kalimpong, a city in the north-east of India that was populated with a growing number of displaced Tibetans. There, Patterson sought out another Pangdatshang brother and met with a number of Tibetan officials. That summer, Patterson began passing information from Tibetan officials in Kalimpong to the American government through Bob Lynn and Bill Gibson, CIA operations officers at the American consulate in Calcutta.[33] And thus the process began.

Covert probes

New Year's Day 1950 had marked the end of a difficult six months for the US President, laced with uncommon vitriol, as both Truman's domestic and foreign policies were now under withering attack from the Republican Congress, the China Lobby, and the media. Among other things, it was urgent that he clarify his approach to the growing Soviet menace and the reality of Mao's victory in China. On 31 January 1950 the president directed the secretaries of state and defense to undertake a secret 're-examination of our objectives in peace and war in light of the probable fission bomb capability and possible thermonuclear bomb capability of the Soviet Union.'[34] The president's request triggered an extensive assessment of US capacity and priorities, Soviet intentions, the implications of a communist China, and proposed responses. The result of this directive was NSC 68, authored by Paul Nitze, director of the Policy Planning Staff in the State Department. NSC 68, in brief, established the future direction of American foreign policy, calling for an increase in military spending and the expansion of the containment policy. To his dismay, Kennan's implicit geographical limits were lifted.

A number of pressing diplomatic issues had arisen seemingly all at once. Just as Washington was struggling to devise a strategy to address communist advances in Europe and China, the US embassy in Delhi in early 1950 was considering the first of many Tibetan requests for military assistance.[35] Secretary of State Dean Acheson cabled Ambassador Loy Henderson in India to ascertain if the government of India was supplying arms and aid to the Tibetans.[36]

With this request, Acheson and Henderson began a detailed exchange over nearly eighteen months centering on the grave issues facing the Tibetans. Through these ongoing memoranda in the form of top secret telegrams, it was clear that both officials were sympathetic to the Tibetan situation. Moreover, a preoccupation with communist advances—in ways that included Tibet—was now reflected in developments in Delhi, Washington, and London.

On 19 April 1950, Acheson sent a telegram marked 'secret' to Henderson in Delhi informing the ambassador that:

As you [are] aware a primary consideration has been our belief [that] active or overt interest [by] non-Communist countries [in] Tibet at this time wld tend [to] hasten or provoke Chi Communist action against [these] areas whereas, in absence [of] such action, [the] cost [of a] full-scale Commie mil expedition against Tibet in [the] face [of] geographic and logistic difficulties might lead [to an] indefinite delay [of] Commie mil action, particularly, if Tibetan mil capacity [is] quietly strengthened.[37]

Thus, 'quietly strengthen[ed]' became the watchword for Acheson's policy in Tibet. The CIA, including the station in Calcutta, anticipated this and supported it.

The next day, 20 April, President Truman spoke to the American Society of Newspaper Editors in Washington and focused on the power of communist propaganda. Calling for a 'campaign of truth,' Truman told his audience that the United States must underscore America's democratic example and the benefits it offered.[38] In what would become the United States Information Agency (USIA), Truman directed Acheson to strengthen the US education and information effort against communism worldwide. Among the first steps was to compile a list of priority countries where the contest between democracy and communism was underway and where the USIA could make a difference. Tibet was on the list.[39]

In May 1950, Acheson attended a foreign ministers' conference in London with the United Kingdom and France. At the meeting the British foreign minister was handed a position paper outlining the administration's thinking on Tibet.[40] Washington, not without Britain's South Asian sensitivities in mind, thought that if Tibet came under communist control it 'might offer a base for the extension of Communist penetration and subversive activities into Nepal and Bhutan and, eventually, India.'[41] The State Department allowed that the Chinese communists had the ability to 'conquer' Tibet.[42] And the point was also made that:

Comparatively little covert assistance in the form of specialized military instruction and supplies to the Tibetans might make a Chinese military expedition prohibitively costly particularly if the Western States manifested no extraordinary interest in attempting to alter Tibet's international status.[43]

A month later, on 16 June, Mr Charles Freeman, director of the State Department's China Desk provided a copy of this paper to the British embassy in Washington. The concluding paragraph is of particular interest:

By reason of its traditional interest in Tibet and its special relationship with India, the British government obviously is in a better position than is the United States government to appraise Tibetan needs, to ascertain the extent of Indian help and to exert influence upon the government of India to assume responsibility for any necessary action respecting Tibet.[44]

Though Tibet was now on the policy map, it was clear that neither Britain, nor the United States, nor India were then prepared to take the lead in addressing Tibet's situation. Full-scale covert operations were thus put on hold.

13

1950

THE PLA INVADES KOREA AND TIBET

While Washington considered how, if, and where military assistance should be provided to Tibet, tensions on the Korean peninsula were escalating. A month after the London foreign ministers' conference, on 25 June 1950, the communist invasion of Korea electrified Washington.

Truman was ever mindful that a Third World War was dangerously close. He was convinced that this time had come when Acheson called him on Saturday night at his home in Independence, Missouri, and said, 'Mr President, I have very serious news. The North Koreans have invaded South Korea.'[1] Truman, along with his national security advisors, believed this pernicious act had been authored in Moscow and Beijing and that he must act with care to prevent the invasion from escalating into a great power confrontation.[2]

Eight army divisions of the Democratic People's Republic of Korea, comprising 9,000 men supported by 150 Soviet medium tanks, mobile artillery, and supporting aircraft, crossed the 38th parallel in three columns and moved rapidly through the Uijongbu Gap to invade the Republic of Korea.

In Washington, Acheson immediately requested a special meeting of the United Nations Security Council to declare that an act of aggression had been committed against Korea. The next day the secretary of state called the president, who was just sitting down to Sunday dinner, to relay reports that an 'all-out invasion' was underway.[3] Acheson said that while the UN Security Council would call for an immediate ceasefire, he believed the communists would ignore it.[4] Acheson was correct; the North Korean offensive continued unabated.

Within an hour and a half Truman was on the presidential plane back to Washington to meet with his senior advisors; he had three long hours to collect his thoughts.[5] He faced a profound crisis and knew that his next step would be among the most difficult decisions of his presidency. Throughout all of Truman's presidential papers, directives, diaries, and memories, it is clear that containing communism while avoiding a Third World War was uppermost in his mind. Recalling that plane trip, he wrote:

In my generation, this was not the first occasion when the strong had attacked the weak. I recalled some earlier instances: Manchuria, Ethiopia, Austria. I remembered how each time that the democracies failed to act it had encouraged the aggressors to keep going ahead. Communism was acting in Korea just like Hitler, Mussolini and the Japanese had acted ten, fifteen and twenty years earlier. I felt certain that if South Korea were allowed to fall, Communist leaders would be emboldened to override nations closer to our own shores. If the Communists were permitted to force their way into the Republic of Korea without opposition from the Free World, no small nation would have the courage to resist threats and aggression by stronger Communist neighbors. If this were allowed to go unchallenged it would mean a Third World War, just as similar incidents had brought on the Second World War.[6]

Truman believed that a communist success in Korea would give 'Red troops and planes' unfettered access to Japan and Okinawa, and that Formosa would be 'open to attack from two sides.'[7] In a meeting with his advisors and members of the House and Senate in the Oval Office on Tuesday 27 June, he said, 'If we let Korea down, the Soviets will keep right on going and swallow up one piece of Asia after another.'[8]

That summer in Washington the 'Red Scare' drumbeat went on. The nation felt itself under siege. Beyond the alarming events in Korea, catastrophe had been narrowly averted in Greece and Italy as communist partisans had nearly prevailed; and few could forget that Eastern Europe was now a part of the Soviet bloc.

Two months later, on 1 September, Truman made an impassioned radio and television address explaining that the United States was at war in Korea to defend freedom and that 'No cause has ever been more just or more important.'[9] It was now apparent that the administration was thinking of the Asian landmass in geostrategic terms. The question was how to 'contain' communist expansion. It was a question that addressed US interests in Northeast Asia, Taiwan, Southeast Asia, and China.

Tibet, because it was vulnerable to Chinese invasion, was a part of these deliberations. Six weeks earlier, in July 1950, just three weeks after the invasion of Korea and after months of discussion between Acheson and Henderson, the administration established a general approach toward Tibet that eventually framed the US role in Tibet's bid for sovereignty. On 15 July Acheson wrote to Henderson to apprise him of the department's thinking: 'Interested agencies were now considering the advisability of approaching the Tibetan Mission currently in India with a promise of secret United States aid in the hope that this would help the Tibetan authorities to resist Chinese Communist encroachment on Tibet.'[10]

Then, on 22 July 1950, the decision was made to extend a concrete offer of aid to the Tibetans. In a 'Top Secret' telegram from to Henderson in Delhi, Acheson wrote: 'Dept now in position give assurances [to] Tibetans re US aid.'[11] This was conveyed as follows:

[In]View [of] current state US Indian relations, [the] Dept believes action designed [to] obtain GOI [Government of India] cooperation [for] such a project should be left to Tibetans. Dept believes [the] procedure shld be as follows: In response [to the] Tibetan approach you inform them that US [is] ready to assist procurement and financing. Tibetans [should] then approach GOI opening with request for more Indian aid. GOI will presumably say Tibet [is] now getting all aid India can give and all aid Tibet can properly use. Tibetans then would ask whether GOI would agree [to] facilitate delivery through India of materiel procured abroad.[12]

The Central Intelligence Agency, referred to as 'the other agency,' had previously confirmed that it could make available the funds and military equipment the Tibetans would need.[13] To maintain the operation's covert status, Dean Rusk, then assistant secretary of state for Far Eastern Affairs, advised other agencies, in an inter-office memo, that there was an 'extreme necessity for secrecy' and that all telegrams on the subject of military assistance to the Tibetans would have restricted access—a restriction largely maintained by succeeding administrations.[14] The calculation in Washington was that if the Tibetans were prepared to 'resist Communist aggression,' then the US was prepared 'to assist in procuring material and would finance such aid.'[15]

In a 'Top Secret' memorandum from Ambassador Henderson to Secretary Acheson on 7 August 1950, the ambassador confirmed that he had conveyed this message to Tsepon Shakabpa, in a meeting in Delhi.[16] Supplying aid to Tibet, of course, was not without difficulty, not only because of its remote location but also because of the need to maintain the delicate balance with India.

In a meeting a little over a month later, on 9 September, Shakabpa, Tsechag Khenchung, and Taringqop Niloqti met with Henderson at his office to consider the specific nature and timing of US military aid and their negotiations with the Chinese.[17] In a very candid conversation, Shakabpa told Henderson that his sources confirmed that Chinese communist troops were massing along Tibet's eastern border near Jyekundo, Nagchen, Degegochen, and Batang.[18] In addition, Shakabpa made clear to Henderson that they sought independence from the Chinese.[19] The delegation had refused a prior Chinese invitation to go to Beijing via Hong Kong for talks, and now they awaited the arrival of the Chinese ambassador, Yuan Chung-hsien, for negotiations.

In a meeting on 16 September, Ambassador Yuan insisted that the Tibetans urge their government and the Dalai Lama to accept Chinese rule.[20] The authorities in Lhasa sought to stall, but of course all the backing and forthing was a moot point: the Chinese had begun their invasion.[21] Mao's plan was simple: first capture the city of Chamdo and then cut off Tibetan routes of retreat to the north and south. From Chamdo they would proceed to Lhasa.[22]

The attack on eastern Tibet

On 7 October, some 9,000 seasoned PLA troops crossed the Yangzte River into Tibet and soon overwhelmed a poorly trained Tibetan force of about 4,000. The

PLA had better tactics, more men, equipment, arms and the experience of a long civil war behind them. Geoff Bull, the Christian missionary whom Patterson had left with the Pandatshangs ten months earlier, was in the Khampa stronghold of Gartok Markham—the first town the Chinese reached. Bull recalled that when the townspeople realized the fall of Gartok was imminent, 'absolute confusion' ensued.[23] 'Social order' broke down and 'servants acting more on their own instinct than their masters' orders rushed hither and thither thrusting valuables in boxes.'[24] Bull himself was taken prisoner. Suspected of being a 'conspirator against China,' Bull was placed in a 're-education' camp where he was mistreated for three years. He was continually interrogated about the events in his life and his contacts from the day he left England until the day he was captured. Everything was scrutinized. He was released on 19 December 1953. He wrote to Patterson from Hong Kong, his spirit unbroken; and until the day he died Patterson expressed his regret over his inability to help his friend.[25]

On 11 October 1950 news reached the regional governor, Ngabo Jigme, that the People's Liberation Army was nearing Chamdo, a large town in eastern Tibet on the route to Lhasa. Ngabo frantically tried to contact Lhasa to alert his government and ask what to do, but there was no response. Four days later, amidst the chaos of Chamdo's fleeing officials and residents, Ngabo's aide-de-camp finally spoke to a Kashag aide-de-camp in Lhasa after three 'urgent' coded messages had already been ignored. Over the wireless came the answer—a response recalled by Tibetans even today: 'Right now it is the period of the Kashags' picnic and they are all participating in this. Your telegrams are being decoded and then we will send you a reply.'[26] With the Chinese just days away from Chamdo, Ngabo's aide yelled back over the wireless, *skyag pa'i gling kha*'('shit the picnic') and hung up.[27] It was 15 October and this was the last communication Chamdo had with Lhasa.

The Tibetan government's profound lack of understanding of their situation and the strategic realities surrounding them is further reflected in a poignant telegram to Mao as the PLA advanced towards Chamdo and Lhasa. Members of the Tibetan National Assembly telegraphed Mao:[28]

Tibet is a sacred place of Buddhism, which does not allow armed force from foreign countries. This type of bullying activity shall not happen. Tibetan and secular people are very frightened and feel uneasy. We hope you order all border troops not to exercise force towards Tibetan soldiers, and immediately withdraw to their original locations. We pray and look forward to your prompt telegraph reply.[29]

Of course, there was no reply.

Eight days later, Chamdo as well was seized by panic as word of the Chinese onslaught spread. The looting quickly became uncontrollable; the soldiers simply deserted.[30] Robert Ford, a British radio operator who had remained in town, remembered the day:[31] 'The Tibetans were overwhelmed; the Chinese captured over half of the 10,000 Tibetan defenders. With no word from Lhasa and no possibility of stopping the PLA, the Governor, Ngabo, fled in the middle of the night, leaving the local people to fend for themselves.'[32] Ford was captured at Chamdo and spent nearly five years in a Chinese prison camp. He wrote:

Panic was breaking out in the town. People were running about in all directions, carrying or dragging their personal belongings. Monks were hurrying towards the monastery, gabbling their prayers. Ngabo had commandeered most of the ponies, leaving the local people without transport.[33]

It was the beginning of the end for Tibet.

The Chinese entered Lhasa carrying portraits of Mao Tse-tung on 26 October. The Dalai Lama, who was just fifteen years old, and not officially enthroned as the Tibetan leader, wrote in his autobiography that he was 'now faced with the prospect of leading my country to war.'[34] The Oracle was consulted and the young Dalai Lama officially became the Tibetan leader on 17 November 1950.[35]

With the Korean War underway, the Chinese now confronted hostilities on two fronts—or perhaps, more accurately, a war and a prospective insurgency. Five days after the PLA invaded Tibet, Mao sent a blunt memo to his ambassador in India for delivery to Nehru. In it he reiterated that 'Tibet is Chinese territory' and so as a 'domestic problem' the PLA 'must enter Tibet.'[36] He also made clear his intentions in Korea:

China cannot tolerate seeing its neighbor being invaded and do nothing. The responsibilities for spreading the war are for the invading countries to bear. The people of China love peace. However, in order to protect peace, they are never afraid of wars against invasion.[37]

Korea: A point of reference

On 16 October UN troops captured Pyongyang, the North Korean capital, and fought their way north to the Chinese border at the Yalu River. Mao responded by sending 300,000 Chinese 'volunteers' across the Yalu into Korea. They pushed UN forces down the Korean peninsula toward the south-east port city of Pusan where, eventually, a defense perimeter was established. On 9 November, in a grave tone, Secretary of State Acheson sent a warning to consular offices around the world: 'the US believes other Asian nations cannot remain neutral toward communism as neutrality amounts to supine acceptance [of] commie domination and is regarded as weakness by [the] enemy.'[38] He urged US diplomats to talk to their host countries in an effort to gain support for what he knew would be a momentous confrontation, but his cable was directed at no one more than Nehru. The Korean War would continue until 1953, when Eisenhower's election and Stalin's death provided a new opportunity for negotiations—which continue, in theory, until this day.

The Indian prime minister's reaction to the Korean War had been a source of great consternation in Washington. His offer of mediation was not welcome, just as his advocacy for the non-aligned movement had been annoying, if not insulting to the administration, when he visited Washington in 1949. At its core, Nehru's views on global affairs contained a great skepticism toward the West; his insistence on viewing the communist bloc and the West as being morally equivalent was thought offensive to the Christian West, and blind to the contest between democracy and tyranny with its implications for subject peoples.

On 17 November 1950, Tibet made its first appeal to the United Nations. Lhasa's message to Secretary General Trygve Lie said, in part: 'The armed invasion of Tibet for the incorporation of Tibet into Communist China through sheer physical force is a clear case of aggression.'[39] Their hope was to obtain a resolution calling for the withdrawal of Chinese troops from Tibetan territory. El Salvador spoke up on Tibet's behalf, requesting that the Tibetan issue be added to the General Assembly agenda.[40] Acheson informed Ernest Gross, acting head of the UN delegation, that United States would not take the initiative, preferring instead that India assume the lead.[41] However, no member of the Security Council or the General Assembly would sponsor Tibet's case at that time. And even though a majority of the Indian cabinet believed that India could not remain an uninterested party regardless of the impact on India's relations with China, India's UN representative, Sir Benegal N. Rau, 'suggested the matter be dropped.'[42] According to Ambassador Henderson, Rau was reluctant to take any action regarding Tibet 'which might dispel Soviet Union and Communist China.'[43] Henderson wrote: 'Apparently Rau was under [the] impression that by not criticizing Communist China in UN re Tibet, he might play [a] more helpful role in mediating between Communist China and western powers following the arrival of Communist Chinese delegates [at the UN meeting] in Lake Success.'[44]

India was caught between its desire to reduce tensions over Tibet and its determination to retain working relations with Beijing. These nearly irreconcilable objectives prevented Delhi from backing a resolution that would alleviate pressure on the Tibetan people. Apparently, neither Whitehall nor the State Department appreciated the profound difficulties that would confront the Nehru government should they acquiesce to Anglo-American requests. Meanwhile, having tacitly coaxed the naive and untutored Tibetans into the international arena, the Americans and British were stymied; there was no viable way forward at the UN.

We now turn to India, and her involvement in the Korean War and Tibet.

14

NEHRU'S NON-ALIGNMENT, THE KOREAN WAR, AND TIBET

Historian H. W. Brands wrote that: 'better than any single event in the first half-decade of Indian independence, the outbreak of the Korean War revealed the divergent perspectives of the United States and India.'[1] From the beginning, India was a reluctant supporter of US efforts in the United Nations against North Korea out of fear of another world war. Nehru had agreed that the action of the North Koreans was 'clear aggression' and supported the UN resolution of 25 June 1950, calling for 'the immediate cessation of hostilities' and a withdrawal to the 38th parallel.[2] But he refused to offer any further support at the United Nations. Within a few weeks the rift between the US and India had evolved into a full-blown test of wills.

Nehru maintained a policy of non-alignment on the Korean War. He urged mediation through the Security Council. Henderson underscored this in his telegram to the secretary of state in June 1950, writing that the Indian government 'hoped it would not be compelled to give up its present policy of development of friendly relations with all countries … an independent policy … determined solely by India's ideas and objectives.'[3] Regarding the prospect of further UN action to stop North Korean aggression, Ambassador Henderson advised the State Department:

[N]ot [to] assume that Nehru is ready as yet to go along with us all the way. He does not like our Formosa and Indo-China polices and it is not impossible he will give vent at some appropriate or inappropriate time to his feelings by [a] critical outburst.[4]

Robert McMahon, who has written extensively on US policy toward South Asia, agreed with Henderson's assessment, observing that it was because India was reluctant to 'tarnish its nonaligned credentials as well as its credibility with the Soviet Union and China' that it would not support UN sanctions further.[5] But while the Indian prime minister would not support a UN vote against the North Koreans, he had in fact entered into the 'diplomatic maelstrom.'[6]

101

That July Nehru wrote to both Stalin in Moscow and Acheson in Washington with the hope of bringing the two powers to the negotiating table over Korea. To Washington, he proposed 'recognition of the PRC as the legitimate government of China' and suggested that the administration admit the communists into the United Nations.[7] And to Stalin, he proposed that the USSR cease their UN boycott and return to the Security Council to negotiate a peaceful resolution of the crisis.[8] In his response to Nehru, Stalin wrote that he welcomed Nehru's peace initiative. Stalin said: 'I fully share your point of view as to the expediency of a peaceful settlement of the Korean question through the Security Council, the participation of the representatives of the Five Great Powers including the People's Government of China being indispensable.'[9]

Nehru, encouraged by Stalin's reaction, and seemingly oblivious to Washington's displeasure, said to Acheson:

My honest belief is that Moscow is seeking a way out of the present entanglement without loss of prestige and that there is a real chance of solving the Korean problem peacefully by enabling the Peiping [Beijing] Government to enter and [the] Soviet Union to resume its place in the Security Council without insistence on conditions.[10]

Of course, Washington would have none of it. Acheson was offended by the underlying premise of the Indian plan, writing in his memoirs that the 'ousting of the Nationalists from the council—for that was the essence of the matter—was to be the price for the privilege of opening discussions about North Korean troop withdrawal.'[11]

Acheson had become fed up with the Indian meddling. But Nehru saw it differently. In a letter to C. Rajagopalachari, his home minister, he wrote: 'I must say that the Americans, for all their great achievements, impress me less and less, so far as their human quality is concerned. They are apt to be more hysterical as a people than almost any others except perhaps the Bengalis.'[12]

The tempest drew strength as the British, who were hopeful of a peaceful agreement in Korea, became annoyed that they were not told that the Indians had opened a dialogue with the Soviets.[13] And to round things out, Acheson believed that the British lacked grounds for their optimism that the Soviets would negotiate on Korea.[14] All of this contributed to what had become a tense and difficult environment, inhospitable to the diplomacy required.

Still, Nehru was unrelenting in his efforts. He sent his sister, Madame Pandit, to see Acheson and plead the case for recognizing the PRC and bringing both the communist Chinese and the Russians to the negotiating table at the United Nations. Acheson, who privately called the Indian prime minister's plan a 'multi-splendored confusion,' was urged by Madame Pandit, in what Acheson called a 'spiritual exhortation,' to accept her brother's plan as an 'act of faith.'[15] Acheson's mindset after Madame Ambassador left his office is revealed in his memoirs. He wrote: 'I have never been able to escape from a childhood illusion that, if the world is round, the Indians must be standing on their heads—or, perhaps vice versa.'[16]

During the summer and early fall of 1950, Nehru's stance of non-alignment and his suggestions for mediation in the Korean crisis become the focus of the American media. Relations between Washington and Delhi continued to be strained, with Nehru openly criticizing Washington for not recognizing the PRC and not negotiating a peaceful settlement in Korea. The headline of a *New York Times* article on 4 August screamed 'Nehru Denounces West's Asia Policy' as veteran correspondent Robert Trumbull in Delhi reported how Nehru 'castigated the Western powers for having adopted decisions affecting vast areas of Asia without understanding the real needs and minds of the people.'[17]

Ambassador Panikkar—summer and fall of 1950

It was ironic that while Nehru was railing against the United States and urging PRC admission to the United Nations, the Chinese communists were readying their troops to invade Tibet. The CIA's decision to 'quietly assist' the Tibetans was clearly not quiet enough because India's Ambassador Panikkar was questioned about US arms in a meeting with the Chinese vice foreign minister in Beijing on 15 August. Panikkar stated to his interlocutors that 'the news that the United States is transporting ammunition into Tibet through India is not accurate.'[18]

Panikkar went further and acknowledged China's sovereignty over Tibet in the same meeting:

The Indian government stated that the Government of India recognizes Chinese sovereignty in Tibet. Although the newspaper claims that the Government of India is concerned about Tibet, in fact, the only concern the Government of India has towards Tibet is being afraid of tribal disturbances along the border due to military activities. Therefore [we] hope that Tibetan problems can be resolved through negotiations between China and Tibet.[19]

Panikkar's use of the word sovereignty instead of suzerainty in discussing Tibet with the Chinese signaled the Indian government's acknowledgment that Tibet was a part of China. The Indian ambassador underscored his point by stating that his government had 'no interest in Tibet except commercially and [for] trade.'[20] Panikkar conveyed Nehru's message that 'Tibetan problems should be resolved between China and Tibet, in which India has no political interest. Other countries will also not interfere with Tibet.'[21]

By the end of August, Chinese troops had taken up positions along the eastern border of Tibet. The Chinese demanded that the Tibetans send a delegation to Beijing purportedly to negotiate an agreement that would establish Tibet's status as a part of China. On 31 August, Mao's intention of 'liberating Tibet' and 'driving the remaining factions of the Nationalist reactionaries out of Tibet' were made clear to Panikkar.[22] In a meeting between the Indian ambassador and Chen Jiakang and Qiao Guanhua of the PRC Foreign Ministry, the Chinese did not mince words. Director General Qiao requested that the Tibetan delegation, then in India, come to Beijing immediately to discuss the 'peaceful solution of Tibet problems,' but in the next breath stated that 'our People's Liberation Army is about to start operations in the western part of Sikang as planned.'[23]

Meanwhile, as mentioned in Chapter 13, the Tibetan negotiating delegation headed by Tsepon Shakabpa had spent the summer and fall of 1950 in Delhi meeting with Nehru, Henderson, and Bajpai. Shakabpa wrote that he clearly underscored the Tibetan position to the Indian prime minister:

I met with Prime Minister Nehru and informed him that our mission was proceeding to negotiate with China in regard to the maintenance of Tibetan independence. I explained to the Prime Minister that if he desired peace in Asia, Tibet should be recognized as an independent buffer State.[24]

Nehru, for his part, was disappointed in the Tibetans. Just as he hoped for a negotiated peace in Korea, so he had hoped that the Tibetans and the PRC would peacefully settle their differences. The Tibetan delegation, having placed their hopes in India and the United States to support their bid for independence, were also deeply disappointed.[25]

A world away in Washington, the Truman administration endured seemingly endless frustrations with Delhi. Despite their annoyance with Indian meddling on the Korean matter, the administration acknowledged Nehru as a force for regional stability—and they also saw that India provided a channel for messages between the US and the PRC. Unfortunately that role fell to Ambassador Panikkar, who was regarded as unreliable at best, and often duplicitous in Acheson–Henderson policy circles.[26]

In Beijing

On 2 October 1950, Panikkar was abruptly awakened at midnight by his steward and told that Chen Jiakang, the director general of Asian Affairs in the PRC Foreign Ministry, wished to speak to him. Panikkar hastily donned his dressing gown to greet Chen, who was waiting in Panikkar's downstairs drawing room and told him that the Chinese premier, Chou En-lai, wished to see him immediately.[27] At Chou En-lai's home a half hour later, the table was set for tea for two. 'Chou,' Panikkar recalled, 'was as courteous and charming as ever,' and while he apologized for rousing him at this unusual hour 'did not give the impression of worry or nervousness or indeed of being in any particular hurry.'[28] He simply stated that 'if the Americans cross the 38th parallel China will be forced to intervene in Korea.'[29]

On 5 October, two days after Chou's warning about Korea, the Southwest Army Corps of the People's Liberation Army crossed into the eastern region of Tibet, known as Kham. Privately, Washington was hopeful that Nehru would now see the duplicity of Mao.[30] But Nehru did not, to Tibet's great misfortune.

In preparation for the 5–6 October 1950 invasion, Mao's troops (the 18th Army) transported 10,000 tons of military provisions to support 8,000 men in the staging areas—4,500 regulars and 3,500 militia.[31] The assault force was split in two; the first group began their assault on 6 October. Each PLA officer carried 40 kilogram back-packs containing their provisions and marched 60 kilometers a day. By 18 October, one-third of the detachment had died along the road and 500 horses couldn't be used due to exhaustion.[32] The battle at Chamdo was quick—it was over by 24 October; roughly 5,700 Tibetans were killed.[33]

The Panikkar–Nehru link: an enigma

Nehru's biographer, Sarvepalli Gopal, served for ten years in India's Ministry of External Affairs and had unrestricted access to all of Nehru's papers. He described the prime minister's appreciation of Chinese intentions regarding Tibet as naïve.[34] This quality was indeed compounded by Panikkar's inclination to present a generally favorable picture of Chinese objectives. Was it idealism, misperception, or deceit? Is it possible that Panikkar deliberately obscured Beijing's objectives in speaking with Nehru? Or did Nehru cleverly use Panikkar to muddy the waters, thus presenting a *tabula rasa* designed to draw out the Chinese position, in order to see where, or if, India could find advantage at some point? We do not know. What is clear is that Panikkar was an uncertain interlocutor who left impressions with his principals that were dangerously inaccurate and, eventually, may have changed the course of history.

In late August, when Nehru wrote to Chou conveying his hopes that a peaceful settlement to the Tibetan situation might be found, he was surprised by the unvar-nished response. The premier bluntly stated that Tibet was Chinese territory and that it would be liberated.[35] Nehru later mused that he was not 'quite clear' from whom Tibet was to be liberated, but he believed that the Chinese intended to solve the issue by 'peaceful and friendly' means.[36]

In a meeting on 25 August between Bajpai and Henderson, Bajpai said that a recent telegram from Panikkar reported that the Chinese did not wish to have an armed conflict with Tibet.[37] Bajpai told Henderson that 'he was convinced from the tenor [of Panikkar's telegram that Peking [*sic*] did not contemplate, at least in the immediate future, [the] dispatch [of] armed forces into Tibet.'[38]

On 12 October 1950, six days after the PLA invaded eastern Tibet, concerns about Panikkar were raised in Washington. In a memorandum from Walter McCo-naughy of the State Department China Desk to Dean Rusk, then assistant secretary for Far Eastern Affairs, McConaughy said:

> Panikkar showed great reluctance to carry out his instructions to counsel the Chinese Com-munist [*sic*] against an armed invasion of Tibet... Even when the Communist Chinese mili-tary leaders were openly voicing threats against Tibet, he was discounting the possibility of any military action there.[39]

The next day in Delhi, Henderson asked Bajpai whether Panikkar had confirmed the PLA invasion. Bajpai replied that his government had heard nothing from their ambassador in Beijing, and added that he had sent a strongly worded telegram to

Panikkar on Tibet which was read to Henderson in the 'utmost secrecy.'[40] Bajpai insisted that Panikkar again ask:

whether reports of [a] Chinese invasion had any substance, and when so doing indicate [the] earnest hope [of the] GOI that [the] Chinese would show restraint and patience in dealing with Tibet and would not be hasty in resorting to violence.[41]

Panikkar was also informed that if communist China should indicate that it had already invaded Tibet or that it was planning to do so, 'the GOI would be compelled to follow up his representations with[a] still stronger approach.'[42]

In what must be considered a dramatic breach of diplomatic practice, although Panikkar was informed by Vice Minister Zhang on 12 August that 'military operations toward Tibet have begun, or will begin shortly,' he chose not to inform Nehru that the People's Liberation Army was massing in certain preparation for invasion.[43] Indeed, it appears that Panikkar was intent on pursuing his own version of Indian–China relations. It was not surprising therefore that when the invasion did occur, both the Indians and the Chinese expressed surprise at each other's behavior. Gopal wrote: 'Because of the shortcomings of Indian diplomacy in Beijing, the Chinese reacted to India's protest with a surprise which was not wholly feigned.'[44] The Chinese insisted that they had clearly stated they would be 'liberating Tibet,' 'defending the frontiers of China,' and that this was a 'domestic problem in which no foreign interference would be tolerated.'[45] Chou wrote to Nehru:

On August 31, 1950, the Chinese Ministry of Foreign Affairs informed the Indian Government through Ambassador Panikkar that the Chinese People's Liberation Army was going to take action soon in west Sikang according to set plans, and expressed the hope that the Indian Government would assist the delegation of the local authorities of Tibet so that it might arrive in Peking [sic] in mid-September.[46]

When the Chinese invaded, Panikkar was forced to explain the 'change' in Chinese policy toward Tibet. Meanwhile, in what might not have been a perfect analogy, Bajpai, the secretary general of the Indian Ministry of External Affairs, observed that 'Panikkar's protests on Tibet compared closely with Neville Henderson's protests in Nazi Germany on behalf of Czechoslovakia.'[47]

In what appears to have been a diplomatic 'Hall of Mirrors', the Chinese were right to be surprised over India's surprise. Director General Chen of the Ministry of Foreign Affairs informed the first secretary of the Indian embassy in Beijing that he had specifically informed Panikkar on 30 August that the PLA would be going into Sikang.[48] He said:

We are indeed taking military actions around Chamdo in the western part of Sikang Province. This is not a new plan. This is a determined plan. I remember informing Ambassador Panikkar of the point on August 30th while visiting the Ambassador with Director-General Qiao Guanhua.[49]

A declassified Chinese Ministry of Foreign Affairs memorandum of the discussion between Panikkar and the Chinese Deputy Minister Zhang on 21 October 1950, after the PLA had begun their invasion of eastern Tibet, makes the communnist position clear. The Chinese deputy minister bluntly informed the Indian ambassador at the end of their conversation that 'Any person who obstructs the liberation of Tibet and opposes our peaceful liberation must bear all responsibilities.'[50]

Nehru: Shocked at the PLA's 'liberation' of Tibet

At the end of October the Chinese expressed 'shock' that the GOI and other govern-ments were 'claiming' that the Chinese Army had suddenly 'invaded or encroached' on Tibet.[51] From Beijing's vantage point the Indian ambassador had been fully apprised of their intention.[52] Deputy Minister Zhang told Panikkar:

The problem of Tibet is a domestic problem of China. The liberation of Tibet and consolidat-ing the border are sacred rights of the People's Republic of China, and no foreign interference shall be tolerated.[53]

Zhang made the additional point that the PRC had evidence of 'foreign powers and foreign elements within Tibet and encroaching upon Tibet.'[54] One of the 'foreign elements' that the Chinese referred to was US Vice Consul Mackiernan in Tihwa, as discussed in Chapter 11. It is clear from these declassified Chinese documents that the PRC had followed Mackiernan and the Tihwa consulate for some time and with-out obvious alarm. Certainly, the activities at Tihwa did not rise to form a *casus belli*.

In the final analysis, Panikkar's disingenuousness and partiality distorted the reality confronting Nehru. Beyond that, the prime minister lacked concrete options; India did not have the capacity to resist the Chinese invasion or to provide effective assis-tance to the Tibetans so that they might resist. An Indian effort, in Nehru's words, would have been a 'political folly of the first magnitude.'[55] To complicate matters further, declassified Chinese Foreign Ministry documents show that Panikkar, under instruction from the government of India, told Chinese Minister Zhang and Chen it was the 'opinion from the Government of India that Tibet will not resist strongly now and in the future, therefore military actions can be taken at any time.'[56] Thus, if these documents are to be believed, Nehru—absent a clear understanding of Chinese intentions—was effectively reaffirming the Chinese position.[57]

Amidst all of the confusion, Nehru chose to present himself as a victim, lamenting in a letter to his sister that he felt 'that the Chinese Government has not played fair with us in regard to Tibet. I feel hurt about this.'[58] Still, he maintained that his poli-cies had pursued the right path. In a second letter to his sister four days later, he again referred to the situation in Tibet. He wrote that some had felt 'let down' by the Chinese and were angry. But he said, 'I do not think this is all justified and we have to be careful to not overdo it.'[59]

On 26 October Bajpai sent Panikkar a 'strongly worded' telegram to be passed to the communist Chinese government; it was read aloud to Henderson in a meeting on 31 October.[60] Bajpai accused the Chinese of 'contrasting statements' made to the GOI regarding the Tibet situation, alleging they had acted 'with deceit' and had 'ignored Indian feelings and friendly suggestions re Tibet.'[61] Bajpai called China's action 'deplorable' and 'not in the interest of world peace.'[62]

On 30 October the Chinese, in turn, accused the GOI of interfering in the Tibetan situation. Nehru then wrote a 'Top Secret' letter to Chou expressing 'amazement' that the Chinese government would accuse the GOI of trying to influence the Tibetans in any way.[63] He insisted that he had merely 'given friendly advice' to the Tibetans, and emphasized that Indian policy was one of non-involvement in pursuit of peaceful resolutions.[64] Nehru reiterated that 'the basic policy of the Government of India [was] to work for friendly relations between India and China, [with] both countries recognizing each other's sovereignty, territorial integrity and mutual interests.'[65]

Good relations with India were also important to China. Chou En-lai worried that should the Dalai Lama decide to seek asylum in India, difficulties in the Sino-Indian relationship might arise.[66] Chou wished to resolve outstanding issues with India through normal diplomatic channels, peacefully, and yet, perhaps as an opening gambit, told Panikkar: 'if the Dalai Lama leaves Tibet and goes to India it would cast a shadow over the Sino-Indian relationship.'[67] 'Therefore,' Chou continued, 'the attitude of the Government of India toward this issue will affect the peaceful resolution of the Tibetan problem.'[68] Meanwhile, Acheson was hopeful Nehru would now see China in a more realistic light and wrote:

Dept believes Tibetan developments so soon after Chinese Commie duplicity in dealing with GOI re Korea and in assisting Ho in Indochina shld leave no doubt re absence moral principles Peiping [Beijing] regime and its cynicism in conducting internatl relations. At minimum it shld cause GOI to reassess its view re character Peiping regime, as it serves [to] confirm our own views.[69]

In the end Nehru held his course: obeisance toward China, and a critical wariness toward Washington. Yet, as the brutal details about the Chinese invasion came to light in the press, this could not have been easy. Several members of Nehru's cabinet openly expressed their displeasure at his policies. Henderson wrote to Washington of dissent in high government circles and said, 'even those members of [the] Cabinet who are Nehru adherents appear to be convinced that [the] time has come for India to recognize that international communism is [the] country's chief danger and to make corresponding shifts in policy.'[70] Sardar Patel, India's deputy prime minister, became an outspoken critic of Nehru's policies. He wanted to reverse India's direction to develop closer ties with the West and particularly the US.[71] Patel openly condemned the PRC for the invasion of Tibet.[72] He was quoted in the *Hindustan Times* on 11 November 1950, saying 'to use the sword against the traditionally peace-loving Tibetan people was unjustified.'[73]

In a letter to the prime minster, dated 7 November 1950, Patel asserted that 'the Chinese Government has tried to delude us by professions of peaceful means.'[74] Patel called the Chinese actions 'perfidy and tragic' and accused Ambassador Panikkar of being at 'great pains to find an explanation or justification for Chinese policy and actions.'[75] Patel advised Nehru to take action to secure India's borders, most particularly the northern and north-east frontiers—the borders with Nepal, Bhutan, Sikkim, Darjeeling, and Assam—and to improve India's roads, rail, and air in these frontier areas.[76] In addition, Patel believed that Nehru should take steps to secure the trade routes from India to Tibet, fearing that now China would expand its frontiers 'almost up to our gates.'[77] Patel had also pressed this view with Bajpai. In a 4 November letter he wrote to the secretary general that:

The Chinese advance into Tibet upsets all our security calculations. Hitherto, the danger to India on its land frontiers has always come from the North-West. Throughout our history we have concentrated our armed might in that region. For the first time, a serious danger is now developing on the North and North-East side.[78]

Indeed, in the coming years China realized Patel's fears all across India's northern border. The PLA would build roads in Aksai Chin, claim Arunachal Pradesh including Tawang in the north-east, pressure the Sikkim, Bhutan, Nepal borders and the tribal areas of Assam; and, eventually, support some 300,000 troops between Lhasa and the Indian border with four military airfields.

Due to tensions arising from Nehru's continuing criticism of America's refusal to recognize the PRC and to accept Soviet overtures related to the UN, Washington was hesitant to pressure Nehru to take action in Tibet. Interestingly, Sardar Patel pointed out to Nehru that India was 'practically alone in championing the cause of Chinese entry into the UN.'[79] Administration officials were, in fact, so concerned about the delicate and strained relationship with India that State Department officials were warned that:

[T]here should at the present time be no public discussion in Washington of the Tibetan matter by Department representatives in order that there be no compromise or adverse influence of the India position by reason of statements which might be made in Washington.[80]

Washington walked a fine line: the Department knew that, on balance, Nehru meant to accommodate Beijing, but they also believed that good US relations with a healthy and economically sound India were essential for stability in Asia. Separately, Washington was quietly determined to support Tibetan resistance and hoped, in time, to use the Dalai Lama to rally the opposition to speak out against communism.

In a private dinner meeting with the Indian prime minister on 3 November 1950, Henderson was able to discuss the issues at hand and relay Acheson's message that the US would be willing to help in any way possible.[81] In his practiced fashion, Henderson assured Nehru that the US 'did not want to say or do anything which would increase this burden.'[82] Then, the ambassador asked the prime minister how the US could help. Nehru's well-known response neatly wrapped the predicament the US faced of trying to help the Tibetan people while placating the prime minister. Nehru responded that the 'US could be most helpful by doing nothing and saying little just now.'[83] Nehru told Henderson that any announcements that the United States made regarding Tibet, either condemning China or supporting Tibet, might 'lend [a] certain amount [of] credence to Beijing's charges that great powers had been intriguing in Tibet and had been exercising influence over India's Tibet policies.'[84] Nehru had been made aware through Bajpai that Henderson might extend an offer of help with the Tibetan situation. He had written to his sister the day before the dinner declaring that 'if [Henderson] asks me, I shall gratefully decline the suggested help. Nothing could be more damaging to our cause, and us, than asking for American help to deal with the Tibetan situation.'[85]

This begs the question as to why Washington was hopeful that the Nehru government could be persuaded of the danger posed to India and Asian stability by Mao's totalitarian government. While the answer to this is elusive, it may be that Bajpai's confidential meetings with Henderson in 1950 gave Henderson the impression that Delhi could be drawn toward the American position. Henderson believed that Bajpai had been frank in his discussion of Panikkar in Beijing and that Bajpai had an 'attitude of genuine friendless towards the United States.'[86] In Henderson's words:

Sir Girja [Bajpai], on a number of occasions, has told me in confidence that he is not at all satisfied with the policies of his Government with regard to Communist China. In fact, I am inclined to believe his is almost as much ashamed of some of the instructions which have gone to Panikkar as he is of some of Panikkar's reports.[87]

Having quietly offered help, the Truman administration, for its part, acknowledged that 'India ha[d] become the pivotal state in non-Communist Asia by virtue of its relative power, stability and influence.'[88] It could not risk unsettling relations with Delhi by extending overt aid to Tibet or by making overtures to the Dalai Lama to leave Tibet to lead an anti-communist movement. Yet Henderson's analysis of the situation was prescient. In response to Bajpai's query about what the American ambassador thought China would do regarding Tibet, he said:

…basing myself entirely on actions [in] Communist-controlled states of past, Peking would continue conquest of Tibet regardless of Indian sensibilities. After completion, it would turn friendly disarming face on India; express its regret at being compelled [to] take action disagreeable to India; reiterate feelings of friendship for India and desire as much closer neighbors to cooperate with India in ridding Asia of last vestiges of colonialism, etc. It would then work out new adventures.[89]

Washington was in the game, however, and had developed a complex and subtle plan through Henderson, who would jeopardize his career in support of the Dalai Lama. The Henderson plan and the US reaction to China's invasion are the subject of the next chapter.

15

THE DALAI LAMA AND HENDERSON'S PLAN

While Acheson was reluctant to openly accuse the Soviets of complicity in the Korean invasion, he saw China differently.[1] Acheson told the president and others present at the October 1950 NSC meeting that: 'As for the Chinese Communists we ought to draw a line and not try to walk both sides of the street. There is no use denying they are fighting us, so we had better stir up trouble for them.'[2] Whatever Acheson had in mind at this meeting, it was clear that US involvement in Tibet would certainly stir up trouble for the Chinese.

After the attack

The US embassy in Delhi formally learned of the Chinese assault on eastern Tibet by PLA troops on 28 October from India's Foreign Secretary Menon.[3] By mid-November the Chinese, having taken over eastern Tibet, issued a statement saying, in effect, that Tibet was now part of the motherland and under the 'protection' of the PLA.

A month later, on the night of 16 December 1950, the Dalai Lama, dressed as a commoner and accompanied by two tutors and members of the Kashag, left Lhasa for Yatung, a town just 12 miles inside the Tibetan–Indian border. The Dalai Lama recalled that he felt both 'a mixture of anxiety and anticipation'—he did not want to leave his people but was excited about the prospect of travelling.[4] Several weeks before the date of departure, Tibetan government officials had sent caravans carrying personal items and treasures, including bars of silver and gold, from the Potala Palace.[5] The Phala, the Lord Chamberlain, told the young leader to dress in disguise so that the people of Lhasa would not prevent him from leaving the Palace.[6] They left at night; the Dalai Lama remembered it was cold but very bright as the sky was filled with stars.[7] Altogether the party consisted of almost two hundred Tibetans; some were monks and others were high officials. The journey of some 200 miles would take ten days and included Heinrich Harrer, who would capture the journey through his photographs for the world to see. The temperature was frigid and the winds blew with gale force; they travelled from 4 a.m. until 10 a.m. when the winds were not at full force.[8] On some days they could only travel six miles, but on average they covered more than thirty.[9] The Dalai Lama rode in his sedan chair. His Holiness would dismount from his horse at every town and alternate sets of servants would carry him a few hundred yards at a time into town. It was a grueling journey which included traversing three mountain ranges of 16,000 feet each and then crossing swift rivers in fragile yak-skinned boats.[10]

Ambassador Henderson's plan

On arrival at Yatung, the new enthroned Dalai Lama hoped to negotiate a measure of autonomy from Beijing by dispatching another delegation to Beijing for talks. The head of the delegation was the former governor of Chamdo, Ngabo Ngawang Jigme. It was this delegation that five months later, in May 1951, would be forced to sign the infamous 17 Point Agreement.

Ambassador Henderson, sympathetic to the Tibetan plight, saw the writing on the wall and knew that talks in Beijing would not alter Mao's plans for Tibet. In March 1951, as the delegation was en route, he decided to take things into his own hands. Without departmental approval, Henderson sent a 'Top Secret' memo to Elbert Matthews, the director of the State Department's Office of South Asian Affairs. It said: 'without instructions I am taking certain action with regard to Tibet to which I hope the Department will not take undue exception.'[11] Henderson planned to approach the Dalai Lama directly—a bold and risky endeavor.

Ambassador Henderson had been introduced to Heinrich Harrer, an Austrian who had tutored and befriended the Dalai Lama in Lhasa.[12] Harrer shared his thoughts and insights on Tibet with Henderson, explaining that the Dalai Lama and his government were eager to establish closer ties to the United States and were 'very much in need of advice.'[13] Among the points made by Harrer was that the Dalai Lama was being pressured to come to terms with Beijing and return to Lhasa from Yatung. Harrer emphasized with the ambassador that the Dalai Lama had not given the delegation now proceeding to Beijing 'any plenipotentiary powers.'[14] It was after his meeting that Henderson wrote to the Department in Washington:

I am convinced that if the Dalai Lama goes back to Lhasa with his treasures both he and his treasures will eventually fall into the hands of the Chinese Communists... On my own initiative, therefore, I am endeavoring to send to the Dalai Lama a message... The paper on which the messages are written has been purchased in India and will bear no indication of origin. I realize that a considerable amount of risk is involved in sending a message of this kind. My judgment is that it is better for this risk to be taken than to see the Chinese Communists succeed by trickery in taking over Tibet and in gaining control of the Dalai Lama... I have not informed the Department of this matter by telegram or asked for its authority, because of my fear of a leak. Furthermore, if my message should become public, the Department is free, if it desires to disclaim any responsibility in the matter. My taking of this action does not mean that I have any intention of following the practice in the future of going ahead in matters of this kind without proper authority. I realize the danger of officers in the field committing acts on their own which might not be in line with the policies of the Department. It seems to me, however, that this was one of the rare occasions when I should move forward fast, taking upon myself the entire responsibility for the consequences. Please inform George McGhee and Dean Rusk of my action. The appropriate members of the un-nameable agency should, of course be informed.[15]

Henderson was deeply moved by the plight of the Dalai Lama and his people and was willing to risk rebuke by the Department and damage his career in order to act on what he thought was a matter of principle and great urgency.

The next day, 30 March, Henderson sent a copy of the Matthews letter to the US ambassador in Ceylon, L. C. Satterthwaite, who responded in a lengthy memo: 'My belief is that the Government of Ceylon would be very glad indeed to grant asylum to the Dalai Lama if he should request it...'[16] In his final paragraph Satterthwaite said, 'you are, in my opinion, to be highly commended for the courageous course of action you have taken and I am sure that you will have the full backing of the Department.'[17] Satterthwaite sent a copy of his response letter to Washington, and a little over a week later he received a response from Elbert Matthews at the Department, saying that Henderson's plan had 'full Departmental backing.'[18]

On 13 May Fraser Wilkins, a US Embassy officer in Delhi, George Patterson, and an interpreter met with Dzasa Liushar, the Tibetan foreign secretary, handed him Henderson's letter, and asked for it be delivered to the Dalai Lama in Yatung. The meeting was in Kalimpong, which had become a home to Tibetan refugees and was also popular with Tibetan officials attached to the Tibetan trade mission. The subject of the meeting, according to a heavily redacted document, was: 'Blue Letter for the Dalai Lama.'[19] There was no indication that it came from an American source, and instructions for its delivery were explicit: the letter was to be hand-delivered without delay to the Dalai Lama who 'should be informed only by word of mouth that it came from the Ambassador.'[20]

Henderson's message to the Dalai Lama was: Do not return to Lhasa. He wrote:

The Peiping [Beijing] Communist regime is determined to obtain complete control over Tibet. No concession made to that regime by His Holiness can change this determination. The Chinese Communists prefer to gain control through trickery rather than force... Until changes in the world situation would make it difficult for the Chinese Communists to take over Tibet, His Holiness should in no circumstances return to Lhasa... It is suggested that His Holiness send representatives at once to Ceylon...to obtain permission for His Holiness and His Household to find asylum... If His Holiness and His Household cannot find safe asylum in Ceylon he can be certain of finding a place of refuge in one of the friendly countries, including the United States...[21]

From Henderson's actions it is possible to see the tension between Washington's Cold War calculus, which demanded an adroit and dispassionate diplomacy, and the personal anguish he felt in executing this policy.

His instincts regarding the outcome of the Tibetan delegation's talks in Beijing were correct. Even before the Tibetans arrived, their fate had been sealed; the document known as the '17 Point Agreement,' which made Tibet a part of China, had already been drafted.[22] Not only had there been no negotiations, but Chinese troops near the border had begun to improve infrastructure and other facilities in the areas adjacent to Tibet. Well in advance of the invasion, the Chinese had constructed a supply headquarters, vehicle repair shops, telephone and communications systems, and food and clothing factories at Chengtu and readied mobile hospitals.[23]

The Chinese noose tightens

On 24 May 1951, the day after the document was signed, a distressed Tsepon Shakabpa and his translator, Jigme Tering, met with Fraser Wilkins in Calcutta.[24] Shakabpa made it clear that the Tibetan delegation lacked the authority to sign an official treaty and he now approached the United States for help.[25] Shakabpa asked if the Americans would approach the government of Ceylon to request asylum for the Dalai Lama and his followers, and if that was denied would the United States be willing to accept the Tibetan leader and members of his retinue.[26] In addition, he inquired if the US government would provide financial and military assistance to the Tibetans; and finally, would they also provide refuge in America for the Dalai Lama's brother.[27]

Shakabpa's queries were conveyed to Washington. Two days later Secretary of State Dean Acheson, in a lengthy top secret memo to the embassy in New Delhi, requested an assessment of the situation in Tibet.[28] Fully appreciating that Washington would have little traction on this issue in the UN General Assembly—and might possibly harm the Tibetan cause—Acheson wanted to know if the government of India would 'now take the initiative and support Tibet's case in UN?'[29] The Americans correctly felt that Tibet's case could attract a much broader world appeal if countries other than the US supported Tibet at the United Nations, and to that end they were eager for India to take the lead. Another central theme in the US position on assistance to Tibet was the issue of Tibetan resistance. Acheson said:

US prepared provide limited assistance in terms light arms depending upon POLIT and MIL developments in Tibet proper, and depending also on whether GOI attitude WLD make such supply feasible. US GOVT feels aid CLD effectively be given only while there may be within Tibet POLIT and MIL forces willing and able resist... Strong stand by Tibetan GOVT against any clear aggression WLD encourage world support for its position, whereas surrender in Outer Tibet WLD almost certainly be followed by collapse interest elsewhere. US unwilling commit itself to support any such undertaking from outside, but if resistance is maintained in Tibet from beginning WLD contribute insofar as attitude GOI makes possible.[30]

Washington's position was conveyed to Shakabpa by Wilkins, in conversations that took place on 7 and 8 June in Kalimpong.[31] The Dalai Lama, ensconced in a monastery near Yatung, worried about the Tibetans in eastern Tibet and feared that the

Chinese would continue on to Lhasa. He had been stunned when he had heard on an old 6-volt Bush radio receiver that his delegation had signed an agreement (the 17 Point Agreement) with the Chinese.[32] He wrote: 'I could not believe my ears. I wanted to rush out and call everybody in but I sat transfixed.'[33] The Chinese talked about the imperialists in Tibet and that the Tibetans were 'enslaved and suffering.'[34] The young leader recalled how he 'felt physically ill as [he] listened to this unbelievable mixture of lies and fanciful clichés.'[35] Some of his advisors and his brother, Taktser, urged him to leave Tibet and take refuge in India, while the monks of the largest monasteries in Tibet wanted him to return to Lhasa. In a letter from his brother, who had now been promised safe passage to the United States, the Dalai Lama was told that the United States was willing to help the Tibetans—though Washington preferred to offer asylum as a last resort.[36]

Washington was hopeful that the Dalai Lama would become a countervailing voice against communism. This was evident in a telegram delivered by assistant secretary of state for Far Eastern Affairs, Dean Rusk, to the Thai ambassador in Washington. That May the Committee for a Free Asia (CFA) had been established, and among their objectives was to help strengthen Asian resistance to communism.[37] The CFA was apparently funded by the Central Intelligence Agency.[38]

The letter given to the Thai ambassador was on CFA stationery and stated that 'it is our belief that [the] Dalai Lama is both a symbol and potential leader of Asian resistance to Communism.'[39] The CFA offered to facilitate asylum in a Buddhist country for the Dalai Lama and 150 members of his retinue, and offered to provide financial assistance in the hope that the young leader would repudiate the 17 Point Agreement, made under duress. Acheson wanted the Dalai Lama to oppose 'COMMIE aggression' and support resistance in Tibet.[40]

The State Department and CIA made certain that communications remained open and that they stayed abreast of the Dalai Lama's thinking. Nicholas Thacher took over the Fraser Wilkins talks in Calcutta and continued with Shakabpa and his translator in Kalimpong.[41] Eager for information, he asked the two Tibetans for any news from Yatung of the Dalai Lama's plans 'whether of importance or not,' believing that the more he received, the more he could convey to Washington and 'the more convincing evidence we would have of the Tibetan Government's genuine desire to cooperate and resist.'[42]

At the end of June Shakabpa reported to Thacher that the Dalai Lama had received the US government's letters and had questions on the nature of US aid and assistance.[43] He wanted to know if the US aid would 'be directed simply toward assisting the Dalai Lama's flight... and would some aid be forthcoming for resistance.'[44] Thacher replied that 'certainly the US Government was willing to help both.'[45] The American objective was for the Dalai Lama to publicly repudiate the newly signed 17 Point Agreement with China, and Thacher made it clear to Shakabpa that this was the most important requirement for obtaining aid. Reflecting the Truman Doctrine and also rising anti-communist emotion, US policy was to help those who helped themselves and to that end 'signs of vigorous action and vigorous resistance by the Tibetan Government was of the utmost importance.'[46]

The Tibetans, naturally, were concerned about the ramifications of taking such a strong position against a powerful enemy. To strengthen their resolve—or increase their fear—Thacher outlined the consequences for Tibet if they agreed to Chinese terms, referring to unfolding events in Czechoslovakia and Poland. In his report to Washington, Thacher noted that it might be helpful for the Tibetans if the US government would, at the appropriate time, 'give sympathetic consideration to Tibet's claims for complete independence.'[47] But Washington's response to this was swift and clear and summed up by three brief lines in a cable from the State Department to the embassy in New Delhi:

Dept does not wish to commit itself on what it may or not say re legal status Tibet. If Shakabpa SHLD press suzerainty point, he CLD merely be told that his views had been made known to this GOVT.[48]

Thacher added at the end of his report that he thought the Tibetans opportunistic and 'may forget broader duties to save own skins and are strongly tempted to come with their gold and jewels to Kalimpong for safe haven, rather than to take the risks and hard work of opposing China.'[49]

Of course agreements between nations and non-state actors are complex and this was no exception. The US was, in effect, seeking to move a significant piece on the Cold War chessboard and, amidst the intense and very human drama surrounding the Dalai Lama, progress came slowly and with much frustration. Still, Thacher was impatient for a response from the Dalai Lama, as was the embassy, which now referred to Tibetan communications as 'archaic.'[50] The question was whether Tibet would resist the communists and approach the government of India for asylum.[51] But Washington suspected that if Shakabpa was pressed any harder to try to get the Dalai Lama to act against the Chinese, it would 'provoke a negative reaction' which would of course defeat the American goal.[52]

Thubten Jigme Norbu: the Dalai Lama's brother

While American officials were waiting for a response from the Dalai Lama on whether he would leave Tibet, his brother Thubten Jigme Norbu, known as Taktser Rinpoche, had begun to take steps to leave India.[53]

It was at this point that George Patterson, who was residing in Kalimpong, assumed a fuller role. Norbu, also now in Kalimpong, asked Patterson to tea at the home of his mother and sister. Later that evening, when Patterson returned to his home, Norbu paid him an unexpected visit. He arrived, Patterson recalled, with 'heavily armed guards' and an air of secrecy.[54] Norbu requested that the curtains be drawn, adding further drama. He was carrying two letters from his brother, the Dalai Lama, and asked Patterson to help him leave the country. The letters, intended for officials in the United States, were a plea for assistance and for Washington to protect

Norbu from the Chinese.[55] (He had been in a monastery when the communists invaded; they had tried to indoctrinate him and ordered him to depose his brother—but instead he warned the Dalai Lama of the plan.) Patterson requested that the letters be left with him to read, and a few days later, on 17 June, he travelled to Calcutta and passed them to the American consulate.[56]

Washington decided that honoring his Holiness' request for his brother to travel to the United States might solidify US–Tibetan relations and so plans were made.[57] A visa was granted. Norbu would be sponsored by the Committee for a Free Asia.

Taktser Rinpoche goes to Washington

On the steamy afternoon of 30 June in Vice Consul William Gibson's Calcutta flat, the Dalai Lama's brother along with Evan Wilson, the consul general, Robert Linn, a consular attaché, and George Patterson acting as interpreter, gathered to make final arrangements for Taktser's trip to Washington.[58] It was thought dangerous for Taktser to stay in India much longer.[59] A few hours after their meeting, the consulate in Calcutta cabled Washington to say that Taktser and his servant Dhondrup would arrive in New York on Monday 5 July. The State Department wanted a quick departure, fearful that the Chinese might harm him or that the Indian government might cause delays.[60]

Meanwhile, the Tibetan negotiating delegation and Chinese officials returned to Calcutta from Beijing en route to see the Dalai Lama in Yatung. Their arrival alarmed the Americans and the Dalai Lama's brother, who was by then ensconced at the Grand Hotel with George Patterson and preparing to leave. The US was worried about Taktser's safety, but even more concerned that unless the Dalai Lama spoke out soon, the opportunity for Tibet to rebuke the Chinese publicly would be lost. US officials told Patterson that Washington was disturbed by the inaction on the part of the Tibetan government; the Tibetans must make a decision. This was emphasized in a memo to the secretary of state from Henderson. He wrote: 'So long as Tibetan Government remains silent it is difficult for US [to] denounce agreement as effort [to] deprive Tibet [of] its autonomy pressure and threat of force.'[61] Patterson replied that Taktser would contact his brother and request urgent action.[62]

On the evening of 5 July Taktser and his servant left Calcutta on Pan American Flight 3 for London, where an American embassy official met them at the airport.[63] (It was noted in the file that the police and customs officials 'showed every courtesy at the airport' and that the consulate assured the officials at Pan American that the 132 pounds of excess baggage that they were carrying, totaling $282.17, would be paid.)[64] He then flew on to Washington on 8 July, where government officials debriefed him, leading the State Department to believe that he might influence his brother to take a stand against the Chinese.[65]

Taktser's secretive departure would not have been out of place in a John le Carré thriller. Many of the details, including the remarkable role of George Patterson, have only recently been declassified. Previously unavailable documents were released to the authors in 2008 when the CIA acted on a four-year Freedom of Information request. One of the memos, dated 16 July 1951, provides a glimpse of Patterson's role:

The contribution George Patterson has made with regard to the visit of Taktser to the United States should be noted. It was through Patterson that first contact was made with Taktser Rimpoche, including acquisition of the full text of the letter, which Taktser was carrying from the Dalai Lama to the United States Government. It was also the efforts of Patterson that brought Taktser to Calcutta, where he arranged all meetings between the Consul General and Taktser, acted as interpreter, and gave invaluable assistance in helping us to successfully effect Taktser's departure for the United States.[66]

George Patterson was, indeed, an unusual man. A principled visionary and activist, he was devoted until his death in 2011 to the idea of an independent Tibet.

Talks continue

Relations between the US and China further deteriorated in the summer of 1951. While North Korean and Chinese forces had been driven from Seoul in March, a late spring stalemate on the battlefield blunted further military progress. Meanwhile, in Washington, the Truman administration was on the offensive, fighting off claims of being soft on communism and losing China. Within this acid political environment, Washington was ever hopeful that the Dalai Lama would leave Tibet and publicly rebuke the Chinese. During that June and July there had been more than twenty meetings between Tibetan officials in Kalimpong and American diplomats.[67]

On 12 July a message was sent to His Holiness. One copy was given to Shakabpa, and one was given to Yapshi Sey, the Dalai Lama's brother-in-law. The message began: 'at this hour of crisis in Tibetan history' and urged the leader to 'show the highest courage … act against Communism' and leave Tibet.[68] The letter continued:

We make this last appeal realizing that if it fails, it will be almost impossible to help you further. Tibet will become the slave of Communist China, and the age-old glories of Tibetan civilization and religion will be lost forever.[69]

On Shakabpa's copy, the closing paragraph read: 'Please send a final message at once, stating whether or not you would be willing to leave for India. If it is your desire to leave, we have a plan to help you.'[70] A code was adopted for future communication. If there were a message for the Americans, the messenger would state 'I am from the Potala' or simply mention the word 'Potala.'[71] If the Dalai Lama planned to take refuge in India, the message would be 'the Potala is moving.'[72] In the end, however, Washington's efforts were futile as the Dalai Lama decided to return to Lhasa. He was convinced of this when, in the Tibetan tradition, he literally 'rolled the dice': two bits of paper that were rolled into dough balls, one saying 'Go to Lhasa', the other saying 'Go to India.' The balls were then placed in a bowl and rotated in front of an image of the Buddha; the 'Go to Lhasa' ball came out first.[73]

The Dalai Lama ordered most of the Tibetan officials in Kalimpong back to Tibet; Shakabpa was granted permission to remain in India.[74] On 24 July the young Tibetan leader left Yatung for Lhasa with his retinue, under the watchful eye of General Chang Ching-wu, the newly appointed commissioner and administrator of Civil and Military Affairs for Tibet. By the end of 1951 there would be nearly 8,000 Chinese military personnel in Lhasa.

A last effort

Fearing that perhaps their past messages had not been relayed through the proper Tibetan officials to the Dalai Lama, the Americans made yet another attempt to convince the Dalai Lama to leave Tibet. On 18 July the consul general in Calcutta, Evan Wilson, wrote a letter to the Dalai Lama that was subsequently hand-delivered to the Tibetan Defense Minister, Ragashar Shape, who was riding with the His Holiness' party back to Lhasa.[75] The letter, like the others that had been passed to the Dalai Lama, was unsigned and made no direct reference to the source. Ragashar was told orally the letter was from the US government and asked to tell the other Tibetan ministers of US intentions.[76] But he sent a message back to the Americans saying that he could not convince the other members of the Kashag without 'a signed letter on US letterhead.'[77] Washington's reply was clear: an official government letter carried too many risks, especially if fell into the wrong hands.[78]

Washington's frustration was palpable and reflected in correspondence with the embassy in Delhi.[79] Acheson commented that it would be most unfortunate if a simple misunderstanding had caused the leader not to seek asylum.[80] On 15 August the American consul general, Evan Wilson, again met with Yapshi Sey, the brother-in-law of the Dalai Lama, to send a final message to the leader.[81] Yapshi was asked by the Americans to translate the message into Tibetan and take it directly to Lhasa.[82] The message shown, just three sentences in Tibetan, took nearly two hours to be translated.

In a message from the Calcutta consulate to the State Department in Washington, W. O. Anderson wrote in the margins of his reporting cable from Calcutta: 'it's in the lap of the gods now.'[83]

Thus the US, and more particularly Ambassador Henderson, had made every effort to convince the Dalai Lama that he could best serve the Tibetan people by seeking asylum outside Tibet. Meanwhile, US officials were learning a hard lesson about the dangers of delicate negotiations with remote cultures. Their effort to use the young leader as a powerful Buddhist voice against the communist Chinese had caused the Tibetans to conclude that this vast American effort, including financial assistance, could only mean that Washington supported Tibet's bid for independence. This view may have been encouraged by a letter sent by the US in July 1951 which said:

You will be of greater help to Tibet outside of Tibet where you will be the recognized leader and will symbolize the hopes of the Tibetans for the recovery of Tibet's freedom…[84]

Linguistic nuance was not, however, the only issue that bedeviled US policy. Cultural differences, including the intercession of the state Oracle, Chinese promises of financial support for a self-serving aristocracy who feared losing their lifestyle should the Dalai Lama depart, and the view among many Tibetan elites that it would be dishonorable to abandon Tibet also played a part. Swept into the treacherous diplomatic waters of South Asia, Washington struggled to sustain US strategic interests while managing politics in Washington. This meant retaining workable relations with Nehru's India and containing the Chinese—including their thrust into Tibet, while rebuffing increasingly vitriolic attacks from the China Lobby at home—a challenge more than sufficient for Henderson, Acheson, and the White House.

In the end, many in Lhasa believed the American offer was flawed; that the Dalai Lama's legitimacy would be questioned if he abandoned Tibet; and that, in any case, the Chinese would not interfere substantially with Tibetan life. In July government officials met at Yatung near Sikkim's border to debate the issue of the Dalai Lama's return to Lhasa. Most, including senior monks, Kashag members, and aristocratic government officials, believed the young leader should return; while members of the Dalai Lama's family, Tsepon Shakabpa, and Phala, the Dalai Lama's Lord Chamberlain, among others, felt he should instead accept the American offer and depart.[85] At Yatung, Tsipon Namseling, a Revenue Office official, delivered an emotional argument opposing the Chinese 17 Point Agreement.[86] He said 'that by going into exile they would not only refute Chinese claims to sovereignty over Tibet but keep the flame of Tibetan independence alive.'[87] Others insisted that the Dalai Lama could best serve his people by returning to Lhasa and working with the Chinese. The Dalai Lama's dilemma increased with a letter from his brother, who confirmed that the Americans would assist in his arrangements to go into exile and provide support.[88] The Dalai Lama wrote in his autobiography:

Should I really leave before even meeting with the Chinese? And if I did, would our new-found allies see us through thick and thin? As I pondered these thoughts, I continuously came up against two particular considerations. Firstly, it was obvious to me that the most likely result of a pact with America or anyone else was war. And war meant bloodshed. Secondly, I reasoned that although America was a very powerful country, it was thousands of miles away. China, on the other hand, was our neighbor and, whilst materially less powerful than the United States, easily had numerical superiority. It might therefore take many years to resolve the dispute by armed struggle. And after it was all over, the Tibetans would again be on their own.[89]

In the end, the Dalai Lama decided to meet with PLA General Chang Ching-wu: 'He must be human after all,' his Holiness temporized.[90]

While the US had agreed to help the Dalai Lama find asylum, India was not as forthcoming. US officials in Delhi had heard from 'several' Tibetan sources that the Dalai Lama perhaps could have taken refuge in India 'but had been discouraged' by the apparent lack of sympathy from the Indian government.[91]

Lloyd Steere, in the US embassy in Delhi, discussed this with Girja Bajpai of the Indian Ministry of External Affairs in October 1951 after the Dalai Lama's return to

Lhasa. In his cable to Acheson, Steere wrote that his Indian interlocutor gave 'vent to some expressions of regret' but 'pointed out that there had been little that India cld offer Tibet in way of polit or practical support.'[92] As Tibetan historian Tsering Shakya noted, the relationship between India and Tibet at this critical point was at 'its lowest ebb.'[93] 'The Tibetans,' he wrote, 'were convinced that India had lost interest in Tibet and was at pains to maintain friendly relations with China.'[94]

16

MR NEHRU ... AGAIN

Washington had no illusions about Beijing's motives in invading Tibet and entering the Korean War. Acheson's assessment was blunt: he wrote to Ambassador Henderson that this 'SHLD leave no doubt re absence [of] moral principles Peiping regime and its cynicism in conducting international relations.'[1] Even so, he warned Henderson to avoid a 'told you so attitude' when speaking with Nehru.[2] Washington was walking a fine line. With deep disappointment about the inability to recast the Dalai Lama as a galvanizing anti-communist figure in Buddhist Southeast Asia, and the expanding Korean War, the US could not afford to have a weak India in the face of a strengthening communist China. As 1950 came to a close, India's millions of inhabitants needed food and aid. Washington now confronted a multidimensional challenge in Asia, requiring a full range of diplomatic and military efforts that extended from Tibet to India to China to Korea. Jawaharlal Nehru remained central in this delicate equation—charming, quixotic, self-absorbed, and vital to US interests.

In December 1950, through his sister Ambassador Pandit, Nehru made his first official request for aid. In a private meeting with the secretary of state, Ambassador Pandit requested two million tons of food grains to help alleviate India's growing food shortage.[3] Nehru pointedly told his sister that he wanted 'no political strings attached to it.'[4] Understandably the Truman administration was very concerned about India's looming food crisis, but getting an aid package through Congress for a nation that had seemingly dismissed American values and disapproved of the American way of life promised to be difficult. Moreover, Nehru was correct in anticipating the requested concessions that are often a condition of US aid, and clear in his instructions to his sister, Ambassador Pandit.

Anything savoring of political conditions or pressure or the possibility of such pressure being exercised in the future would of course be totally unacceptable to us. We have therefore to be a little careful in considering proposals of financial help. There is a tendency in the US to treat the countries they help as some kind clients to it, which are expected to toe their general policy.[5]

In January 1951, as Washington considered the nature of an aid package to India, Ambassador Henderson wrote to Acheson to say that while Nehru's attitude to the Far East situation 'was not conducive to [a] receptive atmosphere in [the] US and particularly Congress,' failure to assist them would only 'add grist' to the mill to 'those elements unfriendly to the US,' and in the end assistance could 'strengthen chances [of] survival [of the] free world.'[6]

George McGhee, the assistant secretary of state for Near Eastern, South Asian, and African Affairs, prepared a lengthy and detailed report for Acheson, stating that it was imperative to provide food grains to India not only because ties between the United States and India would be strengthened but that not to provide aid would likely cause 'millions [to] die of starvation.'[7] He wrote that then 'we shall find it difficult to live with our own consciences, and our dwindling credit in much of Asia will be further reduced.'[8]

McGhee's report reiterated the importance of a stable India for the region, noting that 'if South Asia falls under Communist control, a strategic area containing half a billion people will be denied to us, and its resources, including strategic material, can be utilized against us.'[9]

The *New York Times*, which had been critical of Nehru a few months earlier, now called for support to aid India's hungry millions. In a 27 January 1950 editorial entitled 'Hunger Is Not Political' the paper called for no further delay in granting India's request for grain.[10] The newspaper further urged Congress not to become embroiled in the politics of Nehru's refusal to go along with United States policy toward communist China.[11] But the contest was set: Senator Tom Connally of Texas, the Democratic chairman of the Senate Foreign Relations Committee, had made clear to McGhee: 'you are going to have one hell of a time getting this thing through Congress.'[12]

Food for India

Acheson supported McGhee's recommendations and the secretary met with President Truman on 1 February 1951.[13] While there was some dissent in Congress over support for India, a group of bipartisan members had written to Truman urging his endorsement on a food aid package.[14] On 12 February Truman endorsed a grant for India, allowing it to purchase 2 million tons of grain, and strongly urged Congress to 'take immediate steps to put this program into effect.'[15] On 1 March 1951 the House Committee on Foreign Affairs approved the legislation, but political emotions remained high. Due to a deadlock in the House Rules Committee and the Senate Foreign Relations Committee's reluctance to schedule hearings, it wasn't until three months later, on 15 June, that Truman could sign the bill into law.[16]

Congressional haggling over aid further strained US–India relations. In India Henderson was aware that 'propagandists for Moscow [and] Peking [are] actively criticizing' Indian officials for seeking help from the United States, and that elements fundamentally hostile or suspicious [to the] US [are] becoming more triumphantly cynical.'[17] Henderson worried about the growing anxiety in India over the issue and sent a telegram to the State Department on 24 March detailing these events, with the hope that the troubles would resolve quickly.[18] At the same time, Nehru sent a request to Beijing inquiring about the price and quantities of food available.[19] Two days later both the Indian ambassador, Panikkar, and his first counselor, T. N. Kaul, met with the director general of Asian affairs in the Chinese Foreign Ministry, Chen Jiakang, and discussed both a range of issues regarding Tibet and also the possibility of supplying food to India.[20] When Kaul met with Chen Jiakang subsequently, he told him:

In October 1949, Prime Minister Nehru visited the United States to discuss purchasing 2 million tons of wheat from the US. However, the wheat never came. Rice from China arrived in India one or two weeks after Nehru's discussion. This made a good impression in India. Nonetheless, 50,000 tons of food is too little. We are also purchasing from the Soviet Union.[21]

Underscoring Henderson's insight, Kaul ended his conversation by saying: 'Mutual assistance among Asian countries will block instigation attempts from Britain and the United States.'[22]

Undersecretary McGhee, equally concerned about the slow progress in Congress, wrote to Acheson that further delay would:

[D]eny us the benefits we should otherwise expect from our response. Failure to act will be confirmation to the Indians of what they have alleged in the past, that we talk as if we want to help them but do not come through.[23]

Nehru's critical public outbursts against the United States did not endear the prime minister to members of Congress then enmeshed in the aid debate. When members of the deadlocked House Rules Committee finally reached an agreement to provide the GOI with a loan of $190 million for food, provided this was repaid in strategic minerals, Nehru was outraged. He was further offended by the conditions Washington placed on the distribution and management of the aid. The United States insisted on 'unrestricted observation' of its distribution and a role in deciding how the funds received in India from the sale of the US grains were allocated.[24] On 30 April, speaking in Uttar Pradesh, Nehru told his Congress Party workers that 'India is not so down and out as to accept any conditions dictated by any foreign country in the matter of importing food that sullies our honor.'[25] The next day in a speech broadcast on All India Radio he relayed what he had privately told his sister five months earlier: he 'would not accept food from any country if it had any political strings attached.'[26]

This pushed the leadership in both Houses of Congress to postpone the upcoming debate about the bill. The US Congress demanded a clarification of India's position in the form of a public statement. Nehru thus confronted a difficult decision. India clearly needed the grain that Washington would authorize; there was intense domestic pressure to alleviate the food crisis. Moreover his sister, as ambassador in Washington, had made clear that political differences were growing, not contracting, and could soon render the relationship dysfunctional. It was also clear that much of the friction was a matter of political style, pride, lifestyle, and differing perspectives toward the Cold War, rather than the ideological gulf—turning on the distinction between democratic and authoritarian governance—which existed with the newly minted Maoist government in Beijing. In the end, Nehru accepted the conditions of aid set by Congress: on 10 May, before the Indian Parliament, he accepted the aid package which was given on the basis of a half loan, half grant.[27]

Early covert contacts

By the time President Truman had signed the legislation to alleviate a potential famine in India in June, the CIA, in keeping with the administration's restructured national security and intelligence apparatus, had begun a clandestine relationship with the Tibetans.

On 5 April 1951 Truman sent a presidential directive to the secretary of state, the secretary of defense, and the director of the CIA establishing a Psychological Strategy Board (PSB) that would coordinate US psychological operations. The board was to be the nerve-center for these programs and would both coordinate psychological operations and evaluate their effectiveness to ensure they were consistent with overall national aims.[28] The phrase 'psychological operations' was used as 'a cover to describe those activities of the United States in peace and in war through which all elements of national power are systematically brought to bear on other nations for the attainment of US foreign policy objectives.'[29]

In October the concept was taken further. The National Security Council and the Central Intelligence Agency approved the 'intensification of covert operations.'[30] The directive, known as NSC 10/5, was designed to place 'maximum strain on the Soviet structure of power' which included its satellite, communist China.[31] This 'reaffirmed' the 1948 covert mandate of NSC 10/2, which approved extended covert actions as part of the 'national responsibility' of the United States to 'strengthen the resistance of those in free nations against Communism' as well as to 'develop underground resistance and facilitate covert and guerrilla operations in strategic areas.'[32]

By November 1951 the new PSB under the direction of Gordon Gray (he would later chair the special committee that handled covert operations for Tibet) came up with detailed guidelines for the president to review. The eleven-page 'Top Secret' classified report outlined eight objectives for a national propaganda campaign.[33] Overall the objectives were consistent with the aims of Truman's policy: to stem the spread of communism from the USSR and satellite governments and encourage resistance to communist regimes.[34] Strategies employing guerrilla warfare and the use of aggressive intelligence against communist regimes were formulated and tested under the aegis of the PSB and the CIA. Clandestine programs under this directive were expanded 'threefold' between 1949 and 1959.[35] Between 1949 and 1952 alone, the CIA grew from 300 employees to over 6,000; in the same period its budget increased from $4.7 million to $82 million.[36]

While Henderson was working with Nehru on the wheat loan bill in 1951, he was, as previously noted, secretly talking with members of the Dalai Lama's family, George Patterson, and others to formulate an escape plan for the Tibetan leader and his brother. The United States had offered, unsuccessfully, to facilitate asylum in a Buddhist country for the Dalai Lama and his retinue, in addition to financial assistance.

Thus, Ambassador Henderson and Secretary Acheson now found themselves, as they must have known they would, pursuing US–India relations on two tracks— overt and covert. The US knew this was unquestionably a critical time for the Tibetans, who had been forced into signing the 17 Point Agreement. As seen, the State Department had spared no effort to entice the Dalai Lama to denounce the agreement publicly in the hope that he would provide a rallying point for Tibetans against the PRC.

The Truman administration's effort had been extraordinary given the fact that Tibet represented an utterly alien culture, the Tibetans spoke no English, and all contact had to proceed without Indian knowledge. And, of course, India's non-aligned status and its determination not to offend Beijing meant that the Indians would not actually propose to China that a compromise be reached on the subject of Tibet. In a top secret telegram from Acheson informing the American embassies in London and Moscow of Henderson's clandestine meetings with the Tibetans, the US frustration with Nehru is evident:

Present attitude GOI obviously is one of the chief limiting factors in [the] situation.… [E]vidence so far available indicates Nehru unwilling [to] take steps which WLD antagonize COMMIE CHINESE.[37]

The extended six-month wrangle surrounding the wheat loan had furthered strained Washington's relations with Delhi. Henderson emphasized this point in a memo to Acheson, in June 1951, when he wrote: 'we do not believe … Nehru's stated willingness [to] accept US grant aid [indicates any] appreciable change in [his] degree [of] friendliness.'[38] Henderson, in the same memo, then referred to the Sino–Tibetan treaty signed a month earlier, saying that given the tensions in US–Indian relations it was not the best time to tell the GOI or the UK about the delicate conversations they were engaged in with the Tibetans. This is further reiterated in a telegram from Lloyd Steere, the chargé d'affaires in Delhi, to Acheson in mid-June:

Emb has not (rpt not) discussed subject [of] recent conversations with Brit nor does it intend to do so this stage because of belief on past experience Brit may feel their relations with India wld require them at least hint at fact and substance US–Tib discussions to GOI. Emb continues, however, exchange normal info re Tibet with Brit.[39]

The British, ever curious, must have had some indication of American clandestine engagement in Tibet. On 2 July the British Embassy requested a meeting at the State Department in Washington specifically to discuss Tibet. (As the meeting was taking place, the Dalai Lama's brother was waiting for his flight from Delhi to the United States, and the American embassy in Delhi and the consulate in Calcutta were both in secret ongoing conversations with the Tibetan government.) The assistant secretary of state for Far Eastern Affairs, Livingston Merchant, and others attended. The British, who were not privy to Washington's intentions, 'were concerned with bringing the Indian Government more into the picture, particularly as regards [to] any moves the US government might make or contemplate making.'[40] The British wished the State Department to believe that the GOI could be helpful in facilitating 'the very aims' that the US wished to achieve, and that contrarily, 'if the Indians were left without any knowledge of such matters ... their attitude could be adverse.'[41] The British counselor, Mr Burrows, evidently acting under instructions, made it fairly clear that the British government's attitude and action toward the Tibetan question, including the possible repudiation by the Dalai Lama of the Beijing agreement, would be likely to follow closely the lead of India (whether or not India had first been brought into the discussions).[42] Britain's sensitivity toward its special relations with Delhi is on indirect display here, as is more broadly its concern about Washington's expanding presence in South Asia.

A new era begins: the Dalai Lama returns to Lhasa; the PLA settles in...

The fall of 1951 saw a deepening political concern with Nehru on several fronts. In September the CIA produced a National Intelligence Estimate (NIE) entitled 'India's Position in the East–West Conflict.'[43] Nehru had refused to sign the Japanese peace treaty, as did the Soviets, and Washington was concerned about how to convince the GOI that their policy of neutralism and stance against collective security was favorable to the Soviet Union.[44] The NIE was unequivocal in stating that India's failure to commit itself to either side in the East–West conflict 'resulted in a tendency to appease world Communism and in failure to support the West in its program of combating world Communist aggression.'[45]

In an early reflection of what would later be called the 'Domino Theory', the CIA believed that the 'threat of Communist domination of Southeast Asia is already serious' and 'Communist domination of India would almost certainly result in Communist domination of the South and Southeast Asian region, including Indonesia.'[46] With these ideas informing discussions about Nehru and India policy in Washington, there were three significant developments on the ground in India and Tibet in late summer and fall.

The first was that the Dalai Lama returned to Lhasa on 17 August 1951 rather than accept US aid and offer of asylum. By withholding public repudiation of the agreement, he hoped to re-negotiate the 17 Point Agreement, to obtain more favorable terms from Beijing, and do more for the Tibetan people.[47] The second development came in the fall: in October 1951 Chester Bowles, then governor of Connecticut, was appointed by Truman to be Washington's new ambassador to India and Nepal. Bowles took up his new responsibilities and the Indian cause with 'unbridled enthusiasm and near-missionary zeal.'[48] Historian McMahon wrote: 'Beginning almost from the day of his arrival in the subcontinent, the American envoy to India had undertaken what must rank among the most vigorous one-person lobbying campaigns on behalf of a foreign country ever conducted by an American diplomat.'[49]

The new ambassador's embrace of all things Indian could not, however, erase the palpable distrust and vitriol in Washington's relationship with Delhi.[50] Bowles, an energetic man of the people, succeeded in conveying a new image of Americans—though not surprisingly this had only limited effect on relations between the two governments. Bowles, like his predecessor Henderson, felt that the US should help the Tibetan people and should make 'at least one final effort' either orally or by a letter to encourage the Dalai Lama to resist the Chinese.[51] And while he believed that overt aid—planes, arms, and supplies—would not be practical at this time, perhaps Washington could send 'small gifts such as [the] newest photographic equipment' or a new colored film.[52] Bowles concluded that this would represent 'tangible evidence to DL [Dalai Lama] of US friendship and wld have effect far out of proportion to their monetary value.'[53]

The third development of significance in the India–Tibet theatre occurred sixteen days after Bowles took up his new post in Delhi. General Zhang Guohua, the commander of the PLA 18th Army Corps, and General Tan Kuan-san arrived in Lhasa on 26 October 1951. Over the summer PLA troops had begun to arrive in Lhasa, although they had few vehicles and Tibet had even fewer roads. By October approximately 2,000 were quartered there and 2,000 more were camped in the immediate vicinity. An additional 3,000 PLA accompanied General Zhang upon his arrival, swelling to 10,000 in Lhasa and the surrounding area by the end of 1951. By this time Lhasa was suffering from food and housing shortages, made worse by rampant inflation. The Chinese, not prepared for the extreme winter climate, paid exorbitant sums of money to the aristocratic families for the use of their homes.[54] It was PLA policy to attempt to woo the Tibetans, which they did by hosting lavish banquets for the wealthy to soften resistance among the elite. Tibetan land lying fallow or used for grazing was turned over to the Chinese for cultivation, which in turn helped to sustain the increasingly pressed region.

Mao's early policies in Tibet from 1951 until 1956 can be described as emphasizing gradualism. His hope was to avoid alienating the Tibetans, and to this end he chose General Zhang to lead the occupation due to his knowledge of Tibetan traditions. Zhang, who served as secretary of the CPC Tibet Committee from 1950 to 1952, was instructed to 'to do united front work' by respecting the local religion and customs. Beijing's aim was slowly to 'win over the elite, and particularly the Dalai Lama, and through them the common people.'[55] In an editorial published in *The People's Daily* in May 1951, Mao admonished the PLA to 'strictly observe our ethnic and religious policies, [you] must observe the peaceful agreement, must obey discipline, must trade fairly with Tibetans…'[56] Mao ordered his armies to respect the Tibetans and 'prevent and correct the tendency of big nationality chauvinism.'[57] Mao hoped the Tibetans would seek out and accept reform themselves.

TIBET: AN UNFINISHED STORY

Despite Beijing's propaganda, banquets, and benefits, Tibetan attitudes, emanating partly from the monasteries but also from a population offended by the 'liberation' drumbeat, ranged from skeptical to hostile. Though Beijing implied that life would continue as it had before, but without the 'feudal oppression' that sustained the monasteries, the 17 Point Agreement had ushered in far-reaching change—which began with the creation of a Military and Administrative Committee and a Military Area Headquarters in Lhasa. The PLA quickly put these in place and began building roads and bridges allowing the transport of food, men, military equipment etc. They created, in effect, a parallel administrative structure in Lhasa which proceeded to displace traditional Tibetan facilities. The PLA assumed control of the educational system, commercial licenses, housing, and transportation within the city.

With the creation of the Tibetan Military District Headquarters in February 1952 the Tibetan army was incorporated into the PLA—the first step in establishing firm control of Tibet. General Zhang Guohua, commander of the PLA 18th Army Corps, who first took control of the city, commanded the headquarters; General Tan Kuan-san served as political commissar.

It was the beginning of a new era for Tibet. The PLA invaded to claim territory—indeed all of Tibet—and to extend the Han enterprise. They were in Tibet to stay, no longer a political fiction, as Curzon had noted at the turn of the century. Mao was clear: Tibet was a part of China and, even if done gradually, the Tibetans would be integrated into the motherland, both politically and economically.

* * *

Now, as the full impact of the Korean War gripped Washington, the US rededicated itself to a non-communist South Asia, to sustaining relations with India (the key to South Asian stability), and to containing Chinese and Soviet expansion. US policy gained focus on these points as the war unfolded and it strengthened its military presence in the Western Pacific, including Formosa (Taiwan), which became a staging area for military operations in Korea and for covert programs directed against the Chinese mainland, including Tibet.

17

FORMOSA

THE UNSINKABLE AIRCRAFT CARRIER

Dean Acheson made his feelings on Formosa clear to president Truman in a meeting at Blair House on 26 June 1950. He told the president that 'he thought it undesirable that we should get mixed up in the question of the Chinese administration of the island.'[1] The president agreed, responding that Washington was 'not going to give the Chinese [Nationalists] a nickel for any purpose whatever ... all the money we've given them is now invested in United States real estate.'[2] But regardless of his personal views, the President ordered the 7th Fleet to the Taiwan Strait both to prevent an attack on Formosa and to make sure that the Nationalists did not attack the mainland, provoking further war and creating a backlash in the United Nations.[3]

The president issued a statement on 27 June 1950 informing Americans that he had 'ordered United States air and sea forces to give the Korean government troops cover and support.'[4] He continued:

In these circumstances the occupation of Formosa by Communist forces would be a direct threat to the security of the Pacific area and the United States forces performing their lawful and necessary functions in that area. Accordingly I have ordered the Seventh Fleet to prevent any attack on Formosa. As a corollary of this action I am calling upon the Chinese Government on Formosa to cease all air and sea operations against the mainland. The Seventh Fleet will see that this is done.[5]

The start of the Korean War on 25 June 1950 had ushered in a new set of issues; strategic threats and requirements in the Western Pacific were fundamentally changed. The US was now engaged on the Asian mainland, which portended almost limitless liabilities, so Formosa, one of Washington's few assets in the region, assumed new significance. It was now both a staging platform for Korea and an anti-communist redoubt on China's periphery.

In Washington, the onset of war in Korea had spurred Truman to sign NSC-68, the proposed reorganization and strengthening of US security capabilities, carefully drafted and fully debated—and seemingly forgotten on his desk for six months. It also reinvigorated Chiang Kai-shek and the China Lobby who now lived to fight another day. Historian Ross Koen wrote '[the war] virtually assured the Chinese [Nationalists] of increased American aid to enable them to take more of the responsibility for the defense of Formosa.'[6] And so as long as the United States was fighting in Korea, it was unlikely that the communist government of China would be recognized. Sinologist Nancy Bernkopf Tucker observed that 'only among the Nationalist Chinese and their supporters did the Korean War engender delight. If the fighting would just last long enough, they reasoned, the Kuomintang might succeed in thoroughly re-entangling American wealth and power in Nationalist affairs.'[7] A jubilant Senator Alexander Smith (R-NJ) believed his prayers had been answered and wrote that 'the saving of Formosa was clearly God guided.'[8]

The Korean War brought out distinct opinions on how to treat the Nationalists, most particularly differences between General Douglas MacArthur, who believed that defending Formosa, at all costs, would strengthen US supremacy in the Pacific, and the administration. Truman and Acheson both maintained that the shift in policy toward the Generalissimo was temporary and a function of the Korean War. Truman clarified the US position toward Formosa in his message to Congress on 19 July which emphasized that the United States had no intention of 'seizing Formosa unilaterally for US mil exploitation.'[9]

On 27 July 1950, a little over a month after the war began, the joint chiefs of staff conducted a review of US policy toward Formosa and forwarded their recommendations to the secretary of Defense.[10] The JCS recommended that in order to deny Formosa to the communists the US would have to provide supplies and military aid.[11] They wanted the Nationalists to be able to resist attack 'but not start a conflict with the Chinese mainland,' nor did they desire to 'widen the conflict in Korea.'[12] One month later the president authorized more than $14 million for military assistance to Formosa.[13]

On 30 November 1950, at the end of a very tumultuous year, John Foster Dulles, in his capacity as consultant to the secretary of state, prepared an assessment of the situation in Asia. He outlined the dangers and risks facing the United States in light of the war with North Korea and the 'evident cooperation between the Moscow and Beijing.'[14] Dulles wrote that:

It would seem that there should be a review of our attitude towards Formosa. Our sea and air power and the presence of the Chinese Nationalists should make it possible to salvage Formosa, and perhaps use it as a base for covert and perhaps open Chinese activities against the China mainland, which would at least divert the Chinese government (communist).[15]

Now there was no turning back. The Nationalists had become critically important. The window had shut. From this point forward overt support for Tibet would be impossible.

FORMOSA: THE UNSINKABLE AIRCRAFT CARRIER

Indispensable Taiwan

Washington's wish to avoid an all-out war with the communists did not impede the administration from training and deploying the Nationalists and indigenous Formosans as guerrillas on the mainland to impede communist efforts to consolidate their victory. The CIA had responsibility for these operations, which grew exponentially over the decade. Intelligence historian Richard Aldrich called this a 'pinprick war,' carried out 'wherever the West could gain access to the perimeter of China.'[16]

The men were delivered to their drop-points by Civil Air Transport, a 'CIA airline,' which came out of the shadows in June 2001, when the director of the Central Intelligence Agency publicly acknowledged:

[its] unwavering service to the United States of America in the worldwide battle against communist oppression. From the mist-shrouded peaks of Tibet, to the black skies of China, to the steaming jungles of Southeast Asia, the legendary men and women of Civil Air Transport and Air America always gave full measure of themselves in the defense of freedom.[17]

Civil Air Transport (CAT), owned by the Central Intelligence Agency from 1950 to 1970, was an integral part of the agency's covert program in the Korean War, Tibet, Indonesia, Laos, Thailand, Burma, and South Vietnam. Later renamed Air America, this 'official' airline of the CIA was not without controversy and is remembered by some as the most colorful, mysterious, and romantic airline in the world, complete with 'enough shady deals, dragon ladies and international intrigue to keep their sheet metal repairmen busy patching bullet holes.'[18]

It had its genesis in World War II with General Claire Chennault, the legendary founder of the Flying Tigers who had trained Nationalist pilots and flown in support of the Nationalist cause. When the war ended, Chennault and his partner Whiting Willauer, a Washington lawyer, started their own airline in 1946, under the name of China National Relief and Rehabilitation Administration Transport (CNRRA) and carried cargo and relief supplies for the United Nations Relief and Rehabilitation Administration.[19] A year later CAT was formed and by 1948 they were helping Chiang Kai-shek transport supplies and cargo during the civil war; CAT became an integral part of the Nationalist war effort.[20]

But as the Nationalists floundered so did CAT, and by early 1949 the airline was in decline, lacking both funding and air missions. In May 1949 Chennault approached the State Department with a proposal to continue funding the airline as a part of the anti-communist resistance effort.[21]

Finally, in March 1950, the Departments of State, Defense, and the joint chiefs of staff 'concluded that continued support of CAT was in the national interest.'[22] CAT would provide 'a deniable source of transportation to move personnel, air drop supplies to guerrillas on the mainland, and engage in various clandestine operations.'[23] A memorandum of a conversation on 25 May 1950 between Major General Lyman Lemnitzer, at the Department of Defense, and Dean Rusk, assistant secretary of state, summed up Washington's position. It said: '[T]hat covert action in support of resistance on Formosa, while of limited possibilities, is authorized by existing US policies and that augmentation and intensification of the covert effort is desirable.'[24]

The CIA advanced Chennault and his partner $350,000 to clear their debts and agreed to provide another $400,000 in June 1950.[25] On 24 March 1950 the two owners of CAT signed an agreement with the CIA: the CIA now had their own airline.[26] And within a year, the US was supporting pro-Nationalist guerrilla parachute training on Formosa.[27]

By early 1951 the Truman administration had concluded its analysis of the viability of supporting guerrilla activity on the mainland from Formosa.[28] The State Department advised that while the US should maintain support for the Nationalists, it should avoid 'committing US strength or prestige to returning that Government to the Mainland.'[29] Meanwhile, Washington would 'covertly support the development of any resistance movement.'[30] In a lengthy report prepared by the joint chiefs of staff, provided to both the secretary of defense and the secretary of state, Dean Acheson, the JCS concluded that the Nationalist forces constituted 'the only immediately available ground forces for use on the mainland.'[31] This report submitted to the National Security Council on 21 March 1951 envisioned:

[A]n increase in the tempo of guerrilla activity and sabotage within Communist China would be promoted while, at the same time, the threat of Nationalist landings on the China coast would prevent further CCF [Chinese Communist Forces] withdrawal from South China for transfer to Manchuria and Korea. Furthermore, this trend combined with possible large-scale guerrilla activity in Kwangsi and Yunnan would materially reduce pressure on Hong Kong and Macao, and reduce support of the Viet Minh.[32]

Ultimately, according to Ambassador James Lilley, a 'China hand' and CIA operative in Taiwan, the US engaged in a 'three-pronged' effort on Taiwan.[33] The CIA wanted to train the indigenous population on Taiwan, called the Third Force, who were loyal to neither Chiang Kai-shek nor Mao, although many had been former Nationalist officers. They would be trained on Saipan or Okinawa and then infiltrated into mainland China in an effort to incite revolts. Secondly, the US wanted to support what was said to be over a million KMT guerrillas left on the mainland; this operation was carried out with the support of the Taiwanese intelligence services. And finally, the CIA would send in their agents for reconnaissance and collection on the Chinese mainland.[34]

Covert activities on Formosa mushroomed as the Korean War intensified, eventually becoming what one official called 'rather spectacular.'[35] Responsibility for the operations fell to both the CIA and the Air Force and was managed through Truman's Office of Policy Coordination, who had more than 600 individuals on Formosa.[36] The commercial cover for these employees was provided, at the time, by a company called Western Enterprises Incorporated (WEI) that became known to agency personnel as Western Auto.[37] Frank Holober, a Far Eastern paramilitary specialist who arrived in Taiwan in June 1951, wrote that guerrilla activity was aimed at:

China's soft underbelly that comprised the coastal areas lying opposite Taiwan. Assuming that the Communists had assigned their most astute and seasoned generals and troops to the Korean venture, military and political action along the coast might encounter something less than crack troops and serve to drain away resources needed to fight in Korea.[38]

There was an 'amalgam of CIA paramilitary types' at Western Auto, including World War II Office of Strategic Services (OSS) operatives, intelligence specialists, retired and active army, navy and marine officers, smoke jumpers, and newly recruited college graduates—including several football stars.[39] The new recruits were first met at Sung-shan Airport by General Claire Chennault, 'acting in his capacity of member of an unpublicized guerrilla committee, which also included Madame Chiang Kai-shek'; she was known as the 'Mother of Guerrillas.'[40]

There were a number of missions to which they could be assigned: 'guerrilla training, logistical support, over flight capabilities, mainland propaganda programs—both radio and leaflet balloon,' among others.[41] In time, CAT's short drops of agents and supplies on the coast were augmented and by March 1952 the CIA began long-range penetration missions from Taiwan.[42] Resistance fighters were often dropped in remote areas to build up resistance efforts, while commando raids using small boats sought to destroy key installations.[43] Many times flights were made at night using celestial navigation and moonlight and without accurate maps. By 1957 CIA Station Chief Ray Cline (his official title was Chief, United States Naval Auxiliary Communications Center) was running a dozen missions a month. But success had become an ever more precious commodity: the PLA, the People's Armed Police, and local party watch groups had become better at detecting new arrivals. Cline told one of the authors that in 1957–8 he had trained and parachuted some 300 agents into China and towards the end of that time none of the two-man teams lasted more than three days on the ground. 'We'd be in radio contact and then it would just stop.'[44] In 1962 Cline left Taiwan to return to Washington as deputy director of CIA, where he enjoyed markedly greater success.

* * *

With this chapter, discussion of Formosa, its Korean War role, and the installation of a broadly-based clandestine capability in Asia, we draw Part I of this volume to a conclusion. Of course Taiwan remained both an asset and a liability over time, as the US addressed the difficult but necessary task of developing relations with the People's Republic of China—a multidimensional challenge that has framed US–Asia policy for half a century and, with National Security Advisor Henry Kissinger's 1971 secret agreement in Beijing, directly impacted Tibet.

Harry Truman's presidency, formed in the aftermath of WWII, confronted the world anew. He entered office as the Soviet Union swept through Eastern Europe, presaging a convulsive post-war era that posed a bewildering challenge to an untutored and untested 'haberdasher from Missouri.' Yet, as have seen in Part I, the Truman presidency was able to draw deeply on the most fundamental principles of

American life and governance to fashion a new global order from the destruction of the war. Defining the Soviet challenge for the American people, his administration advanced the 'containment' narrative which, while directed at the USSR, extended to the Soviet satellites, including China, and in time established a way of thinking about Tibet in Cold War terms. It was during this presidency that the US developed the institutional capacity to manage the Soviets and their allies. The National Security Council, the CIA, and a range of special committees were formed that would, over time, make the decisions that guided US relations with Tibet. In fact, as the Korean War evolved and communist China gained influence in Asia, the Special Operations Committee of the National Security Council considered the possibility that the Dalai Lama's influence among Asian Buddhists might aid in resisting communist inroads into South Asia—though this proved not to be the case. Still, Tibet came to be seen as an asset through the sympathetic and perceptive minds of Ambassador Loy Henderson in Delhi and Secretary of State Dean Acheson in Washington; both considered it a buffer, and perhaps under the right circumstances a barrier, that might resist the flow of communism to South Asia.

Many of the themes that inform Part I of this volume arise from the challenges defined and confronted by the Truman administration. As Truman entered the last year of his presidency, 1952, South Asia was in play yet US influence remained limited. The Chinese, the Dalai Lama, and US Ambassador Chester Bowles each now confronted unique challenges in the crucial period 1950–2—and each had a vital role in the drama then playing out. The geostrategic stakes could not have been higher. Truman and his administration, pummeled by charges of losing China, would be defeated in the 1952 election. India's assessment of Chinese intentions—and China's promises to respect Tibetan traditions and religion—would prove worthless. And the Dalai Lama's decision to return to Lhasa to renegotiate the 17 Point Agreement, rather than accept the US offer to arrange asylum either in the US or elsewhere, proved to be the wrong choice.

Britain, India, and the US had proven unreliable interlocutors to the fledgling government in Lhasa as it sought to make its way on the world stage. But Tibet wasn't buffeted and mispositioned by geostrategics alone; there was treachery courtesy of Panikkar, dysfunction in Washington brought by the 'Red scare', a self-absorbed Nehru enthralled by the 'non-aligned movement,' and Tibet itself—chaotic, introverted, and utterly unprepared for the station it sought.

K. M. Panikkar, however, stands out among these vexing personalities and political currents. Nehru relied upon him to interpret events in Beijing where his decidedly anti-Western and anti-American bias was well known. A Secret Memorandum dated 12 October 1950 from Walter McConaughy of the Office of China Affairs to Dean Rusk, then assistant secretary for Far Eastern Affairs, provides an excoriating assessment of Panikkar's reports, which are termed 'misleading in the extreme.'[45] McConaughy said, 'It is unfortunate that he is our principal foreign diplomatic source of information in Peiping' and then provided a detailed analysis of Panikkar's personality and views.[46]

Panikkar's position at the intersection of the China–India relationship complicated Washington's efforts to befriend India. He was decidedly unsympathetic to a continuing US role in Asia, underscoring Ameri-skeptic views in Delhi. As we proceed to Part II, we can see why, during the Eisenhower administration, the US turned to Pakistan as a ready and willing regional ally. Pakistan had begun courting Washington from the moment it achieved independence; Islamabad supported the American commitment to fight communism and, more broadly, accepted Western security objectives in the Middle East.[47] This was a welcome change from Nehru's distilled criticism and non-aligned posture, which had been so frustrating to the Truman administration. It wasn't until President Eisenhower took office in 1952 that a concrete military agreement was signed with Pakistan. Many historians, among them Robert McMahon, maintain that Washington's security agreement with Pakistan signed in May 1954 'had-far reaching implications for the triangular relationship among the United States, Pakistan and India.'[48] Among those implications, discussed more fully in the next chapter, was that India sought closer relations with both the Soviets and the PRC which both directly and indirectly impacted Tibet.

Eisenhower's national security policy flowed naturally from the Truman administration—even though the men were of different political parties and not on overly familiar terms. But Eisenhower, partly encouraged by his secretary of state, John Foster Dulles, brought an added dimension—his strong personal faith—to the office. Deeply opposed to communism, he believed that there was 'no area too remote to be ignored, there is no free nation too humble to be forgotten.'[49] This, of course, included Tibet.

PART II

18

THE EISENHOWER ERA

General Dwight D. Eisenhower was sworn into office on 20 January 1953. His tone was somber. He told the nation that America, responsible for 'the free world's leadership,' would face the threat of communism 'not with dread and confusion but rather with confidence and conviction.'[1] Before a gathering of 750,000 people spread along the Ellipse toward the Lincoln Memorial, Eisenhower departed from his prepared remarks and withdrew from his pocket a brief prayer he'd written that morning.[2] To a sea of bowed heads he spoke quietly of his belief in God, his dedication to freeing the oppressed, and his opposition to communism, thus setting both the tone and the direction of his presidency and the nation for the years ahead.

Like Truman before him, Eisenhower was dedicated to stemming the spread of communism. In his first State of the Union Address a month later, the new president issued a ringing declaration to Congress and the nation, promising that his administration would make the 'free world secure.'[3] His address reflected the passion of an earlier campaign speech delivered in the August heat of Madison Square Garden in 1952, when he had spoken of 'Communist barbarism' and included Tibet in a list of nations subject to its tyranny.[4]

Emphasizing security

One of Eisenhower's first tasks was to revamp the National Security Council (NSC). In February 1953 the new President explained to Congress how he would utilize the NSC to assist him in 'domestic, foreign, and military policies' in order to make the nation more secure.[5] He also spoke about the importance of how America was seen by other nations and the strategic importance of reflecting national values in telling the American story abroad. He told the 83rd Congress that he intended to 'make more effective all activities of the Government related to international information.'[6] Each of these initiatives—the determination to fight communism, his management

141

reform at the NSC, and the creation of the United States Information Agency—were part of his broader effort to tell the American story worldwide. And ultimately, each of these initiatives directly or indirectly impacted Tibet.

On entering office Eisenhower began a National Security Council review to establish a long-range, integrated, national strategy and an effective means of executing it.[7] Robert Cutler was appointed to the newly created position of assistant to the president for National Security Affairs—a title since held by Henry Kissinger, Zbigniew Brezinski, Robert McFarlane, and Brent Scrowcroft, among others. Cutler, a veteran of the Truman administration's Psychological Strategy Board (PSB), reviewed the national security process and delivered his recommendations two months later, in March 1953.

Cutler's proposals streamlined and structured the NSC process to make it more consistent with Eisenhower's style. 'Eisenhower,' Cutler wrote, 'transformed the Council into a forum for vigorous discussion against a background of painstakingly prepared and carefully studied papers.'[8] And the president made it clear that he intended to use the NSC to help him make 'decisions of high and necessarily secret policy.'[9] With the NSC in place, Eisenhower proceeded with a global assessment of communist initiatives. In the spring of 1953, as the French Indochina conflict assumed an increasingly ominous cast, he made clear that the US would not let Indochina fall to a Chinese-sponsored insurgency or 'display any weakening of our determination to maintain the defense of Formosa or to support any other threatened area.'[10] Eisenhower asserted in his memoirs that 'we as a nation could not stand aloof unless we were ready to allow free nations to crumble, one by one, under Communist pressure.'[11] To that end, NSC directive 5409, updating US policy toward South Asia, was passed on 4 March 1954. The directive reiterated the president's view that the loss of Southeast Asia 'would be a serious psychological and political defeat for the West.'[12] Further, the directive stated that in the event of a communist seizure of power in a South Asian country, the United States would consider contributing military support if necessary, while attempting to secure support from other free nations.[13]

In this context Eisenhower, like Truman, was particularly concerned about stability in India. The administration wanted to encourage Delhi to 'consult more frankly' with the US and, though it was a member of the 'non-aligned movement,' Eisenhower wished to 'develop India's eventual participation in a common front against communism.'[14] When challenged by his secretary of the treasury, who was worried about the financial capacity of the United States to aid so many nations at once—the count at the time was thirty-five—Eisenhower responded:

The United States has passed the point of scrutinizing its programs to assist foreign nations in a single year. Instead, we should be thinking in terms of decades or even of generations from the point of view of our country's welfare. As a result of looming destructive power and the psychological appeals of Communism, this country is going to be confronted with very great and very tangled problems. We should therefore look upon the assistance we give to foreign nations as an investment.

The American people were clearly concerned both about sustaining the post-war recovery that had begun to build a solid middle class, and also about the spread of communism. Yet the American 'investment' in South Asia had shown poor results. By the time Eisenhower took office the mutual distaste between Washington and Delhi was palpable. As in the prior administration, the dissonance arose not simply from divergent policy approaches to the international problems of the day, but also from cultural differences laced with strong views—an unfortunate combination.

Tensions were also rising between India and Pakistan in the continued debate over Kashmir: both countries looked to the United States for support. And while Pakistan made clear it would stand with the US in the fight against communism, its principal purpose, as Washington learned, was to correct the 'asymmetry of the US relationship with India.' Of course, the White House knew at the time that having Pakistan as an ally would complicate US South Asia policy by provoking Nehru and adding tension to the already unhappy state of US–Indian relations. But, as one diplomat pointed out, the administration 'misjudged the extent of the response.'[15] Ambassador Dennis Kux put it this way: '[W]hile differences over the containment policy and nonalignment involved abstract concepts, the US military alliance with Pakistan, just seven years after the trauma of partition, was a different matter, striking a deeply emotional nerve throughout the Indian body politic.'[16]

Relations between Washington and Delhi quickly declined to a deep chill. Not only was it now almost impossible for Eisenhower to approach Nehru with his intention to provide Tibet with covert support, but it also had the unintended consequence of pushing Nehru closer to both the Soviets and the Communist Chinese.

19

PAKISTAN

A NEW AMERICAN ALLY

Eisenhower and his secretary of state, John Foster Dulles, believed that Pakistan could be useful not only in stemming the further spread of communism but also in promoting stability in the Middle East. These factors inclined the new administration to assist Pakistan where it was practical.

Shortly after the new administration came into office, the foreign minister of Pakistan, Sir Zafrulla Khan, arrived at the State Department with an urgent request for more aid to stave off their growing food shortage.[1] As with India's food crisis, Washington understood the importance of extending aid to Pakistan on humanitarian grounds. But now there was also a geopolitical benefit to be had. To that end, the administration placed a high priority on arranging the appropriate financial assistance for Khan and dispatched a delegation to review the situation.

The delegation arrived shortly before the new secretary of state made his first visit to the Middle East and South Asia in May 1953. Dulles' tour of the region was partly promotional and allowed him to gain an impression of the region and its leaders.[2] But discussions with Pakistan were clearly a priority. Dulles sent a glowing report back to Washington about the 'genuine feeling of friendship' he encountered in Pakistan.[3] This was, of course, quite distinct from the impressions he had in India, where he had just been.

Every fiber of Dulles' being—moral, religious, political, and strategic—told him that there could be no higher policy priority than halting the spread of communism. The secretary had little tolerance for the policies of nations that did not reflect his worldview. Neutralism, he maintained, was immoral.[4] He stated that 'neutral governments do not seem to realize that the Communist intentions are so diabolical and so hostile to their freedom and independence.'[5] Dulles' views had been well known before he entered the State Department. In a *Life* magazine article in May 1952, he told the world that America must be able to 'retaliate instantly against open aggression by Red armies, so that if it occurred anywhere, we could and would strike back where it hurts, by means of our own choosing.'[6]

It was no surprise that Dulles and Nehru, seeming to dwell in parallel realities, agreed on very little. In Delhi, Dulles met with the Indian prime minster and, hoping to avoid one of Nehru's tirades, chose not to mention that the United States was considering including Pakistan as part of a regional security agreement.[7] In a convoluted if not disingenuous statement, he told Nehru that the United States 'had no present plans that would bring it into a military relationship with Pakistan which could reasonably be looked upon as un-neutral as regards to India.'[8]

Neither man liked the cut of the other's jib. In a 13 October 1953 letter to K.P.S. Menon, his ambassador in Moscow, Nehru wrote that he was 'not at all impressed' with Mr Dulles.[9] A year later, when meeting Mao in Beijing, he said that Dulles was 'a man of exceedingly limited outlook but with some kind of bigoted zeal about it, he is a danger in a position of high responsibility.'[10] In response to Mao's comment that 'Dulles talks quite well!', Nehru said: 'A man like Dulles is a great menace. He is a Methodist or Baptist preacher who religiously goes to church and he is narrow-minded and bigoted.'[11] Dulles returned Nehru's sniping. At a National Security Council meeting in June 1953, Dulles told the president and vice president, among others, that he found Nehru to be 'an utterly impractical statesman.'[12] The die was cast.

The following month, while continuing to brief the NSC on his South Asia trip, Dulles offered his thoughts on how best to stabilize the Middle East region and create a defensive bulwark against the Soviets. Questions about regional stability had become paramount as it became clear that turmoil over the British base at Suez destabilizing in Egypt. Dulles made it plain to the NSC that in his opinion Egypt could no longer be Washington's key partner in the Middle East.[13] Instead, he thought, Pakistan could be 'the loyal strong point' along with Turkey, and perhaps later these nations, with Iraq and Syria and Iran, could form a loosely structured alliance, 'a defense Pact of a northern tier of nations.' This was subsequently incorporated into NSC 151, which set out US policy in the Middle East.[14]

Washington believed that Pakistan could 'play a potentially significant military role in the Middle East if global war between the Soviet Union and the West should suddenly erupt.'[15] Administration officials thought that the Pakistanis could be particularly helpful in 'monitoring Soviet activities in the region and providing access to the oil fields of the Persian Gulf in the event they were cut off by hostilities.'[16]

By the end of September 1953, Washington signaled to Pakistan that it was ready to discuss military assistance within the context of a mutual defense agreement. By November the two governments agreed to meet. Ostensibly, the meeting was to be held in secret: the sensibilities of the outspoken and emotional Nehru were not to be taken lightly. The State Department instructed that: '[All] United States officials concerned [should] bear in mind the extreme delicacy of our relations with India at the present moment until we are ready to give the Indians [an] appropriate explanation regarding our plans for Pakistan.'[17]

Unfortunately, US intentions did not remain a secret for long. It appears that John P. Callahan, a *New York Times* correspondent in Karachi, obtained a 'press release' from the Pakistani government announcing the talks.[18] Although Washington denied the report, on 2 November the *New York Times* reported that the United States and Pakistan intended to enter into an arms pact during the Pakistani governor general's visit to Washington on 12 November.[19]

Nehru enraged

This dispute, like earlier Nehru dramas, played out in the American press. The *New York Times* reported that in a meeting with the Indian ambassador, G. L. Mehta, in Washington, Dulles revealed that the US 'was considering some form of military agreement,' but played the issue down.[20] Two days later, President Eisenhower held a press conference after meeting with the Pakistan governor general, Ghulam Mohammed. In an attempt to deflect the worst and placate the Indians, the president told reporters that the 'US would be most cautious about doing anything that would create unrest and disaster, or failure or hysteria in India.'[21]

But the moment could not be made to disappear; in all, the *Times* ran nine editorials and eleven detailed analyses over a four-month period. Nehru could not be placated. In a public statement the Indian prime minster said that a military agreement between the United States and Pakistan would have some very far-reaching consequences in the whole structure of things in South Asia.[22] A week later, a *Times* headline read 'Pakistan's Hopes of US Pact Fade: Indian Objection to Military Aid Cools Karachi Ardor—Reds Exploit Issue in Kashmir.'[23]

The *Times* had been given the details of a personal letter that Nehru wrote to Pakistani prime minister Muhammad Ali Bogra earlier that month. Nehru told Ali that while 'it is not for us in India to come in the way of Pakistan's foreign policy ... we cannot ignore it.'[24] The Indian prime minister wrote bluntly that an alliance with the United States would put Pakistan into the Cold War, and emphasized that this would mean that the Cold War 'has come to the very frontiers of India.'[25]

Among the charges India heaped on the Pakistanis was that a US–Pakistan alliance 'would provoke Russia with dire consequences for the whole subcontinent.'[26] But it wasn't just the threat of bringing the Cold War to the region that so bothered India. Delhi was concerned that a stronger Pakistani military with US backing would exert pressure on the situation in Kashmir; or perhaps, even worse, that Pakistan's newly acquired military superiority would be used to start an all-out war with India.[27] Nehru was persuaded that Washington's intentions were to 'outflank' India's policy of neutralism in an effort 'to bring India to her knees.'[28] Nehru's emotion and paranoia were all too apparent, not only further constraining US–Indian relations, but also sharply limiting any prospective cooperation with the US on Tibet.

The Nixon visit

The situation was not helped when Vice President Nixon and his wife took a fact-finding tour of the Far East and South Asia in the fall of 1953, and Nixon indicated support for bringing Pakistan into the fold.

The politically savvy governor general of Pakistan, Ghulam Mohammed, who had made American intentions public, now in private meetings pressured the Vice President for US military aid.[29] The governor pleaded urgently with Nixon, insisting that the effects of not providing the aid would be disastrous, and telling him that if the 'US were not to grant aid now, especially in view of all the publicity, it would be like taking a poor girl for a walk and then walking out on her, leaving her only with a bad name.'[30]

Nixon was impressed by the anti-communist stance of the Pakistani officials, and was particularly impressed with Ayub Khan, the head of the military.[31] And indeed, many in Congress shared Nixon's sentiments. Senator William Knowland, the Republican majority leader and China Lobby supporter, urged the president to 'ignore India's objections and extend military aid to Pakistan.'[32] In an interview with the *New York Times* he said: 'to withhold aid because of the protest of neutralist India would be discouraging to those nations willing to stand up and be counted on the side of the free world.'[33] In Washington's view Pakistan was a 'true friend.'[34]

Nixon's experience in India could not have been more different. Taking a page from Dulles' report, the vice president called Nehru 'the least friendly leader' he had met during his travels.[35] While Nixon was being served tangerine juice and cashews from a smartly dressed Indian servant, Nehru spoke in what Nixon called his 'softly modulated British voice obsessively and interminably about India's relationship with Pakistan.'[36] The Indian prime minister vacillated between this mild demeanor and 'railing' against Pakistan.[37] Little time was devoted to US–Indian relations or, indeed, other Asian issues.

In the end it must be said that the Pakistanis played their hand extremely well. They had purposefully leaked the details of Washington's intentions that sparked Nehru's public outcries. Nehru made such 'threatening noises that he backed the US administration into a corner.'[38] Ambassador Kux summed up Washington's conundrum: 'the question became less whether to go ahead with arms for Pakistan than whether to back down because of India's protests.'[39] And given the climate in Washington in the early 1950s, the answer to the second question was much clearer than to the first.

Military aid for Pakistan

On 15 January 1954 a Special National Intelligence Estimate (SNIE) detailed the arguments for and against granting military aid to Pakistan. While there was much discussion about the impact of such aid to Pakistan on US–Indian relations, and how this might reverberate in the future, many senior officials in Washington believed that to deny Pakistan aid now 'would mean a loss of US prestige.'[40] And that:

US denial of military aid to Pakistan would be looked on in India as a reluctant concession to India[n] pressure. While it would remove a source of friction, the beneficial effect on US–Indian relations would probably be negligible. In fact, India would probably be encouraged to use similar pressure tactics against the US on other occasions.[41]

Moreover, it was thought that having Pakistan and Turkey as allies against the threat of communist advances in the region (and the prospect of future air bases) mitigated all other concerns.

A few days before the US–Pakistan agreement was announced, Eisenhower sent Prime Minister Nehru a personal letter outlining the US decision through his ambassador in Delhi, George Allen. Eisenhower wanted Nehru to know that providing military assistance to Pakistan would 'not in any way affect the friendship we feel for India.'[42] Eisenhower reiterated the administration's objective of 'opposing aggression in the Middle East' and 'that consultation between Pakistan and Turkey about security problems will serve the interests not only of Pakistan and Turkey but also of the whole free world.'[43] To allay Indian fears that a military build-up for Pakistan would not threaten its neighbor, Eisenhower emphasized that:

I am confirming publicly that if our aid to any country, including Pakistan, is misused and directed against another in aggression I will undertake immediately, in accordance with my constitutional authority, appropriate action both within and without the UN to thwart such aggression.[44]

On 25 February 1954 Washington announced that the US government would provide Pakistan with military assistance to promote peace and security in the Middle East.[45] Following Pakistan's agreement with the US, Pakistani officials signed the 'Friendly Cooperation' agreement with Turkey on 2 April. The Mutual Defense Assistance Agreement between Washington and Karachi was signed on 19 May 1954; Pakistan was now allied with the West.

One immediate consequence of Pakistan's new alliance was the end of any hope for a peaceful resolution to the Kashmir stand-off. Nehru refused to allow Americans to be among the United Nations observers in Kashmir, bringing the bilateral talks between Pakistan and India to a halt. Moreover, though India had agreed to a plebiscite in 1954, it now refused to discuss these arrangements.[46]

Meanwhile India, as discussed in the following chapter, had signed the wide-ranging Panchsheel Agreement with China on 29 April; it covered, among other things, mutual respect for each other's nation's territorial integrity and sovereignty, mutual non-aggression and non-interference in each other's internal affairs. The implications for Tibet were profound.

Further fallout from the new US relationship with Pakistan was the forced downsizing of Washington's propaganda effort in India. Nehru, stung by the administration's decision, began to rethink his position on the size and nature of the US mission in India. In light of the new treaty, the newly formed United States Information Agency had made it a top priority to counteract negative Indian opinion of that alliance.[47] Washington was intent on casting its new relations with Pakistan in the best possible light, being aware that information management and the promotion of the American story were as important as its military capabilities.[48] Nehru's action would now make that more difficult.

In a letter to his chief ministers in April 1954 Nehru wrote: 'The US military aid to Pakistan affects us, and we have to say something, and say it clearly and definitely.'[49] In his pique over US aid to Pakistan, Nehru refused US aircraft access to Indian airspace, limited Americans entering India, and discouraged Indians from seeking training in the United States.[50] Nehru felt that there was a widespread network of Americans in India and, while not all were involved in what he called 'undesirable' activities, he felt certain that some were directly or indirectly involved in 'doing intelligence and propaganda work,' promoting pro-Western, anti-communist values. And he was particularly suspicious of the large staff of the United States Information Service, which included community centers, a leadership program, fellowship exchanges, professors, students, and missionaries.[51] Nehru was discomfited by the agency's opening of new reading rooms at four Indian universities and the plan to open six more at the beginning of 1955. He complained to his secretary general:

[I]n view of the new developments connected with the US military aid to Pakistan, this kind of widespread activity in India is particularly objectionable and, to some extent, dangerous. The activity of any foreign mission or any foreign element of this kind must be considered objectionable.[52]

Today, many historians feel that Eisenhower's decision was a 'deeply flawed strategic concept.'[53] The Eisenhower administration, like Truman's, saw India's neutralism as disappointing and inconsistent with the goal of fighting communism. Looking back, it is not surprising that Washington's strategic objectives took precedence over what it knew would further sour US–Indian relations. Ultimately, US military arms to Pakistan impacted the power balance between Delhi and Karachi—and, of course, many blamed the US. Historian Stanley Wolpert characterized the alliance with Pakistan as 'surely the worst single blunder in US South Asian policy and easily the most costly,' and laid the blame on the secertary of state's 'hell and brimstone' concern with 'the Russian menace.'[54]

As the months passed, relations between Delhi and Washington worsened. In a lengthy letter to his chief ministers on 26 April 1954, Nehru clarified his concerns. He wrote that the shift in US policy favoring Pakistan, which now received military, economic, and technical assistance, had produced an 'ill will between India and the United States.'[55] Over time Nehru continued to accept US aid, but he began to distance himself from Washington.

In December 1953, as Washington was solidifying arrangements for Pakistan to play a pro-American role in South Asia, Nehru proceeded to sign a trade agreement with Moscow. But not only was Nehru edging closer to the Soviets, he now moved—perhaps in reaction to the new US–Pakistan treaty—to formalize an agreement with Beijing on the conditions and arrangements governing trade in Tibet.[56] The consequences of this agreement, known as the Panchsheel Agreement, have reverberated down through the decades, providing a part of the political–diplomatic framework impacting Tibet today. This agreement, and Nehru's rise to power among the nations in South Asia, provides the focus for the next chapter.

20

THE PANCHSHEEL AGREEMENT

AN INDO–CHINESE CONDOMINIUM

While the United States, Pakistan, and India formalized their bilateral and regional arrangements, the PLA had become more firmly entrenched in Tibet. Toward the end of 1953, India and China began talks over the status of Tibet. The agreement that emerged, known as the Panchsheel, unfortunately was very much at Tibet's expense. Indian and Chinese attitudes are revealed by the toast of the India's ambassador in Beijing to Chou En-lai upon signing: 'To the Panchsheel Agreement: Let us drink to the settling of all our differences through this Agreement.' Chou responded: 'to settling all those points which are ripe for settlement.'[1]

Preliminary discussions with the Chinese over Tibet had begun in June 1952 when T. N. Kaul, the chargé d'affaires at the Indian embassy in Beijing, met with PRC Vice Foreign Minister Zhang Hanfu.[2] Since the British withdrawal from India five years earlier, there had been no formal discussions between Delhi and Beijing regarding Tibet. Though Nehru had not discussed things formally with Mao, Nehru believed that the Chinese were now responsible for Tibetan affairs—a point made clear by a small incident in the fall of 1952.

In early September, S. Sinha, the head of the Indian mission in Lhasa, wrote to Nehru to say he had been approached by a group of Tibetans who, as 'champions of Tibetan freedom and culture,' were in 'need of funds to build support in Tibetan villages and amongst the middle class'.[3] Sinha wrote that 'funds were available from foreign countries particularly from the USA,' and the Tibetans sought a loan from India for the amount of 200,000 rupees.[4] Nehru's response was swift and pointed. He told Sinha that he found all of this 'rather disturbing as it indicates that our policy is not fully understood.'[5]

Nehru wrote:

Our policy is to recognize that Tibet is under Chinese suzerainty... [W]e do not wish to interfere in internal affairs of Tibet and we can certainly be no parties to any secret or other activities against the Chinese. That would be both practically and morally wrong. It is for Tibetans and Chinese to settle their problems. Our interests now within Tibet are limited and our chief concern is proper maintenance of our frontier line. We are naturally friendly towards Tibetans, as we have been in the past, but we must not give them any impression of possibility of interference or help.[6]

Delhi and Washington were on divergent paths over Tibet, viewing regional security matters, and China, through very different lenses. As Nehru had made clear in his note to Sinha, the prime minister's main concern by 1952 was the vulnerability of India's northern frontier now that Mao's army was in Tibet.

The border between China and India had ostensibly been established by Sir Henry McMahon who, on behalf of the British, had mediated between British India and Tibet at the Simla Convention of 1913–14 (in the end the Chinese had not signed the agreement). Nehru wanted to ensure that these boundaries remained intact and voiced his concerns to his ambassador in Beijing, K. M. Panikkar. Indeed the Indian prime minister thought it 'rather odd' that the Chinese had not commented on the issue.[7] Nehru also made a point of stating that 'he would not tolerate any intrusions' into India's border states of Bhutan, Sikkim, or Nepal.[8] Panikkar responded that 'India must stick to the position that the Frontier had been defined and there was nothing to be discussed.'[9]

Although Mao was silent on the issue of the border, the Chinese had informed the GOI in April 1952 that they wished to change the Indian mission in Lhasa into a 'proper Consulate General.'[10] Nehru was agreeable to this request, and in return allowed the Chinese to open a consulate in Bombay.[11] His acquiescence to this rather benign request effectively acknowledged that the Chinese now controlled Tibet—a point the Indian prime minister fully understood. It reflected a point he made at a press conference on 21 June, when he told journalists that since the Chinese government exerted suzerainty over Tibet, 'we cannot treat Tibet as an independent country with an independent representation from us.'[12]

Nehru made clear in a letter to his chief ministers that Tibet was a part of China and that his intention was to maintain an amicable relationship with the country that shared '2,000 miles of frontier' with India. He wrote that 'where these interests were not vital or important or were such that we could not define them, such as Tibet, we were prepared to adjust ourselves to changes.'[13] Nehru was both intractable on the matter of India's borders with China while also accepting the PRC's claim on Tibet.[14] This marked the first of several concessions that Nehru made to China on the issue of Tibet over the next two years.

The following year, in September 1953, Nehru broached the subject of formal talks with the Chinese. He sent a letter to Chou En-lai explaining that his government was 'anxious to come to a final settlement about pending matters so as to avoid any misunderstanding and friction at any time.'[15] The Indian prime minister wrote:

It has been a matter of deep satisfaction to me to note the growing cooperation between our great countries in international affairs. I am convinced that this cooperation and friendship will not only be to our mutual advantage, but will also be a strong pillar for peace in Asia and the world.[16]

By the end of 1953, Nehru's ambassador in Beijing, Raghaven, had conveyed the Indian position on Tibet to Chou En-lai. A declassified account of this conversation on 21 December 1953 is instructive in that it illustrates the Indian government's outrage at the US–Pakistan security agreement, and that the parties believed progress on a Tibet agreement would publicly affirm the developing India–China relationship.[17] Raghavan told the Chinese premier that:

As the United States is working hard trying to push aside the Sino–Indian relationship, Prime Minister Nehru hopes that the negotiation between China and India on the Tibetan problem can succeed soon. Because this will show that there are no difficulties and disagreements between China and India.[18]

Chou responded: 'A solution [to Tibet] will show the world, especially the Western world, that our Asian nations and people are united.'[19]

This was another nail in the Tibetan coffin. Nehru's pique, pride, and narcissism were all in play and buttressed his effort to curry favor with the powerful and unpredictable regime to the north. The new US–Pakistani agreement had brought much of this to the fore and, significantly, had removed any possibility of US–Indian cooperation on Tibet.

To be sure, the Chinese were eager to 'win over India' to avoid any challenge to their claim of sovereignty over Tibet.[20] A lengthy and detailed Top Secret report, prepared by the Chinese representative in Lhasa, Zhang Jingwu, was sent to the Chinese foreign ministry in October 1953. This declassified report, which the authors obtained from the Chinese foreign ministry archives, provided guidelines for the PRC negotiations with India and clearly illustrated the sensitivity of the issue.[21] The Chinese foreign ministry instructed that the discussions with India over Tibet be kept secret from the Tibetan government; only after decisions were finalized would the Tibetans be informed.[22] Beijing's intentions were clear: 'to regain diplomatic power' in Tibet, China planned to take over India's trading and communications rights and to integrate Indian outposts into China.[23] Beijing also began to place military personnel in the Tibetan foreign bureau (Tibet's foreign ministry) in Lhasa. In a detailed memo to the PLA cadres on the 'Tibet Work Committee,' the foreign ministry simply stated:

In this way we will have the control of foreign affairs and can build a foundation to completely take over diplomatic power. For the cadres who want to stay in the old way they shall be educated with patience and applied with strong political influence.[24]

One might ask why, if Tibet was already a part of China (as Beijing claimed), it was necessary to place Chinese military personnel into the Tibetan foreign bureau. Beyond Beijing's provision of patience and political education to the Tibetans, the report also indicated that it would be necessary to play a long and patient hand with the Indians. It stated that:

Since Tibet has been deeply influenced by Britain and India for a long period, it will be difficult to reverse the current relationship between Tibet and India; we shall adopt the principle of patiently explaining, slowly discussing, gradually unifying and steadily moving forward. We shall not be in a hurry.[25]

Discussions on Tibet, known as the Beijing Conference, began on 31 December 1953.[26] T. N. Kaul, now the joint secretary in the Ministry of External Affairs, did most of the negotiating with the Chinese in Beijing. He remembered the talks as long and tedious. In his memoir he wrote, 'The Chinese are past masters exhausting the patience of people with whom they are negotiating. They are more adept in this art than the Russians, the Japanese or the Americans.'[27] Kaul, with the ambassador and an advisor, went to the Chinese foreign office every other day and in these meetings the same topics were discussed: the frontier issue between Tibet and India; the three Indian trade agencies that were presently in Gartok Gyantse, and Yatung; the ability for Indian and Tibet traders as well as pilgrims to move freely between India and Tibet; the issue of passports and visas; Indian postal and telegraph facilities and Indian hospitals in Tibet; and the problems with Indian security guards and escorts.[28]

In January 1954, Kaul met with officers at the British mission in Beijing to apprise them of his talks.[29] Notes of this conversation were sent to London and then to Acheson in Washington with the request that the 'information be treated carefully to avoid any leak that British [are] passing on Indian confidences.'[30] Two months later Raghaven, the Indian ambassador in Beijing, met with the British to apprise them of the progress being made. Raghaven was upbeat about his negotiations with the PRC and relayed to the British chargé d'affaires, Humphrey Trevelyan, that 'so far, the Chinese have observed their agreement with Tibet very strictly, and that the Tibetans have autonomy without much Chinese control.'[31] The Indian ambassador wrote that India and China had 'no differences, in principle.'[32] Notes of this conversation, like the previous ones, were sent to Washington marked 'US Eyes Only.'[33] In the early 1950s the PRC proceeded with caution in implementing major reforms and changes in Lhasa. They were focused on the longer term.

On 29 April 1954 the Panchsheel Agreement was signed; the Indian government accepted that Tibet constituted an integral part of China.[34] A few months later the *Calcutta Statesman* ran an article about Chinese officials in Lhasa who were 'borrowing important State papers and historical documents from the Tibetan government and are carrying them to China for detailed study.' Washington correctly assumed the documents were those upon which Tibet based its claim to being a 'sovereign nation' and 'those which define Tibet's historical borders.' The PRC was beginning their process of weakening Tibetan claims to sovereignty and 'writing Tibet's history to suit the purposes of the Chinese government.'[35]

Nehru reasoned that 'we have only given up what in fact we could not hold and what in fact had, in reality, gone.'[36] However in concrete terms Nehru effectively ended any future discussion over Tibet and also lost the chance of 'securing a clear and explicit recognition of India's frontier at the time when India had something to offer in return.'[37] Two months after signing, in July 1954, the Chinese complained that Indian troops were in Barahoti, Uttar Pradesh. There followed a series of incursions numbering in the hundreds which culminated in the PRC attack on India in October 1962.[38]

Some members of the Indian parliament criticized Nehru, referring to these events as the 'melancholy chapter of Tibet.'[39] To that criticism he responded:

What did any honorable Member of this House expect us to do in regard to Tibet at any time? Did we fail or did we do a wrong thing? Where did we come into the picture unless we wanted to assume an aggressive role of interfering with other countries?[40]

The agreement, in the words of Hugh Richardson, was 'a practical admission of the fact that Tibet had ceased to be independent' and that the Indian government's acceptance of 'frequent references to "The Tibet Region of China" acknowledged that Tibet was a part of China.'[41]

The former head of mission in Lhasa wrote: 'That is something which no Indian Government had previously admitted; and in the circumstances of 1954 it amounted to the countersignature by India of the death warrant of Tibetan independence.'[42]

* * *

Thus, one sees the line as it proceeded from Dulles' anti-communist fundamentalism, to his embrace of a willing Pakistan, to Washington's disapproval of what it perceived to be India's amoral non-aligned status, to tensions between India and Pakistan over the US relationship, to India's accommodation with Beijing. From this first comes an unwillingness to support Tibet's attempt to gain independence, then a seamless move by India via the Panchsheel that accepts China's sovereign control of Tibet.

Of course, it must be said that from Nehru's perspective it was the Americans who were immoral not only with reference to the Cold War but also because, while the US chose not to publicly embrace Tibetan sovereignty, it sought to persuade Delhi that its security would not be put at risk if it challenged China on the sovereignty issue. Critically for Tibet, Nehru's position made it more difficult for Washington to explore the provision of covert assistance and to support Tibet's attempt to remain free of Beijing's control.

Yet, there is indication that Delhi was aware of covert activities in northern India and turned a blind eye, which suggests a more nuanced policy than might at first be apparent. B. N. Mullik, the head of India's Intelligence Bureau, recalled in his autobiography that Nehru asked in 1952 that officials 'befriend all the Tibetan refugees in India, help them in every way possible and maintain their morale.'[43] Mullik said that Nehru 'could not publicly announce these policies nor was there any use in publicly denouncing China' but had asked Mullik 'to keep in touch' with Gyalo—the Dalai Lama's second elder brother—who could be 'much benefit to us from the security point of view'.[44]

Cambridge professor Christopher Andrew wrote in his authoritative history of the MI5:

What strikes me about the MI5 relationship with India is how close it was. The MI5 representative and the first head of the intelligence bureau in Delhi, TG Sanjeevi, worked very well together. Amongst a host of other things, they shared a significant distrust of Krishna Menon. The relationship between Sanjeevi's successor, BN Mullik, and the heads of MI5 were based on close personal friendship. At least in Mullik's time, the head of the Indian intelligence bureau was in greater sympathy with the head of MI5 than with the Nehru government.[45]

Thus it appears that from at least 1952 the British, via the Indian Intelligence Bureau, may have had access to the émigré Tibetan communities in India. Moreover, suspicion of Foreign Minister Krishna Menon and the Nehru government by the security service was in keeping with British and American views.

Perhaps, due to the apparent differences between the Nehru government and the Indian intelligence services, the sensitivity of the Tibet question within government circles, and certainly because of the chilly environment between Washington and Delhi, there could be no discussion of covert options regarding Tibet between the US and India. And in little time, India's disappointment and then anger at Washington's newly intimate relationship with Pakistan would push Delhi further into the arms of Stalin and Mao, making such discussions even less likely.

21

NEHRU'S BID FOR GLOBAL PROMINENCE

The five principles for peaceful coexistence in the preamble of the Panchsheel Agreement became the guide for India's foreign policy. The Indian prime minister first announced these principles in the context of his non-aligned philosophy at the Colombo conference in Ceylon in late April 1954.[1] But the Geneva conference, which began two days earlier, received far more attention—for it was here that the Chinese foreign minister, Chou En-lai, grabbed headlines worldwide and the principles of the Panchsheel truly came into play.

The fact that India had not been invited to the 1954 Geneva conference—a gathering to discuss the restoration of peace to Southeast Asia and an end to the Korean War—did not stop the brash Indian minister of defense, Krishna Menon, from crashing the party, so to speak. Newly appointed as minister of defense, Menon arrived in Geneva with his own plan for an Indochina settlement. Primed to present the Indian point of view, he set up shop near the conference headquarters and ultimately played a pivotal role in his unofficial capacity.[2] But he was not unopposed.

Secretary of State Dulles approached the conference with the same zeal as Menon, but with quite different aims. The United States was fearful that the conference might push communist aims in Southeast Asia and Dulles thought it his job to push back. To that end, he conducted himself with the 'pinched distaste of a puritan in a house of ill repute'; rude and ill-tempered, Dulles allegedly refused to shake Chou En-lai's hand—though this was denied—and would have nothing to do with the Chinese delegation.[3] Dulles' critics, and there were many, labeled him the 'arch villain.'[4] There was no love lost between Dulles and Menon, or between Eisenhower—who considered him 'a menace and a boor'—and Menon, for that matter.[5]

The Chinese saw the conference differently. For them it was an opportunity to demonstrate their commitment to peaceful relations and, importantly, to boost their international visibility.[6] Writing on Chinese objectives at the Geneva conference, University of Virginia historian Chen Jian said: 'Mao and his fellow Beijing leaders then had powerful grounds on which to claim that international society—friends and foes alike—had accepted China as a real world power.'[7]

Chou En-lai had a strong presence at the conference and held evening strategy sessions before actual discussions began with Soviet and Viet Minh leaders to form a communist strategy.[8] Chen Jian again:

After the conference failed to reach any agreement on Korea, Zhou endeavored to adjust and coordinate the strategies carried out by Beijing, Moscow and the Viet Minh, while at the same time developing working relationships with the delegations from Britain, France, Laos and Cambodia.[9]

The Chinese, with Moscow's backing, pushed their Vietnamese comrades hard.[10] In early July the strategy paid off. The Chinese and Vietnamese reached a consensus that only a peaceful settlement at Geneva would avoid America's direct military intervention in Vietnam.[11]

Nehru, to no one's surprise, also wanted a role in the drama at Geneva. Flush from his success at Colombo, where he had proclaimed the principles of peaceful coexistence, he plunged into the knotty complexities of the Korean and Indochina conflicts. A month later he briefed his parliament on what he'd told the Geneva attendees: that the way to collective security in Asia was 'to learn to accept the notions of live and let live, not attack one another, threaten one another.'[12] He then returned to the five principles that had been the basis of the recently negotiated Panchsheel Agreement.[13] Presenting these principles as the foundation of the 'non-aligned movement,' Nehru positioned himself as a counterweight to Dulles' proposed South-East Asia Collective Defense Treaty (SEATO). The stage was now set for a clash of two monumental egos promoting diametrically opposed concepts of global order and principles of governance.

The genesis for SEATO is found in Dulles' speech at the Overseas Press Club in New York just a month before the Geneva conference. Here he stated that 'Communist Russia and its Chinese Communist ally' posed a threat to Southeast Asia and that they 'must be met by united action.'[14] He viewed this security arrangement as the way to thwart communism in the wake of the French military collapse in Indochina. With the Geneva conference in mind, Dulles sought to create a 'united front,' a loose coalition of states—including the US, UK, France, Thailand, Australia, New Zealand, the Associated States (Laos, Cambodia, and South Vietnam), the Philippines, and perhaps Indonesia—that would provide collective security 'to deter Communist aspirations in Asia.'[15] Dulles pursued this plan of action with great intensity as Indochina consumed his attention between March 1954 and the middle of 1955.[16]

Before the end of the first phase of the Geneva conference in June 1954, however, Menon, after separately talking with Eden, Chou, and Molotov, gained an agreement on Laos and Cambodia which provided for a ceasefire, followed by the withdrawal of all foreign troops.[17] This offered a less confrontational approach to the region's problems and diluted the rationale for Dulles' proposal. India, along with Canada and Poland, was asked, according to Menon's plan, to serve on the International

Control Commission (ICC) which had been established as a monitoring agency.[18] Nehru savored the moment, his biographer wrote: 'Never had India's—and Nehru's—reputation stood higher in the world.'[19]

India's relationship with China was further burnished in a brief recess from the Geneva conference when Chou En-lai visited Delhi. The Chinese premier's stop coincided with Churchill and Eden's discussions in Washington. Thus, East rivaled West on front pages around the world. Nehru gleefully wrote to Menon noting this 'curious coincident' and asserting that the 'significance of this will not be lost on others.'[20] The Chou visit was, for Nehru, a great occasion, casting the geopolitics of the moment in primary colors. As Chou and Nehru reviewed events at the Geneva conference, a settlement of the Indochina War and their new trade agreement, Nehru told Chou:

If we can lay down principles like respect for sovereignty and territorial integrity, non-interference in internal affairs, non-aggression, equality and mutual benefit and peaceful co-existence, as we have laid down between our two countries, this would create a large area of peace.[21]

Chou agreed with Nehru, hoping to make the treaty applicable to all states of Asia.[22] Chou said: 'In this way we can prevent US attempts to organize military blocs in this area.'[23] The PRC's agreement with India enabled the Chinese to present themselves as the 'new China'—a rational actor seeking a better world.[24]

Chou, skilled and seductive, treated Nehru with great deference, bordering on fawning: 'Your Excellency has more knowledge about the world and Asia than I have,' he assured the prime minister.[25] Not immune to flattery, Nehru warmed to Chou, describing him as a man who 'speaks with authority' and is 'frank and forthright.'[26] Chou had worked his charm. On 28 June Nehru and Chou issued a joint statement reaffirming the principle of 'peaceful coexistence,' expressing the hope that not only would Asian countries follow in their wake, but also that this agreement would inform the settlement at the Geneva conference.[27] Events had conspired to fashion what seemed an Indo–Chinese condominium in which the two nations advanced a concept of world affairs, a 'big idea,' that would propel both forward but for different reasons. Just as Nehru's egoism is seen in the authorship of this proposed 'new reality,' so Chou En-lai's China enjoyed a moment in 'sheep's clothing' that disguised the territorial ambitions soon to play out on the Indian, Soviet, and Vietnamese borders and that had been on display in the brutal seizure of Tibet.

Yet for now, both were playing for major stakes on the global stage. India sought to promote and lead the 'non-aligned movement' which Nehru believed would reframe global interaction. And Beijing had used its relationship with India and the Geneva conference to enhance its legitimacy and facilitate its entry into the world community. Tibet was an afterthought in the foreign ministries of Beijing and Delhi—eclipsed by 'big power politics'; even more, any prospect of US–Indian cooperation on Tibet had vanished.

The SEATO agreement

Less than two months after the Geneva Accords were signed on 21 July, events conspired to separate Tibet further from the region's main concerns. SEATO, which now included Pakistan, was signed on 8 September 1954 in Manila, producing further tensions in the US–Indian relationship. SEATO, Nehru believed, was a defensive pact and 'would add tensions and suspicions and thus lead us away from the new atmosphere of peace which has resulted from the Geneva settlements.'[28] Washington, mindful of the growing influence of India in the region, had hoped to avoid alienating Nehru further. The US ambassador in Delhi, George V. Allen, underscored that US military aid to Pakistan was 'already [an] important reason for India's increasing relations with Red China.'[29] Allen concurred with Washington that Pakistan's participation in SEATO 'would increase hostility against [the] collective security arrangement for Southeast Asia.'[30]

Nehru had gradually moved away from Washington and now seemed more inclined to entertain the views of the world beyond the West. In October 1954 the Indian prime minister traveled to China. Playing to Nehru's aspirations to global acclaim, Chou prepared an arrival that has been described not unlike a coronation: nearly a million people greeted him at the airport. Nehru rode in an open car with Chou past people lining the 12-mile route to the capital to welcome him.[31] He met with Mao, and among the many issues they discussed were the SEATO agreement, the United States, and their mutual hope to maintain close relations.[32] Chou and Nehru discussed the Taiwan issue, arrangements for the conference in Bandung, and the issue that wouldn't go away: Chinese maps that now showed parts of Burma and India belonging to China.[33] In a speech before the Indian parliament, Nehru told members that Chou's visit to India and now his own trip to Beijing 'assumed a significance of historic importance.'[34] The era of 'Hindi–Chini bhai bhai' (Indians and Chinese are brothers) had begun.

By the middle of the decade, India had emerged as an established global player. In April 1955, India invited twenty-five Asian and African nations, some of them newly independent, along with Burma, Pakistan, Indonesia, and Sri Lanka, to meet in Bandung, Indonesia to discuss matters of mutual interest. By that spring Nehru approached the 'zenith of his world influence': the events of the preceding year and now the conference at Bandung showed the Indian prime minister to be a colossus astride the world stage.[35] For Nehru, Bandung provided the platform to advance the principles of non-violence and to promote the 'non-aligned movement' as an alternative to the antagonistic notions of global order held by the West and by the communist world.[36]

The neutral—even friendly—territory showcased Chou En-lai as a rising world statesman.[37] Nehru wrote to his chief ministers that Chou was 'a rather mysterious figure' and had 'attracted the most attention both in public and in the Conference.'[38] Nehru had been duly impressed with Chou from his two earlier meetings and wrote that the Chinese premier 'spoke with authority' and was 'obviously anxious that the

Conference should succeed and, therefore, tried to be as accommodating as possible. He was patient even when he had to put up with rather offensive behavior, which sometimes happened.'[39] In a personal letter to Lady Mountbatten, he again praised Chou, calling him a 'star performer' representing a country which was playing an important and perhaps dangerous part in the world.'[40] And Nehru wasn't only referring to the Chinese minister's persona. The Air India plane chartered to bring the Indian delegation to Indonesia crashed en route and early reports put the Chinese premier on the plane.[41] But Chou showed up and 'after his death-defying entrance' he 'stole the show' and to the surprise of many in the West proved to be 'the soul of moderation.'[42] Ambassador Winston Lord, who was part of both the secret meeting between China and the US in 1971 and also the meetings between Mao, Chou, and Nixon, recalled that Chou had an 'elegant discourse.' Both he and Kissinger thought Chou was among the most 'extraordinary and impressive' world figures they had ever encountered. By contrast, Lord thought that Mao was 'peasant-like' and 'grunted' in 'short incoherent sentences' when in discussions. The two men's styles were total opposites.[43]

Life magazine showed a smiling Chou and Nehru; the caption noted 'Communist Chou En-lai and Neutralist Nehru have a short, happy huddle.'[44] 'Nehru,' the article said, 'chaperoned Chou about as Chou courted delegates with soft speech and silken smiles.' The Philippines delegate, Carlos Romulo, a former president of the UN General Assembly, commented that the men reminded him 'of a debutante and her mother at a coming-out party.'[45]

The Sino–Indian love-fest animated events at Bandung, conferring a measure of legitimacy on the Beijing regime. This only strengthened Beijing's Tibetan claims in the eyes of the world. At the same time, the People's Republic of China and the United States were on the verge of war over the PLA shelling Quemoy and Matsu, two islands in the Taiwan Straits governed by Nationalist China.[46]

India and the Soviets: new horizons

In February 1955 the Soviets inaugurated a large-scale economic assistance program for India, with an agreement to build a 1 million ton steel mill.

Five months later, in the summer of 1955, basking in the glow of his new celebrity, Nehru made a visit to Moscow. Among his main purposes was to solidify the arrangements and conditions under which the Soviets would provide military supplies and economic support.[47] According to historian Stanley Wolpert, with the US–Pakistan alliance providing the context for a 'rapidly escalating' arms race in South Asia, the Russians wasted no time in offering expanded support to India.[48]

Nehru was greeted in Moscow by tens of thousands of curious well-wishers.[49] The *New York Times* wrote that the welcome was stunning and 'foreigners were amazed.'[50] Moscow had 'rolled out the reddest of red carpets' in a choreographed affair to honor the leader of the non-aligned nations.[51] 'Never had a foreign visitor had such a reception from the Russians as India's Prime Minister Nehru received in Moscow last week,' wrote *Life* magazine.[52] Celebrations lasted for four days with sightseeing, state banquets, and high-level meetings; and then Nehru travelled the country for ten days.

Nehru's meetings with the Soviet leadership further irked Washington. Particularly annoying was the joint call by India and the Soviet Union for a ban on nuclear weapons (which Washington knew the USSR could not and would not honor) and Soviet Premier Nikolai Bulganin's expressed hope that the 'legitimate rights of Communist China on Formosa could be satisfied by peaceful means.'[53]

In a farewell speech at Moscow's Dynamo stadium before an audience of nearly 90,000, Nehru thanked Moscow for the wonderful welcome and affection that had been showered upon him.[54] Referring to Washington, Nehru told his audience that: 'Countries make pacts and alliances, often through fear of some other country or countries … Let our coming together be because we like each other and wish to cooperate and not because we dislike others and wish to do them injury.'[55]

Toward the end of 1955 Washington had become convinced that Nehru was dangerously naïve and had entered into a Faustian bargain with a Soviet 'Mephistopheles.' The State Department's Bureau of Policy Planning and others surrounding the secretary believed that this could only ease the flow of Soviet influence into Southeast Asia and the Near East. CIA Director Allen Dulles supported this view before the National Security Council on 15 November 1955. He reported that the agency had 'been piecing together and collating all available information from all available sources on moves by the Soviet bloc' into underdeveloped areas of 'the free world.'[56] In assessing Soviet intentions, the CIA believed they were trying to 'advance Communist influence' in countries such as India through coordinated 'long-term and high-level operations.'[57] Washington feared that if India were to succumb to Soviet blandishments, this would smooth the way for others in the region to follow. US ambassador to India John Sherman Cooper cabled the State Department to reassure them that the 'Embassy is losing no opportunity [to] point out to responsible Indians the folly of taking Russians at their word…'[58] He said:

Even though they offer help [of] relatively modest gift at this time they will probably score impressive propaganda gain because they are presenting themselves to India as dynamic, cheerful, friendly, robustly self-confident, while India—on basis [of] press reports, right or wrongly—are beginning to wonder whether Washington is inconsistent, cool and wavering.[59]

At an NSC meeting six weeks later, Vice President Nixon did not mince words on the direction and outcome of the Delhi–Moscow relationship: 'The assisted country first becomes an economic satellite of the Soviet Union and shortly thereafter a political and military satellite.'[60]

While Nixon, in retrospect, seemed to grasp only part of the story, his comment belies the frame of mind of many in the administration. Personality and cultural differences had largely curtailed productive communication, leaving Washington to compete with Beijing and Moscow for Nehru's favor and, further, for influence in South Asia. Meanwhile Nehru had obtained assistance through the course of the

Eisenhower administration's first term, while holding Washington at arm's length and then currying favor and assistance from both the USSR and China.

This led to Washington's alliance with 'like-minded' Pakistan, which had the effect of furthering Nehru's relations with Moscow and Beijing where he sought support for 'non-alignment.' But it was Chou En-lai's seduction of Nehru—elegant and complete—that rang alarm bells for Washington, dedicated to stemming the flow of communism into the vulnerable post-colonial nations of South and Southeast Asia.

Bearing these reversals in mind, we turn now to the administration's two-pronged effort to fight communism in South Asia. It entailed the reorganization of national security management and clandestine capabilities, but it also emphasized an innovative (though ultimately unsuccessful) program to project 'soft power' through spreading the tenants of Tibetan Buddhism. It was hoped that Tibetan traditions and spirituality, though distinct from other forms of Buddhism, could provide a path to the cultures of Southeast Asia and thus strengthen anti-communist values in a non-political realm.

22

NSC DIRECTIVE 5412

STRUCTURING CIA OPERATIONS

Eisenhower embraced covert operations as an essential tool to fight communism early in his first term. His administration redesigned its national security and intelligence apparatus to make covert operations easier to manage and more effective.[1] Unlike Truman, who arrived in the White House 'almost totally ignorant of intelligence,' Eisenhower understood from his WWII service as supreme allied commander the role and capacity of intelligence to bring added crucial information into the policy process, so he incorporated the full range of clandestine programs into the conduct of his foreign policy.[2] Beyond the use of 'human intelligence' in India and Tibet, he revolutionized the use of 'signals intelligence,' spy planes, and satellites.[3]

In the same way that the president revamped the NSC to reflect his policy requirements, he changed the way America approached and conducted its intelligence operations. More specifically, Eisenhower institutionalized the nation's capacity for covert operations. To avoid what he feared might trigger World War III, he clearly delineated the role of the Central Intelligence Agency (CIA) and its director. He narrowed and focused the scope of the agency to undertake political and military operations, and specifically excluded the nation's nuclear options.[4]

In March 1954, the president approved the first in a series of important National Security Directives establishing the scope and objectives of US national security policy and the framework which would guide covert operations in Tibet. The National Security Council approved NSC 5412, which stated in part:

The National Security Council, taking cognizance of the vicious covert activities of the USSR and Communist China and the governments, parties and groups dominated by them (hereinafter collectively referred to as 'International Communism') to discredit and defeat the aims and activities of the United States and other powers of the free world, determined … that, in the interests of world peace and US national security, the overt foreign activities of the US Government should be supplemented by covert activities.[5]

Citing the impact and disruption caused by the Soviet and Chinese secret services, this directive, in effect, added a similar covert dimension to the conduct of US foreign policy. It gave the Central Intelligence Agency full responsibility for 'espionage and counterespionage operations under the over-all control of the Director of Central Intelligence(DCI).'[6]

The DCI was to coordinate with representatives of the secretaries of state and defense to ensure that these operations remained consistent with US policies. The Operations Coordinating Board would coordinate and support covert operations between state, defense, and CIA. And before undertaking major clandestine initiatives, CIA was to obtain agreement and secure support from State and Defense.[7]

Most importantly for Tibet, Directive 5412 gave the CIA authority to:

Create and exploit troublesome problems for International Communism, impair relations between the USSR and Communist China and between them and their satellites …[d]iscredit the prestige and ideology of International Communism …[r]educe International Communist control over any areas of the world … and to the extent practicable in areas dominated or threatened by International Communism, develop underground resistance and facilitate covert and guerrilla operations…[8]

Contrary to the advice of some among the joint chiefs of staff and in the cabinet, President Eisenhower was determined not to use atomic weapons against China, but to 'wage a more aggressive covert offensive' against Chinese assets.[9] He was aware that the CIA was controversial and for that reason, and because he intended to use it as 'his chief instrument for waging the Cold War,' he convened a panel of consultants to conduct a study of the CIA a few months after NSC 5412 was approved.[10] The objective of the 'Panel of Consultants on Covert Activities of the Central Intelligence Agency,' called the Doolittle Committee (after the chairman, General James Doolittle), was to ensure that the CIA was the 'appropriate mechanism' for the United States government to carry out 'its over-all intelligence responsibilities and the related covert operations.'[11] In a memo to General Doolittle outlining his thoughts, Eisenhower wrote: 'I consider these operations are essential to our national security in these days when international Communism is aggressively pressing its world-wide subversive program.'[12]

The panel's findings wholeheartedly reaffirmed the president's conviction on using covert operations. In a remarkable statement, the committee urged that America 'reconsider' its commitment to 'fair play,' accept that '[h]itherto acceptable norms of human conduct do not apply,' and in effect use any means necessary to prevail against China and the Soviets.[13] It said:

[I]t is now clear that we are facing an implacable enemy whose avowed objective is world domination by whatever means and at whatever cost. There are no rules in such a game. Hitherto acceptable norms of human conduct do not apply. If the United States is to survive, longstanding American concepts of 'fair play' must be reconsidered. We must develop effective espionage and counterespionage services and must learn to subvert, sabotage and destroy our enemies by more clever, more sophisticated and more effective methods than those used against us.[14]

NSC 5412/2: Moving towards Tibet

A year after NSC 5412, two directives were issued that transformed the way in which intelligence matters under Eisenhower would be handled. The Security Council issued NSC 5412/1 on 12 March 1955, designating the Planning Coordination Group as 'the body responsible for coordinating covert operations.'[15] But it was the next directive, NSC 5412/2 issued in December 1955, that most profoundly affected covert operations around the globe and in Tibet.

This was the genesis for the 'NSC 5412 Group.' Intelligence expert and author John Prados wrote that this directive and the formation of the group 'provided the secret warriors with the broadest possible charter.'[16] Known as the '5412 Committee' or 'Special Group,' they met regularly to review and either approve or deny covert actions proposed by the CIA.[17] The 5412 Group was responsible for all covert decisions relating to Tibet and was the point of coordination for the implementation of Eisenhower's broader covert policies.

Thomas Parrott, the secretary of the committee, recalled that from around 1959 they met at least once a week and sometimes more; he attended 'hundreds of meetings' and believed the committee was 'the most efficient in the government.'[18] The group usually met at the State Department. Speaking as the group's secretary, Parrott said 'we were efficient because we were small and didn't have to coordinate with a bunch of assistants, we could make a decision immediately.'[19] Jokingly referring to himself as 'just the hired help,' Parrott said that the group included the deputy secretary or under secretary of state, Allen Dulles, the DCI, the national security advisor Gordon Gray, and the deputy secretary of defense.[20]

Gordon Gray, heir to the R. J. Reynolds tobacco fortune, became Eisenhower's national security advisor in 1958 and was the first chairman of the group. Subsequent administrations have had similar panels: the Johnson administration had the 303 Committee; and the Nixon administration had the 40 Committee. Successive national security advisors have chaired the committee in accord with the NSC 5412's directive, which, in addition to delineating covert programs, provided the president and the US government with 'plausible deniability.' It stated:

[A]ll activities conducted pursuant to this directive which are so planned and executed that any US Government responsibility for them is not evident to unauthorized persons and that if uncovered the US Government can plausibly disclaim any responsibility for them.[21]

The 5412 Group was a way to 'protect the President,' according to Gray.[22] Plans for covert action were initiated at the Central Intelligence Agency and then brought to the Special Group for scrutiny. The Director of the CIA usually set the agenda for discussion.[23] By all accounts, knowledge of the deliberations, decisions, and implementation of actions approved by the group was made available on a need-to-know basis. While the NSC directive stated that the Special Group should keep representatives in the State and Defense Departments apprised of operations that were approved, this was not done on any 'standardized basis.'[24] Operations approved in the group were closely held, in accordance with the strictures imposed by the director of the CIA, Allen Dulles. There is still much that the public does not know about the inner workings of the group; thus, there are still gaps in understanding the full scope of the Tibetan operation.

In an interview with the now deceased Thomas Parrott in 2004, nearly a half-century after covert operations in Tibet began, Mr Parrott remained reluctant to answer direct questions about why the United States helped the Tibetan resistance effort.[25] He answered, in typical 'agency speak': 'I'm a bit hazy on that.'[26] However, he was able to provide other specific details about how the 5412 Group functioned, and even provided the exact date of CIA Far Eastern Division Director Desmond Fitzgerald's death, which occurred almost forty years earlier.[27]

The exchange with Thomas Parrott is emblematic of the broader problem of penetrating the wall of silence surrounding the government's operations in Tibet. Materials relating to events occurring over five decades ago remain classified, and the authors found that several former CIA officers interviewed on the events of the time became silent at more or less the same point in the story, namely when they were asked exactly what was promised to the Tibetans in return for them actively resisting the Chinese.[28]

On the related and very important matters of what the president knew and when he knew it and, more broadly, the context in which the committee proceeded, Parrott was able to provide a helpful perspective. He recalled that 'Occasionally the State Department man would say, "I have to check with Foster Dulles"; or Gordon Gray would say he'd have to check with my boss, which of course would be the President.'[29] Laughing heartily, Parrott added: 'we all found that very amusing because none of us would ever use the word "President." Gordon Gray would always say that "I'd have to take it up with my associates."'[30] Whether this was to adhere to the notion of plausible deniability, Parrott did not say; but he was firm in his conviction about the president's knowledge of their meetings, remarking in our meeting that 'the President knew of the committee and its meetings: Allen Dulles did not make decisions alone.'[31]

This point was underscored in our 2008 interview with former CIA Director and Defense Secretary James R. Schlesinger. Schlesinger said that Eisenhower was a 'hands-on manager' who knew exactly what was going on and promised to fire anyone who failed to inform him and get his approval of operations beforehand.[32]

Though the 5412 Group and its successors have been the subject of much comment and criticism, it is clear from this crucial interview and a review of available archival documentation that President Eisenhower was aware of and approved of the group's activities.[33]

Professor Christopher Andrew of Cambridge University has observed that 'the most covert part of Eisenhower's use of covert actions was his own responsibility for them. He believed these kinds of operations provided an effective option in fighting the Cold War and felt no "squeamishness" or any "doubts" in the use of them.'[34] Reflecting this point, some historians, notably Fred Greenstein, have called Eisenhower the 'hidden hand president,' in that he managed to 'minimize the visibility of the political side of his role and play up his chief of state status.'[35] General Andy Goodpaster, Eisenhower's chief of staff, confirmed in 2000 many of the points made today by Professor Andrew and Fred Greenstein.[36] Goodpaster had observed first-hand what he called Eisenhower's 'two personas': the 'smiling Ike' for the public and the 'behind the scenes, highly organized Ike, taking careful notes.'[37] The president took full responsibility for his decisions. Goodpaster added, 'we did not wear the President's coat. It was Eisenhower who defined the policy.'[38]

With Tibet in mind, we turn now to the administration's use of peacetime propaganda—an innovation that reflected Eisenhower's belief in the power of religion and his determination to gain support among populations in the world beyond the West. An important aspect of this involved the promotion of religious traditions, including Buddhism, which the White House believed would generate resistance to communism.

23

MOBILIZING RELIGION

Historian Blanche Wiesen Cook noted the vital role that propaganda played during World War II and particularly throughout the Eisenhower presidency.[1] Indeed, Woodrow Wilson and Franklin D. Roosevelt used propaganda as a vital wartime instrument, but Truman and Eisenhower were the first presidents to institutionalize the use propaganda in peacetime.[2] In a campaign speech in 1952, Eisenhower spoke of making more 'subtle' and 'pervasive' approaches in the Cold War a pivotal part of his presidency.[3] Accordingly, he used various outlets to project the American story onto the global stage and particularly to the Soviet and mainland Chinese populations. Cook described C. D. Jackson, Eisenhower's special assistant, who had been a vice president at *Time–Life*, Inc., as a 'master manipulator of the media.'[4] Wiesen Cook credited Jackson for a successful propaganda effort that became a large part of the government's psychological warfare program.[5] Jackson wrote to Eisenhower that he believed that psychological warfare was 'just about the only way to win World War III without having to fight it.'[6]

Eisenhower envisioned a range of strategies that extended 'from the singing of a beautiful hymn' to the 'most extraordinary kind of physical sabotage.'[7] Both the Truman and Eisenhower administrations embraced unconventional approaches of this kind, with, as one scholar noted, 'almost unflagging faith.'[8]

A crucial element of this was the belief that religion could generate resistance to communism—at home and abroad. Eisenhower's goal was to use the nation's church-going Christian sentiments as a point of departure for a broad embrace of religion—any religion as a defining factor in the well-being of human kind, and to project this attitude to the world through the offices of the United States Information Agency. He had made religion and the notion of a 'higher being' a part of his domestic political discourse, which provided the nation with direction and a measure of comfort. This fitted in with a religious revival that had begun in America at about the time the Soviets detonated their first nuclear weapon in September 1949, and remained strong.[9]

Eisenhower's religiosity was reflected, in part, by the carefully structured staff he maintained in the White House for handling religious matters.[10] He incorporated religious references into his everyday remarks and used them to mobilize the American people to join the nation's sacred mission against communism. The president attended prayer breakfasts at the White House with members of Congress and attended private meetings with Billy Graham, a friend and prominent evangelical leader, who preached against communism to the Christian world. Graham's first tent revival in late 1949 drew 350,000 Americans; his 'staccato manner' and 'machine gun style' of delivery gave his denunciation of communism a 'strident urgency.'[11] By 1952 he had a weekly television program and a newspaper column that was syndicated in 125 newspapers.[12] In the first decade of the twentieth century, American religious affiliation was at 43 percent.[13] By the 1940s it had risen to 49 percent, then 55 percent by 1950, 62 percent by 1956 and 69 percent at the end of the decade.[14] In answer to the American Census Bureau asking Americans in 1957: 'What is your religion?', 96 percent of the population 'could cite a specific affiliation.'[15]

The tone for the administration had been set when Eisenhower, at his inauguration, asked God for His guidance; it would be an enduring theme.[16] The administration added the words 'In God We Trust' to all US currency, and the phrase 'Under God' to the Pledge of Allegiance, thus distinguishing Americans from the 'little Moscovites who were solemnly pledging to their hammer and sickle flag.'[17] Lighting the nation's Christmas tree in 1953, Eisenhower said, 'the Communists can find no reserve of strength in prayer because the doctrine of statism denies the dignity of man and consequently the existence of God.' 'Prayer,' he said, 'places freedom and communism in opposition to the other.'[18]

Of course, that message would make its way to the peoples of Eastern Europe and Southeast Asia—but the administration was not about to leave it to chance. To that end, the United States Information Agency (USIA) was established in August 1953. Its mission was to 'submit evidence to peoples of other nations by means of communication techniques that the objectives and policies of the United Sates are in harmony with and will advance their legitimate aspirations for freedom, progress, and peace.'[19] Eisenhower told the new staff that they were 'individuals set apart from all others' and that they must advance the notion that the American government 'is solidly based on some religious concept.'[20] With the creation of USIA, Eisenhower gave propaganda a 'permanent place in the foreign policy apparatus of the US government.'[21] He asserted the centrality of religion in the human experience and he routinized the inclusion of an anti-communist discourse in America's voice to the global community. Eisenhower used religion as a point of departure 'for both supporting and criticizing government behavior … internationally.'[22]

None of this was lost on those fashioning US policy toward Tibet. Tibet, in many respects, was the ideal place to advance such an initiative, as it was a tightly integrated society in which religion was seamlessly welded into daily life. The pivot, of course, was Tibetans' commitment to Buddhism and the Dalai Lama as their spiritual leader, which together were antithetical to both the tenets and practice of communism, which required obeisance to only the Party. Eisenhower's administration would now use religion simultaneously to establish a moral framework for governance and to confirm the relevance of the Dalai Lama and Buddhism as the alternative to Chinese communism in Tibet.

In 1954 a declassified Operations Coordinating Board report addressing the utility of religion as part of the administration's global effort against the communists noted that 'the potential effectiveness of such a program in combating Communism is universally tremendous.'[23] The memo stated:

Religion is an established basic force, which calls forth men's strongest emotions. Because of the immoral and un-Christian nature of Communism and its avowed opposition to and persecution of religions, most of the worlds' principal religious organizations are already allied with the community of free nations. Our over-all objective in seeking the use of religion as a cold war instrument should be the furtherance of world spiritual health.[24]

Specifically, the administration was concerned with the growing spread of communism in Southeast Asia. In September 1954 Vice President Nixon, also concerned with this issue, wrote to the under secretary of state, Walter B. Smith. He enclosed a proposal written by Dr Charles Lowry, a Southern Baptist evangelical, on how religious activism might 'intensify local anti-Communism' and 'lessen the Communist influence in Southeast Asia.'[25] Nixon wrote:

As you know, I have a deep and continuing interest in the peoples of Southeast Asia, as well as a firm conviction that we have not done enough to convince the people themselves, as distinct from the government leadership, that their ideas and aspirations are similar to, and held in common with, ours.[26]

Lowry's report concluded with the observation that 'History is on the verge of repeating itself in Asia. China was lost because the Communists out-thought us and because we could not make up our minds to act boldly. This must not happen in Southeast Asia.'[27]

Selling over twelve million copies a week through 1972, *Life* magazine provided general-interest photojournalism to families across the United States. With Henry Luce at the helm, it was the perfect vehicle to echo the administration's commitment to use religion as a means of highlighting the nature of communism. To that end, *Life* featured a visually stunning report on Buddhism in March 1955. The twenty-five-page magazine article, with numerous pictures, featured a golden Buddha on its cover.[28]

The magazine informed its readers that Buddhism was 'the sole important positive force around which opposition to Communism can be built in this area of the world.'[29] The article continued: 'Communist propagandists among the intellectuals try to find similarities between their philosophy and Buddhism. They emphasize the rational basis of Buddhism.'[30] Not unexpectedly, having emphasized the distinction between a politically-driven authoritarian schema and a transcendental philosophy, the article concluded that 'most intelligent Asians agree that Buddhism and Communism are basically incompatible and opposed.'[31]

Buddhism: The administration's Tibetan gambit

By 1956 the administration had decided to introduce programs that emphasized the strength and validity of Buddhism through fact-based programming in Southeast Asia and established a link with the Dalai Lama and the Tibetan Buddhist community.[32] At the same time, using a dual-track approach, the United States had authorized covert assistance to the Tibetans through the CIA's Directorate of Operations to resist the PLA. Importantly, the administration wished to 'avoid the appearance of official interest in Buddhism for political purposes.'[33] In May 1956, USIA prepared both an official message and extensive programming to mark the celebration of the 2,500th anniversary of Buddhism, known in Tibet as the *Buddha Jayanti* celebration.[34] The administration saw this commemorative event, which would be celebrated over two years, as an effective platform upon which to highlight the stark differences between communism, Christianity, and Buddhism.[35] A declassified NSC memo shows that both the 'State Department and Agency field posts' believed a message from the United States about the celebration would have substantial impact.[36] The memo underscored the point that if the world did not receive a statement from 'some appropriately high authority in the United States it will be taken as a serious affront to their religion by leaders in Buddhist countries throughout the Far East.'[37] The administration, cognizant of the impact of the religious issue in the 1956 elections in Ceylon, was intent on using the capability of each relevant government agency, including the CIA, to reinforce its objectives and point out 'the inconsistencies between Communism and freedom of religion among all religious faiths.[38] Further, the State Department recommended that to expand and strengthen existing US government activities towards Buddhists, the OCB explore the possibility of 'expanding English language training for Buddhist monks and lay leaders and look at the feasibility of increasing travel grants to Buddhist leaders.'[39]

Discussions on this issue were held on 31 May 1956 and again on 28 June, when a committee on Buddhism, with representatives from the CIA, USIA, State Department, and the Operations Coordinating Board, met at OCB offices in the White House Executive Office. Minutes of the meetings show that the discussions centered on how the Buddhist dimension could be utilized to advance US policy objectives in Thailand, Burma, Cambodia, and Laos.[40] They also discussed the problems inherent in implementing programs of this kind, noting that 'the Chinese communists would do their best to subvert Buddhist priests in Southeast Asia.'[41]

USIA broadcasts were directed to Buddhist audiences to show interest in their religion by recognizing Buddhist holidays, festivals, and personalities.[42] But it was the Buddhist clergy and lay groups in Ceylon, Burma, Thailand, Laos, and Cambodia that the United States Information Service (USIS) was specifically targeting. In addition to Buddhist radio broadcasts including daily prayers, USIS distributed brochures, motion pictures, and newsreels, that were shown in Laos and Burma.[43] USIS also provided English classes in Laos and Cambodia and urged that 'contacts' be developed with Buddhist clergy.[44]

Life magazine's cover story in December 1957 was a special issued dedicated to the efforts of the United States Information Service (USIS) all over the world. The cover showed Hank Miller, chief of the USIS in Laos, stating that the job of an USIS officer is to 'encourage pro-US sympathies among Laos' two million citizens.'[45]

Special broadcasts by Buddhist leaders in Southeast Asia were aired for the 2,500th anniversary celebration of Buddhism and a service was conducted for Buddhists in the nation's capital.[46] The USIA made available for local media at 'all posts' special radio broadcasts and print stories detailing how individuals in the United States were observing the Buddhist anniversary.[47]

Of course, the spirituality of Buddhist Tibet was not lost on the administration. Declassified memos show that Operations Coordinating Board focused on Buddhism in both Tibet and China.[48] Notes of the meetings make clear that OCB members believed that while Tibetan Buddhism was not the same as the Buddhism practiced in Southeast Asia, every effort must be made to reach the Tibetans. In a closed session before the Senate Foreign Relations Committee, Allen Dulles explained that many Buddhists regarded Tibetan Buddhism as 'unorthodox.'[49] The director said:

SEA [South East Asia] Buddhists are a little scornful of Tibetan Buddhism as 'polluted'. This doesn't mean that they don't have sympathy for Tibetans as Buddhists—and we try to underline this by pre-fixing the term 'Buddhist' to Tibet whenever we carry news stories or commentaries. In other words, we must generalize on this one.[50]

Thus the administration made it up as they went along. It was far from perfect and there was no way to measure the effectiveness of the program. What can be said is that the US supported broadcasts and events all across Asia that promoted Buddhism as a guide for societies in transition.

24

MEANWHILE, A WORLD AWAY...

In Washington, the OCB's committee on Buddhism could not have imagined that a world away the young Dalai Lama 'desperately wanted sympathetic, wise advice.'[1] In his memoirs the Dalai Lama recalled the 1956 period with sadness: 'I cannot exaggerate our feeling of political solitude in Tibet.'[2] Indeed, it was a disturbing and uncertain time; the events that convulsed Lhasa and reverberated in the United States would have profound consequences—and continue to do so a half century later.

Mao's reforms

Mao, as mentioned, had employed a 'gradual' approach in Lhasa and the environs that had been traditionally under Tibetan control. But the eastern and northern provinces, which included Amdo and Kham. were treated differently. In the early part of the twentieth century these areas had been nominally ruled by China.[3] Mao thus treated these areas as 'China proper' and the fierce Tibetan warriors known as Khampas there were subject to faster and stricter Chinese controls and reforms. These areas were not bound by the 17 Point Agreement and Mao's changes in the region were more drastic and sudden.

By the end of 1954 Mao completed the construction of an extensive road system in Tibet. The PLA, with the help of more than 30,000 Tibetan workers, built 2,000 kilometers of road including the show piece Qinghai–Tibet Highway. Now vehicles had direct access to Lhasa from China.[4] With infrastructure and new administrative offices in place and functioning, Mao was now ready to implement the next phase of reforms. These initiatives had been noted and agreed in the Panchsheel Agreement which formally acknowledged China's rights to Tibet and enabled the PLA to gain an increasingly firm grip.

In the summer of 1954 the Dalai Lama, his family, and a retinue of more than 400 others, including officials and servants, traveled at Mao's invitation to Beijing. Mao wanted the Dalai Lama to be a part of the signing of the new constitution at the Chinese National People's Congress. It is unclear if the Dalai Lama knew, before departing for Beijing, that the new constitution included an amendment barring minority groups from secession.

Mao lavished hospitality on his Tibetan guests; no expense was spared. The young leader attended a round of festivities, conferences, dinner parties, and meetings with Mao, Chou En-lai, and Prime Minister Nehru. The Dalai Lama was impressed with Mao and China's modernization.[5]

It was during this visit that His Holiness was told that Mao was ready to proceed to the next step in Tibet's full integration into the motherland. In March 1955 the Dalai Lama, the Panchen Lama, and several other selected Tibetan officials attended the 7th Plenary Session of the State Council where a resolution was passed creating a new administrative body, the Preparatory Committee of the Autonomous Region of Tibet, commonly called PCART.[6] PCART would be used for consultation and planning during Tibet's transitional period before full integration into China.[7] Most of the committee members were 'indirectly or directly' appointed by the PRC. This allowed Beijing to override proposals made by Tibet's cabinet and national assembly in the decision-making process.[8]

When the Dalai Lama returned to Lhasa in June 1955, thousands of Tibetan well-wishers lined the streets. The people had been uneasy about their leader's trip to China and were thrilled to have him back. The Dalai Lama remembered that summer as 'undoubtedly the best we were to experience during the decade of uneasy coexistence between the Chinese authorities and my own Tibetan administration.'[9] But as the young leader noted, the Tibetan summer is short and by the fall reports of harsh unilateral reforms implemented by the PLA in the eastern regions of Tibet were filtering into Lhasa.[10]

In policies that foreshadowed the Cultural Revolution a decade later, the Chinese imposed punishing taxes on houses, cattle, land, and the contents of monasteries.[11] The monastery tax was paid directly to the local Chinese cadres. Large estates were confiscated and 'redistributed' to the local Chinese cadres, while the Tibetan landowners were publicly humiliated and punished for 'crimes against the people.'[12] Thousands of monasteries were destroyed and their entire wealth, including sacred scriptures and images, seized.[13] Young Tibetans were now drafted by force into the Chinese army. The PLA routinely and publicly harassed monks and nuns, demonstrating that there was no place for religion in the new Tibet.

The PLA demanded that the Khampa warriors hand over their personal weapons. The Khampas, who carried swords and a gun for protection but also as tribal ornaments, refused to surrender them. This led to sporadic violence, just as it had when they refused to surrender their weapons to Major Younghusband a half century earlier at Guru.[14]

The PLA then struck at the very base of Tibetan society and tradition. They rounded up the nomad farmers, who had grazed their animals and farmed on open lands for centuries, and attempted to settle them on assigned lands. Particularly offensive was the attitude of the PLA overseers, who made clear that nomadism was 'repugnant and smacked of barbarism.'[15] The clash of cultures and traditions left little room for harmony.

Uprisings

By the end of 1955 spontaneous uprisings had become common. Khampas, in small guerrilla units, attacked Chinese soldiers throughout Kham and Amdo, wiping out Chinese garrisons in Lithang, Bathang Chamdo, and Kanzu.[16]

The first major revolt erupted at the Sampeling Monastery in the Lithang area. As the PLA attempted to secure the area, some of the fighters fled to the mountains but thousands of armed Khampas took refuge in the monastery. The Sampeling Monastery had a history of defiance: they had fought against tighter controls after the Younghusband expedition, but were eventually put down in 1906. Now in February 1956 some 3,000 monks, many of whom were armed, fought again. But these Khampas and monks were no match for the massive Tupolev-4 bombers that turned the massive fortress into rubble with heavy losses.[17]

Hundreds of Khampas now came together in 1956 as the Chinese moved into the Lithang area of eastern Tibet. The Khampas were subdued; extensive torture and executions accompanied the desecration of monasteries.[18] Men and boys were deported to China; children were taken from their parents for 'reeducation' and Han 'settlers' were given the Khampa property.[19] The Khampas in the surrounded villages attacked the Chinese again when hundreds came to defend the 5,000 monks holed up in the Lithang Monastery, but they could not prevail against the PLA's mechanized weapons. After a month of fighting it too was reduced to rubble by a single bomb.[20]

The Buddhist festival

Events in eastern Tibet were deeply disheartening for the Dalai Lama, who was then isolated in the Potala Palace. He had hoped to attend the Buddhist 2,500th anniversary festival in India, the *Buddha Jayanti*, believing it was a unique opportunity for him to see friends and relatives and perhaps gain new perspectives on the best way forward for Tibet. There also existed the possibility that he might make arrangements to stay in India—though his memoirs suggest that these thoughts were only just being formed.

The government of India had invited him to attend the celebrations, but the Chinese government chose not to pass the invitation along to him, nor did the Chinese reply on his behalf.[21] Only after a direct invitation from the crown prince of Sikkim, who had visited Lhasa, and after the Indians extended an invitation to the Panchen Rinpoche, who represented the pro-Chinese faction, did the Chinese reconsider and permit him to leave Lhasa for the celebrations.[22] The invitation, wrote the young leader in his memoirs, 'came at the depth of my despondency.'[23] Among other things, the young Dalai Lama hoped to obtain advice from the Indian prime minister.[24]

Ultimately, the decision to allow the Dalai Lama to make the journey to India was made by Mao, who granted permission for him to leave Tibet—but with conditions. On his departure, he received a stern lecture from General Chang Ching-wu, the Chinese representative in Lhasa, who referred to 'the little trouble' in Hungary and Poland, where popular uprisings were being brutally suppressed by communist governments but no American rescue was forthcoming. He warned the Dalai Lama not to try to defect and to be aware that there were 'reactionary elements' and 'spies' in India.[25] The general then said, 'If you try to do anything with them, I want you to realize that what happened in Hungary and Poland will happen in Tibet.'[26] As the Dalai Lama prepared to depart for India, the moment was defined by Soviet tanks rumbling through the streets of Budapest while the world listened to heart-rending pleas for help by the Hungarian resistance—and responded with silence.

Mao: Reassuring the cadres

In China, Chairman Mao and his generals were following world events closely. In a lengthy address to the Chinese Communist Party on 15 November 1956, a few days before the Dalai Lama's departure for India, Mao said derisively, 'Buddha has been dead for 2,500 years, and now the Dalai and his followers want to go to India and pay homage to him. Shall we let him go or not?'[27] He went on to outline the politics in play at the festival and the link to Tibet. He told his audience: 'It must be anticipated that the Dalai may not come back, that, in addition, he may abuse us every day, making allegations such as the Communists have invaded Tibet …[28] He might even declare the independence of Tibet in India.'[29] Mao went on to say that if the Dalai Lama issued a 'call for major disturbances,' the PLA would be ready to defend themselves.[30]

In the end it was as if Washington had heard the Dalai Lama's plea, for in the summer of 1956 a decision was reached on Tibet. While the OCB was considering how best to reach out to the global Buddhist community, the Central Intelligence Agency was planning a summer operation that would provide covert support to expand Tibetan resistance to the People's Liberation Army inside Tibet.

The Dalai Lama in India

The Dalai Lama arrived at Sikkim, an Indian protectorate, on the first leg of his journey to the *Jayanti* celebrations. Just inside the border he was greeted by a military band playing the Tibetan and Indian national anthems and a party of Indian officials.[31]

The next day he, the group of officials, and his two brothers made their way to Gangtok, the capital of Sikkim, to be welcomed by a crowd of people casting scarves and flowers in celebration of his arrival.[32] The Maharajah of Sikkim, whose car proudly displayed the flags of Sikkim and Tibet on the front fenders, joined the Dalai Lama.[33] But when the car stopped amidst the crowd of onlookers, the Dalai Lama

182

and his escort were startled when a 'solitary Chinese gentleman' (the Chinese ambassador's interpreter) tore down the Tibetan snow lion flag and replaced it with the Chinese flag.[34]

A few days later, on 25 November 1956, the Dalai Lama was welcomed with further fanfare in New Delhi by Prime Minister Nehru and his vice president, officials of the diplomatic corps, and surging crowds of Tibetans, many of whom had fled the PLA. But for all the celebration and festivities in the streets, tension was mounting behind closed doors in Beijing and Delhi: while the Dalai Lama wanted to remain in India, both the Chinese and the Indians wanted him to leave. The *Jayanti* celebrations thus provided a joyous facade for a tense political drama in which Mao, Nehru, and the Dalai Lama had distinct agendas.

In a meeting on 26 November the Tibetan leader told Nehru that he did not want to return to Tibet but wished to remain in India instead. Specifically, he wished to explore the 'possibility of seeking political asylum.'[35] The Dalai Lama pointed out that the Chinese had invaded a 'peaceful land' and that he was afraid that the uprisings in Kham and the Chinese reprisals 'could end up destroying the whole nation.'[36] He made clear that his people felt they had no alternative but violence, but that he was unable to participate in that.[37] According to Nehru's 'jottings' of the meeting, the Dalai Lama said that Tibetans had 'grown desperate' under the present conditions; they were 'prepared to die'; and that 'hope lies in India.'[38] But Nehru, now under Beijing's watchful eye, was unmoved.

Nehru, disingenuously, stated that the Dalai Lama should 'accept Chinese *suzerainty*,' having previously, through Panikkar, described China's authority in Tibet as '*sovereign*.' He added that 'if he [the Dalai Lama] contested' this, the 'Chinese would try to take over Tibet entirely.'[39] The Indian prime minister made it clear that India 'was not in a position to give any effective help to Tibet nor were other countries in a position to do so.'[40] He explained that 'nothing could be done for Tibet at present' and advised the leader to return home.[41]

Nehru's cold rejection of the Tibetan leader's plea contrasted with his ecstatic welcome for the Chinese premier the next day. Nehru greeted Chou En-lai, who was ostensibly visiting India to attend the *Jayanti* celebrations, at the airport on November 28. At a banquet honoring Chou the next evening, Nehru spoke in glowing terms about the Panchsheel Agreement that India and China had signed in 1954.[42] The preamble to this agreement had effectively ended any hope the Tibetans might have had for pursuing their independence, as India had accepted Tibet as a part of China. The prime minister welcomed Chou 'with affection' and told his dinner guests that 'wherever he [Chou] goes, he will hear the slogan which is becoming more and more popular: *Hindi–Chini bhai bhai*' (India–China are brothers).[43]

While Nehru had made it clear that his political alliance was with the communist Chinese, he seemed to feel a spiritual tie with the Tibetans through Buddhism. In a speech on 24 November for the *Jayanti* celebrations he told the audience, which included the Dalai Lama, that 'Whenever I think about the lives of Gautama Buddha and Mahatma Gandhi, both the products of India's soil, there is turmoil in my mind and my eyes fill with tears.'[44]

On 1 January 1957 the Dalai Lama met with Chou En-lai for discussions in Delhi. The notoriously opaque Chou listened carefully and smiled appropriately as the Dalai Lama voiced his concerns about the treatment of his people under the 'reforms' being implemented by the PLA in Tibet.[45] The Dalai Lama recalled Chou's nickname, 'Chew and Lie,' as he was told he must return to Lhasa because his 'country' needed him.[46] Chou was just as he had remembered him: 'full of charm, smiles and deceit.'[47] Chou later spoke to the Dalai Lama's brothers Gyalo Thondup and Thubten Norbu (Taktser Rinpoche): Norbu had strong words for the Chinese minister and made it very clear that they, at least, could not be persuaded to return to Lhasa.[48] Chou was indeed concerned that the leader would be convinced by his brothers and other family members to remain in India—so much so that that topic overshadowed his talks with Nehru the next day.

Chou, Nehru, and Tibet

Between 30 December 1956 and 1 January 1957, Chou En-lai and Nehru had lengthy conversations about the Bhakra Dam Project in Nangal. Some of the conversation was on the train ride back to Delhi in the evening and early hours of 30–31 December.[49] The Indian prime minister had been eager to discuss US–Sino relations, the Middle East, Poland, Hungary, and China, but was cut short abruptly when Chou insisted on discussing Tibet first.[50] The Chinese minister then proceeded with a lengthy monologue, beginning with the history of Tibet and leading up to current issues.[51] He talked about the Dalai Lama, Panchen Lama, explained Inner and Outer Tibet, Buddhism, and added that the Tibetans were at the moment in a semi-feudal and semi-slave system with compulsory service to the temples.[52] The Chinese minister discussed the Tibetan émigré community in Kalimpong and claimed that 'subversive activities' encouraged by 'US agents' were taking place.[53] He said that Thubten Norbu, the Dalai Lama's brother who had recently arrived in India from the United States, had informed the young leader that 'the United States would support [an] independence movement in Tibet.'[54]

When Chou paused for breath, Nehru interjected: 'Your Excellency has said a good deal.'[55] Nehru knew of the 'nest of spies' in Kalimpong, but was surprised by Chou's claims that there were 'tens of thousands' of Tibetans now residing there.[56] Nehru, of course, understood the real message of the long discourse and, reflecting his government's careful calculation—which dictated non-involvement—responded that his government's policy was to prohibit anti-Chinese propaganda.[57] The next day Chou discussed Sino–American relations, but still couldn't resist a few more words on Tibet. He again mentioned the 'subversive activities' in Kalimpong, making the point that the Chinese government believed that the US was the instigator and was considering similar activity in Tibet.[58]

At the same time that Nehru was meeting with Chou, the Dalai Lama was deciding whether he should visit the Tibetan community in Kalimpong and, more importantly, if he should stay there permanently. Chou met with the Dalai Lama on the morning of 1 January 1957, a few hours before his second day of talks with Nehru.[59] He told the Dalai Lama of the worsening situation in Tibet and again advised him to return and not to visit Kalimpong; Chou made the point that the Chinese would employ force to put down any resistance.[60] The next morning PLA General Ho Lung, who oversaw the invasion of Lhasa in 1950, spoke sternly to the Dalai Lama, reiterating Chou's position. Ho, who was now in charge of administering Tibet, had accompanied Chou to India. He quoted a Chinese proverb which the Dalai Lama remembered: 'The snow lion looks dignified if he stays in his mountain abode, but if he comes down to the valleys he is treated like a dog.'[61]

Despite the threats and cautions the Dalai Lama made the trip to Kalimpong to visit his family. Many of his former officials now resided there with Tibetan refugees who were fleeing the escalating violence in Tibet. At the beginning of February 1957 the Dalai Lama arrived in Kalimpong to stay in the family home of the Bhutanese prime minister. Nehru was right that the city had become home to thousands of Tibetan refugees. His two brothers, Gyalo and Norbu, their mother, a number of friends, and former ministers of his cabinet were all in Kalimpong. They 'begged' the young leader to remain in India.[62]

It was a pivotal moment: he decided after consultations with the Oracle that the gods believed he must return to Lhasa. As he made his return in March 1957, his brother Gyalo was emerging as a vital figure linking the Khampa resistance to the CIA, which we discuss in the next chapter.

25

THE ENIGMATIC GYALO THONDUP

Here we digress for a moment to provide background and perspective on Gyalo Thondup, the Dalai Lama's older brother. Alone among the Dalai Lama's brothers, Gyalo chose not to pursue a monastic life. Instead, over time, he emerged as an integral part of the US–Tibet clandestine program, assisting the CIA and the State Department in India, the US, the Western Pacific, Hong Kong, and Taipei.

Gyalo was an enigmatic figure and remains so today. Eight years the Dalai Lama's senior, he left Lhasa in 1946 for Nanking, the nationalist Chinese capital, where he enrolled in a political institute formed by Chiang Kai-shek.[1] Two years later, to the consternation of his family, he married the daughter of a Han Chinese KMT General, Chu Shi-keui.[2] Being both the Dalai Lama's brother and now the son-in-law of a prominent general placed him in elite social and military circles.[3]

When the People's Liberation Army took over Nanking in April 1949, Gyalo escaped to Hong Kong, went briefly to India and then to Hong Kong in the hope of continuing to the United States.[4] A brief stop in Taipei en route turned into a year-long stay under the watchful eye of Chiang Kai-shek who, to his dismay, refused his request for an exit visa to visit his brother Thubten Norbu in the US.[5] Eventually, under pressure from Washington, he was granted an exit visa.[6]

By this time Gyalo had become 'of interest' to US intelligence officials. He spoke Tibetan and Chinese and rudimentary English and had access to his brother, the Dalai Lama, and though he had indiscreetly requested funds via public telegraph from the US consulate in Calcutta, he had passed a preliminary vetting by US diplomats in Hong Kong while there.[7]

On arrival in the United States, he met with William Anderson at the State Department's Office of Chinese Affairs in late September 1951 and again in early November.[8] Even though he was enrolled in university and able to stay in the US, he decided to join his mother and sister who planned to return to Lhasa from Kalimpong in February on a special mule caravan.[9] His journey, however, was not without controversy. Like the Maoists, Gyalo supported land reform as well as political and social change in Tibet. These views, and the fact that he had Chinese family and friends, aroused suspicion among the Tibetans and resulted in a poor reception on his trip.[10] Indeed, Gyalo was also thought to be an American spy—as relayed to the American consul general by Mrs Thondup at a July 1952 meeting at Calcutta.[11] She told Wilson that Gyalo was 'very discouraged by what he had seen in Lhasa' and found his presence there a source of embarrassment for his brother.[12]

On 19 July, before departing for Darjeeling the next day, Gyalo confirmed to Wilson the disturbing news that the Chinese were 'everywhere' in Lhasa and 'there was nothing the Tibetans could do to oppose them.'[13] Food was short, prices were high, and 'there were many Chinese soldiers to be seen.'[14]

In the same period Gyalo met with his brother to say that the US remained 'keenly interested' in Tibet. The Dalai Lama was grateful for this assurance but had decided to remain in Lhasa for the Tibetan people.[15]

When General Chang, the PLA commander in Lhasa, asked that he head up a mission from Lhasa to Beijing that summer to see Mao, he knew his situation had become precarious.[16] He decided that he had little choice but to return to India, so slipped across the Indian border at Tawang while inspecting one of his brother's estates.[17] In the authors' conversation with him at his home in Darjeeling in December 2012, he recalled this period with some dismay.

Meanwhile, in the unsettled environment surrounding the PLA's consolidation of power in Lhasa during the summer of 1952, the Americans had also become suspicious of Gyalo. Gyalo had many Chinese friends in India from his days at the Central Political University of Nanking.[18] And while they resided in Calcutta, his wife was the principal of the Chinese communist primary school which caused concern among American officials.[19] Still, Washington continued to consider him a useful source of information about personalities and developments in Tibet. As the State Department made clear in a top secret memo: 'While the political reliability of Mrs Thondup has not been ascertained, the Department does not wish to discourage the occasional relaying of messages from Tibet, provided appropriate arrangements can be made.'[20] Washington was concerned that contact with the Thondups in Calcutta or Darjeeling would arouse 'comment.'[21] But with no Tibetan-speaking CIA operatives in Tibet at that point, information was scarce, and Washington had few alternatives. In fact the US was using intelligence collected from monthly reports written by the Indian representative at the mission at Lhasa. These were passed through the American embassy in London with the note: 'In view of the possible repercussions should the Indian Government learn that a copy of this report has been made available to the Embassy by the Foreign Office, it is requested that his dispatch should be treated as 'Eyes Only-US. Official' material.'[22]

In September 1952, at the request of Consul General Evan Wilson, the vice consul in Calcutta, Gary Soulen, met with Gyalo and Mrs Thondup at their home in Darjeeling and had a lengthy conversation. The sixteen-page file has been declassified and sheds light on Gyalo's relationship with the State Department and his thoughts on a prospective Tibetan resistance effort.[23]

Gyalo provided a detailed account of his time in Lhasa and relayed information on the various Tibetans who were arriving in India. They discussed the economic situation in Tibet, the growing presence of a Chinese political cadre, the Dalai Lama's situation, and his receipt of Washington's messages.[24]

In addition, Gyalo reported to Soulen that 'the Tibetans have an internal espionage network operating against the Chinese' and that he was presently working on establishing a secret resistance organization to be headquartered in India.[25] Gyalo had discussed this with Tsepon Shakabpa (who had earlier headed the Tibetan Trade Delegation to the US and was now in Kalimpong) and said they communicated with Tibetans in Lhasa through an established code.[26] He explained that the code was numerical: 'A cup of tea would be, for instance, 134 [and] a shoe would be number 11 …'[27] Soulen, noting Gyalo's utter lack of preparedness for such methods, reported:

I tried to point out to Gyalo some of the pit-falls of amateur codes. I tried to impress [upon] him the fact that a broken code is much worse than none at all. His inexperience and lack of understanding of basic principles will make it extremely dangerous for him to engage in sending wireless code messages to Tibet as he contemplates.[28]

Gyalo also told Soulen that Mr Venoy Kumar, an Indian intelligence officer, had asked him to help organize 'intelligence activities in the border areas.'[29] This reflected the rift that had developed between B. N. Mullik, the director of Indian Intelligence (which had remained close to Britain's MI5), and other parts of the Nehru government. It also confirmed how convoluted things had become. Kumar had two further requests: first, he offered Gyalo 'money for information' stating that the 'GOI was anxious to help him establish a secret organization to infiltrate the Chinese position in Tibet';[30] and second, he asked Gyalo's assistance in apprehending Tibetan or Chinese Communists entering India surreptitiously.[31]

Gyalo had other priorities, however. He twice asked Soulen if the American government could provide arms to be smuggled into Tibet. Soulen explained that would be impossible because, as US diplomats, they were 'guests of the Indian government and could not engage in that kind of activity.'[32] Soulen emphasized to Gyalo and his wife 'the absolute need for them to practice the utmost discretion in conversation or discussion with anyone about Tibet and about their own ideas and plans.'[33]

In the end Soulen concluded that:

Despite Gyalo's naiveté and possible indiscretions it is believed that he may continue to be a source of information that, with other information available to the Department, might evolve into worthwhile intelligence. For that reason the Consulate General will, as opportunities arise, continue this discreetly.[34]

A few weeks later Consul General Evan Wilson met with the Thondups during a brief visit to Darjeeling.[35] Gyalo told him that when he was in Washington he had been asked by Mr Anderson at the State Department to convey an oral message to

189

the Dalai Lama that the US government was still greatly interested in Tibet and was still hopeful that the Dalai Lama would leave Lhasa for India.[36] Gyalo now reported back that his brother was 'very appreciative of our effort' but could not leave Tibet at this time.[37] Gyalo gave a letter, written in Chinese, to Wilson to transmit to Anderson to apprise him of events in Tibet and to confirm that the Dalai Lama had received his message.[38] A memo, declassified for the authors, indicates that in fact Gyalo's 'Chinese letter' contained a plan for an 'anti-Chinese Communist action program to be carried out in Tibet under of aegis of Indian domiciled Tibetans and requested the US Government's reaction to such a plan.'[39] Washington's reply to Gyalo was ambiguous at best, 'expressing US sympathies for Tibetans but pointing out the necessity for Government of India cooperation.'[40]

The US government decided, at that time, to 'defer all further contacts' with Gyalo and his wife.[41] The final meeting with the Thondups took place at Soulen's Calcutta home on 3 December 1952.[42] Washington's instructions were clear: 'that no (rpt no) message to be sent to Gyalo at this time.'[43] In the marginalia are found the words: 'Noted,—alerted interested agency,' which suggests that at this early date there was more in play than met the eye.[44]

Washington experienced growing pressure in 1952 from the Nehru government to restrain, if not terminate, all contacts with the Tibetan community resident in India. Acheson, however, found this difficult, and instructed the embassy in Delhi to 'take first appropriate opportunity remind GOI that US officials will CONT receive courteously persons fleeing from COMMIE control when they RPT they take initiative calling on US officials.'[45]

Gyalo again

Two years later, in January 1954, Mrs Thondup telephoned Mrs Soulen to say that she and her husband Gyalo were in Calcutta for a few days and would like to call on the Soulens.[46] Tea was arranged on 7 January and for two hours Gyalo spoke of earlier events. Soulen now found Gyalo more mature and confident. His command of English now allowed an extended conversation in English.[47]

What had prompted US officials to cease contact with the Thondups? In his report, Soulen wrote that after their last meeting in December 1952 Ambassador Chester Bowles insisted that Indian officials be notified that the US was in touch with them.[48] At that point, the GOI, attempting to limit American access, objected strongly to further US interaction with Gyalo and 'threatened to move him to another part of India if he continued contacts with foreign representatives.'[49] They were adamant in their position. Wilson wrote: 'GOI has made very clear their desire that American officials, and by implication other Americans, should not visit Gyalo Thondup and have given clear evidence that their secret police were keeping a close watch on him, his movements and his associates.'[50]

Gyalo related that one month after seeing American officials in Calcutta an Indian political officer in Gangtok Sikkim, Mr Kapur, visited Gyalo and his wife when they returned to Darjeeling. Kapur made it plain that he came as a 'special emissary' on behalf of Nehru to warn the Thondups about the political activities that Gyalo wished to carry out on Indian soil.[51] In what could only have been a stunning—and upsetting—revelation for Gyalo, Kapur revealed that the GOI knew of the letter he had sent to Anderson in Washington 'regarding the Tibetan situation and the political activities in India which Gyalo wanted to carry out.'[52] Kapur then queried Gyalo on how he had sent the letter and then demanded a copy of it, which Gyalo said he did not have.[53]

Soulen was clearly irritated. He wrote to Washington:

I consider Kapur's remarks to Gyalo, that the US Government was discussing his activities with the GOI, to have been a gross indiscretion and probably were made deliberately to discredit the US Government in Gyalo's eyes or at least to have lowered his respect for US Government officials in India as regards their discretion and their ability to keep confidences.[54]

'Kapur,' Gyalo told Soulen, 'was very, very serious' and insisted that 'Nehru had specifically said they were to stop seeing foreigners.'[55] This of course had been quite confusing for Gyalo. He told Kapur that other GOI officials had urged him to establish a Tibetan resistance effort and had offered to pay for intelligence related to Tibet. Kapur said to Gyalo at several points, 'this situation is too complicated—I cannot go into it now.'[56] Even though Gyalo was warned, US intelligence sources reported that the GOI was using Gyalo for 'intelligence collection' as Gyalo had many contacts with the Tibetan refugees and traders in Kalimpong.[57]

After revealing that he now knew the double game the State Department was playing, Gyalo 'very politely' mentioned to Soulen that he had never received an answer to his letter of October 1952 that was passed to Anderson in Washington, and of course wondered why the US government would have discussed it with the GOI.[58] Soulen, in good diplomatic fashion, 'passed over his remarks as lightly as possible and remained noncommittal.'[59] But underneath he was apparently incandescent.

The depth of Soulen's frustration is revealed in his next comment. 'US efforts to help the Tibetans and gain intelligence,' he wrote, 'were thwarted by the Indians.'[60] He reminded his colleagues that personal contact in the field is of the utmost importance and that these contacts must 'have confidence in us.'[61] India's demand that US officials cease to contact informants, combined with the fact that confidential information had been leaked to Gyalo, clearly made it more difficult and almost impossible for Soulen and his staff to gather any intelligence information.[62] Soulen wrote: 'Over the past 10 months those sources of information have been progressively drying up.'[63]

He ended the angry memo in a barely restrained tone: 'The field has always been cognizant of the potential effect of its actions on Indo–American relations. However, policy of higher authority, culminating in the decision to discuss Gyalo with the GOI, has been to predicate all field actions and discussions with contact on GOI sensitivities (to which there appears no limit).'[64]

Soulen continued: 'the fact [that] for the whole of the past year we have not known that the GOI divulged secret discussions to Gyalo has placed us in a most disadvantaged position.'[65] In the end, he recommended that the US field officers 'be authorized, as suitable occasions arise, to discuss frankly and sincerely with its contacts, including Gyalo, the continuing US interest in and sympathy for the Tibetans.'[66]

The Tibet Relief Committee

The signing of the Panchsheel trade agreement with Beijing in 1954 had shocked and anguished all Tibetans. Gyalo, in India, was determined to find a way to resist the Chinese in Tibet.[67] That summer, Gyalo, Tsepon Shakabpa, the former head of the Tibetan delegation, and Khenjung Lobsang Gyentsen, a monk, began to meet regularly under the pretext of a picnic. They called themselves Jenkhentsisum, an acronym that stood for 'the older brother, the khenjugn, and the tsipon.' Their intentions were defiantly grand: they planned to 'develop a strategy for organizing opposition to the Chinese from Indian soil.'[68] The three men initiated the Tibet Relief Committee to help Tibetans in Tibet who were drastically affected by a tragic flood; and at the same time they organized the Association for the Welfare of Tibet, covertly a political group, that called for Tibetan independence.[69] In September 1954 Tsepon Shakabpa approached the American embassy in New Delhi for a donation to the Tibet Flood Relief Committee, which the embassy noted was in fact part of an anticommunist organization and effort.[70]

After the ruthless bombing and killings of thousands of Tibetans in eastern Tibet in 1956, Gyalo and his Tibetan Welfare Association prepared a lengthy document detailing the atrocities and horrific events unfolding inside Tibet.[71] This was sent to President Eisenhower, Nehru, and the prime minister of Pakistan.[72] As the Dalai Lama arrived in New Delhi for the *Buddha Jayanti* festivities, the *New York Times* ran a lengthy article which began: 'The Chinese Communists are carrying on a program of colonization in Tibet that is slowly changing the entire political and security picture in the strategic Himalayan zone.'[73] At the same time the Far East Bureau at the State Department prepared a very comprehensive 'Top Secret' report detailing the Chinese 'reforms,' the uprisings, the deaths, and the resistance efforts of Tibetan guerrilla groups in eastern Tibet.[74] The implications of China's 'liberation' of Tibet were now made plain at the upper reaches of the US government.

Through the course of 1956 Gyalo continued to build an Indian-based resistance effort in India, where he had received emissaries from the Khampas fighters seeking aid and weapons from abroad.[75] In the summer of 1956 he approached the US embassy in Calcutta for assistance, and the timing was right.[76] Washington now took his Tibet plan from the drawing board to the field.

A few months later, when Washington learned that the Dalai Lama would attend the *Jayanti* Buddhist festival in India, they knew they must not waste the opportunity. CIA operative John Hoskins, based in Calcutta, received an urgent message from Washington to make contact with the Dalai Lama's brother Gyalo, then residing in Darjeeling.[77] Gyalo, an avid tennis player, was often invited to play at the prestigious Gymkhana Club—established in 1909 by the British.[78] Having been informed that Gyalo enjoyed a good game, Hoskins picked up his racket and made his way to Darjeeling, where he quietly introduced himself.[79] In a short time Gyalo became an important part of Washington's plan, not only for covert operations on the ground, but also for his ability to pass messages to his brother.

* * *

We return here to where our digression began. February 1957 found the Dalai Lama and Gyalo in Kalimpong. Gyalo was working with the CIA to select a group of fit and willing Tibetans for resistance training at American bases. He had met and would recommend to the agency twenty-seven determined young Khampas who had fled Lhasa and were inspired by the prospect of regaining their homeland.[80] Covert operations in Tibet had long been a topic of whispered conversations in Lhasa, Delhi, London, and Washington, and had now taken form.

26

WASHINGTON'S CLANDESTINE PROGRAM IN TIBET

As Washington refined its covert program for Tibet, anxiety over communism's revealed brutality rose quickly in the West.

On Sunday, 21 October 1956, Secretary of State John Foster Dulles was asked on *Face the Nation*, 'If there was a blood bath against the Polish people, what would the United States do?'[1] Dulles, in a mangled paraphrase of John Quincy Adams, said America 'has no desire to roam the globe slaying dragons,' adding 'Washington would not send in troops, or intervene or meddle' because 'interference from abroad in the internal affairs of another country often is counter-productive.'[2] He continued: 'Our job is only as exponents of freedom, to keep alive the concept of freedom, because it is a contagious thing, and if anybody is apt to catch it, it's going to be the Poles.'[3] It was one of those moments that crystalized the disingenuous and (to be kind) uninformed nature of government.

Not only was the US at that moment preparing a covert intervention in Tibet, but the next morning the world awoke to news that Hungary, not Poland, had erupted in revolution. The difference in location did not change the non-intervention stance Dulles had described, despite contradictory signals that Washington supported those resisting communist oppression. Moreover, Hungary had been a priority for Radio Free Europe and the Voice of America. The former broadcast twenty hours a day to Eastern Europe, where it also dropped leaflets by balloons 'at a rate of fourteen million a month,' all to preserve the hope of freedom for the 'enslaved peoples' under Moscow's 'hobnailed boot.'[4]

Eisenhower called the situation tragic and the US accepted thousands of refugees, but would not use American forces to quell the slaughter underway in Hungary.[5] On two separate occasions the President 'rejected proposals to airdrop arms to the Hungarians,' even after their plea for help was heard around the world.[6]

As Eisenhower biographer Stephen Ambrose noted, 'in grand strategy, geography dictates the options.'[7] Hungary shared a border with the Soviet Union, was surrounded by communist states, and had no port, all of which made it extremely difficult to access, let alone sustain military operations.[8] Moreover, Eisenhower did not want a direct confrontation with the Soviets.[9] Journalist Scotty Reston summed up the prevailing sentiment in his *New York Times* column: 'It is generally agreed that the State Department should do the prudent thing and watch developments closely and keep quiet …'[10] Thomas Parrott, the secretary of Eisenhower's 5412 Committee, said to one of the authors with regret:

People say we should have supported the Hungarian freedom fighters but we couldn't, we just couldn't, we didn't have the facilities. I'm afraid we were just talking rather big about pushing back the iron curtain but when the chance came to push it back we weren't really able to do it.[11]

Eisenhower wrote in his memoirs that there were no alternatives because Hungary was 'as inaccessible to us as Tibet.'[12] But ironically, the remote nation in the Himalayas was actually more accessible than the war-torn European country. Tibet's very remoteness meant that it was not normally covered in the daily news flow, and because instability in Tibet would not impact the USSR's hold on Eastern Europe, American involvement there ran little risk of triggering a confrontation with Moscow. What is more, such an operation offered the opportunity to harass and unbalance the Chinese in a focused and discrete manner. Thirdly, though it remained remote, there was a possibility of success. It was impossible to know what progress the Khampa resistance fighters might make.

Hungary and its implications were also on the Chinese chairman's mind and became recurring themes in his remarks in early 1957. At the party conference in mid-January, Mao said the 'disturbance' that had taken place in Hungary could not happen in China where 'at most, a small number of people may create trouble here and there and clamor for so-called great democracy.'[13] A week later he noted that the US would not give up its efforts to fight communism in every possible way: '[Eisenhower] will continue his hardline policy toward the Communists and pin his hopes on disturbances breaking out in our midst.'[14] He admonished his party not to be intimated by 'imperialism' or be 'afraid of students creating disturbances or kicking up a row in a cooperative.'[15]

In a January 1957 speech, delivered in Mao's period of democratic reform (also known by the phrase 'Let a hundred flowers bloom, let the hundred schools of thought contend'), there is some indication Mao knew at least some of the CIA's intentions. He declared that the unrest in both China and Tibet was the 'result of the operations of both domestic and foreign counter-revolutionary elements' in an effort to 'stir up disorder.'[16] He told his party 'comrades' he would not be deterred and vowed that the 'secret agents' who were sent by the United States and 'the Chiang Kai-shek clique' to carry on disruptive activities would be 'rooted out by a firm hand.'[17] Perhaps the Chairman had concrete intelligence, or perhaps it was a gambit to raise vigilance and stir nationalist impulses. Either way, Mao's comments about foreign and 'counter-revolutionary' elements in China and Tibet reflected a decision to raise the profile of resistance groups challenging the PLA on the ground. The Chairman's accusations were, of course, correct: as he spoke that February, resistance supported by Tibetans based in India had formed in Tibet and the first six Tibetan resistance fighters were being readied by the CIA.

The Khampas: Four rivers, Six ranges

Within a few months of the Hungarian crisis, the CIA began transporting and training the first small group of Tibetan resistance fighters. Who were these people?

As the violence escalated in eastern Tibet in 1956, one of Tibet's better known Khampa leaders, Gompo Tashi Andrugtsang, the scion of a wealthy business family in Lithang whose monastery dating to 1588 had been destroyed by the PLA, took steps to bring the various Khampa clans together to wage guerrilla war under one flag. These Khampas, members of clans based in Kham and Amdo, all had the same goal: to drive the Chinese out. In December 1956 Gompo Tashi contacted Khampa leaders and others in Tibet and India, saying:

The time has now arrived to muster all your courage and put your bravery to the test. I know you are prepared to risk your lives and exert all your strength to defend Tibet… In this hour of peril, I appeal to all people, including government servants, who value their freedom and religion, to unite in the common struggle against the Chinese.[18]

To bring people together, Gompo Tashi asked Tibetans to contribute money and valuables to build a golden throne: a gift for the Dalai Lama that would show respect and love for their leader. Accordingly, the faithful from all over Tibet donated in the name of Buddhism and His Holiness. The process had a secondary purpose, however. It provided the chance for Khampa leaders and their followers to plan the resistance movement further.

Gompo Tashi and his men received large quantities of gold, silver, diamonds, pearls, onyx, coral, and turquoise, as well a personal religious ornaments.[19] Everyone contributed. In all, forty-nine goldsmiths, five silversmiths, nineteen engravers, and a host of others took several weeks to make a spectacular throne made of gold and gemstones.[20] As thousands of his followers looked on, the throne was presented to the Dalai Lama in a ceremony at the Norbulingka Palace on 4 July 1957.

One year later, on 16 June 1958, a united Khampa army took the name *Chushi Gangdrug*, or Four Rivers and Six Ranges, in reference to the rivers and mountains of Kham.[21] They came together to fight the Chinese, but it wasn't just the Khampas who formed the new resistance effort. They were joined by Tibetans from different walks of life and all parts of the country. As Gompo Tashi wrote, their decisions to join 'were taken on an individual basis as nationalists who could not see their people butchered.'[22] The *Chushi Gangdrug* soon reached beyond Kham and eastern Tibet to become a pan-Tibetan resistance movement.[23]

With an elaborate parade, the new 5,000-strong volunteer army, calling themselves volunteer freedom fighters, unfurled their flag and established a headquarters.[24] Four commanders were selected, and in addition there were field commanders, community liaison officers, captains, and units grouped by 'district of origin. They were assigned names corresponding to letters of the Tibetan alphabet.'[25] As anthropologist and Tibetan historian Carole McGranahan wrote, 'The founding of the *Chushi Gangdrug* served not just to unify disparate groups in their resistance to the Chinese, but also to institutionalize international resistance activities already underway.'[26]

Sky boats and secret agents: training begins

At the beginning of February 1957, when the Dalai Lama was in Kalimpong deciding whether to go or stay in India, six of the Khampas chosen by his brother Gyalo were readied for training at a US base at Saipan in the Mariana Islands.[27]

On 20 February 1957, dressed in Indian *longhis*,[28] the men crossed into Pakistan and eventually boarded a 'sky boat'—the first airplane any of them had ever seen—which took them to the CIA training center. It was a secret operation described (in a declassified CIA document) as one of the most 'romantic' covert action programs ever undertaken.[29] In a truly remarkable account, Athar Norbu, a Khampa survivor from the PLA attack on the Lithang Monastery, recalled his journey:

That day, Gyalo Thondup had told us not to wear anything Tibetan. We ate a big dinner and, after dark, we slipped out of town to a place called 'The Ninth Mile.' … At nine o'clock, Gyalo pulled up in a jeep … and his attendant, Gelung, sat next to him … and he told us guys to be very quiet … Gyalo left us at Siliguri … We had a new driver for the rest of the way, which was almost to the East Pakistani border … From there, we went on foot. Gelung led the way down a small path that went through a tea plantation. He was using a compass, which I had never seen before. We walked for several hours in the jungle, and during the hike Gelung showed us how to use the compass and explained why it was useful. Our objective was to find a big river that marked the Indian–East Pakistani border. We walked two hours before finding it. It took us another hour to find a crossing that was shallow enough for us, because only one of us could swim. Once we got to the East Pakistani side of the river, we walked inland and came to a narrow road. We had been instructed to wait there.

The moon was out, so we could see if anybody was approaching. We saw a guy walking toward us. He was definitely armed and, at first, we thought he was an Indian. But then Gelung got up, clicked a signal with his flashlight and got the appropriate signal clicked back at him and we knew he was Pakistani.

We followed the Pakistani down the path … there was a jeep hidden in the bush. It was brought out and we drove in that for about a half-hour before reaching a small building, which was an East Pakistani check post. Inside was an American, sound asleep snoring. We had never seen an American before. He had brown hair, blue eyes and a big nose. And he was hairy and we thought this was very funny. We made a joke about how the Chinese had an American imperialist in their backyard and didn't even know it. He woke up and was very kind to us. He shook all of our hands, made us tea and served us fancy biscuits.[30]

From here they all piled into a jeep, were driven to a railway station and then traveled to the capital, Dhaka. They were lodged in a safe house in Kurmitola, just north of the city where the Americans had a landing strip. Here a C-118 stripped of all its markings and with blackened windows landed, picked up the mysterious passengers, and took off.[31]

Saipan

The plane landed briefly in Bangkok. Then the men were taken to the Kadena airbase in Okinawa for medical exams, before being dropped at their final destination. They spoke no English but their aptitude, according to one test, showed they 'exhibited good native intelligence.'[32]

They were greeted in Okinawa by Norbu, who after spending time in the United States now spoke English, and then they all traveled to the Marianas. Here they began four and a half months training in basic covert operations at the CIA's Saipan Training Station, known as the Naval Technical Training Unit.[33]

The officer in charge, Roger McCarthy, trained the Khampas in the use of parachutes, pistols, rifles and mortars, demolition and sabotage, for ambushes and detonating bridges.[34] Under his tutelage and that of other CIA specialists, including paramilitary specialists, the six Khampas learned how to operate hand-cranked radios, how to use Morse code and to 'code and decode messages using a system of numbers that represented letters.'[35] But training had its hurdles. It was a challenge for the Khampas to grasp numbers and the concept of a twenty-four-hour clock, which made it difficult to schedule meetings or radio transmissions. They also had no idea of distance, which made it hard for them to understand some of the most basic concepts in covert tradecraft.[36]

It wasn't just that the Tibetans didn't speak English, they had no formal education: their reading and writing skills were also minimal, creating further difficulties.[37] For example, they had to be taught Tibetan grammar before they could even begin the process of understanding how to code messages. It was, as McCarthy said, 'a lot to ask of these men' but they had the stamina, the will, and the intelligence, and they did eventually become assets to the CIA.[38] 'They were good men,' McCarthy told the authors. He quickly bonded with the Tibetans he trained over the years, and even sixty years later recalled how he respected them for their dedication and contributions.[39]

As the training period concluded, the issue of where to air drop the Khampas arose. The CIA lacked updated maps and did not know the names and locations of all the towns in eastern Tibet. It was clearly preferable that the men be inserted into a generally friendly area. To that end, the Khampas were queried about their hometowns, people in the town and the surrounding vicinity.[40] Eventually two drop zones were selected: the first was roughly 37 kilometers south-east of Lhasa close to the Brahmaputra River; the second just south of Lithang, in Khampa territory.[41]

The men would be dropped back into Tibet at an altitude of 15,000 feet and needed special parachutes that had good maneuverability. It was also important to devise a way for the Khampas to jump with equipment, arms, and rations weighing up to 250 pounds—which would stay with the jumper.[42] Roger McCarthy remembered the specially devised parachutes to help the Tibetans land safely and quickly at such a high altitude and felt confident, after trying them out a few times, that they'd work.[43]

In October 1957 the six Tibetans were flown to the US Strategic Air Command recovery field in Kurmola, East Pakistan.[44] Here they boarded an unmarked B-17 Civil Air Transport (CAT) plane for their journey into Tibet.[45] The planes used for these air drops were generally not equipped with modern navigation instruments so it was necessary to use the light of the moon, as there was no radio contact from the ground.[46] Indeed, those involved in the Tibet operation 'cite navigation as the fiercest test of the operation.'[47] Lawrence Ropka, an Air Force navigator on the Tibet project, recalled:

The major challenges were, first and foremost, equipment. We had none. The airplanes did have crude radar but there were no other means of navigation other than celestial and dead reckoning and, of course, eyeball navigation: looking out the window and trying to determine your position relative to various terrain features. There were no radio beacons. There was nothing.[48]

With a full moon as their guide, two of the Khampas—Athar, who was now called Tom; and Lhotse, now Lou—were dropped south of Lhasa. They landed on target on the soft river banks of the Brahmaputra and quickly buried their cache of weapon, grenades, and radio gear. Changing their clothes they appeared as nomads to the unsuspecting villagers, although they each kept a pistol and grenade under their garments.[49] Ten days later they sent a coded message so that Washington knew their first Tibetan trainees were alive. Tom and Lou had been instructed to rendezvous with Gompo Tashi. Fortunately they met up with some Khampa pilgrims, two of whom they knew from the *Buddha Jayanti* festival.[50] Taking them aside and swearing the pair to secrecy, Tom and Lou asked them to take a message to Gompo Tashi and to Lou's younger brother in Lhasa.[51] Their meeting took place outside Lhasa in November 1957; Lou was happy to see his younger brother, who had been staying in Gompo Tashi's household.[52] Tom and Lou's instructions from the CIA were to meet with the Dalai Lama's personal secretary/head of household, the Lord Chamberlain Thupten Woyden Phala.[53] Phala, a trusted confidant, had direct access to His Holiness and Gompo Tashi had access to Phala. Gompo Tashi arranged for Tom and Lou to disguise themselves in monk's robes and the three men met the Dalai Lama's advisor in Norbulingka palace.[54] Here they conveyed Washington's request: would the Dalai Lama make an official request for American assistance?[55] The answer was 'No.' The Dalai Lama did not want to 'provoke Beijing.'[56]

The CIA was not deterred, however. Tom and Lou joined the ranks of the *Chushi Gangdrug* a few months later and the agency proceeded to support the resistance effort which came together the following year.

Due to weather problems, the second group of four Khampas did not parachute back into Tibet until November. Their drop did not go as well: one of the men, Tashi (Dick), hyperventilated and passed out just before the jump; and the others, Wangdu Gyatotsang (Walt), Thondup (Dan), and Tsawang Dorji (Sam), landed on a hillside in a stand of pine trees to the crackle of distant gunfire, believed to be a PLA–Khampa engagement.[57] They landed nearly ten miles from their intended drop zone in Lithang. Still, they were safe and radioed their coordinates. Walt, whose uncle was Gompo Tashi, had been instructed to contact his brothers who were Khampa fighters. Walt, Dan, and Sam made contact with Walt's third brother, but their unit came under Chinese attack and Dan and Sam were killed.[58]

Even though three of the Saipan-trained Tibetans were eventually killed, the CIA viewed the operation as a limited success. CIA support for the resistance certainly bolstered morale among the Khampas. Throughout 1958 and into 1959 the CIA dropped arms and materials to resistance groups using Civil Air Transport and later from Air America C-118 military aircraft. While the C-118 was a bigger airplane, the CAT crews did not like the plane. It had limited 'altitude capacity' which forced the pilots 'to weave their way through the high Himalayas, rather than fly over them.' The radar on the plane was for 'weather avoidance' not for navigation and the side door could not be opened in flight. The door therefore had to be totally removed, meaning the cabin could not be pressurized. This forced the crew and men to wear oxygen masks.[59] The CIA recruited off-season smoke jumpers as pilots to drop supplies and arms into Tibet. The Tibetans would radio their request for an air-drop and provide the location and an alternative location.[60] Then, bearing in mind the possibility of a PLA interception, the CIA would map out the route in and out of Tibet using photos from U-2 spy planes.[61] By the end of November 1958, Khampa fighters had received 18,000 pounds of weapons, ammunition, and communications gear and 300,000 Indian rupees.[62] And by this time, a second group of Khampas were being trained at Camp Hale in Colorado.

The year 1956 was pivotal for two important reasons. First, Washington initiated a covert assistance program in Tibet; and second, despite early difficulties, relations between India and the United States had improved following Nehru's successful December visit to Eisenhower's farm at Gettysburg. Washington recognized India's critical importance to regional stability and had moderated its objections to India's non-aligned policy. Still, even though India's relations with China had begun to fray, there could be no discussion of covert American aid to the Khampas.

1. President Roosevelt and Prime Minister Churchill fishing at Shangri-La, the Presidential retreat in the Catoctin Mountains in 1942. © Popperfoto/Getty Images

103.91802/687

President Roosevelt to the Dalai Lama of Tibet

WASHINGTON, July 3, 1942.

YOUR HOLINESS: Two of my fellow countrymen, Ilia Tolstoy and Brooke Dolan, hope to visit your Pontificate and the historic and widely famed city of Lhasa. There are in the United States of America many persons, among them myself, who, long and greatly interested in your land and people, would highly value such an op-portunity.

As you know, the people of the United States, in association with those of twenty-seven other countries, are now engaged in a war which has been thrust upon the world by nations bent on conquest who are intent upon destroying freedom of thought, of religion, and of action everywhere. The United Nations are fighting today in defense of and for preservation of freedom, confident that we shall be victorious because our cause is just, our capacity is adequate, and our determination is unshakable.

I am asking Ilia Tolstoy and Brooke Dolan to convey to you a little gift in token of my friendly sentiment toward you.

With cordial greetings [etc.]   FRANKLIN D. ROOSEVELT

---

[1] *Infra,* as signed.

2. President Roosevelt's letter to the 14th Dalai Lama, Tenzin Gyatso. © Popperfoto/Getty Images

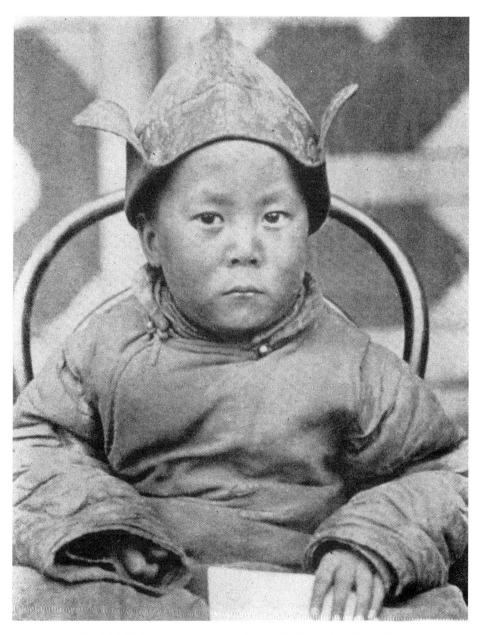

3. The 14th Dalai Lama at the age of nine. © Popperfoto/Getty Images

LOWELL THOMAS

HAMMERSLEY HILL

PAWLING, NEW YORK

November 17, 1950

Dear Mr. Acheson,

Enclosed is a letter and a copy that I would like to send to the Britisher I told you about a year ago -- the last survivor of the Indian Civil Service. Hugh Richardson has just crossed the Himalayas from Lhasa. If Tibet is the key to Central Asia, which I believe it is, then, Richardson is the number one authority on that part of the world.

Wednesday of this week I was asked to come down to the Pentagon and talk to three groups. They kept me holding forth on Tibet continuously for three and a half hours. My son and I have perhaps the most recent information. But, if our Government is taking a serious interest in what is happening out there, Hugh Richardson should be called over for immediate consultation. And when he comes, it might be a good idea if I, or someone else, who knows the subject, would gather together the few other people available who have any worthwhile information. I know that Frank Bessac, the student who just came back from that Sinkiang-Tibetan border tragedy, spent some time in Washington. But, it would be useful to have him. Likewise Colonel Ilia Tolstoy who made the war-time journey across Tibet, and who is now in Los Angeles; and the aged Swedish explorer Sven Hedin, if he is able to come to this country.

As I explained at the Pentagon, the present Chinese invasion of Tibet probably has four major objectives: One, to offset defeats in Korea; two, so they will have a chance to find out something about the mineral and oil resources of Tibet; three, control of Lhasa, Vatican of the Buddhist World; four, to put them along the two thousand mile Indian frontier from which point they will be in a strong immediate trading position, and if they have a long-range plan for controlling the continent of Asia it would give them a much better opportunity to get at India with propaganda. Then, of course, Tibet a few years from now might be an almost perfect air base

X 021436

LOWELL THOMAS

HAMMERSLEY HILL

PAWLING, NEW YORK

2

for any move they might make in the direction of India. It could serve in that way almost immediately. The problem of flying in Tibet will be no different than it is in Bolivia.

Last winter you told me that you thought the least we could do would be to get all the information possible. The number one source for this is our British friend, Hugh Richardson, who at this moment probably is at Government House, Gangtok, Sikkim, doing something about all his possessions which he has just brought by caravan from Lhasa.

Very respectfully yours,

Lowell Thomas

4. Lowell Thomas letter to Secretary of State, Dean Acheson following his difficult trip to Lhasa in 1949. © Heinrich Harrer, VMZ 400.07.04.002 © Ethnographic Museum of the University of Zurich

5. Tibetan army, 1950. © Heinrich Harrer, VMZ 400.07.04.002 © Ethnographic Museum
of the University of Zurich

6. George Patterson, a Scottish missionary arriving in India in March, 1950. He brought
news of the PLA's coming invasion of Tibet. © Heinrich Harrer. VMZ 400.06.242 ©
Ethnographic Museum of the University of Zurich

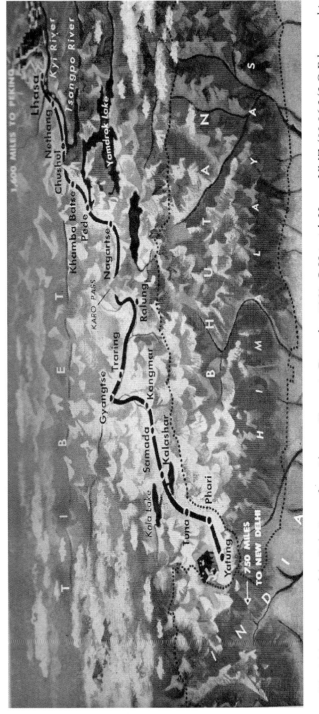

7. The 284 mile route of the Dalai Lama from Lhasa to Yatung in December 1950. © Heinrich Harrer. VMZ 400.06.242 © Ethnographic Museum of the University of Zurich

8. Khampa tribesmen protecting the Dalai Lama on his journey from Lhasa to Yatung in December 1950. © Heinrich Harrer. VMZ 400.06.242 © Ethnographic Museum of the University of Zurich

9. The Dalai Lama in his sedan chair making the trip from Lhasa to Yatung in December 1950. The chair was so heavy that different teams of servants could only carry him for a few hundred yards at a time. © Heinrich Harrer. VMZ 400.08.01.176 © Ethnographic Museum of the University of Zurich

F810001-2013

Enclosure 2 to despatch 68 from Amconsul, Calcutta, August 18, 1951

COPY OF MESSAGE TO THE DALAI LAMA

We understand and sympathize with the reasons
there exist which might lead to your remaining in
Tibet at this time. However, we desire to repeat
our belief that you can best serve your people and
country by evading Communist control at earliest
opportunity and by denouncing agreement with Communist China after you will have reached safe asylum
in India or in Ceylon. Taktser is well and safe in
our country and hopes that you will consider favorably our pledge of assistance previously made you
and your entourage in asylum.

- - - -

EMWilson/blo

10. A Top Secret unsigned letter from the American government to the Dalai Lama. ©
ITAR-TASS/Alamy

11. Prime Minister Nehru greeted by huge crowds in Moscow in 1955. The banner in Hindi and Russian says, "Greetings to Prime Minister Nehru! Welcome!". © ITAR-TASS/Alamy

12. Prime Minister Nehru in Moscow with Prime Minister Khrushchev and Foreign Minister Andrei Gromyko. © ITAR-TASS/Alamy

13. Tibetans gather to support the Dalai Lama at the Potala Palace in March 1959. He fled to India on March 17, 1959. © AFP/Getty Images

14. Chinese Proclamation in Lhasa in April 1959 after the March uprising calling on Tibetans to give their allegiance to the Panchen Lama after the Dalai Lama's departure. ©
Gamma-Keystone/Getty Images

15. Lezlee at home with Gyalo Thondup, the Dalai Lama's brother in Darjeeling, India in December 2012. © Lezlee Brown Halper

16. The exile of the Dalai Lama in India 1959. © Paris Match Archive/Getty Images

17. The Dalai Lama offering Prime Minister Nehru a traditional scarf (khata) on his first visit to Delhi in September 1959. Public domain.

18. Henry Kissinger and Zhou En-lai meeting in Beijing in 1971. © AFP/Getty Images

27

THE SOUTH ASIAN RUBIK'S CUBE

In the early months of 1956, US–India relations had hit rock bottom. Now Washington was not only concerned about India's relationship with the PRC but also their improving relations with Moscow. In the summer of 1955 Nehru had issued a joint communiqué with Soviet Premier Nikolai Bulganin, calling for strengthened relations between the two countries 'in the economic and cultural fields as well as in scientific and technical research.'[1] The prospect of a communist-non-aligned movement axis gaining momentum and progressing to marginalize the West and America's post-war achievement cast a chill over Washington.

When, at the beginning of 1956, Nehru considered purchasing weapons systems (including bomber aircraft) from the Soviets, the Eisenhower administration was outraged.[2] In private meetings at Nehru's residence in March 1956, John Foster Dulles made it clear that such a move would 'greatly vex' the US–Indian relationship.[3] Dulles, who was so unpopular in India that he needed a security detail to protect him from New Delhi protesters, bluntly told Nehru that the consequences of purchasing aircraft from the Soviet Union 'would be very bad indeed.'[4] He asked:

Why do you do this? You can buy planes from the British. You can buy planes from us. I cannot see why you should buy planes from the Russians knowing that it would make it almost impossible for [the] US to carry on its efforts [to] assist you materially in your second five-year plan.[5]

In the end Nehru concluded that he did not want 'to slam the door on American aid nor to carry the *Hindi–Russi-bhai-bhai* business too far' and purchased British planes.[6]

Remarkably, Dulles wrote that he and the prime minister had been able to 'take our hair down' and have an animated and intimate discussion.[7] Dulles wrote that he 'was amused that toward the end of the conference he [Nehru] was sitting on the back of the sofa with his feet on the seat.'[8] What struck Dulles most about the exchange was Nehru's vehemence on the US alliance with Pakistan. Dulles wrote to the President that:

I never appreciated before the full depth of their feeling. I had assumed that India with its far greater population and economic strength would feel relatively immune from any serious threat. However, they feel that Pakistan, or at least West Pakistan, is essentially a military state, largely run by the Army, that they are a martial people, that they are fanatically dedicated to Islam and may develop the urge to attack India …[9]

Dulles' comments on the US alliance with Pakistan underscored his limitations, according to historian Robert McMahon, who was highly critical and wrote: 'Dulles's admission that he never really understood the reasons for the Indian furore over US aid to Pakistan almost defies comprehension.'[10] And while the secretary of state came away with a greater understanding of the deep resentment Nehru felt for the US–Pakistan military alliance, he still could not understand or accept Nehru's policy of non-alignment. A few months later he told an audience at Iowa State University that he thought that 'except under very exceptional circumstances, neutralism was an immoral and short-sighted conception.'[11] This view was not unlike that of Vice President Nixon who, while on tour in Southeast Asia a few weeks later, said, in what seems a contradiction, that the United States respected the right of a country to 'chart its own course,' but 'the US had no sympathy for the kind of neutralism which draws no moral distinction between the Communist world and the free world.'[12] As dysfunctional as the bilateral relationship was, the US could not fail to see the continued—and growing—importance of India in the region. As the largest free country in Asia—indeed, in the world—the United States saw India as the 'key to keeping further Communist aggression from infiltrating the region.'[13] With that in mind, Dulles extended President Eisenhower's invitation to visit Washington later that year, in the hope that relations would improve.[14]

Nehru's second visit to Washington

Nehru visited Washington for a second time in December 1956. After his disastrous 1949 visit, Washington officials were cautious and better prepared. President Eisenhower was thoroughly briefed. The administration was aware that the two leaders would not always find common ground on certain foreign policy issues, but was determined to establish 'a closer personal relationship' with Nehru.[15] The president not only read detailed background briefs on India, and was briefed on relevant foreign and economic issues, but also received a comprehensive list of Nehru's personal preferences. There would be no excessive displays as there had been seven years earlier.

Leaving no room for cultural misunderstandings, administration officials contacted the staff at the Indian embassy in Washington. The president learned that Nehru was an incessant smoker, and 'usually refrain[ed] from drinking any alcoholic beverages' although 'he may sip various selections of wine during a meal, but fruit juices should be served before and during meals.'[16] While it was noted that the Indian prime minister had 'no dietary limitations,' US officials were told that it was considered 'inadvisable to serve beef or pork at formal luncheons and dinners.'[17] Perhaps most amusing were the rather lengthy 'step-by step' instructions on how Nehru's tea was to be prepared and served. The Indian embassy offered to provide Nehru's special brand of tea. State Department officials (noting 'apparently this is something of a ritual') were told: 'Place the tea leaves in a pot using one teaspoon of tea "for the pot". At the moment that the water begins to boil it should be poured on the teas in the pot.' The prime minister liked his tea 'stronger than most Americans.'[18]

Policy-makers had clear objectives for the prime minister's visit: to 'develop good will … increase the Prime Minister's understanding of US foreign policy [and] bring out the broad significant area of agreement between the United States and India.'[19] Of course administration planners knew that Eisenhower and Nehru would ultimately 'agree to disagree' on foreign policy issues like Kashmir and aid to Pakistan, but were keen 'to give a sympathetic hearing to the Prime Minister's views and make him feel he has been consulted on the problems discussed.'[20] At a minimum, it was hoped that the meetings would, perhaps, allow a 'closer personal relationship' between the two leaders.[21]

Washington's preparation and open mind paid off, and Nehru and Eisenhower did not have any major disagreements. In light of the Suez crisis and particularly the Soviet response in Hungary, each of which highlighted for the world the dark side of communism, Nehru was more receptive to Eisenhower's overtures. Nehru commented to the president that the Hungarian affair 'spelled the death knell of International Communism.'[22] He continued:

[T]his is a propitious moment—because of this great blunder of the Soviets—for the free world to move in by strengthening the faith and hope of those who would naturally like to live in independence and freedom, but who have been at least partially misled by the Communists' doctrine.[23]

Reporting to the State Department, the embassy in Delhi broadly agreed: 'the moment of history has arrived which if seized and exploited, can give [the] US much firmer anti-Communist and anti-Red China counterpoise in India.'[24] Still, one would like to know who, exactly, Nehru thought had been 'misled by the Communists' doctrine.' Perhaps of greatest significance to Tibet, by 1956 Nehru had begun to experience a growing 'sense of disquiet' over border tensions with China.[25]

Eisenhower and Nehru did not sign any major protocols, nor did they significantly narrow their differences on issues such as admitting communist China to the UN or Washington's military alliance with Pakistan. Significantly, there were no disputes or even informal debates of any kind.[26] They met privately at Eisenhower's farm in Gettysburg, Pennsylvania. At the time of the Nehru visit no other foreign statesman had been taken to Gettysburg for talks with the President.[27] It had not, however, been entirely easy for the president. Eisenhower told Dulles that the talks had been 'pretty good' and that they were 'in the realm of philosophy'—but that Nehru was 'practically impossible to hear.'[28]

In a glowing report of his US trip Nehru wrote that 'the US government went out of their way in showing me honor.'[29] Nehru was pleased that he and his daughter were invited to lunch at the White House upon their arrival and that he was taken to Eisenhower's farm.[30] Talks had covered a wide range of global personalities and issues, including India–China relations, India's relations with the Soviet Union, and Soviet policies. Not surprisingly, however, some topics were not discussed, including the president's authorization for training Tibetan resistance fighters.

US–India relations: Some progress

A month after his meeting with Nehru, Eisenhower approved directive NSC 5701 which outlined the administration's policy toward South Asia. The region's importance in the global effort to stem the spread of communism was stressed. The report said that 'India has emerged as a foremost representative of the Asian–African or "Bandung" region and is the leading political contender with Communist China in Asia.'[31] Further it was noted that 'It is in the US national interest that the genuine independence of India be strengthened and that a moderate, non-Communist government, succeed in consolidating the allegiance of the Indian people.'[32]

Significantly, administration views toward nations embracing a policy of non-alignment shifted that year. NSC 5701 indicated that the administration had begun to view relations with India in less than Manichean terms, arriving at a more nuanced understanding of Nehru's position. It noted that non-alignment was 'not merely a philosophical attitude'; rather, Indians considered that 'their own national interests will be best served by an independent international policy.'[33] It posited that Nehru's policies posed 'an undeniable dilemma' for the United States that 'on occasion' would bring India 'into opposition with US programs and activities.'[34] But 'over the long run, the risks to US security from a weak and vulnerable India would be greater than the risks of a stable and influential India.'[35] NSC 5701 went on to state that:

A weak India might well lead to the loss of South and Southeast Asia to Communism. A strong India would be a successful example of an alternative to Communism in an Asian context and would permit the gradual development of the means to enforce its external security interests against Communist Chinese expansion into South and Southeast Asia.[36]

Eisenhower now concluded that America 'was better off with India following a policy of non-alignment than actively joining our side, with the consequent added burden on the American taxpayer and 2,000 miles more of active frontier' (with a communist state).[37] And while some officials believed that 'India is Asian, and Indians no matter how westernized are Asians and often unpredictable to Westerners,' it would be administration policy to give economic assistance to India's second five-year plan.[38] In accordance with the directive, Washington increased its aid package to India in 1957 by $225 million. During Eisenhower's second term aid to India grew from $400 million in 1957 to $822 million by 1960.[39]

Importantly, just as India had begun to gain Washington's favor, Pakistan began to lose it. The administration was frustrated over Pakistan's 'chronic political instability and recurrent economic crises.'[40] The president wasted few words when he told his cabinet before the adoption of NSC 5701 in January 1957 that it had been costly to have Pakistan as a military ally and that 'in point of fact we were doing practically nothing for Pakistan except in the form of military aid.'[41] This, the president said, was 'perhaps the worst kind of plan and decision we could have made. It was a terrible error, but we now seem hopelessly involved in it.'[42]

Historian Robert McMahon concurs with the caveat that if 'Indo–American relations had been spared some of the tensions present since independence, perhaps US officials would have been less willing to run the risks associated with choosing Pakistan as an ally.'[43] Washington concluded that: '[S]o long as India remains non-Communist and democratically oriented, no serious problem is posed to present American policy. On the contrary, Indian influence contributes to the stability of parts of free Asia.'[44]

India and China

As tensions eased between India and the United States, India's relationship with China continued to deteriorate over border issues. Nehru had agreed not to delineate a border at the time of the Panchsheel signing. But by 1959 this folly could no longer be pushed aside. Nehru could not keep the growing number of 'border incidents' from his parliament or the media. The disputes were centered in the region of Ladakh, as both China and India claimed the Aksai Chin plateau. China was forging ahead with airfield and road construction in Tibet, some of which had extended into Aksai Chin. In addition there were disputes and incursions along the north-eastern border of Arunachal Pradesh, which India shared with China.[45]

When Nehru saw Chinese-drawn maps including Indian territory as part of China in a *China Pictorial* magazine of July 1958, he was incandescent.[46] He wrote to Chou En-lai to remind him of their past conversations about border issues. Chou reassured him that the Chinese maps were outdated and would be corrected. In response, Chou further reminded Nehru that 'no treaty or agreement on the Sino–Indian boundary had ever been concluded between the Chinese central government and the Indian government.'[47]

A declassified top secret CIA report sums up the Chinese strategy:

It was basic Chinese policy early in Peiping's relations with New Delhi not to claim territory in writing or orally, but only on the basis of maps. Thus the Chinese claim to NEFA [North East Frontier Agency] appeared only as a line on Chinese maps dipping at points about 100 miles south of the McMahon line. Chou En-lai, in talks with Nehru in 1954 and 1956, treated the Chinese maps not as representing Peiping's 'claim' but, on the contrary, as old maps handed down from the previous regime which had 'not yet' been corrected. This provided the Chinese premier with a means for concealing Peiping's long range intention of surfacing Chinese claims at some time in the future.[48]

With roads built across the Askai Chin plateau, the Chinese now had a permanent military presence in the region and easy access to Tibet. They had begun construction in 1956 and finished in the latter part of 1957. The Chinese knew that the Indian prime minister lacked the will and the means to challenge their claims. Even when the Askai Chin incursions were brought to Nehru's attention by Subimal Dutt, the Indian foreign secretary, it wasn't until months later in April 1958 that the prime minister called for an inspection of the area. When Dutt wrote to Nehru about the road, the prime minister responded:

I shall gladly discuss this matter with you, JS and Gopalachari. Meanwhile, my reaction is that we should send a reconnoitering party there in spring with clear instructions that they should not come into conflict with the Chinese. I do not think it is desirable to have air reconnaissance. In fact, I do not see what good this can do us. Even a land reconnaissance will not perhaps be very helpful. However, it may bring some further facts to our notice.[49]

Indeed, India confronted a fait accompli. Now any negotiations would have to begin from this point and not the McMahon line.

Chou's guile

CIA analysts called the Chinese plan a 'five-year masterpiece of guile, executed—and probably planned in large part—by Chou En-lai.'[50] Indeed, each time Nehru brought up the issue of maps through Panikkar, Beijing's response had been that there had not been time to revise them, which gave Nehru the expectation that at some point in the future they would be revised. 'Chou played on Nehru's Asian, anti-imperialist mental attitude, his proclivity to temporize, and his sincere desire for an amicable Sino–Indian relationship.'[51] Above all, in these early years, the Chinese plan was to maintain cordial relations with Nehru in an effort to avoid any hostility. Chou and his advisors were certainly aware that Nehru was more conciliatory toward them than toward his opposition, the press, and even some of his own members of the cabinet.[52] To that end, angering Nehru was to be avoided. The preferred avenue for exchange on this matter was the diplomatic channel, where Panikkar was the perfect foil. In this way, neither the border discussions nor the discussions regarding Tibet came under public scrutiny—the public was simply unaware.

Sino–Indian relations began to sour as events spiraled downhill, culminating at the end of 1958 with the Chinese ambush and capture of an Indian military patrol on the Askai Chin plateau. This began a costly and bitter Sino–Indian border dispute which, along with recriminations over Tibet, created a maelstrom which eventually devolved into a brief war in 1961–2. The border dispute remains unresolved to the present day.

Tibet and Sino–Indian relations

The Tibet question had now become a significant factor in Sino–Indian relations. Nehru thought that the Chinese had relaxed their control over Tibet after the Tibetan uprising of 1956 and was convinced that the PRC would respect Tibetan autonomy if other powers did not intervene.[53] But by September 1957 he began to see the situation differently. When the Indian political officer in Sikkim paid a visit to Tibet that month, the PRC had instructed the Dalai Lama and the Panchen Lama 'to accord him no welcome' because, Mao claimed, 'Western imperialists were influencing Nehru and he might side with them.'[54]

In a note given to the Indian chargé d'affaires in Beijing, the Chinese accused India of 'carrying on subversive and disruptive activities against China's Tibet region under the instigation and direction of the US and the "Chiang Kai-shek clique" in Kalimpong'—a possible reference to Gyalo.[55] While available documents are unclear on whether Nehru knew about US covert contacts with the Kalimpong enclave (possibly through his intelligence service's links to MI5) Nehru acted with surprise to China's accusations, asserting that the Indian government 'had no evidence that the US Government and the Kuomintang regime are using Kalimpong as a base for disruptive activities against China's Tibet region.'[56]

Even with these outward signs of trouble, Nehru would not sanction any change in Indian policy nor take any action on behalf of the Tibetans.[57] In the summer of 1958 Nehru decided, at the Dalai Lama's invitation, to make a trip to the land in question and see for himself how the Chinese were treating the Tibetans. But Beijing denied Nehru entry to Tibet and he was only briefly able to glimpse the situation in eastern Tibet while visiting Bhutan that fall.[58] On 5 October 1958 Nehru wrote to Menon that 'Tibet was occupied territory whose people lived in fear of their masters and where the Khampas were in revolt.'[59]

Nehru's assessment was correct. It was hardly imaginable that within six months the Dalai Lama and thousands of his followers would be on Indian soil and in need of support, and that his improvised and apparently imprudent relationship with Beijing would unravel.

28

THE DALAI LAMA LEAVES TIBET

The year 1958 came to a close amidst heightened tensions; uprisings had become commonplace and events began to spiral out of control. In the east the PLA continued their determined destruction of monasteries and villages, leaving the impression that no one was safe. In August of that year the Chinese had demanded that the Tibetan Kashag dispatch Tibetan troops to confront and disarm the Khampas. Amidst rising tensions this was blocked by the Dalai Lama, who thought it 'unthinkable to send out a Tibetan army to fight against Tibetans whose "crime" was to defend Tibet.'[1] In Lhasa the breaking point had been reached. The Dalai Lama recalled that he was 'very near despair.'[2] And then, he wrote in January 1959, 'either by accident or design, the Chinese brought the final crisis on us.'[3]

In early 1959 the Dalai Lama agreed to accept the Chinese authorities' invitation to attend a theatrical production at their military headquarters in Lhasa, though no date had been set. It was during this period that the young leader was to take his final examinations, which involved a lengthy public debate before monks and lamas from the monasteries in and around Lhasa. The intense preparation and study had meant that, despite Chinese insistence, the Dalai Lama was hesitant to commit to a date. But the Chinese authorities were insistent. After two curt messages demanding the Dalai Lama's presence, delivered personally by the officers on the staff of General Tan Kuan-san, the 'political commissar' in Lhasa, the date of 10 March was agreed.[4] The Dalai Lama was ordered to attend the performance by himself without bodyguards at the military camp located just under two miles from his Norbulingka palace.[5]

That March, Lhasa was crowded with people participating in a religious celebration called the Monlam festival. Included were refugees from eastern Tibet, Lhasa residents, monks, and Khampas, who had come from every corner of the country to celebrate. As the festivities were concluding and many began to filter back to their homes and villages, the rumor spread that the Dalai Lama was expected at the PLA military headquarters and had been instructed to arrive alone and without bodyguards. Even though many had left the city, thousands of monks and Khampas still remained—the Dalai Lama estimated there were upwards of 100,000 visitors still in Lhasa, more than the city had ever seen.[6] The religious nature of the festival and the massive influx of people on the streets formed a combustible mix, especially when ignited with the rumor that His Holiness would be abducted. 'Rumors were falling like hailstones,' recalled one Lhasa resident.[7]

On the morning of 10 March thousands of Tibetans—some estimate close to 30,000 people—gathered in front of the Dalai Lama's summer palace, the Norbulingka. The crowd opposed His Holiness' attendance at the 'theatrical event' at the Chinese military camp and were determined to prevent this 'at any cost.'[8] It was an ominous moment. Neither the Tibetan Kashag nor the Chinese could disperse the crowd which quickly turned to violence, attacking those suspected of pro-Chinese sympathies.[9]

In the coming days the Dalai Lama played for time. Confined in the Norbulingka, he wrote a letter to General Tan Kuan-san and sent three of his ministers to the military headquarters hoping to diffuse the situation.[10] The Chinese response was to train their howitzers on both the Norbulingka and Potala palaces.

A week had passed and then on the morning of 17 March two rounds were fired; the shells landed near the Norbulingka. The Dalai Lama heard the shots and thought 'the end had come': the Chinese had begun their attack and would destroy the palace.[11] The Kashag and the state Oracle were consulted: it was decided that the Dalai Lama would leave Lhasa. He wrote: 'The decision was not a small matter: the stakes were high: the whole future of Tibet depended on it.'[12]

They left under the cover of night; Phala, the lord chamberlain, organized the small parties which consisted of the Dalai Lama's mother, his youngest brother, his eldest sister, four ministers, his two tutors and bodyguards. Before leaving, the Dalai Lama went to his chapel for a silent farewell—the monks praying had no idea they would not see him again.[13] At the altar he left the traditional white Tibetan scarf as his symbol of farewell.[14]

At the designated hour he removed his saffron robes and dressed as a soldier, complete with a fur hat and a rifle to complete the disguise. His mind was 'drained of all emotion.'[15] He was led outside the palace by a soldier. There, he took off his glasses and slung the rifle over his shoulder.[16]

The small party crossed the Brahmaputra River and met with his other family members—his mother and sister were dressed as Khampas—and soldiers and Khampas to protect him on the long and difficult journey to India. They made their way toward the difficult 16,000 foot Che-la mountain pass which separates Lhasa from the Tsangpo Valley. At the top of the mountain pass, the Dalai Lama notes he turned for a last look at his homeland.[17] After five days of travel they were welcomed at the Chongye Riwodechen Monastery in the Chongye valley in southern Tibet.[18] Phala, through his Khampa contacts, had managed to get a message to Tom and Lou (the Khampas who had been trained on Saipan island), who met the party at Chongye.[19]

Using his small battery-operated radio Tom contacted Okinawa and passed the coded message that the Dalai Lama was alive and well.[20]

From here it was a week's travel over high mountain passes to Lhuntse Dzong. 'Every day that week,' the Dalai Lama recalled, 'we had to cross a pass.'[21] At the top of the Sabo-la pass at 19,000 feet they encountered a blizzard.[22] In some places along the pass the snow had not melted and it was sheer ice. After a week's travel with Tom and Lou as escorts, the party reached their final destination in Tibet, Lhuntse Dzong, a stronghold base of the Volunteer Freedom Fighters, 60 miles from the Indian border.[23] This dzong or fort was like a small Potala palace and they were met with fanfare by officials, Khampas, and monks; more than 1,000 people greeted the young leader.[24]

A few days after the Dalai Lama left Lhasa the Chinese began a full assault with artillery and bombs. Much of the Norbulingka was destroyed, in addition to other monasteries and schools. Although the Tibetans fought back with arms received from monasteries and the government arsenals, the Chinese flag was raised over the Potala Palace on 23 March. Hearing the news of the devastation in Lhasa, and aware the Chinese had dissolved the Tibetan Kashag, the Dalai Lama repudiated the 17 Point Agreement and officially proclaimed the renewed Tibetan government.[25] On 29 March Phala asked the two CIA operatives to send a message to Washington to request asylum in India; not knowing whether or not Nehru would agree, the party began the trek toward the Indian border.[26]

On their final night in Tibet, at a small settlement called Mangmang, the party learned that the Dalai Lama would be granted asylum.[27] He spent his last night on Tibetan soil huddled in his leaking tent as the skies opened up, soaking all and sundry in heavy rains. It had been a week of appalling weather, the Dalai Lama remembered, with blizzards and snow glare and now rain.[28] By morning the Dalai Lama was too ill to travel. On 31 March a weak and ill Dalai Lama was helped onto the back of a dzomo (a cross between a yak and a cow), 'an equable animal with an easy gait.' It had been an inauspicious beginning, and 'on that primeval Tibetan transport' the young leader left for India.[29]

Reaction in Washington: 'Nothing is ordinary in Tibet'[30]

The next day, 1 April, CIA Director Allen Dulles received a desperate cable from Tom and Lou that was passed to the president. The emotional tone is palpable:

Many Tibetan Monks and lay people were killed. Please inform the world about the suffering of the Tibetan people to make us free from the misery of the Chinese Communist operations. You must help us as soon as possible and send us weapons for 30,000 men and airplane. All Tibetans and Khambas are suffering from the Chinese Communists.[31]

At the end of April, more than two years after the CIA had approved and initiated covert operations in Tibet, Allen Dulles now briefed the Senate Foreign Relations Committee. His comment that 'nothing is ordinary in Tibet' had the added advantage of being true.[32] He explained to committee chairman Fulbright, thirteen senators, and the accompanying CIA staff that the CIA 'had been following the Tibetan situation very closely since 1956 when we began to receive reports indicating the spread of a Tibetan revolt against the Chinese ...'[33] DCI Dulles briefed the senators on the history of Tibet and the events leading up to the 1959 revolt and the Dalai Lama's dramatic escape to India. He responded to questions about the Dalai Lama's two brothers and answered questions on the relationship between the Dalai Lama and the Panchen Lama.[34]

On the question of the Dalai Lama's brothers, had Dulles been in a more forthright mood, he would have said that his brothers were actively involved in the resistance, but in keeping with his and the president's concerns about intelligence, Dulles said little about their relations with the CIA. Senator Mansfield asked the DCI what the Dalai Lama's brothers were doing in the United States. Mansfield inquired, 'Are they at Johns Hopkins?'[35] Dulles responded, 'I don't think they are now. We are in close touch with both of them. They have been pretty busy recently on other matters.'[36] On more important issues, Dulles told the committee that the Chinese were now 'mopping up the rebels' and that he had messages from 'our people with the Chamdo tribesmen' that they are 'short of food and ammunition.'[37]

Dulles himself was obviously moved, having told attendees at a 23 April 1956 NSC meeting that the CIA received pathetic reports about the 'people on the frontier.'[38] Dissents, patriots, and insurgents had been severely beaten and driven to the border areas where they were hungry, vulnerable, and exposed to the elements; they were desperate to cross into India and safety.[39] Tibetans were in fact starving, and the messages became more and more desperate pleading for Washington's help.[40] In our interview with Thomas Parrott, he strongly reiterated this point. 'The messages from Tibet were pathetic; the men were starving to death, picking up nuts and anything they found on the ground to eat. They were begging for our help,' he said with great sadness.[41] Not only was there an extreme food shortage, but also there was little ammunition to fight the Chinese. Dulles knew before appearing at the Senate Foreign Relations Committee that the Khampa rebels had been 'pretty well knocked to pieces.'[42]

That April day, speaking before a select group of Foreign Relations Committee members, the DCI reflected Eisenhower's earlier calculation on the Soviet invasion of Hungary when he compared the situation in Tibet to the 'Hungarian operation.'[43] He was brutally clear when Fulbright asked whether there was any possibility of the Tibetans resisting the Chinese. His answer was a simple 'No.' He added:

They haven't the ammunition; they haven't the organization. They may be able to reassemble in certain mountains areas there and hold out for some time. But this is terribly difficult country. I mean there is no cover. There isn't the cover that there is for guerrilla operations.[44]

Before Dulles was finished with his appraisal of the Tibetan situation, Fulbright interrupted to say: 'This is interesting but I don't believe there is something we can do about it.'[45] To which Dulles responded: 'We can, I think, do this, and we are.'[46] Although the next line is redacted, one assumes Dulles stated the obvious, namely that an operation was already underway in Tibet providing arms, food, and medicine.[47] He went on to say that it was important to get the 'Southeast Asians to understand what has gone on here.'[48] Again, Dulles' words to Fulbright underscore the US government's intention to be certain that the world learned of the horror and savagery of the Chinese assault on Tibet and its culture. He said:

Hungary was done openly right before the world, and they could not suppress the news of this. Here in these great mountain areas they can suppress the news. The facts are not really known. What we are trying to do, not tied into the United States or anything the United States has done, but in other ways, is to get this information out. For example, we have played back information that we received to the Dalai Lama and then from the Dalai Lama to Nehru and to the Indians.[49]

Fulbright accepted the point, saying: 'I agree it has propaganda value to impress upon Southeast Asia the danger of the Chinese Communists. It would be very valuable.'[50] Taken with the urgency of the situation, Fulbright asked Dulles if there was any 'direct physical assistance' that could be given, to which Dulles answered, 'at this time it would be best to help the refugees coming across into India.'[51]

Dulles left much unsaid in the Senate Foreign Relations Committee hearing room that day. Proceeding under presidential directions, he offered sufficient information to describe the policy and generally assess the progress. Further detail would have required decisions to release information about specific operations, sources, and methods—something the CIA rarely does.

The discussion thus centered on how best to utilize Tibet's dramatic struggle—the brutality, starvation, and decimation of Tibet's religious culture—against the seasoned PLA troops, newly recycled from, to condemn China in the global discourse of the time. The memo, parts of which remain heavily redacted, read:

The Tibetan revolt is a windfall for the US particularly since it tends to harden Asian sentiment against the Chicoms. Therefore, regardless of other considerations, it would appear to be in the US interest (1) to keep the rebellion going as long as possible and (2) to give it maximum emphasis in all public information media. Physical support for the rebels will be extremely difficult, both logistically and politically.[52]

It is clear from the memo and from Dulles' closed meeting with the Senate Foreign Relations Committee that the revolt in Tibet helped to advance US interests in the region. Accordingly, the government was willing to help the Dalai Lama because it believed that a government-in-exile 'would be a political asset for the Free World.'[53] As the secretary of defense, Neil McElory, told Dulles at the NSC meeting a week earlier, Washington had to make sure to keep 'the ruthless Chinese Communist action against Tibet on the front pages.'[54]

In McElroy's view the Tibetan situation should be treated as a 'new Hungary.'[55] Secretary of State Christian A. Herter summed up what seemed to be the president's and the State Department's policy when he said: 'We must be careful that we ourselves do not appear to stimulate reactions to the Chinese Communists' action in Tibet, but rather covertly assist the Asian people themselves to keep the Tibetan action prominently before the world.'[56]

On 23 April, the same day that Dulles was briefing the NSC, the CIA station in Delhi sent a full briefing on the Dalai Lama's first meeting with an official of India's Ministry of External Affairs.[57] The Dalai Lama, very weak from dysentery, had crossed into India on 31 March, and after a five-day journey finally found rest at the ancient monastery in Towang. Here he was met by an Indian official who accompanied him further south to Bomdila, a Buddhist enclave, where he would meet P. N. Menon,[58] a career civil servant in the Indian Ministry of External Affairs.[59] At Bomdila the Dalai Lama spoke critically of Nehru to Menon, saying that the prime minister had misled him in 1951 and again in Delhi in 1957. The Dalai Lama made his point clearly: he would not 'betray his people a third time.'[60] From Bomdila the Dalai Lama went to Tezpur, where he was met by a cluster of journalists and well-wishers; and there he made his first public statement.

The Dalai Lama began his press statement at Tezpur by saying: 'It has always been accepted that the Tibetan people are different from the Han people of China. There has always been a strong desire for independence on the part of the Tibetan people.'[61] He told reporters that, contrary to Chinese reports, he fled Lhasa of his own free will and was not under duress; and then the world heard of the events in Tibet over the past nine years. On his journey from Tezpur to Mussoorie to meet Nehru, thousands gathered on the streets to greet him as his convoy drove by, chanting 'Long Live the Dalai Lama.'[62] Finally, on 24 April, the Dalai Lama met Prime Minister Nehru in a face-to face meeting at Birla House in Mussoorie.

The Dalai Lama made it clear to the Indian prime minister that Tibetans must have their independence.[63] The meeting was emotionally charged—Nehru banged his fists on the table a number of times. He could not restrain himself and angrily shouted: 'That is not possible! You say you want independence and in the same breath you say you do not want bloodshed. Impossible!' Reprising his infamous exchanges with US Ambassador Loy Henderson, Nehru's lower lip quivered with anger.[64]

The Dalai Lama now clearly understood Nehru's position and thus his own. He had been granted asylum and would now proceed to establish his government in exile at Dharamsala in northern India. Meanwhile, though the future of his people was less certain than he had hoped, his story and the story of China's perfidy in Tibet had swept the globe, drawing millions to his cause.[65] Importantly, the Tibet story was now, among those familiar with it, of a piece with the Korean struggle against communist invasion in 1951 and Hungary's brave attempt to resist the Soviet invasion in 1956.

29

TIBET AT THE UNITED NATIONS

By the time the Dalai Lama reached Tezpur he had been reunited with his brother Gyalo, who was now his advisor and a reliable channel to Washington. In their discussions, the Dalai Lama was told of the full extent of American involvement in Tibet and then gave his brother a message to be passed to Washington. The CIA received the Dalai Lama's request on 23 April, the day before he met with Nehru. It was passed to the State Department and then to the president.[1] The Dalai Lama thanked the American government for its past help and requested supplies for the Tibetan resistance. But more importantly he asked the Americans, just as he intended to ask Nehru the next day, to recognize the 'Free Tibetan Government' and hoped Washington would influence other countries to do the same.[2] Acting Secretary of State Douglas Dillon urged, in a memo to the president, that 'we should avoid taking a position which may appear to encourage the Dalai Lama to seek international recognition in the absence of clear knowledge of the firmness of his plans or of the attitudes which other friendly states are likely to have.'[3] The State Department was concerned about the possible ramifications for US–India relations should the US recognize the Free Tibetan Government, particularly as the Dalai Lama was now on Indian soil. In addition, Washington was hopeful that other Asian states would support the Dalai Lama. This point and another more salient point were made in an attachment from the CIA sent to the State Department on 23 April for the president:

As Dalai Lama has not publicly asked for international recognition of Free Tibetan Government, Department assumes his request for US recognition is probably intended to feel out US attitude as guide to his future moves. While US recognition could be granted if it proves in our national interest, such step will have to be carefully considered in light of reactions of other friendly governments were the US to take such step.[4]

The matter of exactly what the national interest was, or was not, was partially addressed in a rather timid memo from Assistant Secretary of State Parsons to Secretary of State Christian Herter in October 1959.[5] Arguing that recognition was not in the US national interest, the assistant secretary said that few countries would follow the US lead and that such an action would damage the prestige and influence Washington then enjoyed among Asian leaders. He urged that Washington consider world opinion and, in a mystifying phrase, added, 'above all Department does not wish [to] give impression we are endeavoring to take advantage of Tibetan situation for general Cold War purposes.'[6]

Washington responded to the Dalai Lama in June, underscoring its concern and sympathy for the Tibetan struggle against the Chinese communists and assuring the young leader that the US desired to be helpful.[7] The president made it clear that the message was to be given to the Dalai Lama orally and in strictest confidence.[8] Eisenhower's final point was clear; he said:

[H]e [Dalai Lama] should be told that it is obviously in his best interest to avoid a break with Nehru if such a break can be avoided without prejudicing his own basic principles and negotiating position. If a break nevertheless occurs, the Dalai Lama should avoid aggravating it. However, if he is forced to leave India permanently, we will assist in supporting him and an appropriate entourage, and we will also undertake to help him in finding asylum elsewhere.[9]

The president wanted the Dalai Lama to know that 'if he should decide to go to the United Nations, the United States would do whatever it appropriately could to assist him.[10] Clearly the Dalai Lama would have preferred a more fulsome endorsement. The Tibetans were also unhappy that the message had been transmitted orally—just as they had been when oral messages were passed by Ambassador Henderson. Acting Secretary of State Murphy recommended a brief written communication, to which the president agreed.[11]

At the 30 July NSC meeting CIA Director Allen Dulles addressed events in Tibet. He commented on Nehru's conundrum, saying: 'Nehru was in a dilemma between widespread sympathy in India for Tibet and the need to conciliate Communist China.'[12] He noted that Nehru was attempting to remain neutral and give the Dalai Lama asylum while avoiding 'political support of the Tibetan independence movement.' Dulles also told the NSC:

[T]he US has put feelers in Buddhist countries about accepting the Dalai Lama, but no country has been receptive, probably because there is reluctance to alienate Communist China and because there are so many different sects of Buddhism.[13]

Dulles said, 'in any case the US is faced with the problem of what to do about the Dalai Lama.'[14]

The US had options, of course, but it also had a wide range of considerations that included bilateral relations with India, prospective relations with China, and concern, in the context of Cold War tensions, about making the Dalai Lama seem a creature of US interests. Washington was also aware of the delicacy of even tacitly encouraging Tibetan independence in the eyes of US allies who retained colonies.

Britain and France, in particular, sought to prevent the issue from gaining traction in the form of a resolution in the UN General Assembly. On the other hand, the US opposed communist oppression and supported self-determination—hence Dulles' question. The answer should have had something to do with walking between the raindrops…

Tibet and the United Nations

Two days before Dulles' briefing to the NSC, Under Secretary of State Robert Murphy met with representatives of the department's Far East Bureau, the Bureau of Near Eastern Affairs, and the Bureau of International Organizations (which coordinates Washington's relations with the UN) to advise them that Washington would support the Dalai Lama's public appeal—should he proceed—at the United Nations.[15] Secretary Herter made clear that it would be better for the appeal to be made soon. He advised not to accuse the Chinese of aggression as Tibet's status as an independent nation was disputed, but rather to underscore Tibetan suffering and the denial of their human rights.[16] He instructed that this be communicated to the Dalai Lama in India. Washington would then arrange invitations for the Dalai Lama to visit Asian countries to garner their support. Washington had informed the Dalai Lama that it would 'defer' recognition of a Tibetan government-in-exile for the moment, adding that this could perhaps be revisited after the appeal at the United Nations.[17]

And so Washington began the task of contacting its embassies in Buddhist countries to support the Tibetan appeal. Washington was helped by the International Commission of Jurists, which released a 204-page report that June. The report, entitled 'The Question of Tibet and Rule of Law,' found that the Chinese slaughter of Tibetans in Tibet was contrary to the Genocide Convention of 1948, and that these deliberate acts were meant to destroy the Tibetan religion and the Tibetan nation.

But securing support for Tibet's appeal was difficult and complicated, and by September, as the death toll mounted in Tibet, the Dalai Lama had gained a depressing view of the phrase 'in our national interest.' Some of this became evident in the 4 September meeting between the Dalai Lama and Winthrop Brown, the US chargé d'affaires in Delhi. Brown asked if the Dalai Lama had received any indications, particularly from Asian countries, of either sponsorship or support for his case at the UN.[18] Brown reported to the department that the Dalai Lama 'made a rather helpless gesture with his hands indicating he had not had much response—adding that missions with whom he had spoken since arriving in Delhi had not been unable to make any commitments.'[19] Brown concluded: 'I gather he is not too optimistic he will get much support.'[20] The next morning Brown raised the matter with the Indian Foreign Secretary Subimal Dutt who demurred, saying it was inappropriate for India to bring this matter before the UN since the Chinese were not members.[21] Dutt added, 'No one is going to war with China over Tibet'—and so summarized, in a phrase, Nehru's decade-long stance on Tibet.[22]

On 9 September 1959 the Dalai Lama submitted his appeal to Dag Hammar-skjöld, the UN secretary general in New York. The same day Brown was instructed to see the Dalai Lama again before he left for Mussoorie.[23] In a meeting the next day, Brown reiterated US support for the Tibetan people and advised the Dalai Lama that Washington was continuing to contact 'friendly nations' to seek sponsorship in the General Assembly.

On 10 September Dulles again briefed the NSC on events in Tibet. He stated that a sponsor had not yet been found and reiterated what had been told to the Dalai Lama, namely that his case would be stronger if it were based on human rights viola-tions.[24] 'Since Tibet was for many years a part of China,' he said a claim based on aggression would be harder to appeal. Under Secretary Douglas Dillon agreed with Dulles and said that 'the appeal of the Dalai Lama to the UN involved a difficult legal question. Was Tibet an independent nation or not?'

In the end Washington chose restraint, and Ireland and Malaya took the lead in inscribing the Tibet resolution. The issues in play were clarified in a candid exchange between Secretary Herter, the British Foreign Secretary Selwyn Lloyd, and the French Minister of Foreign Affairs Maurice Couve de Murville when they met in New York on 18 September.[25] Selwyn Lloyd was blunt about the British position: he feared that if Tibet's resolution was inscribed at the United Nations, this would set an 'unfortu-nate precedent' adversely affecting British interests in Oman.[26] When Herter asserted that Tibet was like the Hungarian situation, the foreign secretary responded: 'Hun-gary was independent and Tibet is not.'[27] Further, he feared this action could divide the Commonwealth. Herter was aware that many of Tibet's neighbors were reluctant to support Tibet for fear of Chinese reprisals. Couve de Murville worried about Algeria: he knew that the human rights question could be raised there as well.[28] He said: 'even close friends such as Belgium and the Netherlands would find themselves in embarrassing positions because of their overseas protectorates.'[29] Couve de Mur-ville insisted that it was best not to interfere in the relationship between India and China, saying: 'if the white people interfere, it will only result in bringing China and India together.'[30] The French and British later abstained on the Tibetan resolution.[31]

In the second week of October 1959 Gyalo Thondup, who led the Tibetan delega-tion to the UN, arrived in New York to meet with Ambassador Henry Cabot Lodge, Eisenhower's new UN ambassador. Gyalo was accompanied by Ernest Gross, who had been retained by the State Department to advise the Tibetans on the UN pro-cess.[32] Gross had been the deputy US representative to the UN in 1950 during Tibet's first appeal to the United Nations and was now in private practice.

Lodge, like the other US diplomats, made the point to Gyalo that if the Tibetans went to the United Nations and pressed for Tibetan independence, it would fail.[33] The matter of Tibet's legal status was now crucial, as many other nations would not support a resolution decrying Chinese aggression if Tibet's status as an independent nation were unclear. China could, however, be found to have violated Tibetan human rights. To move forward at this point, the State Department realized that it could no longer advance a policy pivoting on an ambiguity. They decided, once again, to address Tibet's actual status. Gyalo was planning a visit to Washington, and officials there were uncertain how to handle what was, clearly, a very emotional issue.[34]

The decision was taken, in the end, on very practical grounds. The Bureau of Far Eastern Affairs concluded that 'on balance the arguments against recognition of Tibetan independence under present conditions are stronger than those in favor.'[35] In the memo, the assistant secretary of state for Far Eastern Affairs, Parsons, wrote:

I consider this conclusion valid from the standpoint of both the United States national interest and from that of the Tibetans. We share with the Tibetans the objectives of keeping the Tibetan cause alive in the consciousness of the world and maintaining the Dalai Lama as an effective spokesman of the Tibetan people. I believe that United States recognition of the Dalai Lama's government as that of an independent country would serve neither purpose well.[36]

The Bureau concluded that since other countries were not likely to recognize the Free Tibetan Government in exile, the Tibetans would seek political support from the US. And 'this would almost certainly damage the prestige and influence [the Dalai Lama] now enjoys as one [of] Asia's revered leaders and would hamper his activities on behalf of the Tibetan people.'[37]

That same week Gyalo had some unexpected support when Gross introduced him to the former first Lady Eleanor Roosevelt; as a staunch anti-communist, she gave her support to the Dalai Lama and the plight of the Tibetan people in her weekly column—though it didn't change the equation neither at the UN nor the Department of State. Years later, in 2004, her grandson William D. Roosevelt, a friend of the authors, commented that his grandmother was indeed a great supporter of the Dalai Lama and the Tibetan people. She had particularly enjoyed long talks about Tibet with Lowell Thomas at her estate of Spring Wood, in Hyde Park, NY after Franklin's death.

On 21 October Resolution 1353 (XIV) was adopted by the General Assembly with a vote of 45 to 9 and 26 abstentions. The resolution called for 'the respect for the fundamental human rights of the Tibetan people and for the distinctive cultural and religious life.' Ambassador Lodge wrote to the secretary of state two days later; in his opinion the resolution was the 'maximum' that could be done.[38] It had taken enormous effort and diplomatic maneuvering on behalf of the State Department. He was with the Department's wise strategy of allowing Ireland and Malaya to take the lead; this enabled the US to avoid Russian accusations that Washington was 'reviving the Cold War.'[39] But he regretted that the United States' closest allies, France and Britain, had abstained. He ended his memo by saying: 'I think you should also know there was widespread distaste for the whole operation.'[40]

A week later Gyalo traveled to Washington and met with Robert Murphy, under secretary of state for Political Affairs. He spoke of the Dalai Lama's desire for American 'guidance and advice,' as well as the need for support and of his intention to 'continue the struggle for freedom.'[41] In this context, Murphy reiterated Washington's support for the right of 'self-determination of peoples,' but avoided specific commitments.[42] Reflecting the US government's determination to make the Tibet story a part of the global political discourse and a continuing liability for communist China, Murphy urged His Holiness to travel in order to keep the situation alive and thus remain a vivid factor in 'world public opinion.'[43] With this comment, Murphy was reflecting the policy of the NSC 5412 Group (which he had attended), whose executive secretary, Thomas Parrott, told the authors:

One of the reasons we were so anxious to help the Dalai Lama was that he was such a visible symbol against Communism and this was part of the Foster Dulles policy to oppose Communism. We couldn't get in a war with China. We had to be careful about our operations and what we said.[44]

While Gyalo departed with encouragement and best wishes from his meeting with Under Secretary Murphy, he also received a bracing lesson in the ways of Washington that gave new meaning to the word realpolitik. When added to the Dalai Lama's discussion with Nehru in Mussoorie, the US position made clear that the Dalai Lama's future and the future of his people were indeed less certain than previously thought.

Meanwhile, though Murphy's careful comments had avoided a crisis, what was a delicate situation became immeasurably worse the following month when the president took a three-week goodwill trip abroad. The schedule called for a stop in India between 9 and 14 December 1959 and the Dalai Lama had requested to see him while he was there. India's foreign secretary, Subimal Dutt, opposed the idea, telling US Ambassador Elsworth Bunker that this would inject a 'controversial matter' into the president's visit.[45] Dutt cautioned that it would fuel allegations that the US was urging Delhi to encourage the Tibetan resistance. Bunker understood Dutt's concerns and also the possible implications for the Nehru government. Delhi was still trying to retain the vestiges of its relationship with Beijing—who had, by now, concluded that India intended to assist the Tibetan independence effort.[46] Accordingly, Bunker, perhaps erring to the side of caution, and with a somewhat narrow concept of US 'interest,' counseled against the meeting.[47]

The Dalai Lama was clearly upset by the president's refusal to meet and was reminded of the hard-edged game of Cold War geopolitics of which he was now a part. This was underscored in a recently declassified memo to the President from Secretary of State Christian Herter in April 1960. Herter recommended that the president meet with the Dalai Lama and his brother, Gyalo Thondup, during a trip to the US tentatively planned for May or June 1960.[48] The memo began: 'Last December, the Special Group under NSC 5412/2 agreed that it would be desirable for the Dalai Lama to travel outside of India and to visit the United States.'[49] The memo went on to note the Dalai Lama's disappointment at being unable to see the President in India, and stated that he was now reluctant to come to the US if a personal meeting with the president could not be arranged. Herter wrote to the president:

From reports we have received it is apparent that the morale of the Dalai and his principal advisors is at an all-time low. We believe that the Dalai Lama's leadership movement can be adversely affected by a continued decline in morale. On the other hand if it is possible for him to call on you for a half hour's visit, at a time and date convenient to you, I believe that this would greatly encourage him to carry on through a prolonged period of enforced inactivity.[50]

As it transpired, the president did not meet with the Dalai Lama. Indeed, on advice from his counselors, the Dalai Lama chose not to visit the United States unless he was received as a chief of state. Washington felt unable to provide that platform at that time for several reasons, but principally due to the China Lobby and the Chiang Kai-shek government on Taiwan which strongly opposed such a designation. The trip was not to be, therefore, as both protocol and Washington's arcane politics would not allow it.

While the president was restrained in his ability to overtly support the Tibetans, he did continue to authorize covert operations funding. On 4 February 1960, President Eisenhower met with members of the 5412 Group to discuss Tibet.[51] Allen Dulles briefed the group with the recommendation that continued support be given for the resistance. After asking a few questions, the President turned to Secretary of State Herter and asked whether he too would recommend covert assistance to the Tibetans. Gordon Gray wrote in his report memo:

Herter felt not only would continuing successful resistance by the Tibetans prove to be a serious harassment to the Chinese Communists but would serve to keep the spark alive in the entire area. He felt that the long-range results could mean much to the free world apart from humanitarian considerations for the Tibetans.[52]

This seemed sufficient for Eisenhower to sign off on the project, providing covert support for the Tibetan resistance which continued until 1964.[53]

Now with the question of a UN resolution resolved for the moment, the Dalai Lama on Indian soil, the resistance movement underway, and increasingly frayed relations with Beijing, Nehru's scope of maneuver had contracted. We turn to our penultimate chapter.

30

THE DALAI LAMA, NEHRU, AND THE CHINESE

A DIFFICULT MIX

Relations with China

When the Dalai Lama arrived on Indian territory in 1959, there were few signs that a Sino–Indian love fest ('*Hindi–Chini bhai bhai*') had ever existed. By late 1958 members of the Indian parliament were openly questioning Nehru about the Askai Chin territory then being claimed by China. Many had seen the map in the *China Pictorial* that showed China's borders intruding into areas claimed by India. Now it had become a public matter. Nehru wrote directly to Chou En-lai, but Beijing had gained its objective and now little would change. Yet Chou still hoped to soothe Nehru somehow, as he had done in the past, and answered his note on 3 November 1958 by saying:

The Chinese Government believes that with the elapse of time, and after consultations with the various neighboring countries and a survey of the border regions, a new way of drawing the boundary of China will be decided in accordance with the results of the consultations in the survey.[1]

Nehru pressed further and wrote in December 1958 that he was 'puzzled' by Chou's response and referred specifically to meetings in 1954 when Nehru had been led to believe that there were no boundary issues to be resolved.[2] The Chinese knew now that Nehru would not back off and thus Chou revealed his hand.

In a letter dated 23 January 1959 to Nehru, Chou finally admitted that 'border disputes do exist between China and India ... and that now there would be difficulties in changing the old maps.[3] The Chinese people,' Chou wrote, 'objected to India's claim to the western part of China.'[4] Yet, still trying to placate Nehru, Chou then wrote:

Our government would like to propose to the Indian Government that, as a provisional measure, the two sides temporarily maintain the status quo, that is to say, each side keep for the time being the border areas at present under its jurisdiction and not to go beyond.[5]

Of course this was unacceptable to Nehru. Chou received Nehru's shocked response on 22 March, the day the Dalai Lama was fleeing to safety; Nehru, Chou, and the Dalai Lama had now taken a clear position.

Even as Nehru saw the stunning duplicity of the Chinese, he hoped to save the relationship from deteriorating completely—partly to save face in his parliament and partly because he did not want a border war that China would surely win. So while he granted the Dalai Lama asylum, he continued to tell his parliament that he embraced the principles of non-intervention; which was encouraging to Beijing, who feared he might help the Tibetan fighters. The Chinese also hoped to maintain the semblance of a cordial relationship, even though the loss of life and dislocation in Tibet approached what today would be called 'ethnic cleansing,' and word of their barbarism had spread with the flight of resistance fighters to India.

After the Dalai Lama's speech on 18 April denouncing the 17 Point Agreement, Beijing demanded that Nehru limit the Dalai Lama's influence to religious activities and ensure that he remained firmly separated from politics. With the influx of more Tibetan refugees and resistance fighters, both the Chinese and Indians began to police their borders more carefully, which invited clashes. This, when added to the border dispute where Nehru believed he had been misled by Chou, brought the complete breakdown in Sino–Indian relations and the 1962 war.

A CIA analyst described the Sino–Indian relationship in the 1950s:

Developments between late 1950 and late 1959 were marked by Chinese military superiority which, combined with cunning diplomatic deceit, contributed for nine years to New Delhi's reluctance to change its policy from friendship to open hostility toward the Peiping regime. It emerges that above all others Nehru himself—with his view that the Chinese Communist leaders were amenable to gentlemanly persuasion—refused to change this policy until long after Peiping's basic hostility to him and his government was apparent. When finally he did re-think his China policy, Nehru continued to see a border war as a futile and reckless course for India.[6]

The CIA: expanded resistance training

Meanwhile, the United States continued to provide training and financial support for the Tibetan resistance. In May 1958 the CIA began training a second group of 500 to 700 Tibetans. They were divided into five groups representing different districts in Tibet. After completing the program the men were dropped back into their own districts to form resistance groups.

Their training was undertaken at Camp Hale, a US base near Leadville, Colorado.[7] The camp had been used for high altitude training during the Second World War and was well suited for Himalayan operations; remarkably, the Tibetans did not know they were in the United States.

Gendun Thargay, one of those who went through the Camp Hale program in 1961, recalled that prior to the airplane journey from East Pakistan, some Tibetans (as in the prior group) had seen Chinese airplanes from the ground when they bombed Kham, but none had ever been close to a '*namdu*' ('skyboat' in Tibetan).[8] Standing on the tarmac, they were startled 'when a small door near the tail of the plane opened, a ladder descended and out stepped a tall, sharp-featured white man smoking a pipe.'[9] Inside the plane a picture of the Dalai Lama was taped to the fuselage. The Tibetans were shown how to fasten their seatbelts and then offered a 'brown drink' that Gendun thought was rum but was actually Coca-Cola.[10] The meal included 'roast beef sandwiches, pickles and salt and pepper shakers,' all of which was new.[11] Beside their plates were small bars of soap, which they ate as well. The Khampas were more comfortable on the floor, so they left their seats to play a popular Tibetan dice game called *sho*.[12]

After arriving at Camp Hale, the men were given green army fatigues and black boots. They were given English names printed on cards affixed to the visors on their hats. They were taught 'weaponry, survival techniques, radio operations, coding, how to organize an underground network, make letter drops and chart contact points'— among other skills.[13] They spent about six months in the small, isolated camp.[14] When their training was complete they were dropped back into Tibet carrying radios and 'lightweight pistols equipped with silencers.'[15]

By 1960, with a swelling pool of Tibetan refugees in India, the CIA decided to train, provide military equipment, weapons, communications, and money to the guerrilla fighters at a location closer to Tibet. Gyalo Thondup was helpful in establishing a training facility at Mustang, a small enclave of land in Nepal that extended into Tibet.

In 1961 the effort paid off. Tibetan resistance fighters ambushed a PLA convoy and seized some 1,600 invaluable documents from the lead vehicle which CIA Director Allen Dulles displayed in a 'bloodstained and bullet ridden' pouch at a meeting of the 5412 Group in November of that year.[16] The documents provided first-hand intelligence on a range of governance problems, including political difficulties that Mao and others were experiencing within the party and in various provinces where minorities were described as being in revolt. The papers revealed that Mao's Great Leap Forward had brought famine and starvation, which now required that food be taken from Tibetan storehouses and trucked to China.[17] Also detailed were Mao's plans to send large numbers of Han 'civilians to Tibet to settle the land.'[18] Most chilling were orders to the PLA to 'eliminate all Tibetan resistance and their families, using whatever means necessary.'[19] The documents served still another purpose important to the resistance: they revealed the magnitude of the violence visited upon the Tibetan people. Between March 1959 and September 1960, more than 87,000 people had been killed in Lhasa alone.[20] Ambassador James Lilley, a career CIA officer and veteran diplomat who served as US ambassador in Beijing and Seoul, told the authors that the documents proved a 'treasure trove of priceless information.'[21]

TIBET: AN UNFINISHED STORY

Lyndon Johnson: Tibet was rarely on the president's agenda

By the time Lyndon B. Johnson was sworn in during 1963, many of the programs and funding for the Tibetans were already in place. That year the CIA supported a broadly based 'political program' that brought 133 Tibetans to the US for training in 'political, propaganda and paramilitary techniques.'[22] In addition the US was funding the Dalai Lama's entourage in Dharamsala, sponsoring Tibetans at Cornell University, and Tibet Houses in New York and Geneva.[23] The budgetary authorization for 1964 to cover the covert program totaled $1,735,000; that figure was raised to $2,500,000 in 1969.[24] The CIA supported the effort through the mid-1970s, but as the program seemed unable to gain traction on the ground, subsequent funding was steadily reduced.

Though Tibet was not a topic of particular interest in the Johnson White House, the president was reluctantly drawn to the region when compelled to address two unconnected South Asian issues in 1965. The first was the Second Indo–Pakistani War over control of Jammu and Kashmir, which cast American interests in South Asia in bold relief. Its resolution involved tricky diplomacy with Delhi, Islamabad, and with Soviet premier Alexei Kosygin, who ultimately chaired peace talks and supported a United Nations mandated ceasefire in 1965.[25]

More delicate from a domestic political perspective was the 1965 famine in South Asia, described by the State Department as 'unprecedented in modern history.'[26] Media coverage and Indian requests for assistance imposed pressure on Johnson to approve PL 480 emergency food relief; but the president, supported by Congress, hesitated. Uncomfortable with Nehru's leadership of the 'non-aligned movement' and warming relations with Moscow, Johnson hoped to 'make them [the Indians] come to us'[27] and approved food shipments for only two months at a time; he became, in effect, 'the US government's "desk officer" for PL 480 food aid to India.' Needless to say this infuriated Nehru.

With it all, Johnson was preoccupied, often convulsed, with the Vietnam War. In an address on 7 April 1964 at Johns Hopkins University to explain why Americans were fighting in Vietnam, he briefly mentioned Tibet and told his audience that:

Over this war—and all Asia—is another reality: the deepening shadow of Communist China. Their rulers in Hanoi are urged on by Peking. This is a regime which has destroyed freedom in Tibet, which has attacked India, and has been condemned by the United Nations for aggression in Korea. It is a nation which is helping the forces of violence in almost every continent. The contest in Vietnam is part of a wider pattern of aggressive purposes.[28]

Washington's neglect of the Tibet issue under the Johnson administration changed with the succeeding Nixon administration. The Dalai Lama and Tibet's struggle for independence would become a part of the conversation, if only a small one, as Richard Nixon and Henry Kissinger pursued a rapprochement with China.

THE DALAI LAMA, NEHRU, AND THE CHINESE

The Nixon–Kissinger gambit

Soon after he took office in 1969, Nixon let it privately be known that he sought improved relations with the PRC. Many in his party, and particularly the Republican right, remained adamant, however, in their refusal to accept the communist regime as a legitimate member of the international community. Yet Nixon's idea arose from geostrategic concerns about the Soviets. Nixon, Kissinger, and a small group of advisors reasoned that the rapid expansion of the Soviet Red Army and strategic tensions with Moscow warranted steps to explore a possible rapprochement with Beijing. In the broadest sense, they envisioned a triangular relationship in which the US and China would achieve greater leverage over Moscow and, ultimately, a more favorable distribution of global power.

Accordingly, the US sought discrete channels for authoritative communication with Beijing. Quiet initiatives were undertaken from several quarters: Kissinger's staff enlisted the support of Jean Sainteny, a former French official who facilitated Kissinger's secret talks in 1969 with North Vietnamese officials. Sainteny sought contact with China, via China's ambassador to France. Kissinger met with Corneliu Bogdan, the Romanian ambassador to Washington, who relayed that Romanian President Nikolae Ceauşescu had sent his vice premier to Beijing to raise the issue with Chou En-lai. Nixon spoke with Pakistani President Yahya Khan; and special envoys, including Vernon Walters, made quiet initiatives in Paris (but with little success) to convey Washington's interest in substantive talks with the Chinese leadership.

It was in this period, in March 1970, that the Dalai Lama, possibly aware of American efforts to open talks with the Chinese, asked to be received on a 'private' visit to the White House in the latter part of 1970. When Kissinger raised this with Nixon, it was decided that the support and attention generated by such a visit 'would create, gratuitously and without a compensating gain, a further point of friction between us [the US] and Communist China.' So the White House demurred and the visit was put off.[29]

This view was further clarified as the president, Kissinger, the NSC staff, the Department of State, and the CIA concluded that a beneficial strategic shift was now a possibility. At a meeting of the 40 Committee in San Clemente, California on 31 March 1971 (renamed 'the 5412' in the Nixon administration), 'all agreed' that the Tibetan operation was an unsuccessful irritant to the PRC and was unlikely to influence that nation's policy, except by hampering rapprochement with the United States.[30] The committee decided, accordingly, to reduce the paramilitary forces at Mustang from 1,800 men to 300 over the next three years.[31]

Eventually, partly through the 'Warsaw talks' that had begun in early 1970, arrangements and protocols were agreed with Beijing. In July 1971 Kissinger feigned a stomach upset in Pakistan—the last stop on his tour of Asia—and was driven to a remote airfield on the outskirts of Islamabad where he boarded a Pakistani airplane for Beijing. Several Chinese were on board and waiting for Kissinger's entourage. They included:

Huang Hua,[32] Ji Chaozhu,[33] Zhang Wenjin[34] and Tang Wenshang and Nancy Tang (who was born in New York and went to China with her mother in 1953, translated for high level meetings throughout this period, she later served in the Chinese People's Political Consultative Conference).[35]

In the Kissinger party's first meeting with Chou En-lai on 9 July 1971, Chou broke the ice by offering cigarettes to the group: 'No one wants one?' Chou said. 'I have found a party that doesn't smoke.'[36]

The discussions proceeded to identify areas where security and other cooperation—including obtaining China's assistance to end the Vietnam War—might be possible. Kissinger declared it was an 'historic occasion.'[37] 'Because,' he continued, 'this is the first time that American and Chinese leaders are talking to each other on a basis where each country recognizes each other as equals.'[38] In response Chou said: 'Of course it would be even a still greater occasion if President Nixon comes to China and meets Chairman Mao Tse-tung.'[39]

'The relationship': a forty-year discourse

As the meetings unfolded, it became clear that there was a range of regional and functional issues of substantial interest to both sides.[40] There were also differences, particularly regarding how Taiwan's status would be addressed. Chou was very direct on this point, underscoring not only that Taiwan had belonged to China for more than 1,000 years but also that 'Taiwan is a Chinese province, is already restored to China, and is an inalienable part of Chinese territory.'[41]

The talks at the Diaoyutai State Guesthouse[42] would touch on Tibet only indirectly, but with profound effect. Though not the *coup de grâce* it could have been, Kissinger framed the evolving US–China relationship in a way that greatly limited both Tibet's options and US options in Tibet. He informed Chou that 'President Nixon has authorized me to tell you that the US will not take any major steps affecting your interests without discussing them with you and taking your views into account.'[43] Tibet's troubled dream of autonomy was now cast in sepia.

In Washington, Kissinger subsequently reported to Nixon that the talks were 'the most searching, sweeping and significant discussions I have ever had in government.' He stressed that dealing with the Chinese required nuance and style and said a grasp of the 'intangibles' was crucial if the US was to 'deal effectively with these tough, idealistic, fanatical, single-minded and remarkable people.'[44]

In a memorandum to Nixon on 14 July, Kissinger described his progress, and the project to 'open' China' that he and the President had undertaken, in these words: 'The rewards and risks will be great [but] if we keep our nerve and are clear about our purposes we can start a new historical course.'[45] Kissinger summed it up by saying:

The progress we have now started will send enormous shock waves around the world. It may panic the Soviet Union into sharp hostility … it could shake Japan loose from its American moorings. It will cause a violent upheaval in Taiwan. It will have [a] major impact on our

Asian allies, such as Korea and Thailand. It will increase the already substantial hostility in India.[46]

Kissinger and Chou met over a three-day period and with each encounter built upon the progress of the last. Kissinger told the president and White House staff that he had spoken with Chou for twenty hours.[47] The Chinese premier had no notes; Kissinger said 'Chou En-lai personally was, next to de Gaulle, the most impressive foreign leader I have ever met.'[48]

The momentous events of these few days in Beijing foreshadowed the reversal of two decades of US policy and also of the anti-communist narrative that had informed Nixon's career to that point. All of that was replaced by a new discourse that would weld Henry Kissinger to 'the relationship' and enhance both over the next four decades. If Chou was the greatest living statesman, Henry Kissinger was his equal; and if Moscow threatened, it would be met by a Washington–Beijing axis conceptualized by Kissinger and Chou and blessed by the Great Helmsman and the leader of the free world.

President Nixon's historic meeting with Chairman Mao took place on 21 February 1972; a joint communiqué was signed on 28 February in Shanghai.[49] The document, which would be instrumental in governing US–China relations, was meant to 'normalize' relations with the Republic of China on Taiwan by the end of the decade. It would 'codify' the 'one China Policy' that recognized Taiwan as part of China. Though Tibet was not specifically mentioned, the document contained varying implications for Tibet, India, and the nations on the South China Sea littoral. Largely because US diplomats were anxious to gain agreement to move normalized relations forward, they accepted China's wide-ranging assertions of its sovereignty and its claims without stating reservations that noted long-standing conflicting claims made by others—including Tibet.

A new geopolitical logic

With Nixon's successful visit to Beijing behind him, and approaching the end of his first presidential term, a certain geopolitical logic had begun to emerge. The US was clearly not alone in its concern about the Soviets' mounting military capacity. In addition to the Soviets' advanced air and naval forces capable of threatening the US, and the fear that Soviet armored divisions would come crashing through the Fulda Gap into central and western Europe, China faced over eighty Soviet divisions across the Amur River on its northern border.

There was, thus, a clear strategic rationale for Nixon's initiative and it is within this context that a point of clarification is in order. Though the resistance training at Mustang was significantly curtailed during Nixon's White House tenure, declassified documents and discussions to date, among US diplomats and their Chinese interlocutors, reveal no specific commitments by the Nixon administration to close the Mustang operation, nor indeed a decision to withdraw support from the broader

Tibetan resistance. NSC senior staff member and former US Ambassador John Holdridge, who attended the Nixon–Kissinger–Chou talks and was a friend and colleague of the authors,[50] told the authors in April 1998 that the topic of Tibet had not been raised in specific terms until President Gerald Ford's state visit in November 1975. This was reconfirmed by Peter Rodman, a senior member of the NSC staff and speechwriter for Henry Kissinger, in 2007.[51]

When Tibet entered the conversation, it was in an offhand and rather jocular way during Ford's third session with the Chinese on 27 November 1975 in the Great Hall of the People.[52] In addition to President Ford, the attendees included Henry Kissinger, Donald Rumsfeld, assistant to the president, George Bush, US representative to the PRC, among others, and Deng Hsiao-p'ing, Chinese vice premier. In a reference to India and the security of the Chinese border, the vice premier said he had no fear that India would attack Chinese borders as he did not think they had the capability. He said: 'The most they can do is enter Chinese territory as far as the autonomous Republic of Tibet, Lhasa. And Lhasa can be of no strategic importance to India. The particular characteristic of Lhasa is it has no air—because the altitude is more than 3,000 meters.' In response Kissinger said 'Really' and then continued: 'it is a very dangerous area for drinking '*Mao Tai*,' to which everyone laughed.[53]

The meetings were, in effect, a continuation and a 'tidying up' of Nixon's normalization policy with China. In this rather light-hearted exchange, the issue of Tibet had been raised by Deng in the context of the many small issues that remained unresolved between the United States and China.[54]

Deng then proceeded to ask about the Dalai Lama's office in the US.[55] He said:

For instance, the question of the Dalai Lama having set up a small office in your country. And during my discussions with some of your visitors I said that was like chicken feathers and onion skin. [Laughter] Do you have such an expression?[56]

Ambassador Bush responded: 'We have an impolite one,' to which Deng said, 'In Chinese it means something of very little weight. Feathers are very light.'[57]

President Ford then stated: 'Let me assure you, Mr Vice Premier, that we oppose and do not support any governmental action as far as Tibet is concerned.'[58]

Thus, if there was a point in time when the US President and the Chinese leadership directly addressed the Tibet question, it was President Ford's statement on this occasion. Tibet was now a prominent casualty of the Cold War and also an early casualty of the Nixon–Ford policy of rapprochement.

There is an interesting back story to the exchange with Deng that illuminates the tensions lying just beneath the surface of these ebullient diplomatic exchanges; it also reveals Beijing's concern about the possible appeal of Tibet's story in the West and determination to block any progress its cause might make in the US.

While the Chinese sought to make light of the Tibet situation in this meeting, six weeks earlier (October 1975) the Chinese had loudly insisted that the US close the Tibetan office in New York. In a *New York Times* article on 15 October, a week before Kissinger's planned PRC visit, the headlines read: 'China Denounces US on Tibetans.'[59] China described the Dalai Lama's office as constituting a 'flagrant violation of the principles of the Shanghai Communiqué.'[60] Speaking with Philip Habib on 13 October, Kissinger, who was then assistant secretary for East Asian and Pacific Affairs, said: 'I saw that the Chinese are screaming about the Tibetan thing.'[61] Habib told Kissinger that the Chinese had 'forced the pace and ... have decided to issue their statement because we haven't responded—or we have the issue under advisement.'[62] Habib advised him it would be best 'if we could duck this issue.'[63] The Chinese were pushing the US to issue a public statement. Habib told Kissinger that 'we have before accepted that Tibet is under Chinese control ... that isn't acceptable to them now. Our relationship with the Dalai Lama makes it hard. We are phasing out of that now though.'[64] To which Kissinger responded, 'Yes.'[65]

Thus the drama unfolded, both in the formal halls of diplomacy where a new geostrategic format for US–China relations was being agreed, and also in the public arena where bombast and posturing exerted pressure through the media.

In drawing this chapter to a conclusion, we see that time in its inexorable way had, by the mid-1970s, teased out the motivations and objectives of the four major actors: Chou En-lai, Nehru, the US, and the Dalai Lama.

In the end, Washington's temporizing, the Dalai Lama's naïvety, and Nehru's vulnerabilities were exploited by Chou En-lai, who had proved to be a ruthless and cunning figure. China absorbed Tibet, crushing its monasteries, traditions, and culture. But, as Stalin and Mao both worried, Tibet was more than a territory. It was now a phenomenon proceeding in two dimensions, to which we now turn.

31

CONCLUSION

This book presents the Tibet story unfolding in the harsh Cold War world of interest-driven diplomacy. These pages also describe an imagined world depicting a place of enthralling beauty that engaged the heart, the eye, and the spirit of travelers and writers from Herodotus to Major Francis Younghusband to James Hilton. But most importantly, these pages chronicle how Chinese might and guile conquered Tibet and how the Tibetan story lives on.

We have examined the people, the fears (real and imagined), the interests, ambitions, and events that combined to deny Tibetan independence. The British Foreign Office, Nehru and his ambassador to China, K. M. Panikkar, the CIA, Mao and Chou En-lai, Dean Acheson and Loy Henderson, the prescient US ambassador to Delhi, John Foster Dulles, the China Lobby and Henry Luce, and of course the Dalai Lama and Presidents Roosevelt, Truman, and Eisenhower—played vital roles in this magnificent drama, informed by 'national interest,' personal ambition, fear, hubris, and imagined destiny.

The story of modern Tibet begins with the fact that when he assumed responsibility for his kingdom in 1950, the fourteenth Dalai Lama was fifteen years old—simply a boy. Isolated in the Himalayan fastness and educated by tutors and palace elders, his knowledge of the issues and personalities, not to mention great power aspirations, was limited. This was made worse by a complex and contentious regional history referred to as the 'Great Game' in the nineteenth century, which became even more difficult in the twentieth century when Tibet fell into the maw of the Cold War.

But it was in the mid-twentieth century, in the vital period from 1947 to 1959, that Tibet might have achieved independence, but failed. The question is why.

There was no one reason, of course, but personalities and the national passions of the great democracies at the time—Britain, India, and the US—combined in one of history's great ironies to deny Tibet the support it needed to resist Mao's communists.

TIBET: AN UNFINISHED STORY

It was a perfect storm: dominant neighboring China, intent on absorbing Tibet; Nehru, who believed India's interests and security required obeisance to Beijing; Britain, whose financial straits and colonial interests limited its ongoing role; and the US, an uncertain trumpet politically constrained at home and engaged abroad with other Cold War priorities. Tibet's inexperienced, untutored—and frankly incompetent—government had nowhere to turn.

Mr Nehru

Unfortunately, Tibet's prospects relied in some measure on the 'good offices' of Indian Prime Minister Jawaharlal Nehru. We have, at various points in these pages, addressed the peculiarities of Nehru's personality and the ambiguities infusing his relations with China. A brief further comment, however, is merited.

Nehru's public persona rested, in combination, on his leadership of the 'non-aligned movement,' his role as guide and steward of independent India, and his 'friendship' with China. The benefits of his relationship with Beijing and his fear of Chinese aggression stilled any formal Indian resistance to Chinese encroachment upon Indian territory, even while his parliament and press became aware of Chinese-built roads and airfields in Askai Chin and Chinese claims to Arunachal Pradesh.

Nehru's 'friendship' with China in the early 1950s bought valuable time and a platform for his moment in the sun at the Bandung conference in 1955. But it was his inability to resist the PLA militarily in subsequent years that led him to deny to himself, and all those around him, the existence of the border dispute which was, in January 1959, bluntly confirmed by Chou En-lai.

While some have argued, not without merit, that Nehru's stewardship of the non-aligned movement delivered important benefits to India, including heightened global stature and a platform for India's—and Nehru's—deeply held belief in non-violence, others found his unwillingness to make a stand against communist authoritarianism unacceptable. In any event, it was not to be 'peace in our time,' just as it was not when British Prime Minister Neville Chamberlain returned from Berlin a generation earlier proclaiming those words in September 1938. Nehru's acquiescence to Beijing ended, as Britain's had, in war.

As the 1950s unfolded, Nehru had found himself in an increasingly conflicted position. His policies strained to accommodate two distinct and strongly held views of Tibet: its status and its people. While Beijing claimed sovereignty over Tibet and insisted on India's compliance with that view, many Indians felt linked to their neighbor both by proximity and by a long and peaceful history. In addition, many Indians had a deep spiritual connection to the Buddhist faith, founded in South Asia over 2,000 years ago, and were sympathetic to the Dalai Lama and the Tibetan people.

Indian Intelligence Chief B. N. Mullick recalled that Nehru reflected these sentiments, advising officials in 1952 'to befriend all the Tibetan refugees in India, help them in every way possible and maintain their morale.' Mullick explained that Nehru 'could not publicly announce these policies nor was there any use in publicly denouncing China' but had instructed Mullick 'to keep in touch' with Gyalo [Thondup] who could be 'much benefit to us from the security point of view.'[1]

Attempting to placate domestic emotions and parliamentary invective, Nehru said in March 1959 that he 'would do his best through diplomatic channels to stop the fighting' and went on to tell the Tibetans to 'use wisdom and patience' and 'ultimate victory will be yours.'[2] And, in fact, Nehru helped the Tibetans in a number of ways. He provided asylum for the Dalai Lama, members of the Kashag and many others, and a location for the Tibetan government-in-exile at Dharamsala in northern India. Funds were provided for schools and social services; and, it appears, Nehru's government may have looked the other way when Tibetan resistance-related activities were underway at Kalimpong.

Still, the support he had offered was limited and he was, sadly, out-maneuvered by the Chinese. Nehru confronted a subtle and very able interlocutor in Beijing. Chou En-lai played cleverly to Nehru's personality, fears, and global ambitions. He was the perfect foil, conducting a fawning seduction that perfectly positioned Delhi for Beijing's purposes.

China sought two things from India: first, to gain India's complicity in delivering Tibet to the PRC without resistance or objection (China wished to avoid circumstances in which India might be drawn by Buddhist sympathies to support Tibet's anti-communist resistance); and second, to gain additional recognition and wider global acceptance, particularly among the non-aligned nations. India's acceptance of China, it was thought, would make China and its policies appear more benign—and acceptable.

Tibet's status

On the crucial question of Tibet's status, which arose in the early 1950s, none of the involved nations was prepared to recognize Tibet publicly as a sovereign nation. Nehru rejected the British view, in which China was regarded to have suzerain rights in Tibet. He could take little comfort from the American non-position, which ranged from rejecting Tibet's claim to independence, to possibly accepting the British position, to accepting the opinion issued in December 1950 by the State Department's legal advisor to Secretary Acheson, which said: 'As a matter of fact, this Office believes that China does not have and has not had sovereignty over Tibet.'[3]

Given the circumstances, Nehru bowed to political reality and accepted Beijing's claim that China possessed sovereign power over Tibet and then attempted to persuade the Dalai Lama and others of the same. His *ad seriatim* concessions to Chinese demands culminated in the 1954 Panchsheel Agreement, in which India formally recognized Tibet as part of China. This failed to quell China's territorial ambitions, either then, as the punishing border wars in 1961 and 1962 bore out, or now, as seen in Arunachal Pradesh (which Beijing calls 'South Tibet'). Indeed, since 2011 China has affixed a map to its passports depicting Arunachal Pradesh as part of China.[4]

While legal scholars assert that claims based on tradition or historical use have no standing in international courts, maps today remain one of Beijing's favored instruments in what has been described as 'law-fare': namely, using the law (often Chinese domestic laws and regulations) to frame contentious international issues in a China-friendly manner.[5]

With friends like these …

Rarely, in the past six decades, have the stars been favorably aligned for Tibet. While Nehru had been viewed by the State Department throughout the 1950s as the key to regional stability, he proved a disappointment. He was unwilling to resist the Chinese, or to assist the Tibetans. His leadership of the non-aligned movement precluded any chance of support in America's confrontation with Soviet communism but, perhaps most significantly, his disdain for American values and culture made productive exchange difficult, at times impossible, despite the painstaking efforts made by Acheson and Eisenhower.

To the further misfortune of Tibet's aspirations, John Foster Dulles, Eisenhower's secretary of state, was, in important ways, the wrong man at the wrong time. He was an ardent anti-communist, could not countenance a relationship of any kind with Beijing, and was uniquely unsuited by temperament and culture (most of the time) to maintaining good working relations with Nehru. Dulles' frayed relations with Delhi (though eventually mitigated by the Eisenhower–Nehru talks at Gettysburg) effectively removed the prospect of Indian cooperation on Tibet. Thus, even as Washington could expect little from Delhi, it was constrained by the relationship from providing overt support to the Tibetan resistance or even discussing it publicly.

Dulles was a Christian with deep links to both China, where his paternal grandfather had been a Presbyterian missionary, and to the Catholic Church, where his nephew Avery Dulles was a Roman Catholic cardinal. Together with publisher Henry Luce, the Catholic Church, and Senator Joe McCarthy, he championed the China Lobby which, in turn, was *primus inter pares* among those supporting his foreign policy. These links welded the administration to the Chinese Nationalists under Chiang Kai-shek, who insisted that no step be taken that would compromise China's sovereignty—which meant that Tibet must be seen as part of China.

Accordingly, both the Truman and Eisenhower administrations, despite their sympathy for the Dalai Lama and his aspirations, were unable to assist without incurring the wrath of the China Lobby and suffering the attendant political damage radiating from the toxic 'Red Scare.' Thus, just as these fervent anti-communists were seduced by the Nationalists, so they, in effect, separated Washington from the real struggle in Tibet where Lhasa fought invasion and occupation by the sharp end of the 'Communist enterprise,' the People's Liberation Army.

Weighing these countervailing pressures and interests, and given Washington's convictions, there was little choice but to provide covert assistance to train, equip, and deploy a force of Khampas to increase the cost of Chinese occupation and, eventually, it was hoped, drive the PLA out. Training was provided by the CIA at US bases in the Marianas and at Camp Hale in Colorado; the operation was later moved to Mustang. Due to vexing logistical issues, however, especially the difficulty of air operations in the Himalayas, and the potential for the PLA to intercept Tibetan fighters as they gathered to receive air drops, the effort was not as extensive as many would have liked. Indeed, the effort had a tentative quality. Added to this was the incoherent, faction-ridden resistance movement, neither fully embraced nor rejected by the Dalai Lama and the Kashag.

Cold War realities prevailed in 1972; and as described, the CIA-supported operation was terminated not long after the fateful 1972 Nixon–Kissinger visit to Beijing, which initiated a policy that would reset the US–China relationship.[6]

What was promised?

What remains is the question of what exactly was promised to the Tibetans, including Gyalo Thondup and the resistance fighters themselves, by CIA officers in the field. US public statements were carefully crafted. Many relevant State Department NSC and CIA files remain classified or redacted, just as the operations themselves in Tibet were structured to ensure plausible deniability. Our interviews with many of the men involved were disappointing, both for what they would not discuss and because of their personal dismay.

Gyalo Thondup has made it clear that US officials promised that the US would help the Tibetans gain their independence, a promise not kept and which he came to resent.[7] He told the authors in Kalimpong in December of 2012: 'The Americans made a lot of promises but they were not kept. They promised to help Tibet get independence after my brother left Tibet. They told me this many times—and all these promises meant nothing.'[8]

Clearly, the Tibetans believed they had been promised that the US would support Tibetan independence, but that is not something US officials will confirm, even now. Thomas Parrott's southern-fried ambiguity is perhaps emblematic: 'If the Tibetans thought they would get their independence from China, well then they were just Whistling Dixie, I guess. We were sympathetic to the Dalai Lama but we had to think of our own interests.'[9]

In the end, the CIA's effort in Tibet was a gambit, a 'check' but certainly not a 'checkmate'; it was simply a move in a larger chess game.[10] The CIA had succeeded in mounting an operation that harassed the Chinese, forcing them to deploy more equipment and expend more management time in the Tibet region than planned. The resulting unrest underscored China's vulnerabilities in its outlying ethnic regions—but did not alter the fact of China's grip on Tibet.

Nor has it to this day.

Conquering a story

Beyond the Tibet of failed politics and diplomacy there is another Tibet. This Tibet, an imagined kingdom wrapped in the exotic magnificence of the high Himalaya, has produced the longest surviving myth in the West. It occupies a unique place in the Western mind. Wrapped in mystery, aspiration, and possibility, it is James Hilton's expression of transcendent hope found in *Lost Horizon*; it is the instinct that caused Roosevelt to name the presidential retreat Shangri-La; it is a diamond in the metaphor for the 'Western creation of a sacred landscape.'[11]

Tibet is one of the first and also the last great unexplored regions on earth. We mentioned, at the beginning of this volume, the early recordings of 'gold digging ants' in the fifth century BC. These were followed by the incredible tales of clerics, mystics, and fortune hunters. In the early fourteenth century, Odoric of Pordenone, a Franciscan friar who sought to spread Catholicism in China, India, and Tibet, combined observation with fantasy in furtherance of the region's mystical qualities. In the early Middle Ages, stories about Central Asia were laced with sightings of grotesque monsters in the region—not unlike those depicted in the fifteenth-century paintings of Hieronymus Bosch. Included were 'the dog-headed men of India, the awkward Antipodes who travelled on a single oversized foot, the giant Cyclops, and bizarre Cephalics with eyes, noses and mouths embedded in their chests.'[12] Thus the elements of the story were compelling and provided not only a glimpse into worlds never seen and rarely, if ever, described, but a platform to take the Tibet story forward.

With the modern era, these fantastical images faded to be replaced by descriptions of a remote and exotic place. Many of these arose from the writings of George Bogle, Francis Younghusband, and others. But it was the British army, and colonial officers of the Younghusband era and later, in the 1930s, who fashioned the myth of a peaceful and tranquil place informed by reason and the miracle of self-discovery.

Peter Bishop makes the point that 'the encounter between Britain and Tibet in the last quarter of the eighteenth century marked the beginning of something new: the sustained creation of Tibet as an important imaginal landscape for Western cultures.'[13]

Tibet's unique 'soft power'

As China seeks a leading role in global affairs, the reality of its mistreatment of the Tibetan people has clashed with Tibet's reified place in the Western mind. The result is revulsion at the deconstruction of a culture, and dismay with a leadership that permits such excess. As this dynamic plays out, it is apparent that Tibet possesses a unique 'soft power' which invites global opinion-makers to condemn China's suppression of the Tibetan people. It is a 'soft power' born of moral condemnation. Accordingly, China's actions have raised probing questions about the values and norms that inform its civil society, not only in Tibet but also in Sinkiang and Inner Mongolia—and by implication its present suitability for global leadership.

The Beijing leadership is reluctant to recognize that Tibet is a phenomenon unto itself. It has a dimension, and presents quite differently from Taiwan, Sinkiang or Mongolia—each of which is either separate from China or has separatist movements. The Tibetan myth stands alone. It cannot be prised from the world's imagination, or suppressed, or set aside. It is celebrated around the world, particularly in the West, and despite China's determined efforts to diminish the Tibetan culture and people.

CONCLUSION

Among the reasons why the Tibetan story remains so much in the public mind, and its 'soft power' retains such traction, is often personal friendship that world leaders, including US presidents, have had with the Dalai Lama; initiatives taken in the UN; legislation passed by the US Congress and Senate; and American and European public concern about human rights and self-determination.

President George H. W. Bush was the first US president to meet with the Dalai Lama in the White House, on 16 April 1991, after which many Western leaders met with him privately each year. On 21 May 1991, in the aftermath of the 1989 protests in Lhasa and the brutality in Tiananmen Square, the US Senate passed Resolution 41 condemning the Chinese 'Occupation of Tibet.' President Clinton and Hillary Clinton (both as first lady and as secretary of state) met with the Dalai Lama informally on several occasions, enjoying stimulating conversations with him; Vice President Gore joined the president to meet with the Dalai Lama at the White House in May 2001. The relationship continued and was expanded by President George W. Bush and First Lady Laura Bush, who received him at the White House both in their official capacities and as friends—a relationship that continues to the present day. President Obama hosted the Dalai Lama at the White House on 18 February 2010. Reflecting Tibet's 'soft power,' the President infuriated Beijing when he used the meeting to criticize China for its policies and urged that China preserve Tibetan identity and respect human rights there.[14]

Partly because of its unique story, Tibet has presented a difficult problem to Western policy-makers. The principle of 'national self-determination' offered by Woodrow Wilson at Versailles to oppressed peoples around the world challenged the US, in subsequent years, to establish clear criteria for supporting one independence or separatist movement but not another. Thus, when the question is raised of why Washington supported Tibet's resistance to China, but not the Basques, Kurds, or Sri Lankan Tamils, the answer must be that Tibet combined both geopolitical advantage and a salve to the spirit; the US saw a platform for containing communist China and recognized the drive of a people to pursue their customs and religion against all odds—and, though sharply constrained both domestically and diplomatically, supported both.

China's choice

The results of China's invasion, now in its eighth decade, have been tragic for both Tibet and for China. The Tibetan culture has been damaged and China has lost credibility due to its brutal practices and failure to find grounds on which reconciliation talks might proceed. Beijing has devoted manpower, management expertise, and billions of dollars of investment with little positive return. One might ask if China wouldn't benefit from a modified policy at this point. The Dalai Lama has agreed that Tibet is part of China. Most Chinese know little about Tibet. This provides the new Chinese leadership with an opportunity to reframe the Tibet issue for domestic audiences and consider a modified administrative structure. Perhaps a suzerain relationship in which Tibet exercised greater control over internal affairs would suit both Lhasa and Beijing, allow Beijing to reduce its massive military garrison in Tibet, eliminate enormous expense, avoid harsh and continuing global criticism, and actually advance its global interests. There is, after all, a precedent for 'One China—Two systems.' Moreover, as China addresses its present challenges—which include a crisis of ideology, a party demographic pattern that will make China old before it is rich, a mis-positioned elitist communist, hostility among its East Asian neighbors over territorial disputes, growing difficulties with the US, corruption and social tensions including a growing gap between rich and poor—the leadership may wish to consider whether China can digest the Tibetan chestnut. Tibet rests, after all, upon a traditional culture wrapped in a pervasive religion providing a coherent identity—none of which China can claim. It is not beyond reason to ask whether Tibet may not only survive longer than the present regime in Beijing but function as an example of ethno-religious solidarity and resistance for other minorities and ethnic groups seeking opportunity and self-expression in China today.

32

POSTSCRIPT

In this final note we offer a brief comment on selected events in Tibet and Washington, marking the waypoints in a deeply troubling story over the four decades since 'normalization' in 1979. The initiatives taken by the US Congress and the White House are significant, as is the continuing unrest in Tibet, China's combined soft and hard power policies, and what US policy is today.

* * *

The making of US foreign policy is an opaque and complex process involving numerous moving parts: public opinion, Congress, the media, the business community, security strategists, and the academy. This has especially been the case when it concerns Beijing and Tibet.

The Dalai Lama had hoped to visit the US in the early 1970s, but largely due to the Nixon–Kissinger overture to Beijing his first trip was delayed until September 1979. Upon his arrival, the *New York Times* announced, to the consternation of the State Department, that the Dalai Lama would 'spend 49 days in the United States advancing the cause of an independent Tibet.'[1] As he proceeded to Washington the *Times*, pressured by the administration, toned down its coverage with headlines that read: 'The Dalai Lama Talks Religion not Politics, on a 2-Day Visit to Washington.' And so, on his first visit to America, the full panoply of interests, contradictions, and compromises as related to China—and thus Tibet—was on display.

The 1980s saw the Tibet policy addressed in Congress, in the White House, and, ominously, on the streets of Lhasa. A series of pro-independence demonstrations took place between September 1987 and March 1989 in the Tibetan areas of Sichuan province, the Tibetan Autonomous Region, Qinghai province, and the Tibetan prefectures of Yunnan and Gansu provinces. These spurred a number of legislative and other initiatives in Congress, particularly between 1987 and 89. In June 1987, the US

House of Representatives passed HR 3590, 'A Bill Concerning Human Rights Violations in Tibet by the People's Republic of China.'[2] Noting the rising violence and the brutal policies of Chinese security forces, the Dalai Lama was invited to address the US Congressional Human Rights Caucus on 21 September, where he presented a five point plan for reconciliation. Mayank Chhaya characterized it this way:

The plan advocated respect for the human rights of the Tibetan people; abandonment of the policy of transferring ethnic Chinese into Tibet; turning Tibet into a demilitarized zone of non-violence; protecting and restoring Tibet's natural environment; and the commencement of negotiations on the future status of Tibet. This plan is a representation of his Middle Way approach, in which he seeks autonomy, but leaves out the idea of independence, which seems unlikely for Tibet since it lacks the political and economic strength to emerge as a serious threat to Chinese control over Tibet.[3]

Though the Dalai Lama's proposals were applauded by Congress, they were criticized by the State Department as having a 'veiled independence agenda.' Significantly, his proposals reverberated in Tibet: in October 1987 six people died in riots at the Sera Monastery. These events brought excoriating criticism of PRC policies in Washington by political figures ranging from Democratic Congresswoman Nancy Pelosi and Democratic Senator George Mitchell[4] to Republican Senator Jesse Helms[5] and President Ronald Reagan.

When the main tenets of HR 3590 were posted on walls in Lhasa in 1988, riots broke out in which between three and thirty people (according to different accounts) died in protests at the Monlam Prayer Festival. On 5 March, a demonstration by monks, nuns, and students marking the anniversary of the 1959 Tibetan uprising led to three days of protest, the destruction of Chinese stores and a brutal police response, followed by the imposition of martial law on 8 March and the closing of the Tibet border.

As the magnitude of the repression became known around the world, the Dalai Lama's proposals were seen to be a possible way forward. In global recognition of this possibility, the Nobel Committee awarded the Dalai Lama the Peace Prize in 1989.

The monasteries: centers of resistance

Meanwhile, resistance on the ground continued. From the 1970s through to the present day the resistance to China's attempt to deconstruct Tibetan culture and society has been centered in the monasteries. Under policies introduced in 1962, the monasteries had been run by monks with only indirect involvement of government officials. That policy was abandoned during the 1966–79 Cultural Revolution, when most monasteries were closed and many destroyed. Former Secretary of Defense James Schlesinger visited China in that period and in 1976 reported on the tensions between Beijing and Tibetans, commenting, 'Propaganda stressing Chinese solidarity with minority nationalities is cover for problems arising out of Han efforts to control tribal cultures. Tibet is nothing more than occupied territory and so-called autonomous regions little better than Chinese provinces.'[6] Lhasa gave him the impression that Tibet was 'an occupied area, pure and simple.'[7]

In the 1980s new policies were adopted that, in effect, allowed the monasteries to again be administered by the monks. In 2011 that changed once more. Despite the guarantees of freedom of religious belief in China's constitution, the authorities forbid the display of the Dalai Lama's likeness and have wired the monasteries with video cameras and microphones. In 2012, the Beijing authorities introduced a system called the 'Complete Long-term Management Mechanism for Tibetan Buddhist Monasteries' that places almost every institution directly under Communist Party officials permanently stationed in each. Moreover, every monk and nun is to have a government 'companion' for 'guidance and education.'

Beijing's hold is anchored by the PLA, which now has more than a quarter of a million individuals stationed in Tibet. It includes several divisions of specialized mountain troops and special operations regiments in Lhasa. The city, administered by some sixty departments and committees directly connected to their national offices in Beijing, has been, with the exception of carefully managed tourist sites, all but 'locked down' since the Olympics riots in 2008. Visitors report squads of PLA soldiers patrolling the streets in groups of three. Concentrations are particularly heavy around the Jokhang Temple, with military present at most intersections.

Beijing's use of soft power

Beijing's Tibet policy has unfolded in several dimensions. Beyond the presence of security forces in Lhasa, Beijing has employed 'soft power' in a complex process designed to improve urban areas while deconstructing Tibetan institutions. The aim is to reconstitute and modernize the cities by replacing Tibetans in most government offices and agencies with Han migrants.

The housing, communications, health, police services, commerce, licensing, and education systems are each, in effect, administered from Beijing. The education system, in particular, has been the institution of choice to socialize the next generation of Tibetans to ensure loyalty to the 'Motherland' and the Communist Party. Emphasis here has been given to primary school curricula and educational materials. At university level examinations are given in Mandarin, not Tibetan, and Mandarin is required for appointment to all municipal and judicial positions.

Beyond avoiding official use of the Tibetan language, a second set of initiatives is designed to extract the gravitas from Tibetan culture and traditions; in effect, to hollow out the culture. This is done by turning the temples, palaces, and monasteries the symbols of Gelugpa (also called yellow hat) Tibetan Buddhism—into Disney-like amusement stops accessed on tours where tickets are collected before entering. The tours are sold in Beijing for holiday-makers to ride the 'Lhasa Express' to Tibet, complete with drop-down oxygen bags. Tickets are then presented for admission to the Potala Palace, the Jokhang Temple, Barkhor Street—the circular prayer route around the temple where the faithful prostrate themselves (tourists are reminded this is 'a good place to buy souvenirs')—the Sera, Drepung, and Tashi-lumpo monasteries (the latter is home to the China-friendly Panchen Lama), and the Norbulingka summer palace of the Dalai Lama (where 'The park is crowded with picnickers and traditional activities during the Shoton, or Yogurt festival, in August').

This hollowing-out process has been accompanied by a third policy referred to above, namely an extensive program to improve Tibet's cities, roads, bridges, rail, and telecommunications. The PRC has poured billions of yuan into an extensive mod-ernization program that has been people-friendly in many ways. Beijing's 'charm offensive,' for which it should receive considerable credit, has delivered several new apartment blocks with hot running water, a great luxury in Tibet. Public transport has been improved (buses have heat) and access to consumer goods has been signifi-cantly expanded. Chinese claims of Tibetan progress are supported by statistics underscoring these achievements. The data also shows, however, that nearly all of the progress has been in urban areas populated by ethnic Han, rather than the country-side where 87 percent of Tibetans live.

The Olympic debacle

These improvements and frustrations combined to form complex currents which, on 14 March 2008, erupted in a series of demonstrations and then riots in Lhasa, Gansu, and Qinghai—the same locations as in 1987 and 1989. This time Tibetans were angered by the inflation which brought higher food and consumer prices. They were disturbed by the 'Lhasa Express' train from Beijing and Cheng-du, which was increasing the flow of Han migrants and creating heightened competition for jobs. But most of all, they were incensed by the assault on their traditions, culture, and spiritual life. And it was this unrest that provided the preamble for the eruption five months later in Lhasa when the Olympic torch passed though the city marking the beginning of the 'XXIX Olympiad' hosted by Beijing in August 2008.

At a cost estimated to be between $15 and $40 billion, the Olympics were to be Beijing's 'coming out party,' designed to show China, now approaching the pinnacle of world power, as a key member of the world community. The events were watched, according to Nielsen Media Research, by some 4.7 billion viewers worldwide, the largest global audience ever. But what could have been a shining moment for Beijing quickly turned into a slow-motion disaster that placed a global spotlight on its dis-turbing subjugation of Tibet and, more broadly, China's troubled civil society.

It began with the optics which seemed to confirm a darker side of China. Chinese Olympic torch carriers were accompanied by a threatening security detail dressed in black; police swarmed the roadways; and as the torch passed through Lhasa, festering grievances erupted in ethnic hatred toward the Han and all that they represented. With massive worldwide media coverage of the event, the ensuing riots, and the police crackdown, world audiences were shocked at the brutal images. Newscasts and the global press connected the Olympic riots to the March unrest and to the wider concern about China's civil society and human rights policies.

POSTSCRIPT

In little time the story of the Olympics was paralleled daily by extensive coverage of China's prejudicial treatment of minorities, its corruption, its dysfunctional legal system, and its treatment of pro-democracy dissidents like Liu Xiaobo, whose empty chair at the Nobel Prize awards in Oslo two years later would stand silent witness to his eleven-year prison sentence for opposing the regime. Termed the 'Genocide Olympics' by Hollywood voices such as Mia Farrow and Steven Spielberg, for supporting pariah regimes such as Sudan and Zimbabwe, it quickly became clear that Beijing could not control the Tibet story, which was now accented each day by official denials and explanations, which were themselves drowned in the news flow.

Unfortunately for Beijing the story repeated itself over the next three weeks, amplified in cities across the globe: the beleaguered men in black now doggedly protecting the torch from jeering crowds laced with 'Free Tibet' placards.

A week after protests broke out in Lhasa, Nancy Pelosi, speaker of the US House of Representatives (who had in 2006 facilitated the award of the US Congressional Medal of Freedom to the Dalai Lama), called upon the international community to denounce China's brutal crackdown on anti-government demonstrations, where officials had accused the Dalai Lama and his supporters of attempting to sabotage the Olympics, and promote independence. In Lhasa during a visit planned before the protests, Pelosi made the following points before a crowd of thousands:

- 'If freedom-loving people throughout the world do not speak out against China's oppression in China and Tibet, we have lost all moral authority to speak on behalf of human rights anywhere in the world.'
- 'The situation in Tibet is a challenge to the conscience of the world.'
- China's claim that the Dalai Lama was behind the protests made 'no sense.'
- An international probe is needed to clear the Dalai Lama's name regarding the violent protests in Tibet.

While Pelosi may have reached for a can of petrol to 'douse' the fire, the Chinese were the true authors of the conflagration that ensued. They had pre-conditioned events with a toxic combination of disdain for local Tibetans and a certain hauteur that accelerated global condemnation of China as the 2008 Olympics unfolded—a condemnation that China failed to contain as its global standing imploded.

And it was the bitter experience of being unable to surmount the powerful Western-based news flow—exemplified by the *New York Times*, the BBC, and CNN—that caused Beijing to decide in January 2009 to invest $6.8 billion in a global network called CNC World run by Xinhua, the New China News Agency.[8] The purpose was to provide a distinct, China-friendly version of the day's news.

Sadly, however, Beijing has misdiagnosed the problem it confronts. Just as China is seeking to legitimize its authoritarian governance today, the effort itself raises questions of credibility. In this instance, Beijing proposes to pit a network run by the Chinese Communist Party against the collective Western press, whose sources and editors are drawn for every corner of society and every strain of political opinion.

TIBET: AN UNFINISHED STORY

US policy today: Plus ça change, plus c'est la même chose⁹

The hope that Washington would fully commit to Tibetan independence in the years following the 1950 invasion by the People's Liberation Army proved to be stillborn. The result today is that Tibet is occupied by Chinese security forces while the authorities emphasize investments, new infrastructure, greater economic opportunities, and the story of a new and revitalized Tibet.

Current US policy was established during the George W. Bush administration by the Tibetan Policy Act of 2002 (TPA), a part of the Foreign Relations Authorization Act of FY2003. It reinforces the US commitment to human rights, religious freedom, humane treatment of political prisoners, and economic development projects in Tibet. It also requires annual reports on Sino–Tibetan negotiations both by the State Department and by Congress and requires US officials to raise issues of religious freedom and political prisoners. Finally, it urges the State Department to establish a US consulate in Lhasa.

In its 2004 report to Congress on Tibet negotiations, the State Department said:

Substantive dialogue between Beijing and the Dalai Lama is an important objective of this Administration. The United States encourages China and the Dalai Lama to hold substantive discussions aimed at resolution of differences at an early date, without preconditions. We have consistently asserted that any questions surrounding Tibet and its relationship to Chinese authorities should be resolved by direct dialogue between the Tibetans and the Chinese. The Administration believes that dialogue between China and the Dalai Lama or his representatives will alleviate tensions in Tibetan regions of China.

The United States recognizes the Tibet Autonomous Region (TAR) and Tibetan Autonomous prefectures and counties in other provinces to be a part of the People's Republic of China. This long-standing policy is consistent with the view of the international community. In addition, the Dalai Lama has expressly disclaimed any intention to seek sovereignty or independence for Tibet and has stated that his goal is greater autonomy for Tibetans in China.

Because we do not recognize Tibet as an independent state, the United States does not conduct official diplomatic relations with the Tibetan 'government-in-exile' in Dharamsala. However, we maintain contact with representatives of a wide variety of political and other groups inside and outside of China, including with Tibetans in the United States, China, and around the world. Our contacts include meeting with the Dalai Lama in his capacity as an important religious leader and Nobel laureate. It is a sign of our country's respect for the Dalai Lama that the President, the Secretary, and other senior administration officials have met with him on several occasions.

We have consistently urged China to respect the unique religious, linguistic, and cultural heritage of its Tibetan people and to respect fully their human rights and civil liberties.

While these matters are raised on a regular basis in bilateral discussions between the US and China, progress has been meager.

* * *

POSTSCRIPT

Finally ... a small anecdote. In a March 2012 meeting at the offices of the National Interest in Washington with a senior PLA general, one of the authors presented a photograph of Jampa Yeshi, the Tibetan protester who immolated himself in Delhi to protest against Chinese President Hu Jintao's visit to India. The general was told that Mr Yeshi is the thirtieth Tibetan to immolate himself that year. The general's response was: 'These people are criminals, this is not our fault, it is terrorism and it will be stopped.'[10]

We commented that the Tibetan situation could not be improved if the problem was not properly understood—and it is not. This was reinforced in 2012 when more worshippers immolated themselves at the Jokhang Temple in the center of Lhasa. They were joined by sixty more, bringing the 2012 number to ninety-two. Since 2009, there have been 127 self-immolations and counting; which is why this modest volume is entitled 'Tibet: An Unfinished Story.'

APPENDIX

SEVENTEEN-POINT PLAN FOR THE PEACEFUL LIBERATION OF TIBET (1951)

THE AGREEMENT OF THE CENTRAL PEOPLE'S GOVERNMENT
AND THE LOCAL GOVERNMENT OF TIBET ON MEASURES
FOR THE PEACEFUL LIBERATION OF TIBET

23 May, 1951

The Tibetan nationality is one of the nationalities with a long history within the boundaries of China and, like many other nationalities, it has done its glorious duty in the course of the creation and development of the great motherland. But over the last hundred years and more, imperialist forces penetrated into China, and in consequence, also penetrated into the Tibetan region and carried out all kinds of deceptions and provocations. Like previous reactionary Governments, the KMT [p.Kuomintang] reactionary government continued to carry out a policy of oppression and sowing dissension among the nationalities, causing division and disunity among the Tibetan people. The Local Government of Tibet did not oppose imperialist deception and provocations, but adopted an unpatriotic attitude towards the great motherland. Under such conditions, the Tibetan nationality and people were plunged into the depths of enslavement and suffering. In 1949, basic victory was achieved on a nation-wide scale in the Chinese people's war of liberation; the common domestic enemy of all nationalities—the KMT reactionary government—was overthrown; and the common foreign enemy of all nationalities—the aggressive imperialist forces—was driven out. On this basis, the founding of the People's Republic of China and of the Central People's Government was announced. In accordance with the Common Programme passed by the Chinese People's Political Consultative Conference, the Central People's Government declared that all nation-

251

alities within the boundaries of the People's Republic of China are equal, and that they shall establish unity and mutual aid and oppose imperialism and their own public enemies, so that the People's Republic of China may become one big family of fraternity and cooperation, composed of all its nationalities. Within this big family of nationalities of the People's Republic of China, national regional autonomy is to be exercised in areas where national minorities are concentrated, and all national minorities are to have freedom to develop their spoken and written languages and to preserve or reform their customs, habits, and religious beliefs, and the Central People's Government will assist all national minorities to develop their political, economic, cultural, and educational construction work. Since then, all nationalities within the country, with the exception of those in the areas of Tibet and Taiwan, have gained liberation. Under the unified leadership of the Central People's Government and the direct leadership of the higher levels of People's Governments, all national minorities have fully enjoyed the right of national equality and have exercised, or are exercising, national regional autonomy. In order that the influences of aggressive imperialist forces in Tibet may be successfully eliminated, the unification of the territory and sovereignty of the People's Republic of China accomplished, and national defence safeguarded; in order that the Tibetan nationality and people may be freed and return to the big family of the People's Republic of China to enjoy the same rights of national equality as all other nationalities in the country and develop their political, economic, cultural, and educational work, the Central People's Government, when it ordered the People's Liberation Army to march into Tibet, notified the local government of Tibet to send delegates to the Central Authorities to hold talks for the conclusion of an agreement on measures for the peaceful liberation of Tibet. At the latter part of April, 1951, the delegates with full powers from the Local Government of Tibet arrived in Peking. The Central People's Government appointed representatives with full powers to conduct talks on a friendly basis with the delegates of the Local Government of Tibet. The result of the talks is that both parties have agreed to establish this agreement and ensure that it be carried into effect.

1. The Tibetan people shall be united and drive out the imperialist aggressive forces from Tibet; that the Tibetan people shall return to the big family of the motherland—the People's Republic of China.
2. The Local Government of Tibet shall actively assist the People's Liberation Army to enter Tibet and consolidate the national defences.
3. In accordance with the policy towards nationalities laid down in the Common Programme of the Chinese People's Political Consultative Conference, the Tibetan people have the right of exercising national regional autonomy under the unified leadership of the Central People's Government.
4. The Central Authorities will not alter the existing political system in Tibet. The Central Authorities also will not alter the established status, functions and powers of the Dalai Lama. Officials of various ranks shall hold office as usual.
5. The established status, functions, and powers of the Panchen Ngoerhtehni shall be maintained.

6. By the established status, functions and powers of the Dalai Lama and of the Panchen Ngoerhtehni is meant the status, functions and powers of the 13th Dalai Lama and of the 9th Panchen Ngoerhtehni when they were in friendly and amicable relations with each other.

7. The policy of freedom of religious belief laid down in the Common Programme of the Chinese People's Political Consultative Conference will be protected. The Central Authorities will not effect any change in the income of the monasteries.

8. The Tibetan troops will be reorganised step by step into the People's Liberation Army, and become a part of the national defence forces of the Central People's Government.

9. The spoken and written language and school education of the Tibetan nationality will be developed step by step in accordance with the actual conditions in Tibet.

10. Tibetan agriculture, livestock raising, industry and commerce will be developed step by step, and the people's livelihood shall be improved step by step in accordance with the actual conditions in Tibet.

11. In matters related to various reforms in Tibet, there will be no compulsion on the part of the Central Authorities. The Local Government of Tibet should carry out reforms of its own accord, and when the people raise demands for reform, they must be settled through consultation with the leading personnel of Tibet.

12. In so far as former pro-imperialist and pro-KMT officials resolutely sever relations with imperialism and the KMT and do not engage in sabotage or resistance, they may continue to hold office irrespective of their past.

13. The People's Liberation Army entering Tibet will abide by the above-mentioned policies and will also be fair in all buying and selling and will not arbitrarily take even a needle or a thread from the people.

14. The Central People's Government will handle all external affairs of the area of Tibet; and there will be peaceful co-existence with neighboring countries and the establishment and development of fair commercial and trading relations with them on the basis of equality, mutual benefit and mutual respect for territory and sovereignty.

15. In order to ensure the implementation of this agreement, the Central People's Government will set up a military and administrative committee and a military area headquarters in Tibet, and apart from the personnel sent there by the Central People's Government it will absorb as many local Tibetan personnel as possible to take part in the work. Local Tibetan personnel taking part in the military and administrative committee may include patriotic elements from the Local Government of Tibet, various district and various principal monasteries; the name list is to be prepared after consultation between the representatives designated by the Central People's Government and various quarters concerned, and is to be submitted to the Central People's Government for approval.

16. Funds needed by the military and administrative committee, the military area headquarters and the People's Liberation Army entering Tibet will be provided

by the Central People's Government. The Local Government of Tibet should assist the People's Liberation Army in the purchases and transportation of food, fodder, and other daily necessities.

17. This agreement shall come into force immediately after signatures and seals are affixed to it.

Signed and sealed by delegates of the Central People's Government with full powers:

Chief Delegate: Li Wei-han (Chairman of the Commission of Nationalities Affairs)
Delegates: Chang Ching-wu, Chang Kuo-hua, Sun Chih-yuan

Delegates with full powers of the Local Government of Tibet:

Chief Delegate: Kaloon Ngabou Ngawang Jigme (Ngabo Shape)
Delegates: Dzasak Khemey Sonam Wangdi, Khentrung Thuptan, Tenthar, Khenchung Thuptan Lekmuun Rimshi, Samposey Tenzin Thondup

NOTES

PROLOGUE

1. W. Dale Nelson, Foreword by David Eisenhower to *The President is at Camp David* (Syracuse, NY: Syracuse University Press, 1995), p. 6.
2. Ibid.
3. 'Drury to Ickes,' 23 April 1942, RG 79, Records of Key Officials, Records of Newton B. Drury, box 4, National Archives, cited in http://www.nps.gov/history/history/online_books/cato/hrs6.htm
4. James Hilton, *Lost Horizon* (London: Pan Books Ltd, 1991), p. 128.
5. Franklin D. Roosevelt, 'Address at Chicago,' 5 October 1937. Online by Gerhard Peters and John T. Woolley, *The American Presidency Project*, http://www.presidency.ucsb.edu/ws/?pid=15476, last accessed 1 June 2013.
6. Letter from James Hilton, 5 October 1937, Franklin D. Roosevelt Library, President's Personal File #5066, labeled James Hilton.
7. Letter to Mr Hilton from President Roosevelt, 20 December 1937, Franklin D. Roosevelt Library, President's Personal File, labeled James Hilton.
8. Ibid.
9. Conversation with William D. Roosevelt, 6 May 2000, in Washington, DC.
10. http://www.nps.gov/history/history/online_books/cato/hrs6.htm
11. The first American to have contact with the Tibetans was William Woodville Rockhill. He met the thirteenth Dalai Lama, who was in exile, at the sacred Buddhist mountain Wu T'ai Shan, in a remote part of northern China. Rockhill was Theodore Roosevelt's Minister to China (1905–9) and headed up the American legation in Peking. He was a Tibetan scholar and spoke both Tibetan and Chinese. Rockhill did not reach Lhasa, although years later he traveled to eastern Tibet.
12. 'The Secretary of State (Hull) to President Roosevelt,' 3 July 1942, *Foreign Relations of the United States* (hereafter known as *FRUS*) Diplomatic Papers, China 1942, p. 624.
13. 'President Roosevelt to the Dalai Lama of Tibet,' 3 July 1942, FRUS, Diplomatic Papers, China 1942, p.625. The present Dalai Lama(Tenzin Gyatso) was born on 6 July 1935, to a farming family, in Taktser, Amdo, northeastern Tibet. He was named Lhamo Dhondup and at the age of two was recognized as the reincarnation of the previous 13th Dalai Lama, Thubten Gyatso.

INTRODUCTION

1. 'Shangri-La and Hyperreality: A Collision in Tibetan Refugee Expression,' in *Tibetan Culture in the Diaspora*, Frank J. Korom, ed. (Wien: Österreichische Akademie der Wissenschaften, 1995), p. 61. Also see Peter Bishop, *The Myth of Shangri-La: Tibet, Travel Writing and the Western Creation of Sacred Landscape* (Berkeley: University of California Press, 1989).
2. Ibid.

1. EARLY BEGINNINGS: THE WESTERN IMAGINATION

1. In 1996, ethnologist Michel Peissel posited through his research that these ants were marmots which, when burrowing, dug up soil which contained gold dust. Peissel studied the Minaro people in the Dansar plain near the Indus River on the border with India and Pakistan. The Minaro told him that they collected the earth dug up by these animals. The area is now an off-limits military zone. Marlise Simons, 'Himalayas Offer Clue to Legend of Gold-Digging Ants,' *New York Times*, 25 November 1996. Also see Michel Peissel, *The Ants' Gold: The Discovery of the Greek El Dorado in the Himalayas* (New York: HarperCollins, 1984).
2. http://ebooks.adelaide.edu.au/h/hakluyt/voyages/odoric/english.html
3. Ibid. Odoric called Tibet both Tebek and Thebet. In his journal he wrote: 'The women of this countrey weare aboue a hundreth tricks and trifles about them, and they haue two teeth in their mouthes as long as the tushes of a boare.' Also see Manuel Komroff, ed., *Contemporaries of Marco Polo* (New York: Liveright Publishing, 1928), p. 244, cited by Christiaan Klieger.
4. http://ebooks.adelaide.edu.au/h/hakluyt/voyages/odoric/english.html
5. Ibid.
6. Peter Bishop, *The Myth of Shangri-La: Tibet, Travel Writing and the Western Creation of Sacred Landscape* (Berkeley: University of California Press, 1989), p. 25.
7. The East India Company was established in 1600 by Royal Charter to promote trade between Great Britain and the East Indies. Subsequently its trade shifted to South Asia where, in addition to trade, it performed administrative and policing functions. There are two numbering systems used in identifying the Panchen Lama. The Ganden Podrang system was used by the Tibetans and the Tashilhunpo system was used by the Chinese. In this book we recognize Lobsang Palden Yeshé as the Third Panchen Lama according to the system used by the Lhasa administration. This title is a combination of Sanskrit and Tibet words meaning 'great scholar'.
8. He held the posts of secretary to the Select Committee, the registrar to the Court of Appeals, and private secretary to the Governor. Clements R. Markham, ed., *Narratives of the Mission of George Bogle to Tibet and the Journey of Thomas Manning to Lhasa* (Cambridge: Cambridge University Press, 2010), p. cxxxvi; and also see Kate Teltscher, *The High Road to China* (London: Bloomsbury Publishing, 2006), p. 11.
9. 'Minute by Warren Hastings,' 4 May 1774, in Markham, p. 3
10. Markham, pp. 7–8.
11. Ibid., p. 8.
12. Ibid., p. 11.
13. Ibid.

14. 'Private Commissions to Mr Bogle, Fort William,' 16 May 1774, Markham, p. 8.

15. 'Memorandum on Tibet, by Warren Hastings,' 16 May 1774, Markham, p. 12.

16. 'From Pari-Jong to Deshripgay' in Markham, p. 68. Samuel Turner, who followed the same route into Tibet a few years later, also commented on this Tibetan burial site. In his journal he wrote that this practice was 'in direct opposition to the practice of almost all other nations.' Samuel Turner, *An Account of an Embassy to the Court of the Teshoo Lama in Tibet* (New Delhi: Asian Educational Services, 2005), p. 198.

17. Markham, p. 77.

18. Ibid.

19. Ibid., p. 121.

20. Ibid., pp. 84–5.

21. Ibid., p. 89. They spoke Hindustani—the Lama had learned the language from his mother—although at times Bogle tried to use his limited Tibetan or have one of the court interpreters at hand. Markham, p. 84.

22. Ibid., p. 84. All the British visitors described in this chapter, Bogle, Turner, and Manning, refer to the Panchen Lama as the Teshu Lama: a reference to his home, the Tashilhunpo Monastery. Later, in his novel *Kim*, Rudyard Kipling refers to the Lama as the Teshoo Lama. The Dalai Lama is the head Lama and the Panchen Lama the second-ranking Lama.

23. Ibid., p. 104.

24. Ibid., p. 177.

25. Ibid.

26. Ibid.

27. Bishop, *The Myth of Shangri-La*, p. 41.

28. Turner, *Account of the Teshoo Lama*, pp. 197–8.

29. Ibid., p. 198.

30. Bishop, p. 40.

31. Ibid., p. 55.

32. The Nepalese Gurkha army of 18,000 invaded Tibet in 1792, plundering the monastery of the Panchen Lama. The Chinese army defeated the Nepalese forces; the peace treaty called for the Nepalese to pay an annual tribute to the Chinese Emperor. The British would not intervene and, according to Markham writing in 1876, the Chinese general who invaded Nepal gave a very negative report about the British, even suggesting that British troops made up part of the Gurkha army. The Chinese were able to firm up their hold on the Tibetans at this time. See Markham, pp. lxxv–lxxxii; Warren W. Smith, *Tibetan Nation: A History of Tibetan Nationalism and Sino-Tibetan Relations* (Colorado: Westview Press, 1996), pp. 134–7.

33. Markham, p. lxxx.

34. Laurie Hovell McMillin, *English in Tibet, Tibet in English* (NewYork: Palgrave, 2001), p. 56; Bishop, p. 72.

35. Markham, pp. 222–3. The diaries of George Bogle and Thomas Manning were first published in 1876, edited by Clements R. Markham. The book was recently reprinted by Cambridge University Press.

36. Markam, p. 223.

37. Ibid., p. 228.

38. Ibid., pp. 214, 216.

39. Ibid., pp. 216, 220, 221.

40. Ibid., p. 220.
41. Ibid., pp. 263–7.
42. Ibid., p. 266.
43. Bishop, pp. 54–5.
44. Ibid., p. 54.
45. McMillin, p. 77.
46. Ibid., p. 77.
47. Ibid.
48. Perceval Landon, *The Opening of Tibet: An Account of Lhasa and the Country and People of Central Tibet and of the Mission Sent There by the English Government in 1903–4* (New York: Doubleday, Page & Co., 1905). Advertisement by Doubleday at the back of the book.
49. Ibid.
50. Bishop, p. 138. Among the various individuals to travel to the region were: Russian, Colonel Nikolai Prejevalsky in 1872; Indian, Sarat Chandra Das in1879; American, William Rockhill in 1888–9; Swedish, Sven Hedin at the beginning of the twentieth century.
51. Bishop, p. 143.
52. Ibid.
53. McMillin, p. 90.
54. FrancisYounghusband, *India and Tibet* (Oxford: Oxford University Press, 1985), p. vii.
55. The Great Game refers to Britain's imperial competition with Czarist Russia for resources and influence in Central Asia.

2. SIR FRANCIS YOUNGHUSBAND: SOLDIER, VISIONARY, ROMANTIC

1. Perceval Landon was born in 1868 and educated at Hertford College, Oxford. In 1899–1900 he was War Correspondent for *The Times* during the South African War. He was also involved, with his close and lifelong friend Rudyard Kipling and others, in a daily paper called *The Friend* which was started during the Boer War. This South African experience launched a career of world travel, journalism, and other writing, so that he described himself in *Who's Who* as 'special correspondent, dramatist, and author.' In 1903–4 he was special correspondent for *The Times* on the British Military Mission to Lhasa, Tibet. Landon's ghost story 'Thurnley Abbey' was originally published in 1908 in his book *Raw Edges*.
2. Edmund Candler, *The Unveiling of Lhasa* (London: Thomas Nelson & Sons, 1905), p. 1.
3. Alastair Lamb, *Tibet, China and India 1914–1950* (UK: Roxford Books, 1980), p. 5.
4. Hon. George N. Curzon, MP, *Russia in Central Asia in 1889 and the Anglo-Russian Question* (London: Longman's and Green, 1899), pp. 13–14.
5. Candler, p. 28. This is stated in a dispatch from Lord Curzon, 8 January 1903.
6. Interview with V. I. Trubnikov, 4 May 2012, in Cambridge, UK. Trubnikov was director of the Russian Foreign Intelligence Service 1996–2000. He confirms that, based upon the archives of the Russian SVR, the 'explorers' were in fact intelligence officers reporting their findings to Moscow.
7. Perceval Landon, *The Opening of Tibet: An Account of Lhasa and the Country and People of Central Tibet and of the Mission Sent There by the English government in 1903–4* (New York: Doubleday, Page & Co., 1905), p. 27.
8. Parshotam Mehra, 'Beginnings of the Lhasa Expedition: Younghusband's Own Words,' Letters to Major General J. W. Younghusband, 'on the way to Simla' May 1903, and 'Simla'

21 May 1903, both p. 10, http://himalaya.socanth.cam.ac.uk/collections/journals/bot/pdf/bot_04_03_02.pdf, last accessed June 2013.

9. Ibid. Malcolm was able to arrange two treaties with the Shah of Persia: one enabled the British to establish factories in Persia; the other gave some islands in the Persian Gulf to the East India Company. See p. 14, ftn 8.

10. Ibid. Younghusband referred to the Russian threat in Tibet: 'though their Ambassador in London has sworn to Lord Lansdowne that such a thing is the very last thing in the world that his government would dream of doing. However, from India, Peking, Paris and St Petersburg identical reports arrive so evidently an attempt at least has been made by the Russians to get hold of Tibet.' Letter to Major General J. W. Younghusband, 21 May 1903, p. 11.

11. Landon, p. xiv.

12. Younghusband, *India and Tibet*, p. 24.

13. Candler, p. 37.

14. Younghusband, p. 153.

15. Ibid., pp. 153–4. After three months at Khamba Jong, Younghusband was unable to negotiate with Tibetan officials. In October 1903 he returned to Simla to seek further directions from the Government of India. Whitehall gave him and his army approval to proceed to Gyantse.

16. Candler, pp. 39–40.

17. Candler, 'Dedication,' in *The Unveiling of Lhasa*, p. v.

18. Lt. Col. L. A. Bethell, Pousse Cailloux, 'A Footnote,' *Blackwood's Magazine*, February 1929, vol. CCXXV, p. 157.

19. Ibid., p. 157.

20. Candler, p. 133; Younghusband, pp. 170–7.

21. Younghusband, p. 178.

22. Ibid., pp. 177–8; Candler, pp. 139–41.

23. Younghusband, p. 178.

24. Candler, p. 144.

25. Ibid., p. 145.

26. In writing the story in his book about the expedition, Francis Younghusband negotiated with Ganden Tri Rinpoche, who was chosen to officiate in the absence of the Dalai Lama. Younghusband wrote that this old and respected Tibetan Lama was the 'Chief Doctor of Divinity and Metaphysics of Tibet.' The Dalai Lama had left him his 'seals of office' and designated him 'Regent.' Francis Younghusband, p. 273. The negotiations between Younghusband and the Regent are discussed in the first-hand accounts of Edmund Candler, p. 363, and Perceval Landon, pp. 445–7.

27. Younghusband, p. 416. Some in the British parliament and press were highly critical of the mission, arguing that Younghusband had interfered with people who desired to be left alone. This was, they said, 'wanton wickedness, and nothing else—except perhaps, inane folly and wastefulness of human life and good money,' p. 417.

28. Lt. Col. Sir Frederick O'Connor, *On the Frontier and Beyond* (London: John Murrary, 1931), p. 46.

29. George Seaver, *Francis Younghusband: Explorer and Mystic* (London: John Murray, 1952), p. 243.

30. Younghusband, *India and Tibet*, pp. 325, 326.

31. Ibid.

32. Ibid.
33. Ibid.
34. George Seaver, *Francis Younghusband* (London: John Murray, 1952), p. 248.
35. Quoted in Seaver, p. 249, from Francis Younghusband, *Vital Religion* (London: John Murray, 1940), pp. 2–3.
36. Ibid.
37. 'Lady Lees' Memories' in George Seaver, *Francis Younghusband* (London: John Murray, 1952), p. 373.
38. *New York Times*, 2 August 1942; Patrick French, *Younghusband: The Last Great Imperial Adventurer* (London: HarperCollins, 1994), p. 202. The bombing raid refers to Roosevelt's comment to reports on the origination of the Doolittle Raid.

3. BRITISH AND NAZI VERSIONS OF TIBET

1. Alex C. McKay, '"Truth", Perception and Politics: The British Construction of an Image of Tibet,' in Thierry Dodin and Heinz Rather, eds., *Imagining Tibet: Perceptions, Projections, and Fantasies* (Somerville, MA: Wisdom Books, 2001), p. 67.
2. The 'Century of Humiliation' is a term used by the CCP since 1949 to refer to the period from the Opium Wars in 1842 to 1911, when the Republic of China was formed by Sun Yat-sen.
3. Edmund Candler, *The Unveiling of Lhasa* (London: Thomas Nelson & Sons, 1905), p. 308.
4. Loc. cit.
5. Loc. cit.
6. McKay, p. 70.
7. Ibid., p. 71. In the years following the Younghusband mission the Tibetans were often described in negative terms by some British officials and writers in order to justify the invasion. In a London *Times* article, for example, a reporter wrote that the Tibetans were 'a stunted and dirty little people.' Ibid.
8. Ibid., p. 73.
9. Ibid.
10. Ibid., p. 75.
11. Ibid.
12. Ibid., p. 78. The 'core image' is also known as the 'historical image.'
13. Hugh E. Richardson, *Tibet and its History* (London: Shambhala, 1984), p. 11.
14. McKay, p. 83.
15. Hilton (references to page numbers of the Pan 1991 edition of *Lost Horizon*), pp. 128–9.
16. Bishop, p. 211.
17. B. R. Crisler, *New York Times*, 26 July 1936. Hilton, who was in Hollywood to discuss the *Lost Horizon* movie, also mentioned that he had found much of his material for the book at the British Museum Library; he read 'Travels of the Abbé Huc.'
18. James Hilton's fame was based largely on two of his novels. In 1920 he published *Catherine Herself*, his first novel. In 1933 he published *Lost Horizon*; in 1934 *Goodbye, Mr Chips*, and in 1941 *Random Harvest*. It was *Lost Horizon* and *Goodbye, Mr Chips* that were international best-sellers and inspired successful film adaptations.
19. Hilton, p. 58.
20. Ibid., p. 63. Conway mentions Shangri-La as being in Tibet. (Interestingly, the High

Lama in Shangri-La is not a Buddhist monk; rather he is Father Perrault, born in Luxembourg in 1681, who became a Capuchin friar, eventually making his way to Tibet.) See p. 104.

21. Hilton, p. 69.
22. Ibid., pp. 102–3. This is the quote used at the beginning of the book (these books are in the rooms of all Shangri-La hotels).
23. Hilton, p. 138.
24. Ibid., p. 138.
25. Donald S. Lopez, Jr, *Prisoners of Shangri-La: Tibetan Buddhism and the West* (Chicago: University of Chicago Press, 1998), p. 10.
26. T. Lobsang Rampa, *The Third Eye* (New York: Ballantine Books, 1964), p. 88. Rampa's father was said to have been an aristocrat, and one of the leading members of the Dalai Lama's government. Rampa entered the monastery at seven years old and, as the story goes, had a hole drilled in his head into which was placed a third eye that gave him the ability to see people as they really were, not as they pretended to be.
27. Martin Brauen, *Dreamworld Tibet* (Somerville, MA: Wisdom Books), p. 90. He also said he had been instructed in 'the art of telepathy, hypnosis, levitation and yoga.'
28. Ibid., p. 94. Tibetologist Donald Lopez makes the unusual point that the book served 'the important purpose of bringing the plight of Tibet to a Western audience of thousands who otherwise would have been unconcerned; an audience who would have no interest in Tibet without the trappings of astral travel, spirituality, and the hope of human evolution to a New Age.' Donald S. Lopez, Jr, 'The Image of Tibet of the Great Mystifiers,' in Thierry Dodin and Heinz Rather, eds., *Imagining Tibet: Perceptions, Projections, and Fantasies* (Somerville, MA: Wisdom Publications, 2001), p. 195.
29. Brauen called this body of fictional work 'neo Nazi literature.' Brauen, p. 51.
30. Christopher Hale, *Himmler's Crusade: The True Story of the 1938 Nazi Expedition into Tibet* (New York: Bantam Press, 2003), p. 11.
31. Ibid.
32. Ibid., p. 64.
33. Ibid., pp. 40–1. Dolan had an alcohol problem that haunted his whole life.
34. Ibid., p. 41.
35. Ibid., p,52.
36. Ibid., p. 53.
37. Ibid., p. 53. He was the second 'white man' to kill a panda; the first was from the Roosevelt family and the panda was sent to the Field Museum in Chicago, p. 52.
38. Ibid., p. 10.
39. Ibid., p. 64.
40. Ibid., p. 137.
41. Ibid., pp. 180–3.
42. Ibid., p. 279.
43. Ibid., p. 298.
44. Ibid., p. 298.
45. Brauen, p. 67.
46. George Curzon, *Frontiers*, Romanes Lecture (Oxford: Clarendon Press,1908), quoted in Peter Bishop, p. 148.
47. Jamyang Norbu, 'Behind the Lost Horizon: Demystifying Tibet,' in Dodin and Rather, p. 375.

4. STILWELL, THE BURMA HUMP AND THE OSS

1. We have chosen to use the Wade–Giles system for Chinese names, the system that was used until Pinyin was introduced in the 1950s. We use the spelling Chiang Kai-shek instead of Jiang Jieshi; Formosa instead of Taiwan, when referring to events before 1949; Kuomintang instead of Guomindang; Mao Tse-tung instead of Mao Zedong; and Chou En-lai instead of Zhou Enlai. For place names, we use the Chinese Postal Map system of romanization, for example Sinkiang, Chungking, Nanking; but Peking only for the historical period, and Beijing from the PRC onwards.

2. This was a sensitive issue with the Tibetans, and in the end they stated that they would allow 'non-military goods' to pass through Tibet. Melvyn Goldstein wrote: 'these supplies were to be sent through Tibetan trading companies on existing pack-animal trails via Central Tibet, Nagchuka, and Jyekundo, bypassing Lhasa.' Melvyn Goldstein, *A History of Modern Tibet, 1913–1951* (Berkeley: University of California Press, 1989), p. 386.

3. 'Telegram from the Secretary of State (Cordell Hull) to the American Ambassador in China (Gauss),' 3 July 1942, *FRUS* China 1942, p. 626.

4. 'Memorandum from the Secretary of State (Hull) to the Ambassador in China (Gauss),' 3 July 1942, *FRUS* China 1942, p. 626. US officials were mindful of the Chinese claim over Tibet. Roosevelt's personal letters show that the question of how to deal with Tibet's status had arisen five years earlier through a largely personal channel. In April of 1937, Helen Cutting Wilmerding, a cousin of Eleanor Roosevelt, wrote a personal note beginning 'Dear Franklin' that requested a 'signed photo' and a 'letter of good will' to the Tibetan government on behalf of her brother, Charles Suydam Cutting, a celebrated ethnographer and botanist going to Lhasa in the summer of 1937. Cutting had already made his first trip to Lhasa in 1935 and had traveled prior to that with Theodore Roosevelt and his son Kermit to Ladakh and Sinkiang. Cutting knew Brooke Dolan, who traveled with Schäfer and later with Tolstoy to Tibet. The correspondence was passed to Assistant Secretary of State Sumner Welles, whose views foreshadowed those of Secretary Hull towards Tibet in 1942. Welles thought it inadvisable for the President to give letters or gifts to officials in Tibet. His note to his Private Secretary, Miss LeHand, read: 'Tibet is still technically under the suzerainty of China and consequently, gifts or a letter of good will from the President of the United States to officials of Tibet would be liable to be misconstrued in China.' See *Franklin D Roosevelt and Foreign Affairs*, vol. 5, April–June 1937 (New York: Clearwater, 1980), p. 385; Ilya Tolstoy, 'Across Tibet from India to China,' *National Geographic*, August 1946, p. 169; India Office Records (IOR) L/P&S/12/4305, British Library, London; Alastair Lamb, *Tibet, China and India, 1914–1950* (UK: Roxford Books, 1989), p. 217, ftn 378; 'Letter from Sumner Welles, Assistant Secretary of State, to Marguerite LeHand, Private Secretary to the President,' 27 April 1937 in Edgar B. Nixon, ed., *Franklin D. Roosevelt and Foreign Affairs* (Cambridge, MA: University Publications of America, 1969), vol. 3, p. 119; and Interview with William (Bill) D. Roosevelt, August 2002, Palm Beach, Florida. Kermit was later in the OSS and the CIA.

5. Interview with George Patterson, 1 May 2005, Scotland.

6. 'Memorandum from the Secretary of State (Hull) to the Ambassador in China (Gauss),' 3 July 1942, *FRUS* China 1942, p. 626. The British were as anxious as the Americans in 1942 about how best to preserve the Chinese front against the Japanese, particularly after the Burma Road was cut. The Foreign Office instructed its ambassador to underscore its view with the Americans in Peking that 'China has made and is making—within the lim-

itations now imposed by her isolation—a real contribution to the united war effort and deserves that we should bend our energies to supporting her.' 'Memorandum from the Head of the Far Eastern Department of the British Foreign Office (Ashley Clarke) to the Counsellor of the American Embassy in the United Kingdom (Matthews),' 7 August 1942, *FRUS* China 1942, p. 144.

7. Ibid.

8. 'Tibetan Précis,' in Hugh Richardson, *High Peaks, Pure Earth: Collected Writings on Tibetan History and Culture* with an edited introduction by Michael Aris (London: Serinda Publications, 1998), p. 600. The Tibetan Précis was originally written by Mr Richardson, the last British Head of Mission in Lhasa, in 1945. It was then published in India and marked 'Secret For Official Use Only.' According to the late Michael Aris, an Oxford Tibetan scholar, there were at one time fifty copies of this produced but only three have survived. See pp. xi and xxi.

9. Brooke Dolan went to Tibet with German zoologist Ernst Schäfer in 1931 and 1934 (see footnote 142 onwards). Dolan was the well-educated grandson of a very wealthy Philadelphia businessman. Dolan studied zoology at Princeton—he didn't complete his degree—and then became affiliated with the Academy of Natural Sciences in Philadelphia. Schäfer and Dolan met in Hanover where the latter was putting together an expedition of zoologists and anthropologists to travel to Asia. See Christopher Hale, *Himmler's Crusade: The True Story of the 1938 Nazi Expedition into Tibet* (New York: Bantam Press, 2003), pp. 41–2.

10. Ilya Tolstoy, 'Across Tibet from India to China,' *National Geographic*, August 1946, p. 169.

11. Papers of Frank Ludlow, 'Report from week ending August 24th 1942,' 'Secret,' India Office Records (IOR), British Library, London.

12. Papers of Frank Ludlow, 'Report from week ending Feb 13th 1943,' IOR, British Library, London. Rumbold's comments were written at the end of Ludlow's report. After Rumbold's note, the under secretary in Delhi wrote, in an almost illegible script: 'It seems extraordinary that the GOI should have sent us no information about the visit until we asked for it. I would be interested to know what is behind this whole thing.' The signature is illegible. Ibid., p. 2.

13. Ibid.

14. Private correspondence from Frank Ludlow, Esquire and OBE, Lhasa, to B. J. Gould, Political Officer Gangtok, Sikkim, sent to H. Weightman, Esquire, Joint Secretary to the Government of India in the External Affairs Department, New Delhi, 31 January 1943.

15. Ibid.

16. Records of the Office of Strategic Services, Miscellaneous Washington Files, History Project, Intelligence Service Personnel, Far East Theatre, National Archives Record Administration (hereafter known as NARA), College Park, Maryland, RG 226, OSS E146, Folder 2720, undated. Although the document is not dated, it is evident from the list of other missions that it is from this time period. Other operation areas listed are: Japan; Japanese Occupied China; French Indochina; Thailand; Burma; and Malaya.

17. Ibid. The Tibet mission was marked 'COMPLETED' on the memo.

18. 'Proposed Psychological Warfare Undertaking in the Far East,' Annex A, RG 226, OSS E146, Folder 2719, 4 January 1943, NARA, College Park, Maryland.

19. Ibid.

20. 'Memorandum from the Director of the Office of Strategic Services (Donovan) to the Secretary of State,' 2 July 1942, *FRUS* China 1942, p. 624.

21. 'Telegram XX, from Foreign Office, New Delhi to Ludlow, Lhasa,' no. 6499, dated 17 August, in the Papers of Frank Ludlow, IOR, British Library, London.
22. 'Confidential Telegram from Gould in Gangtok to the British Foreign Office in New Delhi, Repeated to Ludlow in Lhasa,' no. 8525, 23 October 1942, IOR, British Library, London.
23. 'Extract from Enclosure in India Foreign Secretary's Letter,' no. 4, 20 December 1942, in 'Confidential Memo from Frank Ludlow,' IOR, British Library, London.
24. 'Exchange of Presents in Tibet, Tolstoy–Dolan Mission, 1942–43,' Major Ilya A. Tolstoy, May 1944, RG226, SS E169A, 1178, NARA. Tibetan gift-giving was similar to the Kula gift exchanges of the Trobriand Islanders, researched by anthropologist Bronislaw Malinowski and recorded in his 1922 ethnography, *Argonauts of the Western Pacific*. The Trobriand Islanders of the South Pacific used decorated shells in ritual exchanges designed to establish status, prestige, and social cohesion. The shells would be kept only temporarily and then given away to tribesmen in a gift-giving ceremony. The pair observed, for example, that 'the same eggs often circulated over and over again in the gift-exchanging ritual.'
25. 'Exchange of Presents in Tibet, Tolstoy–Dolan Mission, 1942–43,' Ilya A. Tolstoy, Major, May 1944, RG 226, OSS E169A, 1178, NARA. Presents were exchanged throughout his trip: 'the higher a visiting official you are,' he wrote, 'the better and more numerous presents you are to give.' Ibid. At the nomad camps, Tolstoy and Dolan were given gifts such as grain, meat, eggs, butter, milk, and cheese; it was expected that the chief of the camp would be repaid with money 'wrapped in paper' when the pair moved on. Upon their arrival in Lhasa, they received hundreds of pounds' weight of foodstuffs as welcoming gifts, including 2,800 pounds of grain (barley and peas), 240 pounds of potatoes, and even seventeen sheep. Ibid. Upon their departure from Lhasa they were again given gifts, including rugs, objects of art, a 'religious painting,' various pelt skins, two mules, and a dog. Tolstoy sent the Dalai Lama's gifts of four religious tapestries and gold coins to OSS for delivery to President Roosevelt. Ibid.
26. Hale, p. 339. Apparently Dolan fathered a child while in Lhasa with the daughter of a Tibetan aristocrat. Unfortunately the mother and child drowned a few years after this expedition.
27. 'The Tibetan Foreign Office to Captain Ilya Tolstoy and Lieutenant Brooke Dolan, 13th Day of 1st month, Water Sheep Year' (corresponding to 17 February 1943), *FRUS* China 1943, p. 622.
28. 'Report from F. Ludlow to the Political Officer in Sikkim,' 4 April 1953, in the Papers of Frank Ludlow, IOR, British Library, London.
29. 'Memorandum from Colonel John G. Coughlin at the Office of Strategic Services, Headquarters, USAF, CBI to General William Donovan, Subject: Tolstoy Mission,' RG226, OSS E148, 647, 18 September 1944, NARA.
30. Ibid.
31. George Atcheson thought Tolstoy's initiatives to the Tibetans would be 'politically embarrassing and cause irritation and offence to the Chinese.' See 'Memorandum by the Assistant Chief of the Division of Far Eastern Affairs (Atcheson),' 30 March 1943, *FRUS* China 1943, pp. 624–5. Atcheson wrote that 'the Chinese Government claims suzerainty over Tibet. Therefore, in all probability, the Chinese government would not welcome the introduction into Tibet of such a potent facility as a radio transmitter, particularly as the Chinese are not likely to have any actual control over the transmitter or the material broadcasted.' Ibid.

32. 'The Secretary of State (Hull) to the Ambassador in China,' 3 July 1942, *FRUS* China 1943, p. 626; and also 'The Assistance Secretary of State (Berle) to the Director of the Office of Strategic Services (Donovan),' 23 April 1943, *FRUS* China 1943, p. 629.

5. TRUMAN 1945–1948

1. David McCullough, *Truman* (New York: Simon & Schuster Paperbacks, 1992), p. 463.
2. Ibid., p. 382.
3. Ibid., p. 372.
4. Quoted in Ibid.
5. Ibid.
6. Harry S. Truman, *Year of Decisions 1945* (Garden City, NY: Doubleday, 1955), p. x.
7. Truman wrote this to his daughter, Margaret. Quoted in McCullough, p. 355.
8. Harry S. Truman, p. 10.
9. McCullough, p. 486.
10. 'Memorandum for the Director of Central Intelligence,' in Michael Warner, ed., *The CIA under Harry Truman* (Washington, DC: Central Intelligence Agency), pp. 173–5 and xix.
11. *Foreign Relations of the United States*, 1964–1968 (Washington, DC: US Government Printing Office, 1974), vol. X11, p. xxxi (hereafter cited as *FRUS*).
12. The Truman Doctrine, http://www.trumanlibrary.org/whistlestop/study_collections/doctrine/large/documents/index.php?pagenumber=4&documentdate=1947–03–07&documentid=5–4
13. There were over 100 delegates that attended the conference. Shankar Sharan, *Fifty Years After the Asian Relations Conference* (New Delhi: *Tibetan Parliamentary and Policy Research Center*, 1997), p. 13. India officially gained independence on 15 August 1947.
14. The conversation was reported in a memo from Lord Mountbatten, the Viceroy of India. 'Viceroy to Secretary of State for India, February 26ᵗʰ 1947,' Telegram no. 2903, dated 4 March 1947. It is noted on the invitee list that the Tibetans did not initially acknowledge the invitation to attend, stating: 'Reported that Monks are strongly opposing suggestion the observers should be sent.' See Appendix I, 'States originally invited to the Inter-Asian Relations Conference.' It was also written that 'Reminders have been sent to all States who have not so far acknowledged, except Tibet (to avoid raising with China question of Tibet's independence).' Ibid.
15. Warren W. Smith, *Tibetan Nation: A History of Tibetan Nationalism and Sino-Tibetan Relations* (Colorado: Westview Press, 1996), p. 242; Melvyn Goldstein, *A History of Modern Tibet, 1913–1951* (Berkeley: University of California Press, 1989), pp. 357–9. *Reting Rimpoche is a title held by the Abbot of the Reting Monastery.In keeping with general usage we refer to this Abbot simply as Reting.*
16. Goldstein, p. 359.
17. Smith, pp. 243, 256.
18. Tsepon W. S. Shakabpa, *Tibet: A Political History* (New York. Putala Publications, 1984), pp. 292–3.
19. Goldstein, p. 355.
20. The Kashag, or administrative power, during this period of discussion, consisted of four officials (kalons): three were lay officials and one was a monk official. This council received

all 'secular information'—requests, telegrams, etc. Goldstein describes it as the 'throat between the head (the ruler) and the body (the other secular offices).' While the four officials had equal authority, Goldstein notes that the monk official 'was always formally treated as the senior member, but this was merely ceremonial.' Goldstein, pp. 13–14, The Kashag was responsible to a head official known as the Kalon Tripa. This person functioned as a prime minister who, in turn, reported to the Dalai Lama.

21. In post-war Tibet the Oracle remained a vital figure affecting the security of the fourteenth Dalai Lama. The Oracle would prophesy that in 1950, the year of the Tiger, Tibet would suffer great distress, which of course it did when the Chinese invaded; then, later in 1959, the Oracle advised the Dalai Lama to depart Lhasa for his safety and predicted his flight to India.

22. Sharan, 1997, pp. 27–8.

6. THE IRON TRIANGLE: THE CHINA LOBBY, THE RED SCARE, AND THE CATHOLIC CHURCH

1. 'Memoranda of Conversations with the President, October–November 1949,' Box 66, 17 November 1949, The Papers of Dean G. Acheson, The Truman Presidential Library.
2. Ibid.
3. Ibid.
4. The Truman Doctrine http://www.trumanlibrary.org/whistlestop/study_collections/doctrine/large/documents/index.php?pagenumber=4&documentdate=1947–03–07&documentid=5–4
5. The Dalai Lama, quoted in Thomas Laird, *The Story of Tibet* (New York: Grove Press, 2006), p. 295.
6. Millis, Walter, ed., *The Forrestal Diaries: The Inner History of the Cold War* (London: Cassell & Company, 1952), p. 354.
7. Ibid.
8. Ibid. The Director of the Central Intelligence Agency, Rear Admiral R. H. Hillenkoetter, confirmed what Washington planners already knew that month. In a detailed memorandum to President Truman, the agency outlined the strength and capabilities of the Chinese communist armies throughout China. See 'The Papers of Harry S. Truman,' PSF 1940–1953, Subject File: China 1948, Box 1, Harry S. Truman Presidential Library.
9. Nancy Bernkopf Tucker, *Patterns in the Dust* (New York: Columbia University Press, 1984), p. 80.
10. See Ross Y. Koen, *The China Lobby in American Politics* (New York: Harper and Row, 1974), pp. 28–9.
11. Ibid.
12. Nancy Bernkopf Tucker, p. 81. Most Americans at the time knew little about the China Lobby. A *New York Times* article dated 28 June 1951 identified ten groups in the United States that were working for the 'Chiang regime,' but could not provide any detailed information. Among the other newspaper magnates who supported the Nationalist cause with Luce were William Randolph Hearst; Roy Howard of Scripps–Howard; William Loeb of the *New Hampshire Morning Union* (later the *Manchester Union-Leader*); and Robert McCormick of the *Chicago Tribune*.
13. Robert E. Herzstein, 'Alfred Kohlberg, Global Entrepreneur and Hyper-Nationalist,' a

paper presented to a conference of the Historical Society, Chapel Hill, North Carolina, 3 June 2006, p. 2.

14. Robert E. Herzstein, *Henry R. Luce, Time, and The American Crusade in Asia* (Cambridge: Cambridge University Press, 2005), p. 1.

15. Ibid.

16. Thomas Laird, *The Story of Tibet: Conversations with the Dalai Lama* (New York: Grove Press, 2006), pp. 289 and 296. In a declassified report from the CIA dated 3 November 1950, it is noted that the Dalai Lama not only received and was reading *Life* magazine but that he also enjoyed the *National Geographic* magazine. 'Central Intelligence Agency Information Report,' 3 November 1959, CIA-RDP82–00457R00510020, NARA.

17. Herzstein, 'Alfred Kohlberg', p. 1.

18. W.A. Swanberg, *Luce and his Empire* (New York: Charles Scribner's Sons, 1972), p. 302.

19. John Shaw Billings, quoted in Herzstein, *Henry R. Luce*, p. 2.

20. Ibid.

21. Luce's private papers in the Library of Congress in Washington reveal the personal relationship he had with Dwight D. Eisenhower and John Foster Dulles, who became Eisenhower's secretary of state. Luce began his correspondence with Eisenhower in 1950, when Eisenhower was the president of Columbia University. The two men corresponded on a variety of issues, both political and personal, and Eisenhower handwrote many of the letters. During Ike's campaign for president in 1952, he wrote to Luce: 'There is no way in which I can adequately express to you and Mrs Luce my appreciation for your unfailing support during the months leading up to the convention. Your continued confidence is a source of strength and encouragement.' See 'Letter from Dwight D. Eisenhower to Henry Luce,' 5 August 1952, in the Papers of Henry R. Luce, Box 1, Folder 25, 1950–64, Library of Congress, Washington, DC.

22. Herzstein, *Henry R. Luce*, pp. 21, 37, 63.

23. Swanberg, p. 2.

24. Ibid.

25. Barbara W. Tuchman, *Stilwell and the American Experience in China, 1911*–1945 (New York: Macmillan, 1970), p. 188.

26. Herzstein, *Henry R. Luce*, p. 39.

27. Ibid., p. 40.

28. Mrs Luce was also a great fan of the Generalissimo's wife, the former Soong Mayling. Madame Chiang Kai-shek, as she was called, was the daughter of a Methodist minister, and she and her two sisters were educated at Wesleyan University in Georgia. After meeting her, the Generalissimo converted to Methodism.

29. *Life* magazine, January 1946.

30. Herzstein, *Henry R. Luce*, p. 177.

31. John Shaw Billings, quoted in Herzstein, *Henry R. Luce*, p. 276, ftn 83. Luce put Dulles on the cover of *Time* on 13 August 1951 and 12 October 1953, and featured him on the cover as 'Man of the Year' on 3 January 1955.

32. John Shaw Billings, quoted in Herzstein, *Henry R. Luce*, p. 98.

33. *Life* magazine, 6 January 1947.

34. *Life* magazine, 13 January 1947. Marshall further enraged Luce when he became the secretary of state and authorized only limited funds for the Chiang government. Marshall was a man who did not mince words, and in a three-hour meeting with Chiang Kai-shek on 1 December 1946 he told the Generalissimo, while Madame Chiang translated, that

'You have broken agreements; you have gone counter to plans. People have said you were a modern George Washington, but after these things they will never say it again.' Chiang sat expressionless, but 'his feelings were betrayed by a bobbing foot.' After Marshal had finished, Chiang 'unleashed an hour-long rebuttal … his false teeth clicking as he spoke …' Laura Tyson Li, *Madame Chiang Kai-Shek: China's Eternal First Lady* (New York: Grove Press, 2006), p. 277.

35. Herzstein, *Henry R. Luce*, p. 81; author William Swanberg wrote that Luce 'now saw the most grandiose project of his lifetime in danger of ruin.' See Swanberg, p. 252.

36. John T. Woolley and Gerhard Peters, *The American Presidency Project* [online], Santa Barbara, CA: University of California (hosted), Gerhard Peters (database), http://www.presidency.ucsb.edu/ws/?pid=13678), last accessed 1 June 2013.

37. 'Memorandum of Conversation, by the Secretary of State,' 5 January 1950, *FRUS*, vol. VI, pp. 258–63.

38. Ibid., p. 260.

39. Ibid. Ambassador Stuart was at Shanghai, General Douglas MacArthur was the supreme commander, allied powers and commander in chief, Far East, and Admiral Arthur W. Radford was the commander in chief for the Pacific.

40. Ibid.

41. Ibid., p. 262.

42. Ibid., p. 263.

43. Ibid.

44. John W. Garver, *The Sino-American Alliance, Nationalist China and American Cold War Strategy in Asia* (New York: M. E. Sharpe, 1997), p. 21. Truman did allow the Navy to 'deliver arms previously contracted to Taiwan and approved limited economic aid—but he held firm on the central principle of no US military relation with or military action on behalf of the Nationalists.' Ibid.

45. Dean Acheson, *Present at the Creation: My Years in the State Department* (New York: W. W. Norton, 1969), pp. 355–8. This was an exceptionally tough period in Acheson's life, not only because he was under constant attack in the political arena, but also personally. His daughter, who had contracted TB when she was nineteen, was now in the Trudeau Sanatorium in Saranac, New York. She spent five years there recuperating and eventually lost a lung. The Achesons were caring for her five-year-old son. Ibid., p. 354.

46. Tyson Li, p. 308.

47. Kohlberg made his fortune in the 1920s by purchasing linen and lace from Ireland and shipping it to China, where he employed thousands of Chinese women to produce beautifully finished textile products, including his famous 'kohlkerchiefs.'[47] He exported high quality linen, lace gloves, and silks assembled by cheap labor and twice received 'cease and desist' orders from the Federal Trade Commission for 'passing off his products as Irish crochet lace.' Like Luce, he strongly supported Chiang Kai-shek and used his money to attack critics of the 'Generalissimo' and others who he believed supported communism.

48. Herzstein, 'Alfred Kohlberg, Global Entrepreneur and Hyper-Nationalist,' p. 4.

49. Ibid.

50. Herzstein, *Henry R. Luce, Time, and the American Crusade in Asia*, p. 65.

51. Alfred Kohlberg to Chiang Kai-shek, quoted in Herzstein, p. 68.

52. Tyson Li, p. 301

53. Ibid., pp. 301 and 303. Madame Chiang spent most of her time in the late 1940s in the United States lobbying on behalf of her husband.
54. See discussion in the following chapter of Sprouse and Bacon, Office of Chinese Affairs, Bureau of Far Eastern Affairs.
55. Ellen Schrecker, *The Age of McCarthyism: A Brief History with Documents* (New York: Bedford/St Martin's Press, 2002), p. 76.
56. Ibid.
57. Jack Anderson and Ronald W. May, *McCarthy The Man, The Senator, The 'ISM'* (London: Victor Gollancz, 1953), p. 295. The term 'McCarthyism' came to mean 'any investigation that flouts the rights of individuals, usually involving character assassination, smears, mud-slinging, sensationalism, and guilt by association.' See Donald A. Ritchie, Senate Historical Office, Introduction to 'Executive Sessions of the Senate Permanent Subcommittee on Investigations of the Committee on Government Operations,' vol. I, Eighty-Third Congress, First Session 1953 (Washington, DC: US Printing Office, 2003), p. XVIII.
58. M. Stanton Evans, *The Untold Story of Senator Joe McCarthy and his Fight Against America's Enemies* (New York: Crown Forum, 2008). Also Nicholas von Hoffman, 'Exhuming McCarthy,' *Prospect Magazine*, 19 December 2001.
59. Speech delivered by Senator Joseph McCarthy before the Senate on 14 June 1951.

7. TRUMAN AND INDIA

1. Andrew J. Rotter, *Comrades at Odds: the United States and India 1947–1964* (Ithaca: Cornell University Press, 2000), Introduction.
2. Ibid., p. 1. Mayo's book was originally published in 1927 and by the 'mid-1950s the book had gone through twenty-seven American editions and sold well over a quarter of a million copies in the United States alone'. Ibid. H. W. Brands called the American reaction to Mayo's best-selling book rather astonishing and that 'even the most gullible' of readers should have recognized its fallacies. H. W. Brands, *India and the Cold Peace* (Boston: Twayne Publishers, 1990), p. 7. Newspapers like the *New York Times*, *New York Herald Tribune* and the *Chicago Evening Post* praised Mayo's depiction. Ibid.
3. Rotter, pp. 2–4.
4. Brands, p. 7.
5. Ibid., p. 8.
6. H. W. Brands, *The Specter of Neutralism: The United States and the Emergence of the Third World* (New York: Columbia University Press, 1989), p. 19.
7. 'The Commissioner in India (Merrell) to the Secretary of State,' 10 June 1946, *FRUS*, vol. V, p. 88.
8. Ibid.
9. Ibid.
10. Ibid.
11. Ibid.
12. Ibid., p. 91. The United States opened their Embassy on 1 November 1946. Before Merrell was ambassador he was the chargé/commissioner.
13. Robert J. McMahon, *The Cold War on the Periphery: The United States, India and Pakistan* (New York: Columbia University Press, 1994), p. 20. The fighting was brutal and when the tribesmen threatened to take over Srinigar, the state capital, the Maharajah fled

but first notified the government of India and pleaded for troops. Lord Louis Mountbatten was the viceroy of India and oversaw the British withdrawal. After Partition he became India's interim governor-general until July 1948. Mountbatten insisted that the prince would have to accede to India, and a formal agreement was signed on 26 October 1947. This of course did not hold. Ibid., p. 21.

14. Ibid. and 'The Ambassador in India (Grady) to the Secretary of State,' 5 October 1947, *FRUS*, vol. III, pp. 166–7. The government of India wanted Washington to make available ten army transport planes to fly 50,000 non-Muslim refugees from Pakistan into northern India. Ibid.

15. 'The Secretary of State to the Embassy in India,' 14 November 1947, *FRUS*, vol. III, pp. 171–2.

16. 'Memorandum of Conversation by Mr Joseph S. Sparks of the Division of South Asian Affairs,' 26 December 1947, *FRUS*, vol. III, p. 175.

17. Ibid., p. 177.

18. 'Memorandum of Conversation Mr Joseph S. Sparks of the Division of South Asian Affairs,' 26 December 1947, *FRUS*, vol. III, p. 176–178. Shone was the UK high commissioner. The British, it seemed, were not happy about the stronger position of the United States in India during this period and were, according to Grady, 'trying to salvage everything they can from the separation'. Ambassador Grady was generally mistrustful of the British and felt that they were competitive with the United States. Ibid. Also see Brands, *The Specter of Neutralism*, pp. 19–20.

19. H. W. Brands, *Inside the Cold War: Loy Henderson and the Rise of the American Empire 1918–1961* (Oxford: Oxford University Press, 1991), p. 198.

20. Ibid.

21. Ibid.

22. Ibid.

23. Oral history interview with Loy Henderson by Richard D. McKinzie on 14 June 1973, Harry S. Truman Archives.

24. Ibid.

25. Ibid.

26. Ibid.

27. Ibid.

28. Ibid.

29. Ibid.

30. Menon was put out that the US ambassador to London, Lewis Douglas, 'had not seen fit' to call on him. Menon said, 'But we shall see the time when American ambassadors will feel honored to be received by an Indian High Commissioner.' Ibid.

31. Ibid.

32. T. J. S. George, *Krishna Menon: A Biography* (Edinburgh: J. & J. Gray, 1964), pp. 1–5.

33. Oral history interview with Loy Henderson by Richard D. McKinzie on 14 June 1973, Harry S. Truman Archives.

34. 'Report originally produced by the SANACC Subcommittee for the Near and Middle East' (the State-Army-Navy-Air Committee), an interagency committee on the Near and Middle East. It was entitled 'Appraisal of US National Interests in South Asia,' 19 April 1949, *FRUS*, vol. VI, pp. 8–25. The paper was approved on 31 May and was then referred to the National Security Council on 16 June as the basis of US policy towards Asia. This later became part of NSC 48/1 and 48/2 that was approved by the NSC and the president.

35. Ibid., p. 12.
36. Ibid., p. 17.
37. Ibid.
38. Ibid. See 'Memorandum from the Joint Chiefs of Staff,' Appendix C, 24 March 1949, *FRUS*, vol. VI, pp. 29–30.
39. 'The Ambassador in India (Henderson) to the Secretary of State,' 15 August 1949, *FRUS*, vol. VI, pp. 1732–3; 'The Ambassador in India (Henderson) to the Secretary of State,' 29 July 1949, *FRUS*, vol. VI, p. 1728.
40. Ibid., p. 1733.
41. Ibid., p. 1732. A few weeks later Nehru responded to President Truman's request for reconciliation on the Kashmir issue. The letter was sent by Henderson in the diplomatic pouch to Washington. Nehru wrote: 'In conclusion I wish [to] assure you that India does not wish the Kashmir or any other dispute to be settled by the sword. She will always be ready to consider a solution by any method that would lead to a peaceful settlement of the entire dispute.' See 'The Ambassador in India (Henderson) to the Secretary of State,' 8 September 1949, *FRUS*, vol. VI, pp. 1736–8.
42. Ibid., p. 1733.
43. Ibid.
44. 'The Ambassador in India (Henderson) to the Secretary of State,' 15 August 1949, *FRUS*, vol. VI, p. 1732. Also see 'The Ambassador in India (Henderson) to the Secretary of State,' 8 September 1949, *FRUS*, vol. VI, pp. 1736–8.
45. 'Letter to Dean Acheson,' 18 June 1949, in the Papers of Loy Henderson, Library of Congress, Washington, DC, Subject File: Miscellaneous, India. Henderson's papers provide a fascinating insight into this period.
46. Ibid.
47. Ibid.
48. Ibid.
49. Ibid.
50. Ibid
51. Ibid
52. Ibid.
53. 'Letter to Dean Acheson', 18 June 1949, in the papers of Loy Henderson, Library of Congress, Washington, DC, subject File: Miscellaneous, India.
54. Ibid.
55. Ibid.
56. Ibid.
57. Nehru wrote frequent letters to her during his time as prime minister revealing his most personal thoughts. He always endearingly addressed his letters 'Nan dear.' She was the much-loved 'pet' of the family and they called her Nanhi, which meant 'little daughter.' Her English governess shortened her name to Nan. As English names were 'in vogue' at the time, she became known as Nan Nehru. See Anne Guthrie, *Madame Ambassador: The Life of Vijaya Lakshmi Pandit* (London: Macmillan, 1963), ch.2.
58. 'Letter to Vijayalaksmi,' 24 August 1949, in S. Gopal, ed., *Selected Works of Jawaharlal Nehru*, vol. 13 (New Delhi: Jawaharlal Nehru Memorial Fund, 1992), p. 289.
59. Ibid.
60. Loc. cit.

61. 'Letter to Vijayalakshmi,' 31 May 1949, in Gopal, *Selected Works of Jawaharlal Nehru*, vol. 11, p. 354.

62. 'Letter to Vijayalakshmi,' 8 June 1949, in Gopal, *Selected Works of Jawaharlal Nehru*, vol. 11, pp. 355–6. Nehru felt bullied by State Department officials including Acheson, who threatened to withhold US loans and World Bank assistance if the situation in Kashmir was not brought under control. Nehru thought the Department's diplomacy to be 'immature, or it [the US] is too sure of its physical might to care for the niceties of diplomatic behaviour.' Ibid., pp. 356–7.

63. Ibid., p. 356.

64. Ibid. Nehru pointed out that the Americans wanted India to 'tie ourselves' to US foreign policy but that they would continue with their affiliation in the Commonwealth which leaned towards more 'socialist tendencies.' Ibid., p. 356.

65. Dean Acheson, *Present at the Creation: My Years in the State Department* (New York: W. W. Norton, 1969), p. 251. In his memoirs, Acheson reflected the tenor of Washington and the country that year. Commenting on the Hiss hearings, he wrote: 'It is enough to say of it here that at the time of the hearings what had seemed in the beginning incredible and bizarre had moved into personal tragedy. It was destined to go onto something approaching national disaster, lending, as it did, support to a widespread attack throughout the country upon confidence in the government itself.' Ibid.

66. The China Lobby was a group of lobbyists, business people and officials who were Nationalist Chinese supporters.

67. *Life* magazine, 19 December 1949, p. 24. The emphasis was included in the commentary.

68. Ibid. At the beginning of 1949, *Life* wrote: 'Americans should never forget that a Communist victory in China is a victory for the Soviet Union and a major disaster for the US.' See *Life* magazine, 3 January 1949, p. 24.

69. Dean Acheson, *Present at the Creation*, p. 334. Acheson wrote of a later conversation about Kashmir that when he asked Nehru for a 'frank discussion on a practicable solution of the trouble over Kashmir, I got a curious combination of a public speech and flashes of anger and deep dislike of his opponents.' Ibid., p. 336.

70. *New York Times*, 12 October 1949, pp. 1, 18.

71. *Life* magazine, 7 November 1949, p. 68.

72. Ibid.

73. Ibid. *Life* also looked at the visit more realistically, saying 'the US was quite openly interested in getting a friendly India on its side in the Cold War against a Communist Russia.' Ibid., p. 69.

74. *Time* magazine, 13 October 1949. *Time* furthered the American cultural stereotype about Indians in an article on Nehru. They wrote: 'When India's Prime Minister Jawaharlal Nehru needs to relax, he stands on his head.' Ibid. Overall, though, the article was quite informative and gave American readers insight about the Indian leader. Ibid.

75. Non-alignment and neutralism are used synonymously.

76. Gopal, *Selected Works of Jawaharlal Nehru*, vol. 1, pp. 404–5.

77. McMahon, *Cold War on the Periphery*, pp. 54–5.

78. Ambassador George McGhee, *Envoy to the Middle World: Adventures in Diplomacy* (New York: Harper and Row, 1983), p. 47.

79. Ibid., p. 56.

80. 'Memorandum of Conversation by the Secretary of State,' 13 October 1949, *FRUS*, vol. VI, pp. 1750–1.
81. Ibid.
82. 'Memorandum of Conversation, Department of State,' 13 October 1949, 'Official conversations and meetings of Dean Acheson (1949–1953),' Microfilm (Frederick, Maryland: University Publications of America, 1980), p. 0025.
83. Dean Acheson, *Present at the Creation*, p. 335.
84. Ibid.
85. Ibid., p. 336.
86. Ibid.
87. Ibid.
88. 'Memorandum of Conversation by Mr Joseph Sparks, Advisor to the United States Delegation at the United Nations,' 19 October 1949, *FRUS*, vol. VI, p. 1753.
89. Ibid.
90. Quoted in 'Note to the Secretary General,' 3 November 1950, in Gopal, *Selected Works of Jawaharlal Nehru*, vol. 15, part 2, pp. 524–5. At a private dinner between Ambassador Henderson and Nehru on 3 November 1950, a year after the Indian prime minister's visit to the United States, Henderson, in a frank discussion with Nehru, expressed his unhappiness at the state of US–Indian relations. Henderson asked Nehru if there had been anything specific during his trip to the United States that he might have found disturbing. He asked Nehru if, perhaps, the dinners given in his honor seemed to be 'crude displays.' Nehru agreed and said they were 'ostentatious.' Ibid.
91. Quoted in T. N. Kaul, *Diplomacy in Peace and War: Recollections and Reflections* (Bombay: Vikas Publishing House, 1979), p. 23.
92. Frank Moraes, *Jawaharlal Nehru: A Biography* (New York: Macmillan, 1956), p. 471.
93. Vijaya Lakshmi Pandit, *The Scope of Happiness: A Personal Memoir* (New York: Crown Publishers, 1979), p. 252.
94. Ibid., pp. 252–3.
95. Papers of Loy Henderson, Library of Congress, Washington, DC, Subject File: Miscellaneous, India.
96. Pandit, *The Scope of Happiness*, p. 253. The *pièce de résistance* of the dinner was the gift of a 'gold cigarette lighter with two clasped hands on one side and an inscription on the other!' Nehru was 'shocked.' Ibid.
97. Ibid. Ambassador McGhee also wrote that in Nehru's 'first informal meeting with the President, he was offended by Truman's extended discussion of the merits of bourbon whiskey with Vice President Alben Barkley of Kentucky, who was one of the invited guests.' See Ambassador George McGhee, *Envoy to the Middle World: Adventures in Diplomacy*, p. 47.
98. T. N. Kaul, *A Diplomat's Diary: China, India and the USA: 1947–1999* (New Delhi: Macmillan, 2000), p. 5.
99. Ibid. Kaul wrote that the ambassador 'took these remarks in her usual stride and did not contradict them.' Ibid., p. 5.
100. McMahon, *Cold War on the Periphery*, p. 54.
101. Ibid.
102. 'Nehru's Address to the US House of Representatives and the US Senate,' Washington, DC, 13 October 1949, in Gopal, *Selected Works of Jawaharlal Nehru*, vol. 13, p. 303. T. N. Kaul, who was with Nehru during his Washington visit, said he 'got a knock on the

head from Nehru for suggesting to him that if we were short of food grains, we could get wheat from America at concessional rates.' Kaul wrote, 'Nehru literally flared up and said: What do you think India is, a beggar?' Quoted in T. N. Kaul, *Diplomacy in Peace and War: Reflections and Reflections*, p. 21.

103. 'Address to the Indian residents of New York,' New India House, New York, 15 October 1949, *Hindustan Times*, 17 October 1949, quoted in Gopal, vol. 13, pp. 310–11.

104. 'Letters to Chief Ministers,' in Gopal, vol. 14, part 1, p. 365.

105. Ibid.

8. TIBETAN INDEPENDENCE: RESTING UPON A THREE-LEGGED STOOL

1. 'Nehru's Radio Address on All India Radio,' 7 September 1946, in S. Gopal, ed., *Selected Works of Jawaharlal Nehru* (New Delhi: Jawaharlal Nehru Memorial Fund, 1992), vol. 1, p. 404. Chiang Kai-shek and his wife sent Nehru a birthday card in November 1946, to which Nehru replied: 'In the midst of all our problems here, we think often of you and China and look forward to the day when both China and India having overcome their present difficulties will rapidly advance in friendship and cooperation …' Quoted from *National Herald*, 18 November 1946, in Gopal, vol. 1, p. 544.

2. Hugh E. Richardson, *Tibet and its History* (London: Shambhala, 1984), p. 173. Richardson was the last British Head of Mission in Lhasa and the first under an independent India. India inherited the boundaries with Tibet defined by the British in the Simla Convention of 1914. India also acquired the 'extra-territorial privileges enjoyed under agreement with Tibet-the right to maintain trade agents at Gyantse, Yatung, and Gartok (the last was never a permanent post) with small military escorts.' They also inherited the post and telegraph services. Richardson, p. 175.

3. 'Telegram to K. P. S. Menon,' 14 March 1947, Ministry of External Affairs and Commonwealth Relations, National Archives of India, in Gopal, *Selected Works of Jawaharlal Nehru*, vol. 2, p. 502, ftn 2. When in early 1947, for example, the Tibetans sought to attend the Asian conference in New Delhi as an independent nation, under their own flag, the Chinese raised objections. The Nationalists insisted that there be no discussion regarding Tibet's political status at the conference, and the Tibetan representatives must be included with the Chinese representatives; Tibet was not to be listed as a separate nation.

4. 'Record of Nehru's Talks with the Tibetan Mission,' 8 January 1949, File no. 1 (1)-NEF/48, in Gopal, vol. 9, p. 470, ftn 2. The Tibetans exported a small amount of goods to the United States—wool, yak tails, and musk—and the dollars they received for the sale of these products were held by the Indian government; they were paid the equivalent in rupees. See 'Memorandum by the Second Secretary of Embassy in India,' 30 December 1947, *FRUS*, vol. VII, p. 606; and also 'The Chargé in India to the Secretary of State', 5 January 1948, *FRUS*, vol. VII, p. 755.

5. 'Record of Nehru's Talks with the Tibetan Mission,' 8 January 1949, File no. 1 (1)-NEF/48, in Gopal, vol. 9, p. 470, ftn 2.

6. 'Note to Foreign Secretary,' 31 December 1947, in Gopal, vol. 9, p. 469, ftn 2. The foreign secretary was K. P. S. Menon. The Foreign and Political Department of the British India government became, at the end of 1947, the Ministry of External Affairs and Commonwealth Relations and Menon was the director.

7. Ibid.

8. See Melvyn Goldstein, *A History of Modern Tibet, 1913–1951* (Berkeley: University of Cal-

ifornia Press, 1989), pp. 570–6; Tsepon Shakabpa, *One Hundred Thousand Moons* (Leiden: Brill, 2010), p. 905.

9. A. J. Hopkinson, the former political officer in Sikkim, told an American embassy official in Delhi in a discussion about the Tibetan mission that 'despite their acumen as traders, members of the mission may prove to be "babes in the wood" when they come face to face with exchange and banking regulations and import and export restrictions.' 'Memo from the American Embassy in Delhi to the Secretary of State,' 21 November 1947, 693.0031 Tibet/11–2147, NARA, College Park, Maryland.

10. Tsepon Shakabpa, *Tibet: A Political History* (New York: Potala Publications, 1984), p. 295. Goldstein argues that while this mission indeed did demonstrate that the Tibetans 'had some sort of international identity independent of China, the nature of that identity was far from clear.' Goldstein, *A History of Modern Tibet*, p. 570.

11. 'American Embassy in India to the Secretary of State,' 30 December 1947, 693.0031 Tibet/12–3047, NARA, College Park, Maryland. And also see 'Edward W. Doherty to the US State Department,' 25 August 1948, 693.0031, Tibet/18–748, NARA.

12. 'The American Embassy in India to the Secretary of State, Washington, Subject: Additional Background on Tibetan Trade Mission; Questions Regarding Policy Toward Tibet,' 21 August 1947, 693.0031 Tibet/8–2147, NARA. At the end of the report Donovan, who wrote on the ambassador's behalf, requested a clarification of the US policy towards Tibet. He referred to a 'secret memo' from 28 October 1946 that stated: 'the United States and China both regarded Tibet as an integral part of China' but now wondered whether State had changed the 'official policy.'

13. Ibid. Much of the information that Donovan conveyed to Washington about the Tibetan trade delegation was from a personal letter received from A. J. Hopkinson, the British political officer in Sikkim. Hopkinson believed that not only did the trade delegation seek gold and silver for commercial purposes but also for personal use. He wrote that in Tibet 'you save gold for your own tomb if you are a real bigwig.' Ibid., p. 2.

14. 'Telegram from Nanking to the Secretary of State,' 26 July 1948, 693.0031 Tibet/7–2648, NARA.

15. 'Chinese Government Information Office,' Daily Bulletin no. 214, 7 February 1948, enclosure in Memorandum from E. Anderberg, American Ambassador in Nanking to the Office of Chinese Affairs, Department of State, Washington, 693.0031 Tibet/2–2448, NARA.

16. Ibid.

17. Ibid.

18. 'Telegram from Nanking to the Secretary of State,' 26 July 1948, 693.0031 Tibet/7–2648, NARA.

19. Ibid.

20. Ibid.

21. 'Department of State, George Marshall to American Embassy, Nanking,' 28 July 1948, 693.003 Tibet/7–26–48, NARA. The words 'de jure' are underlined in his memo.

22. Ibid. The words 'de facto' are underlined in the memo. Marshall specifically wrote of the hospitality the Tibetans showed towards Tolstoy and Dolan in 1943. In US government correspondence 'ChiGovt' refers to the Nationalists and 'ChiCom' refers to the Chinese Communists.

23. Ibid.

24. 'Department of State, George Marshall to American Embassy, Nanking,' 28 July 1948, 693.003 Tibet/7–26–48, NARA.
25. Ibid.
26. 'Memorandum of Conversation with Mr Tsui Tswen-ling, Counselor, Chinese Embassy and Mr Sprouse,' 12 July 1948, 693.0031 Tibet/7–1248, NARA.
27. Ibid.
28. This in fact was due to a human error. The US embassy in Nanking would not issue the Tibetans visas for them to travel to the United States until they obtained exit visas from China. The Chinese insisted that exit visas be stamped into Chinese passports and not their Tibetan ones. The Tibetans refused; they would not travel to the US on a Chinese passport. They decided therefore to travel to the US via Hong Kong on Chinese passports issued in Calcutta and then throw away the Chinese passports and use Tibetan ones to travel to the States. They believed at the time they could get a visa to the US in Hong Kong on their Tibetan passport, and indeed they did. Goldstein, p. 581.
29. 'Memorandum of Telephone Conversation with Mr Tsui Tswen-ling, Counselor, Chinese Embassy and Mr Sprouse, Office of Chinese Affairs, Department of State,' 19 July 1948, 693.0031 Tibet/7–1948, NARA.
30. 'Memorandum of Conversation: Request of the Tibetan Trade Mission for an Appointment with the President,' 2 August 1948, 693.0031 Tibet/8–248, NARA.
31. Ibid.
32. 'Memorandum of Conversation with Dr Tan Shao-hwa, Chinese Minister and Mr Sprouse, Office of Chinese Affairs, Department of State,' 21 July 1948, NARA.
33. 'Telegram from American Embassy in Nanking to the Secretary of State,' 8 August 1948, no. 1458, 693.0031 Tibet/8–848, NARA.
34. 'Memorandum of Conversation, Department of State, Re: Visit to the US of the Tibetan Trade Mission,' 6 August 1948, 693.0031 Tibet/8–648, NARA.
35. Ibid. A Tibetan delegation had been sent to India and China with a message of congratulations for the Allies' victory in World War II.
36. Ibid., p. 10.
37. 'Records of Nehru's Talks with the Tibetan Mission led by Tsepon Shakabpa in New Delhi,' 8 January 1949, in Gopal, *Selected Works of Jawaharlal Nehru*, vol. 9, pp. 470–3.
38. 'Department of State, Legal Advisor Conrad Snow to Bureau of Chinese Affairs, Mr Clubb,' 22 November 1950, 793B.00/11–2250, Box 4226, NARA. While the Tibetans were able to purchase gold, which in a sense did assert a measure of their independence, it is clear from declassified memos of their visit to Washington that the State Department preferred to keep the status quo on Tibet. A memo between State and Treasury stated: 'The State Department would perceive no objection to sale of gold to the Government of Tibet and does not believe that such sale would in any way constitute an impairment of United States recognition of China's *de jure* sovereignty over Tibet, since the Department does not intend that such a sale would affect the continuation of this Government's recognition of China's *de jure* sovereignty over Tibet.' See 'Memo from the Secretary of State to the Secretary of the Treasury,' 27 August 1948, 693.0031 Tibet/8–748, NARA. This statement, written in pencil, was reiterated in the marginalia on the document.

9. THE MATTER OF TIBET'S STATUS

1. 'The Papers of Harry S. Truman,' PSF 1940–1953, Subject File: China 1948, Box 1, Harry S. Truman Presidential Library.

2. Ibid. These reports were confirmed to the authors in interviews in Cambridge, UK on 3–4 May 2012 with General V. I. Trubnikov, former director, Russian SVR 1996–2000 and Deputy Minister of Foreign Affairs for the Russian Federation 2000–4.
3. Ibid.
4. 'American Embassy in New Delhi, India to the Secretary of State Washington, Subject: Visit to New Delhi of Tibet Trade Mission,' 8 January 1949, 693.0031 Tibet/1–849, NARA.
5. Ibid.
6. 'Confidential Memorandum to Mr Sprouse, Chinese Affairs from Miss Bacon, Far Eastern Affairs, Subject: US Policy Toward Tibet,' 12 April 1949, 693.0031 Tibet/1–849, NARA.
7. Ibid. Like the Bureau of Far Eastern Affairs, the Office of Chinese Affairs, and particularly its director Mr Sprouse, came under attack. The Nationalists vilified Sprouse in 1948. Sprouse was handling the sensitivities involved in the Tibetan visit as well as trying to work out a uniform State Department policy toward Tibet in addition to managing the volatility of the Nationalists. See 'Oral History Program, Interview with Phillip D. Sprouse,' 11 February 1974, Harry S. Truman Library.
8. 'Confidential Memorandum to Mr Sprouse, Chinese Affairs from Miss Bacon, Far Eastern Affairs, Subject: US Policy Toward Tibet,' 12 April 1949, 693.0031 Tibet/1–849, NARA.
9. Ibid.
10. Ibid.
11. Ibid.
12. Ibid.
13. Ibid.
14. Ibid.
15. 'The Ambassador in China (Stuart) to the Secretary of State,' 8 July 1949, *FRUS*, vol. IX, p. 1078.
16. Ibid.
17. 'Confidential Memorandum to Mr Sprouse, Chinese Affairs from Miss Bacon, Far Eastern Affairs, Subject: US Policy Toward Tibet,' 12 April 1949, 693.0031 Tibet/1–849, NARA.
18. 'Note to Secretary General, Ministry of External Affairs,' 9 July 1949 in Gopal, *Selected Works of Jawaharlal Nehru*, vol. 12, pp. 410–11.
19. Ibid.
20. Ibid., p. 410.
21. Ibid.
22. Ibid., p. 411.
23. 'Press Conference in New Delhi', 16 November 1949, in S. Gopal, ed., *Selected Works of Jawaharlal Nehru* (New Delhi: Jawaharlal Nehru Memorial Fund, 1992), vol. 14, part 1, pp. 185–91.
24. Ibid.
25. Ibid.
26. 'The Ambassador in India (Henderson) to the Secretary of State,' 1 December 1949, *FRUS*, vol. IX, p. 1086.
27. 'The Charge in the United Kingdom (Holmes) to the Secretary of State,' 12 December 1949, *FRUS*, vol. IX, p. 1091. The GOI had already sent a small amount of arms and

ammunition to Tibet. See 'Telegram from the Ambassador in India (Henderson) to the Secretary of State,' 30 December 1949, *FRUS*, vol. IX, p. 1097.

28. 'The Charge in India (Donovan) to the Secretary of State,' 21 November 1949, *FRUS*, vol. IX, pp. 1080–1. Their request for 'aid against the Communists' was also given to the UK. Enclosed was a letter that the Tibetans had written to Mao stating that 'Tibet was independent from earliest times.' Ibid., p. 1081. The Tibetans had also requested help from the United States.

29. 'The Secretary of State to the Ambassador in India (Henderson),' 21 December 1949, *FRUS*, vol. IX, p. 1096. Generally, the United States believed that action taken by the Tibetans to promote their independence or membership of the United Nations would 'hasten' a Chinese communist invasion. Ibid., p. 1097. Ambassador Henderson wrote to Acheson to say it was important that the United States not take any action that would encourage the Tibetans to take action to resist the Chinese Communists based upon '… [the] mistaken idea of help from [the] US.' See 'The Ambassador in India (Henderson) to the Secretary of State,' 15 December 1949, *FRUS*, vol. IX, p. 1092.

30. 'The Secretary of State to the Ambassador in India (Henderson),' 21 December 1949, *FRUS*, vol. IX, pp. 1096–7.

31. Ibid.

32. Ibid.

33. 'Department of State, The Legal Adviser, Conrad E Snow to Mr Clubb,' 5 December 1950, 793b.00/11–2250, Box 4226, NARA.

34. Ibid. The report referred to 'outer Tibet' only. This was the area in and around Lhasa that the Dalai Lama controlled. The British were concerned about the US position toward Tibet and had requested the report.

35. Ibid., p. 9. The quoted source was Hyde, *International Law*, 2nd edn, vol. I, p. 22. Nepal was the only country at this time to recognize Tibet as independent. Ibid.

36. In a discussion about Tibet's foreign affairs Mr Snow, the legal advisor, could not cite a treaty that the Tibetans had entered into since 1914. Even though the Tibetans had received individuals of foreign countries and carried Tibetan passports when visiting abroad, according to Snow, this did not necessarily make them independent. Snow noted that these things alone were 'far from showing that Tibet has entered in full diplomatic relations with other countries.' He noted Egypt and Bulgaria, while vassal states under Britain, sent and received consuls as diplomatic agents. But clearly Washington believed that the Tibetans were autonomous and independent in the internal affairs of their state. '*De jure*' refers to the right according to law; and '*de facto*' as in reality or actually existing.

37. Ibid., p. 10.

38. Ibid., pp. 10–11. Snow pointed out that the word 'sovereignty' had been confused with 'suzerainty' and at various times the US had used each word in describing the relationship between China and Tibet. 'In other words,' he wrote, 'the United States' position has been ambiguous.' He believed that in the end the US 'recognized that China retained some undefined rights over Tibet…'

39. Ibid., p. 11.

40. Ibid., p. 11. The Legal Office viewed the 'armed invasion of Tibet' as a 'question of international concern.'

41. Ibid, p. 12.

42. 'Confidential Memorandum to Mr Sprouse, Chinese Affairs from Miss Bacon, Far East-

ern Affairs, Subject: US Policy Toward Tibet,' 12 April 1949, 693.0031 Tibet/1–849, NARA.

10. LOWELL THOMAS IN TIBET

1. Dalai Lama, *Freedom in Exile* (New York: HarperCollins, 1990), p. 54.
2. Heinrich Harrer, *Seven Years in Tibet* (London: Rupert Hart-Davis, 1953), p. 259. There were also freak births among animals which were considered another ominous sign. Ibid., p. 219.
3. Tsepon W. D. Shakabpa, *Tibet: A Political History* (New Haven: Yale University Press, 1967), p. 298. Shakabpa had impressed upon the Tibetan Foreign Bureau 'the need for the world to know more about Tibet' and they gave the necessary permits to enter Tibet. Ibid.
4. Lowell Thomas, *So Long Until Tomorrow* (New York: William Morrow, 1977), pp. 136 and 141.
5. Ibid., p. 162.
6. Ibid., p. 166.
7. Ibid.
8. Ibid.
9. Ibid.
10. Ibid., p. 168.
11. Thomas told the American public that 'Tibet is the most anti-Communist country in the world.' *New York Times*, 11 October 1949; and also see Lowell Thomas Jr, *Out of This World: Across the Himalayas to Forbidden Tibet* (New York: Greystone Press, 1950).
12. 'Personal letter from Lowell Thomas to Mr Acheson,' 17 November 1950, 793B.00/11–1750 Box 4226, NARA. Thomas spent four hours talking with Pentagon officials. Lowell indicated in his letter that the secretary of state asked him to gather available information about Tibet.
13. Thomas, p. 170.
14. Ibid., p. 171.
15. James Lilley, *China Hands: Nine Decades of Adventure, Espionage, and Diplomacy in Asia* (New York: Public Affairs, 2004), pp. 202–4; Interview with Ambassador Lilley, March 2006, Washington, DC.
16. Ibid.
17. Ibid. Notwithstanding Lowell Thomas' comment to Ambassador James Lilley, the authors were able to uncover no evidence that Lowell Thomas was employed by the US government. Throughout the next two decades Henderson and Thomas corresponded with each other from time to time. On a postcard written from Tibet in 1949, Thomas wrote: 'Greetings from Lhasa, to Ambassador Loy Henderson who performed a miracle and got us into Tibet.' 'Post Card from Lowell Thomas in Tibet 1949' in the Papers of Loy Henderson, Folder T, Box 3 at the Library of Congress, Washington, DC. In 1956 Thomas was part of a US delegation to Nepal and sent his observations of the trip to Henderson. And a year later, Thomas wrote at the close of a letter to Henderson that 'if there is anything more I can do for the State Department, on the air, or in any other way, please let me know.' 'Letter from Lowell Thomas to Loy Henderson,' 20 September 1957 in the Papers of Loy Henderson, Folder T, Box 3 at the Library of Congress, Washington, DC.

11. MAJOR DOUGLAS MACKIERNAN: A TRAGIC INCIDENT

1. Ted Gup, *The Book of Honor: Covert Lives and Classified Deaths at the CIA* (New York: Doubleday, 2000), p. 12. Mackiernan had been an avid amateur radio operator as a young boy—ham radios took up an entire room in his family home and the yard was chock-a-block with antennae. 'If ever a boy was cut out to be a spy, it was Doug Mackiernan,' wrote one author. As a child he would plan war games and designed sophisticated methods of decoding and could plug a penny at one hundred yards with his Remington 30.6. In 1942, at twenty-nine years old, Mackiernan joined the US Army as a meteorologist, later becoming the chief of the US Army Air Force's Crypto-analysis Section in Washington, DC. He spoke Spanish and was conversant in both Russian and Chinese and demonstrated his ability with encryption and codes.

2. Thomas Laird, *Into Tibet: The CIA's First Atomic Spy and his Secret Expedition to Lhasa* (New York: Grove Press, 2002), p. 21.

3. The Kazakh, Kirghiz, and Uyghur tribesmen were fighting in an effort to gain control of the ERT from the minority Chinese rule. In 1944 the Uyghurs staged a revolt against the Chinese and claimed independence. By 1945, the ETR was under Russian control. This changed again in 1949 when the communist Chinese came to power and the Uyghurs became part of Sinkiang province.

4. Until 2008, the CIA would not publicly acknowledge that 'Mac,' as he was known, had been employed by the Agency. See https://www.cia.gov/news-information/featured-story-archive/2010-featured-story-archive/douglas-s.-mackiernan.html

5. 'The Urumachi News Summary of October 1945,' in L/P&S/12/4225, IOR, British Library, London.

6. Ibid.

7. 'Cypher Telegram from the Government of India, External Affairs Department to the Secretary of State for India,' 6 May 1945, L/P&S/12/422, IOR, British Library, London.

8. 'The Ambassador in China (Stuart) to the Secretary of State,' Telegram no. 218 and 'The Ambassador in China (Stuart) to the Secretary of State,' Telegram no. 222, both dated 27 May 1947, *FRUS*, vol. VII, p. 555. J. Hall Paxton, the American consul at Tihwa, had observed Soviet oil wells and other types of mining-heavy minerals that were conceivably for uranium mining.

9. 'Telegram from the Ambassador in China (Stuart) to the Secretary of State: Re: Mackiernan's trip,' 6 July 1947, *FRUS*, vol. VII, pp. 567–8.

10. Gup, p. 16

11. Ibid., p. 568. Osman had fled from the Russians who now occupied his pastoral land in the ETR. The chieftain told Mackiernan that Russians had come to his valley in 1946 on a mining expedition and were now mining four types of minerals. Mackiernan sent mineral samples back to Washington.

12. 'The Minister-Counselor of Embassy in China (Clark) to the Secretary of State,' 25 July 1949, *FRUS*, vol. VIII, p. 1304; 'The Ambassador in China (Stuart) to the Secretary of State,' 28 July 1949, *FRUS*, vol. VIII, p. 1304.

13. 'The Secretary of State to the Consul at Tihwa (Paxton),' 29 July 1949, *FRUS*, vol. III, pp. 1305–6.

14. Ibid., p. 1306.

15. *Time* magazine, 14 November 1949.

16. Thomas Laird, *Into Tibet: The CIA's First Atomic Spy and his Secret Expedition to Lhasa* (New York: Grove Press, 2002), p. 106.

17. Laird, p. 109. Up until his death in December 2010 he refused to discuss his role in Tihwa or affiliation with the OSS or Central Intelligence Agency.

18. Ibid., p. 109.

19. Ibid., p. 110.

20. 'The Vice Consul at Tihwa (Mackiernan) to the Secretary of State,' 24 August 1949, *FRUS*, vol. VIII, pp. 1321–2.

21. Godfrey Lias, *Kazak Exodus* (London: Evans Brothers, 1956), p. 93.

22. 'Log of Mr Frank Bessac's Journey from Tihwa to Lhasa, September 27th to June 11, 1950 in Despatch no. 661, from Lloyd V. Steere, Counselor of Embassy, Delhi to Far Eastern Affairs Department of State,' 21 September 1950, 793B.00/9–2150, NARA.

23. *Life* magazine, 13 November 1950, p. 133.

24. 'Log of Mr Frank Bessac's Journey from Tihwa to Lhasa.'

25. Ibid.

26. *Life* magazine, 13 November 1950, p. 134.

27. Ibid., p. 134.

28. Ibid.

29. Ibid., p. 14.

30. Ibid., p. 15.

31. 'Log of Mr Frank Bessac's journey from Tihwa to Lhasa.'

32. Ibid., p. 16.

33. 'Materials on the Conspiracy Activities by Vice Consul Mackiernan of the US Consulate General in Tihwa,' 10 January 1950, Archive no. 118–0005–02(1), Ministry of Foreign Affairs of the People's Republic of China. Indeed Acheson had sent an urgent telegram to the ambassador in the UK on 16 August 1949 to ask if the British in Tihwa as well as Canton, Chungking, and Kunming would accept custody of American property when the US consulates in those locations closed. The US government would 'make funds available if British personnel were to accept this task.' See 'The Secretary of State to the Ambassador in the United Kingdom (Douglas),' 16 August 1949, *FRUS*, vol. VIII, p. 1319.

34. Ibid. The Chinese wrote: 'the local provincial government in Xinjiang was surprised by Mackiernan's conduct which is unusual according to diplomatic custom … to fulfill its responsibility of protecting foreigners, the provincial government started an inquiry from all sides, and obtained his whereabouts by mid-December.' Apparently some of the White Russians who stayed behind in Tihwa came forward and gave the PLA details of Mackiernan's plans. Ibid.

35. 'Materials on the Conspiracy Activities by Vice Consul Mackiernan of the US Consulate General in Tihwa,' 10 January 1950, Archive no. 118–0005–02(1), Ministry of Foreign Affairs of the People's Republic of China.

36. Ibid. This account was given to the PLA by some of the White Russians who had guided the party along their journey.

37. Ibid.

38. 'Materials on the Conspiracy Activities by Vice Consul Mackiernan of the US Consulate General in Tihwa,' 10 January 1950, Archive no. 118 0005 02(1), Ministry of Foreign Affairs of the People's Republic of China.

39. 'Log of Mr Frank Bessac,' p. 19.

40. *Life* magazine, p. 138.

41. *Life* magazine, p. 141.

42. 'Latest Information from Tibet,' Enclosure no. 1 to Despatch no. 262, American Embassy, New Delhi, 7 August 1950, Top Secret. Declassified 793B.00/8–750, NARA. This series of messages began on 22 May. This report was passed to Washington through Delhi from Major Bijaya Shamsher, Director General of the Foreign Department of the Nepalese government

43. Ibid.

44. Ibid.

45. Ibid.

46. Ibid., p. 2.

47. Ibid., p. 2.

48. 'Impressions of Lhasa,' Enclosure no. 2 to Despatch no. 661, 21 September 1950; 'Various Reports by Frank B. Bessac describing the Journey of the Mackiernan Party from Tihwa and Conditions in Tibet,' 793B.00/9–2150, NARA.

49. 'Ambassador Henderson to Secretary of State, Dean Acheson,' 8 September 1950, 793B.00/9–850, 'Highlights of Bessac's Observations,' NARA.

50. 'Impressions of Military Status of Tibet,' Enclosure no. 1 to Despatch no. 661, 21 September 1950, 793N.00/9–2150, NARA. This telegram contained numerous reports from Bessac from his stay in Lhasa in June and July 1950.

51. Ibid. Bessac wrote that it was known in Lhasa that some of the soldiers were only trained for one month.

52. Ibid. Bessac amplifies this point, saying: 'The commander-in-chief and other high officers, the generals, are members of the higher noble families and have obtained their posts either as a result of bribery or feudal right; pleasant people but without training or aptitude for the position they have occupied. The Tibetans realize their present high officers are not suitable and would welcome American advisors' (author's underscoring), p. 1.

53. Ibid.

54. Ibid. The Tibetans had heard that Chinese General Lui Po-Ch'eng was training his men to eat the Tibetan staple of tsampa (barley ground into fine and coarse flour).

55. Ibid.

56. Ibid.

57. Ibid.

12. 'THE BEARDED KHAMPA': TIBET'S PAUL REVERE

1. 'Department of State to the American Embassy in New Delhi,' 25 May 1950, 793B.00/5–2550, Box 4226, NARA. In a memo stamped 'Limited Distribution—Eyes Only Henderson,' the ambassador in New Delhi was advised that the State Department was not planning to bring Zransov to the US and that he could be better utilized by the intelligence community in India. He would however be reimbursed for his services on the Mackiernan trip. See 'Department of State Telegram,' 19 June 1950, 793B.00/6–650, NARA. Patterson would be reimbursed on a per diem basis of $10 a day in India and $9 in Tibet. Ultimately, however, plans changed and Patterson did not meet Bessac and Zransov at the border.

2. George N. Patterson, *Patterson of Tibet: Death Throes of a Nation* (San Diego, CA: ProMotion Publishing, 1998), p. 99.

3. Ibid., p. 117. An American couple, George and Pearl Kraft, ran the China Inland Mission

compound in Kangting; George Kraft was fluent in the dialect spoken in Kham in the eastern part of Tibet.

4. Many of the Khampas, including the most powerful Khampa chieftain, Topgyay Pangdatshang, and his brother Rapga, were living in Kangting after being exiled from Tibet for their part in a revolt against the Lhasa government in 1934. Kangting was the largest city of the Khampas in eastern Tibet that was technically considered part of China's Sichuan province.

5. Patterson, *Patterson of Tibet*, p. 120. The men were garbed in traditional Tibetan gowns lined with lambskins and were armed with rifles which they put down to listen to Patterson preach about the Prodigal Son.

6. Interview with George Patterson, 3 May 2005 and Patterson, *Patterson of Tibet*, p. 121.

7. Patterson interview, 3 May and Patterson, *Patterson of Tibet*. Topgay was considered a leader of the Khampa tribes in Kham and Amdo, who were united in their fight against the Chinese for their tribal rights.

8. Ibid., and also Patterson, *Patterson of Tibet*, p. 123. They did fight against the Japanese but were able to obtain arms from both official Nationalist sources and unofficially from deserting Nationalists regiments in western China.

9. Patterson, *Patterson of Tibet*, p. 125.

10. Ibid., p. 163.

11. Ibid., p. 163. Fifteen years earlier the Khampa chieftain Topgyay had cleared the area and built crude homes for wives and family. Ibid., p. 183.

12. Ibid., p. 186.

13. Ibid., p. 187.

14. Ibid., p. 188.

15. Ibid.

16. Ibid. The Khampa mission was to bring modernization to Tibet.

17. Interview, Patterson, *Patterson of Tibet*, p. 188.

18. The complete journey cut across Tibet through Zayul and Rima to Sadyia in Assam. See Patterson, *Patterson of Tibet*, p. 193.

19. Ibid., p. 203, interview.

20. 'Peking Radio of 20th January 1950 attachment to Foreign Service of the United States memo dated June 15th, 1950,' 793B.00.6–1550, Box 4226, NARA.

21. Patterson, *Patterson of Tibet*, p. 204.

22. Ibid., p. 204.

23. Ibid., p. 217.

24. Ibid., p. 223; and interview with Patterson, Scotland, 3 May 2005.

25. George Patterson, *Journey with Loshay: A Tibetan Odyessy* (Winchester, UK: The Long Riders' Guild Press, 1956, 2004), p. 207.

26. Ibid., p. 209.

27. Patterson, *Patterson of Tibet*, p. 234.

28. Ibid.

29. Ibid., p. 236, and interviews with Patterson.

30. Ibid.

31. Ibid., p. 237; interview with Patterson, Scotland, 3 May 2005.

32. Patterson, *Patterson of Tibet*, p. 237.

33. 'Telegram from Calcutta to the Secretary of State in Washington,' 26 July 1950, 793B.00/7–2650, Folder 4226, NARA. The Tibetan officials that Patterson spoke to reit-

erated that they wanted aid and arms from the United States and Britain. Patterson's contacts were Bob Lynn and Bill Gibson. Interview with George Patterson, Scotland, 3 May 2005.

34. 'The President to the Secretary of State,' 31 January 1950, *FRUS*, vol. I, p. 142. He also directed that no public information be given about the government's feasibility study on a thermonuclear weapon.

35. 'Foreign Service Telegram from Howard Donovan, Chargé d'Affaires, Delhi to the Department of State,' 13 February 1950, 793H.00/2–1350, NARA.

36. Ambassador Henderson in New Delhi was able to obtain a list of the guns, mortars, and ammunition that the Indian government was supplying to the Tibetans from the British High Commission. India was supplying nominal assistance, having taken over the rights and privileges in Tibet from the British. In January 1950 the Indian government indicated that they would be willing to continue to supply the Tibetans with small arms which the Tibetans paid for. 'Telegram from The Ambassador in India (Henderson) to the Secretary of State,' 10 January 1950, *FRUS*, vol. VI, pp. 272–3; 'Telegram from New Delhi to the Secretary of State via London,' 8 March 1950, 793N.00/3–850, Box 4226, NARA. Also 'The Secretary of State to the American Ambassador in India,' 1 March 1950, 793B.56/3–150, Box 4228, NARA. Not only was Acheson trying to ascertain what kind of aid India was giving the Tibetans, but in addition he wanted to know how the Indian government would react if the US gave military assistance to Tibet. Ibid., 1 March 1950, memo. At this point, if the United States wanted to supply the Tibetans with additional military assistance, they would have to have approval to transit through India.

37. 'The Secretary of State to the Embassy in India,' 19 April 1950, 793B.00/4–1950, Box 4228, NARA. In 1956 the US deployed a full-scale covert effort to assist the Tibetans. However, in April 1950 Acheson understood that 'Owing to its geographical location and close relationship to Tibet, India in best position to carry out measures of this nature.' See 'Secretary of State to US Embassy India,' 19 April 1950, *FRUS*, vol. V1, p. 331.

38. Discussed in 'Memorandum by the Acting Secretary of State to the Executive Secretary of the National Security Council (Lay),' 26 May 1950, *FRUS*, vol. IV, p. 311, ftn 2; and Editorial Note, p. 304. The speech was made on 20 April 1950.

39. 'Memorandum by the Acting Secretary of State to the Executive Secretary of the Nation Security Council (Lay),' 26 May 1950, *FRUS*, vol. IV, p. 312.

40. 'Secretary of State to the Embassy in the United Kingdom,' 15 June 1950, *FRUS*, vol. VI, p. 364, ftn 1; and also editorial note, p. 339. An outline of the State Department's report was given to Mr Graves of the British embassy on 16 June 1950.

41. Ibid., p. 364.

42. Ibid.

43. Ibid.

44. 'Secretary of State to US Embassy in the United Kingdom,' 16 June 1950, *FRUS*, vol. VI, p. 364, ftn 1.

13. 1950: THE PLA INVADES KOREA AND TIBET

1. Harry S. Truman, *Memoirs of Harry S. Truman. Volume Two, 1946–1952: Years of Trial and Hope* (New York: Doubleday, 1955), p. 332.

2. Ibid. Truman wanted to fly back to Washington immediately, but Acheson said to wait.

3. Ibid., pp. 332–3.

4. Ibid.
5. Ibid. He left Independence, Missouri so quickly that two of his aides and many of the reporters who were assigned to him were left behind.
6. Ibid., pp. 332–3.
7. Ibid., p. 355.
8. Ibid., p. 336.
9. 'Radio and Television Report on the Korean War by President Truman,' 1 September 1950, John T. Woolley and Gerhard Peters, *The American Presidency Project* (Santa Barbara, CA: University of California), http://www.presidency.ucsb.edu/ws/?pid=13604, last accessed 1 June 2013.
10. 'The Ambassador in India (Henderson) to the Secretary of State,' 15 July 1950, *FRUS*, vol. VI, p. 376, ftn 1.
11. 'The Secretary of State to the Embassy in India,' 22 July 1950, *FRUS*, vol. VI, p. 386. Specifically Acheson wrote: 'Interested agencies were now considering the advisability of approaching the Tibetan Mission currently in India with a promise of secret United States aid in the hope that this would help the Tibetan authorities to resist Chinese Communist encroachment on Tibet.' 'The Ambassador in India (Henderson) to the Secretary of State,' 15 July 1950, *FRUS*, vol. VI, p. 376, ftn 1.
12. 'The Secretary of State to the Embassy in India,' 22 July 1950, *FRUS*, vol. VI, p. 386.
13. 'Office Memorandum from Mr Bell, Subject: Military Assistance for Tibet,' 9 August 1950, 793B.5/8–1050, Box 4228, NARA. Specifically it was noted that the 'other agency' felt that it had the 'funds available and the source through which to obtain any equipment which might be required.' Ibid. Also see 'Declassified Intelligence Report,' 25 June 1950, 00457R/Box 0051, Folder 0020, NARA; and 'CIA Secret Information Report,' 20 June 1950, CIA-RDP82–00457R00510012000002–4, Box 51, Folder 0012, NARA.
14. 'Office Memorandum from Mr Rusk to Mr McWilliams: Military Assistance to Tibet,' 19 September 1950, NND 981749,NARA. Marginalia read: 'Here we go again!'
15. 'Top Secret Memo from the Ambassador in India (Henderson) to the Secretary of State,' 7 August 1950, *FRUS*, vol. VI, p. 424. Ambassador Henderson relayed Washington's message to Tsepon Shakabpa, who was with the Tibetan delegation visiting in Delhi.
16. Ibid.
17. 'Telegram no. 609 from Ambassador Henderson to the Secretary of State,' 10 September 1950, 793B.00/0–1050, and also *FRUS 1950*, vol. VI, pp. 493–5.
18. 'Telegram no. 609 from Ambassador Henderson to the Secretary of State,' 10 September 1950, 793B.00/0–1050, NARA.
19. Ibid. And also *FRUS*, vol. VI, p. 495. In his memoirs, Shakabpa wrote that he and his delegation met privately with Nehru on 8 September and spoke for two hours. He told Nehru that the Tibetans maintained they were 'free and independent and that there was absolutely no way that we would discuss Tibet's being autonomous and independent within a part of China.' Tsepon Shakabpa, *One Hundred Thousand Moons*, p. 926. Shakabpa had asked Nehru for assistance in negotiations with the Chinese and to act as an intermediary. The prime minister replied: 'it would be difficult to find a suitable arrangement if the Tibetan representatives speak of Tibet's absolute independence (*rang btsan gtsang ma*). As for India's role as an intermediary [required in the Simla Convention] that was from negotiations that took place thirty years ago. That time is not like these days'. Shakabpa, p. 926.
20. Ibid., p. 927.

21. Ambassador Yuan wanted the delegation to accept Tibet as a part of China; relinquish their defense to the PLA; and allow the Chinese to negotiate political and trade matters with foreign countries. Shakabpa cabled Lhasa on 19 and 30 September requesting direction. On 12 October the cabinet sent a telegram stating that the regent, the cabinet, and the secular and monastic officials would not accept the Chinese proposal and that Shakabpa should try to delay any action by the Chinese army who were now on the Tibetan border. On 17 October the delegation received notification from Lhasa that the Communist army had crossed into Tibet.

22. Tsering Shakya, *Dragon in the Land of Snows: A History of Modern Tibet since 1947* (London: Pimlico, 1999), p. 43.

23. Geoffrey T. Bull, *When Iron Gates Yield* (Chicago: Moody Press, 1955), p. 107.

24. Ibid.

25. Interview with George Patterson, Scotland.

26. Quoted by a Kashag aide-de-camp in Melvyn Goldstein, *A History of Modern Tibet, 1913–1951* (Berkeley: University of California Press, 1989), p. 692; interview with Tsering Shakya, June 2002, London; interview with Robert Ford, London, 8 February 1950.

27. Ibid. and also Shakya, *Dragon in the Land of Snows*, p. 44.

28. 'Telegram to Mao Zedong from the Tibetan National Assembly,' 30 September 1950, no. 10500018–06(1), Ministry of Foreign Affairs of the People's Republic of China.

29. Ibid.

30. Ibid.

31. Interview with Robert Ford, London, 6 February 2006.

32. Ibid. Also see Robert Ford, *Wind Between the Worlds* (New York: David McKay, 1957), p. 156.

33. Ibid., p. 156.

34. Dalai Lama, *Freedom in Exile*, pp. 53–4. The Dalai Lama usually ascends to the throne as leader at the age of eighteen.

35. Ibid.

36. 'Instruction from Chairman Mao on Discussion between Menon and Ambassador Yuan,' 12 October 1950, Archive no. 105–00011–01(1), Memo no. 169, Ministry of Foreign Affairs of the People's Republic of China.

37. Ibid.

38. 'The Secretary of State to Certain Diplomatic and Consular Offices,' 9 November 1950, *FRUS*, vol. VI, p. 157.

39. Tsepon Shakabpa, *Tibet: A Political History* (New Haven: Yale University Press, 1967), p. 302.

40. 'The Secretary of State to the United Nations Mission at the United Nations,' 16 November 1950, *FRUS*, vol. VI, p. 577.

41. Ibid. Acheson was hopeful that India would support a UN resolution to condemn China's invasion of Tibet. He wrote that now India would 'have a first-hand opportunity to learn what it is like to deal with USSR in matters in which USSR undoubtedly wld be in opposition.' He was hopeful that 'A widening break in India–Commie China and India–USSR relations, probably resulting from active Indian opposition to CHI actions in this case, might induce India to be less neutral and more realistic about Communism in general.' Ibid., p. 578.

42. 'The Ambassador in India (Henderson) to the Secretary of State,' 20 November 1950, *FRUS*, vol. VI, p. 578. Bajpai told Henderson about these developments on 19 November.

43. Ibid.
44. Ibid.

14. NEHRU'S NON-ALIGNMENT, THE KOREAN WAR, AND TIBET

1. H. W. Brands, *India and the United States: The Cold Peace* (Boston: Twayne, 1990), p. 52.
2. 'The Ambassador in India (Henderson) to the Secretary of State,' 27 June 1950, *FRUS*, vol. VII, pp. 230–1. This was a record of a discussion between Prime Minister Nehru and Ambassador Henderson. At a meeting of the United Nations Security Council on 27 June 1950, the Indian government supported the recommendation that the members of the United Nations would provide assistance to the Republic of Korea as necessary to repel the armed attack and to restore international peace and security in the region. See *editorial note in FRUS 1950*, vol. VII, p. 266.
3. 'The Ambassador in India (Henderson) to the Secretary of State,' 27 June 1950, *FRUS*, vol. VII, pp. 230–1.
4. Ibid.
5. Robert McMahon, *The Cold War on the Periphery: The United States, India and Pakistan* (New York: Columbia University Press, 1994), p. 83.
6. Ibid.
7. 'Memorandum by the Assistant Secretary of State for Near Eastern, South Asian and African Affairs (McGhee) to the Secretary of State: Personal Message for Prime Minster Nehru of India,' 13 July 1950, *FRUS*, vol. VII, p. 372; 'The Ambassador in the Soviet Union (Kirk) to the Secretary of State,' 14 July 1950, *FRUS*, vol. VII, pp. 379–80. Nehru's message was reported in a confidential telegram from the US Ambassador in Moscow to Dean Acheson. Also see 'Text of Message from Prime Minister of India to Hon'ble Dean Acheson, Secretary of State, Enclosure 1 from The Indian Ambassador (Pandit) to the Secretary of State,' 17 July 1950, *FRUS*, vol. VII, pp. 407–8.
8. Ibid.
9. Ibid., p. 408.
10. Ibid.
11. Acheson, *Present at the Creation*, p. 419. Acheson added that 'the next installment, clearly forecast by Bajpai to Henderson, would be the ousting of the Nationalists from Formosa.' Ibid.
12. 'Letter to C. Rajagopalachari,' 3 July 1950 in S. Gopal, *Jawaharlal Nehru, A Biography* (London: Jonathan Cape, 1979), vol. II, p. 101.
13. Ibid., and Acheson, *Present at the Creation*, p. 416.
14. Acheson was skeptical of both the Indian and British efforts at a peaceful settlement and wrote in his memoirs that the 'British Foreign Office believed, with more than evidence seemed to warrant,' that the Russians would negotiate on the Korean situation. Acheson, *Present at the Creation*, p. 416.
15. Ibid., pp. 419–20. The Russians did in fact return to the Security Council without the PRC. In her memoirs Nehru's sister wrote that she believed Dean Acheson's 'knowledge about Asia was limited' and he 'knew very little, past or present' about India. 'Acheson, like the next secretary of State, Foster Dulles,' Madame Pandit wrote, 'divided the world into two categories—friends and foes. They both had tidy minds in which everything was either black or white and the archenemy was Communism.' Pandit, *Scope of Happiness* (New York: Crown Publishing Group, 1979), p. 250.

16. Dean Acheson, *Present at the Creation*, p. 420.
17. *New York Times*, 4 August 1950.
18. 'Discussion on Tibetan Problems During Vice Minister Zhang's Reception of Ambassador Panikkar' in 'Record on India's Interference of our Liberation of Tibet and our Replying Documents,' 15 August 1950, Archive no. 105–00010–01(1), Ministry of Foreign Affairs of the People's Republic of China. The writers were provided access to these previously restricted documents at the Ministry of Foreign Affairs archive in Beijing in September 2007.
19. Ibid. The words were underlined in the notes. The meeting, according to the notes, lasted six hours. Panikkar later realized that he had used the word 'sovereignty' instead of 'suzerainty' in his discussions with the Chinese and in November 1950 wrote to the Chinese to explain the oversight in his language.
20. Ibid.
21. Ibid. These sentences are underlined in the original notes to the meeting. Panikkar was scheduled to meet with Zhou but the Chinese premier was unwell. Panikkar had also been ambassador under Chiang Kai-shek.
22. 'Notes of a discussion between Director Generals Qiao, Chen, and Ambassador Panikkar, 31 August 1950, at Ambassador Panikkar's residence' in 'Memorandum on India's Interference of our Liberation of Tibet and Our Reply,' Archive no. 105–00010–02, Ministry of Foreign Affairs of the People's Republic of China.
23. Ibid. The Chinese province of Sikang refers to eastern Tibet or the region of Kham.
24. Tsepon Shakabpa, *Tibet: A Political History* (New Haven: Yale University Press, 1967), p. 300.
25. 'Memorandum from Ambassador Henderson to the Secretary of State,' 9 September 1950, 793B.00/9–1050, Box 4226, NARA. The delegation met with Nehru in Delhi while waiting for visas to proceed through Hong Kong to Beijing.
26. Henderson, for example, had received a message from Bajpai conveyed by Panikkar about Chinese intentions in Tibet on 25 August 1950. Panikkar thought that the PRC would gradually 'make Tibet a part of China' and he felt 'that there was little India could do to assist Tibet.' See 'Henderson to the Secretary of State,' 25 August 1950, 793B.00/8–2550, Box 4226, NARA. And on 16 September Panikkar was warned that 'the Chinese did not intend to sit back with folded hands and let the Americans come up to their border.' This was relayed to Panikkar in a private dinner with the military governor of Beijing, General Nieh Yen-jung. Panikkar recalled that the general spoke about the PRC intentions in a 'quiet and unexcited manner' as if 'he was telling me that he intended to go shooting the next day.' See K. M. Panikkar, *In Two Chinas: Memoirs of a Diplomat* (London: George Allen & Unwin, 1955), p. 108. The Chinese also took advantage of the Panikkar channel and relayed messages through him that were for Washington. See 'The Ambassador in India (Henderson),' 4 October 1950, *FRUS*, vol. VII, p. 869.
27. Panikkar, *In Two Chinas*, p. 109. On 21 September, Panikkar was pointedly told by Chou En-lai that 'if America extends her aggression, China will have to resist.' Gopal, *Jawaharlal Nehru, A Biography*, vol. II, p. 104.
28. Panikkar, *In Two Chinas*, p. 109.
29. Ibid., p. 110. Acheson was rather cynical about Chou's warning and the validity of the Indian government's reporting of events in the PRC. This current warning was 'discussed at considerable length' in an attempt to ascertain whether it was meant to 'affect the UN vote.' Acheson remarked that the Indians had been saying this 'sort of thing consistently

… and I don't think they are taken very seriously …' Acheson and others in the administration questioned Panikkar's reliability in reporting events accurately. See Secretary of State Dean Acheson, 'Congressional Testimony,' 1 June 1951, and Acheson's comments from the 'Princeton Seminar,' 13 February 1954, Papers of Dean Acheson at http://www. trumanlibrary.org/whistlestop/study_collection s/korea/large/koreapt4_4.htm, last accessed 1 June 2013. The Indian consul at the embassy in Beijing, T. N. Kaul, wrote that Panikkar had been dubbed 'Mr Panicky.' Kaul also wrote that the Indian ambassador 'enjoyed inventing stories and conveying them to the Western diplomats.' T. N. Kaul, *A Diplomat's Diary: China, India and the USA* (Basingstoke: Macmillan, 2000), p. 23.

30. 'Secretary of State, Dean Acheson, to Ambassador Henderson,' 27 October 1950, 793B.00/10–2750, Box 4226, NARA.

31. Michael M. Sheng, 'Mao, Tibet, and the Korean War,' *Journal of Cold War Studies*, vol. 8, no. 3 (Summer 2006), p. 22.

32. Ibid.

33. Ibid., p. 23.

34. Gopal, *Jawaharlal Nehru, A Biography*, vol. II, p. 105.

35. Ibid., p. 106.

36. Ibid.

37. 'The Ambassador in India (Henderson) to the Secretary of State,' 25 August 1950, *FRUS*, vol. VI, p. 449.

38. Ibid.

39. Memorandum for Mr. Jessup and Mr. Rusk: 'Credibility of K. M. Panikkar, Indian Ambassador to Communist China,' 12 October 1950, p. 4, Secret Memorandum, U.S. Intelligence and China: Collection, Analysis, and Covert Action, CI00515, Digital National Security Archive.

40. 'The Ambassador in India (Henderson) to the Secretary of State,' 13 October 1950, *FRUS*, vol. VI, p. 531.

41. Ibid., p. 531.

42. The cable continues: 'It would be pointed out to Peking that the GOI had endeavored to befriend it; that in trying to obtain admission for it in the UN, to support it re Formosa, and to assure it would have [an] appropriate voice in [the] settlement of Korea, GOI had aroused displeasure of certain other members [of the] UN; that GOI had for many years maintained friendly relations with autonomous Tibet; that it believed it was not unduly interfering in Chinese affairs in suggesting that effecting change in [the] status of Tibet by armed force would not be in the interests of [the]international position of China or in that of friendship between China and India for which [the] GOI fervently hoped. Charges that great powers were bringing influence to bear on Tibet were senseless. [The] GOI was the only power which maintained representation. At [the] present time there were no British or Americans in Lhasa.' 'The Ambassador in India (Henderson) to the Secretary of State,' 13 October 1950, *FRUS*, vol. VI, p. 531.

43. Gopal, *Jawaharlal Nehru, A Biography*, vol. II, p. 106. Also see 'Report to Shen Jian in India: Contents of Panikkar's Discussion on Tibetan Trade Problems with Vice Minister Zhang,' 12 August 1950, Document no. 105–00011–01(1), Chinese Foreign Ministry Archives. The file contains forty-one pages. On 10 August Bajpai related the telegram that Nehru had sent to the Chinese regarding Tibet. In part it read: 'GOI has proved on various occasions its friendly feeling for Peoples Government of China … If China should now launch fresh armies of invasion into Tibet, or elsewhere, it might well be contribut-

ing to new world war.' Quoted from 'The Ambassador in India (Henderson) to the Secretary of State,' 14 August 1950, *FRUS*, vol. VI, pp. 440–1, ftn 3.

44. Gopal, *Jawaharlal Nehru, A Biography*, vol. II, p. 107.

45. Ibid. Chou En-lai made these points clear to Nehru in a letter written on 16 November 1950. He expressed his surprise over the Indian government's reaction to 'exercise its sovereign rights' and to liberate the people of Tibet. This archival document, from the files of the Chinese Ministry of Foreign Affairs, had been translated into English from Chinese and sent to Nehru. See 'Letter from Zhou En Lai to Prime Minister Nehru' in 'An Incoming Note on India's Interference of our Liberation of Tibet and our Reply Note,' Document no. 105–00010–03, Chinese Foreign Ministry Archives.

46. The Chinese government blamed the Indian government for the Tibetan delegation's delay in arriving in Beijing. See 'Letter from Zhou En Lai to Prime Minister Nehru' in 'An Incoming Note on India's Interference of our Liberation of Tibet and our Reply Note,' Document no. 105–00010–03. In his memoirs, B. N. Mullik, India's Intelligence Chief, wrote that the Chinese had informed Panikkar that they planned to take action in west Sikang in August and that the Tibetan delegation must quickly proceed to Beijing. See B. N. Mullik, *My Years with Nehru: The Chinese Betrayal* (New Delhi: Allied Publishers, 1971), p. 66.

47. Gopal, *Jawaharlal Nehru, A Biography*, vol. II, pp. 106–7. According to Gopal, to cover the discrepancies Panikkar 'explained to his own Government what he described as a sudden change of Chinese policy in Tibet by their expectation of a general war.' Ibid.

48. 'Discussion at the Ministry of Foreign Affairs of the Central People's Government' in 'A Memorandum of India's Interference of our Liberation of Tibet and our Reply', 16 October 1950, 2 p. m. at Foreign Ministry Headquarters, Document no. 10500010–02. The Chinese were told in the meeting that the GOI did not believe the news reports that the PLA had taken military action in Tibet.

49. Ibid. This was repeated again to the first secretary of the Indian Embassy on 28 October. A member of the Foreign Ministry, Wang Chaocheng, reiterated to the Indian official (Yanai Son) that 'Tibet must be liberated, and the current actions in west Sikang in Chamdo are a predetermined plan.' See Discussion Record, 28 October 1950, at Foreign Ministry Headquarters, Document no. 10500010–02. In Panikkar's memoirs he does not acknowledge knowing about the impending Chinese invasion of Tibet. In fact he wrote: 'to add to my troubles, by the middle of the month [October 1950] rumours of a Chinese invasion of Tibet began to circulate. Visits and representations to the Foreign Office [in Beijing] brought no results. The Wai Chiaopu officials were polite but silent.' See Panikkar, *In Two Chinas*, p. 112.

50. 'Discussion Record with Indian Ambassador' in 'Memorandum on India's Interference of our Liberation of Tibet and our Reply', 21 October 1950, Document no. 105–00010–02(1), Chinese Foreign Ministry Archives. There are fifty-four pages in this file, dating from 26 August to 30 October 1950. Declassified Chinese Foreign Ministry documents show that Chinese intentions regarding Tibet were also made clear to V. K. Krishna Menon. Menon met with Ambassador Yuan and other Chinese officials on 10, 12, 16, 18, 23, 26 October. The discussion records indicated that both Chairman Mao and Prime Minister Nehru were fully apprised of the conversations. Mao personally approved the issues to be discussed and Menon came with personal notes from Nehru. See 'Exchanges between PRC Foreign Ministry and the Chinese Embassy in India regarding India's Interference of our Liberation of Tibet,' Archive no. 105–00011–01(1). Menon specifically

told the Chinese that Nehru recognized that Tibet was part of China. See 'Discussion between Shen Jian and Menon,' 26 October 1950, Chinese Foreign Ministry Archives.

51. 'Discussion Record: Indian Ambassador Panikkar, Secretary Kumar, and Deputy Minister Zhang, and Deputy Director Chen at the Foreign Ministry,' 30 October 1950, Document no. 10500010–02.

52. Ibid.

53. Ibid. This is discussed more fully in Chapter 3. See 'Materials on the Conspiracy Activities by Vice Consul Mackiernan of the US Consulate in Tihwa,' 10 January 1950, Archive no. 118–00005–02(1). Specifically, the Chinese were deliberating whether to make his activities public to bolster their claims. Ibid. The authors were granted access to the Archives of the Ministry of Foreign Affairs in Beijing in 2005.

54. Ibid.

55. Ibid. Also see Gopal, *Jawaharlal Nehru, A Biography*, vol. II, p. 105.

56. 'Discussion Record with Indian Ambassador,' 21 October 1950, 11.30 a.m., Document no. 105–00010–02, Chinese Foreign Ministry Archives.

57. See ibid.

58. 'Letter to Vijayalaksmi Pandit,' 27 October 1950, in Gopal, *Selected Works of Jawaharlal Nehru*, vol. 15, part 2, pp. 517–18.

59. 'Letter to Vijayalakshmi Pandit,' 1 November 1950, in Gopal, *Selected Works of Jawaharlal Nehru*, vol. 15, part 2, p. 523.

60. 'The Ambassador in India (Henderson) to the Secretary of State,' 31 October 1950, *FRUS*, vol. VI, pp. 545–6.

61. Ibid., p. 546.

62. Ibid. Bajpai told Henderson that India would continue to send Lhasa their normal supply of arms, which he doubted would help the Tibetans now. Henderson again offered to provide arms to the Tibetans but asked that the GOI allow the arms to be transported through India. Bajpai thought this unwise and suggested they wait until a more propitious time. Ibid.

63. 'Letter to Zhou En-lai,' included in 'Telegraph exchanges between PRC Foreign Ministry and Chinese Embassy in India regarding Indian's Interference in our Liberation of Tibet,' Document no. 105–00018–01, Chinese Foreign Ministry Archives.

64. Ibid.

65. Ibid.

66. 'Report to Ambassador Yuan Regarding Discussion Between Zhou and Panikkar on Tibetan Problem' in 'Discussion record between PRC Minister Zhou En-lai and Indian Ambassador Panikkar regarding the Dalai Lama's intention of leaving Tibet and India's attitudes,' 28 March, 1951, Document no. 105–00010–04(1), Chinese Foreign Ministry Archives. Panikkar told Chou that the GOI had advised the Dalai Lama not to leave Tibet and that the 'Government of India is willing to use the influence of the lamas to advise the Dalai Lama not to come to India.' By this time the Tibetan leader had fled to Yatung. Panikkar told the Chinese foreign minister that 'the Government of India was not pleased when the Dalai Lama left Lhasa and never encouraged him to leave Tibet.' He continued, 'The Government of India will be glad to use their good offices to advise him not to come to India.' Ibid.

67. Ibid.

68. Ibid.

69. 'The Secretary of State to Embassy in India,' 27 October 1950, *FRUS*, vol. VI, p. 545.

70. 'The Ambassador in India (Henderson) to the Secretary of State,' 10 November 1950, *FRUS*, vol. V, pp. 1474–5.
71. Ibid.
72. Ibid.
73. http://www.claudearpi.net/maintenance/uploaded_pics/19501104PatelonTibet.pdf
74. 'Letter from Deputy Prime Minister, Sardar Vhallabhbhai Patel, to Prime Minister Jahawarlal Nehru', 7 November 1950, http://www.defence.pk/forums/indian-defence/80449-my-dear-jawaharlal-sardar-patel-china.html, last accessed June 2013.
75. Ibid. Patel's 7 November letter to Nehru is most probably based on a letter from Girja Bajpai, secretary general of the Ministry of External Affairs, received on 3 November 1950. Bajpai outlined in detail the events taking place in Tibet during this period and the major security issues the Chinese invasion posed for India in the north and northeast areas. In a letter dated 4 November 1950, Patel responded to Bajpai and wrote that 'This creates most embarrassing defense problems and I entirely agree with you that a reconsideration of our military position and re-disposition of our forces are inescapable … The Chinese advance into Tibet upsets all our security calculations.' 'Letter from Sardar Patel to Sir Girga Shankar Bajpai,' 4 November 1950, http://www.claudearpi.net/maintenance/uploaded_pics/19501104PatelonTibet.pdf, last accessed June 2013. Bajpai must have also included telegrams between Nehru and Panikkar on the ongoing talks between him and the Chinese, as Patel wrote: 'In your illuminating survey of what has passed between us and the Chinese Government through our Ambassador, you have made out an unanswerable case for treating the Chinese with the greatest suspicion.' Ibid.
76. 'Letter from Deputy Prime Minister, Sardar Vallabhbhai Patel, to Prime Minister Jahawarlal Nehru', 7 November 1950, http://www.defence.pk/forums/indian-defence/80449-my-dear-jawaharlal-sardar-patel-china.html, last accessed June 2013.
77. Ibid. He continued: 'The Himalayas have been regarded as an impenetrable barrier against any threat from the North. We had friendly Tibet which gave us no trouble … We have to consider what new situation now faces us as a result of the disappearance of Tibet …' Ibid.
78. Letter from Sadar Patel to Sir Girga Shankar Bajpai,' 4 November 1950, http://www.claudearpi.net/maintenance/uploaded_pics/19501104PatelonTibet.pdf, last verified June 2013.
79. 'Letter from Deputy Prime Minister, Sardar Vhallabhbhai Patel, to Prime Minister Jahawarlal Nehru,' 7 November 1950, http://www.defence.pk/forums/indian-defence/80449-my-dear-jawaharlal-sardar-patel-china.html, last accessed June 2013.
80. State Department officials were not allowed to discuss the 'question of Tibet' with the press or 'outsiders' and could only discuss the issue in the State Department with those 'immediately concerned' with the issue. See 'Office Memorandum of the United States Government from Mr Clubb to All Officers,' 1 November 1950, 793B.00/11–150, Box 4226, NARA. On the issue of Korea, Nehru had refused to brand the North Koreans as the aggressor at a UN vote. Nehru was vilified in the American media over this action.
81. 'Department of State, Secretary of State, Dean Acheson, to Ambassador Henderson,' 27 October 1950, 793B.00/10–2750, Box 4226, NARA.
82. 'Ambassador Henderson to the Secretary of State,' 3 November 1950, 1072 793B. /11–350, Box 4226, NARA.
83. Ibid.

84. Ibid.
85. 'Letter to Vijayalakshmi Pandit,' 1 November 1950, Gopal, *Selected Works of Jawaharlal Nehru*, vol. 15, part 2, p. 524. According to Nehru's account of this conversation, the prime minister said that 'apart from the impracticability of such a proposal…any attempt by the United States would be very harmful.' Nehru's lengthy notes on his conversation with Henderson are in 'Notes to the Secretary General,' 3 November 1950, in Gopal, *Selected Works of Jawaharlal Nehru*, vol. 15, part 2, p. 528.
86. 'The Ambassador in India (Henderson) to the Officer in Charge of India-Nepal Affairs (Weil),' 30 December 1950, *FRUS*, vol. VI, p. 613. Unfortunately Washington felt at the end of 1950 that Bajpai was no longer as forthcoming on Panikkar. Henderson believed this was because some of the very confidential information that he shared with Henderson (Bajpai was obviously not authorized to do this) was passed to Washington and occasionally ended up in the press, particularly in *Newsweek* magazine. This resulted in Bajpai's embarrassment and that of the GOI. Ibid., p. 614. Bajpai asked Henderson not to repeat their confidential conversations to Washington. Interestingly Henderson added that Bajpai 'has made it clear to me on several occasions that if the United States Government should be aware of the contents of Panikkar's telegrams, United States attitude towards Communist China might stiffen. He is therefore withholding some of these contents, since the policy of the Government of India is to prevail on Communist China and the United States to come together. I am inclined to believe that Panikkar is denouncing the United States in his telegrams almost as much Communist Chinese leaders, and that Sir Girga does not wish us to know how far Panikkar is going in trying to sell to his Government the Communist Chinese point of view.' Ibid., p. 614.
87. Ibid., p. 615.
88. 'Department of State Policy Statement: India,' 1 December 1950, *FRUS*, vol. V, pp. 1476–80. Despite all the strain in the US–India relationship, Washington was still hopeful of pursuing a 'policy of friendship and cooperation' and that India would 'voluntarily' associate itself with the US and other countries that were opposed to communism. Ibid.
89. 'The Ambassador in India (Henderson) to the Secretary of State,' 31 October 1950, *FRUS*, vol. VI, p. 549.

15. THE DALAI LAMA AND HENDERSON'S PLAN

1. Truman, *Years of Trial and Hope*, p. 387.
2. Ibid.
3. 'Telegram from Henderson, New Delhi, to Secretary of State, Washington,' 28 October 1950, 793B.00/10–2850, NARA.
4. Dalai Lama, *Freedom in Exile*, p. 58.
5. Ibid.
6. Ibid.
7. Ibid., p. 59.
8. Heinrich Harrer, *Life* magazine, 23 April 1951, p. 136.
9. Ibid.
10. Ibid.
11. 'Top Secret Memo from Ambassador Loy Henderson, New Delhi to Elbert G. Mathews, Director, Office of South Asian Affairs, Department of State, Washington,' 29 March 1951, NND 851052, Box 4227, NARA.

12. Harrer eventually became an informant for the US government, working with CIA operative Bill Gibson. Gibson also worked with George Patterson. He was introduced to Henderson through James Burke, the *Time* and *Life* Bureau Chief in Delhi. Interview with George Patterson, Scotland, May 2005.

13. 'Top Secret Memo from Ambassador Loy Henderson, New Delhi to Elbert G. Matthews, Director, Office of South Asian Affairs, Department of State, Washington,' 29 March 1951, NND 851052, Box 4227, NARA.

14. Ibid. In his confidential memo Henderson remarked that he was inclined to believe Harrer's information about the Dalai Lama and the situation in Lhasa. In the meeting Harrer commented that the Dalai Lama was being pressured to come to terms with Beijing and return to Lhasa from Yatung.

15. Ibid.

16. 'Top Secret Letter from J. C. Satterthwaite, American Embassy, Ceylon to Ambassador Loy Henderson,' 13 April 1951, 793B.11/4–1351, Box 4227, NARA.

17. Ibid.

18. 'Memorandum from Elbert G. Mathews to Joseph C. Satterthwaite,' 24 April 1951, 793B.11/4–1351, Box 4227, NARA.

19. 'Top Secret Memorandum of Conversation, Fraser Wilkins, 1st Secretary of American Embassy, New Delhi,' 13 May 1951, Lot 58 F 95/851052–30, NARA.

20. Ibid.

21. Ibid.

22. 'Declassified Intelligence Document, Office of Current Intelligence, Daily Digest of Significant s/s Cables,' 29 March 1951, 79T01146A, Box 0001, Folder 0025, NARA. Significantly, recently declassified US intelligence reveals that the United States was aware of what the Chinese intended for the rest of Tibet by March 1951. According to the CIA report, Ambassador Panikkar in Beijing had been informed on 27 March by Chou Enlai, then serving as the PRC Foreign Minister, 'that the Tibet question had been settled.' The PLA had already set the terms of the agreement.

23. 'Declassified Information Report,' 23 August 1951, 82–00457R, Box 0081, Folder 39, NARA.

24. 'Telegram from Steere, the American Embassy in New Delhi to the Secretary of State, Washington,' 29 May 1951, 793B.00/5–2951, Box 4227, NARA.

25. Ibid. Also see 'Telegram from Ambassador Henderson in New Delhi to the Secretary of State, Washington,' 11 June 1951, 793B.00/6–1151, Box 4227, NARA.

26. 'Telegram from Steere, the American Embassy in New Delhi to the Secretary of State, Washington,' 29 May 1951, 793B.00/5–2951, Box 4227, NARA.

27. Ibid.

28. 'Department of State, Top Secret Telegram to American Embassy in New Delhi,' 29 May 1951, 793B.00/5–2951, Box 4227, NARA.

29. Ibid. Tibet's first appeal to the UN was made on 17 November 1950. The hope was to obtain a resolution calling for the withdrawal of Chinese troops from Tibetan territory. But India's foreign policy at the time was one of non-alignment; and to keep their relationship with the Chinese intact, they would not back a resolution. Having tacitly coaxed the naive and untutored Tibetans into the international arena, the Americans and British, who looked to the GOI to take the lead on a UN initiative, were stymied. This is discussed in Chapter 13.

30. 'Department of State, Top Secret Telegram to American Embassy in New Delhi,' 2 June 1951, 793B.00/5–2951, Box 4227, NARA.
31. 'The Chargé in India (Steere) to the Secretary of State,' 22 June 1951, *FRUS*, vol. VII, pp. 1713–14. A week later, on 15 June, Nicholas Thacher, the vice council in Calcutta, replaced Wilkins in Kalimpong and stayed until the end of June; he was then replaced by Robert Linn, from the CIA station in Calcutta.
32. Dalai Lama, *Freedom in Exile*, p. 63.
33. Ibid., p. 63.
34. Ibid.
35. Ibid.
36. Ibid., p. 66.
37. Kenneth Conboy and James Morrison, *The CIA's Secret War in Tibet* (Lawrence: University Press of Kansas, 2002), p. 15.
38. Ibid.
39. 'Top Secret Telegram from the Secretary of State to the Embassy in Thailand,' 22 June 1951, *FRUS*, vol. VII, pp. 1713–14. Acheson was hoping to gain asylum for the leader and some of his followers in Thailand, as this was a Buddhist country that had past relations with Tibet.
40. 'Telegram from the Secretary of State to the US Embassy in India,' 12 July 1951, *FRUS*, vol. VII, p. 1748. No emphasis added.
41. They met with US officials on 26, 27, and 28 June 1951.
42. 'Enclosure to Foreign Service Despatch from American Consulate in Calcutta to the Department of State, Washington,' 2 July 1951, Reference no. 615, 793B.00/7–251, Box 4228, NARA.
43. Ibid.
44. Ibid.
45. Ibid.
46. Ibid.
47. Ibid.
48. 'Department of State to American Consul in Calcutta, American Embassy in New Delhi,' 3 July 1951, 793B.00/7–251, Box 4228, NARA.
49. Ibid.
50. Ibid.
51. 'Enclosure 3 to Despatch 3 from Am consul, Calcutta,' 2 July 1951, in 'Foreign Service Despatch from American Consulate in Calcutta to the Department of State, Washington,' 2 July 1951, Reference no. 615, 793B.00/7–251, Box 4228, NARA.
52. 'Telegram no. 26, Calcutta to the Secretary of State, Washington,' 9 July 1951, 793B.00/7–651, Box 4228, NARA.
53. Thubten Norbu was the oldest of the Dalai Lama's brothers and was recognized as the reincarnation of a high lama, Taktser Rinpoche. He was sent to the Kumbum Monastery, which was several hours from their village of Taktser in north-east Tibet. See Dalai Lama, *Freedom in Exile*, p. 8. In US correspondence during this period, Norbu is referred to as Taktser.
54. Interview with George Patterson, May 2005; and George Patterson, *Patterson of Tibet*, p. 281.
55. Ibid. Also see 'Telegram from New Delhi to the Secretary of State,' 16 June 1951, 793B.00/6–1651, NND 851052, Box 4227, NARA.

56. 'Telegram from Wilson in Calcutta to Secretary of State, Washington,' no. 526, 17 June 1951, Secret Files, 793B.005–1151, Box 4227, NARA.

57. 'Telegram by Steere, Embassy New Delhi to Department of State,' 13 June 1951, 793B.00/6–1351, Box 4227, NARA.

58. 'Memorandum of Conversation, Enclosure to Despatch 18 from the American Consulate in New Delhi to the Secretary of State, Washington,' 30 June 1951. Bob Linn and Bill Gibson were CIA operatives.

59. Ibid.

60. 'Telegram from Calcutta to the Secretary of State,' 30 June 1951, no. 555, 793B.00/6–3051, NARA.

61. 'Telegram from Ambassador Henderson to the Secretary of State,' 3 June 1951, 793B.00/6–351, Box 4227, NARA.

62. 'Telegram from Calcutta to the Secretary of State,' 30 June 1951, no. 555 793B.00/6–3051; George Patterson interview, May 2005. Patterson used the name Taktser.

63. Only after Taktser arrived in the United States did the Embassy in Delhi decide to disclose to the British High Commission the full story on the Dalai Lama's brother.

64. 'Telegram from Calcutta to the Secretary of State,' 6 July 1951, 793B.00/7–651, Box 4228, NARA.

65. 'Telegram from the Department of State to the American Embassy in New Delhi and the American Consulate in Calcutta,' Control no. 5109, 12 July 1951, 793B.00/7–1251, NARA. The United States government made it clear to Taktser that they would 'indicate publicly its understanding of the position of the DL as the head of an autonomous state.' Ibid. Washington reiterated its financial support for the Dalai Lama and his entourage and encouraged the leader to seek asylum; it was made clear that 'friends of Tibet in US' would provide appropriate support for the Dalai Lama. Ibid.

66. 'Am consul, Calcutta to the Department of State, Washington,' 16 July 1951, 793B.00/7–1651, Box 4228, NARA. Declassified memo to authors under a FOIA request on 6 August 2008.

67. Lloyd V. Steere, the American chargé d'affaires in Delhi, even went so far as to suggest that a member of the Tibetan negotiating delegation who had just returned to India 'feign[ed] illness'. He could then remain in India and tell the world that the Sino-Tibetan agreement had been signed under extreme duress. See 'Telegram from Steere in New Delhi to Secretary of State, Washington,' no. 100, 8 July 1951, 793B.00/7–851, Box 4228, NARA.

68. 'Final Message to Dalai Lama,' 12 July 1951, Enclosure 6, Despatch 34, from Am consul Calcutta, 21 July 1951, Box 4228, NARA.

69. Ibid., p. 2 of enclosure.

70. Ibid.

71. 'Enclosure 5, Despatch 34, from Am consul Calcutta,' 21 July 1951, Box 4228, NARA.

72. Ibid.

73. 'Telegram from Calcutta to the Secretary of State,' no. 24, 6 July 1951, 793B.007–651, Box 4228, NARA. Interview with George Patterson, May 2005; and also 'Enclosure 2, Despatch 68, from the American Consulate in Calcutta,' 18 August 1951. The young leader was under immense pressure from the Tibetan officials that were with him in Yatung. According to the Dalai Lama's brother-in-law, Yapshi Sey, who was in Yatung, these officials told His Holiness that he should not 'shame' Tibet in its hour of need by

fleeing to India. 'Enclosure no. 1 to Despatch no. 260, 2 August 1951, Letter dated 27 July 1951 from Lloyd Steere, Minister-Counselor, New Delhi to the Department of State,' released to authors under FOIA request. American officials in India used Yapshi Sey as a courier to deliver letters to the Dalai Lama in Yatung.

74. Shakabpa, *A Political History*, p. 304.

75. 'The Consul General at Calcutta (Wilson) to the Secretary of State, 13 August 1951, *FRUS*, vol. II, China, pp. 1776–7.

76. 'Telegram from Calcutta to the Secretary of State,' no. 114, 13 August 1951, 793B.00/8–1351, Box 4228, NARA. Shape's reaction to the US message was one of incredulity—he could not understand how the US would be willing to help the Tibetans if they were unwilling to make a formal pledge.

77. Ibid.

78. 'Department of State to the American Consulate in Calcutta and the American Embassy in New Delhi,' 15 August 1951, 793B.00/8–1351, Box 4228, NARA.

79. 'Telegram from the Department of State, Secretary of State, Dean Acheson to the American Embassy in New Delhi and the American Consulate in Calcutta,' 3 August 1951, 793B.00/8–151, Box 4227, NARA. Acheson questioned whether the problem was unreliable intermediaries or lack of sympathy and support from the GOI. Also see 'Telegram from the Department of State, Dean Acheson to the American Embassy in New Delhi and the American Consul in Calcutta,' 18 October 1951, 793B.00/7–2251, Box 4228, NARA.

80. 'Telegram from the Department of State, Dean Acheson to the American Embassy in New Delhi and the American Consul in Calcutta,' 18 October 1951, 793B.00/7–2251, Box 4228, NARA.

81. 'Telegram from the American Consulate in Calcutta to the Department of State: Conversation with Yapshi Sey Phuntsok, Brother-in-Law of the Dalai Lama,' Despatch no. 68, 18 August 1951, 793B.00/9–1851, Box 4227, NARA.

82. 'Enclosure 2 to Despatch no. 68, American Consul Calcutta,' 18 August 1951, 793B.00/9–1851, Box 4227, NARA. The message was translated into the honorific style to show respect. Yapshi Sey did not speak English and they used the daughter of the Maharaja of Sikkim, known as Kukula. She was also the wife of a member of the Tibetan trade mission and her uncle was Ragashar Shape, the Tibetan minister of defense.

83. 'Memorandum from the American Consulate in Calcutta to the State Department in Washington,' 15 October 1951, Re: Telegram nos. 128 and 185, 1 October 1951, 793B.00/1051, NARA.

84. Letter sent on 6 July 1951 asking the Dalai Lama to leave Tibet permanently. Enclosure no. 1 to Despatch no. 70, 11 July 1951, 793B.00/7–1151, Box 4228, NARA. This letter was purposefully left unsigned for 'reasons of security', wrote Lloyd Steere, the chargé d'affaires in New Delhi. He noted: 'it contains no reference to the United States. Arrangements were made, however, by which the Dalai Lama was informed of its origin.' 793b.00/7–1151, NARA, Cover letter to Enclosure, signed by Lloyd V. Steere.

85. Melvyn Goldstein, *A History of Modern Tibet, vol. 2, The Calm Before the Storm* (Berkeley: University of California Press, 2007), pp. 138–9. Many officials in Lhasa also urged that the Dalai Lama return. Ibid. Also see Shakya, *Dragon in the Land of Snows*, p. 83.

86. Goldstein, p. 140.

87. Ibid.

88. Dalai Lama, *Freedom in Exile*, pp. 65–6.
89. Ibid., p. 66.
90. Ibid. The Dalai Lama indeed found the general to be 'just another human being, an ordinary person like myself.' Ibid. Unfortunately the young leader was unable to see beyond the general's facade. In his monthly report, which was secretly passed to the Americans through Whitehall, the Indian political agent in Lhasa, Sumal Sinha, described the general as an 'extraordinary Lilliputian' who left 'bitter memories behind him' on his journey from Yatung to Lhasa. Sinha wrote: 'At Yatung, in particular, on grounds that scarcely supported his conduct, he lashed the Kashag with his fury, made those venerable gentlemen obey his commands, and give him a seat of equal eminence with His Holiness at a meeting between them. Elsewhere on the road, he urged the common people and the village headmen not to supply transport to officials at lower rates but to demand prevailing market rates, although he himself without the slightest qualm enjoyed these very same privileges, and more, at no cost to himself.' In Lhasa the general lived extravagantly and was a demanding taskmaster. See 'Foreign Service Despatch, Report of Indian Agent, Lhasa for period 16 July–15 August 1951, attached to Telegram from Calcutta to the Secretary of State,' 18 October 1951, Control no. 9094, no. 206, 793B.00/10–1851, NARA.
91. 'Telegram from New Delhi, Steere to Secretary of State, Dean Acheson,' 30 October 1951, 793B.00/10–3051, NARA.
92. Ibid.
93. Shakya, *Dragon in the Land of Snows*, p. 85.
94. Ibid. Shakya says that the Indians had felt that their concerns had been marginalized as the Tibetans had looked to the US for assistance without first consulting them. Ibid.

16. MR NEHRU … AGAIN

1. 'Department of State, Secretary of State Dean Acheson to Ambassador Henderson,' 27 October 1950, 793B.00/10–2750, Box 4226, NARA.
2. Ibid.
3. 'Secretary of State to the Embassy in India,' 30 December 1950, *FRUS*, vol. V, pp. 1481–2; 'United States Aid to India Under the India Emergency Assistance Act of 1951: Memorandum by Mr J. Robert Fluker of the Office of South Asian Affairs,' 15 January 1951, *FRUS*, vol. VI, pp. 2085–6.
4. 'Letter to Vijayalakshmi Pandit,' 13 December 1951, in Gopal, *Selected Works of Jawaharlal Nehru*, vol. 15, part 2, p. 531. Nehru wrote to his sister to say that they were in great need of food aid. But he was an extremely proud leader and told her that while he would have no objection to a free grant of food grains, he could not 'ask for it.' Ibid.
5. 'Letter to Vijayalakshmi Pandit,' 9 May 1950, in Gopal, *Selected Works of Jawaharlal Nehru*, vol. 14, part 2, p. 379.
6. 'The Ambassador in India (Henderson) to the Secretary of State,' 20 January 1951, *FRUS*, vol. VI, part 2, p. 2089.
7. 'Memorandum by the Assistant Secretary of State for Near Eastern, South Asian, and African Affairs (McGhee) to the Secretary of State,' 30 January 1951, *FRUS*, vol. VI, part 2, p. 2097. McGhee had consulted with the Treasury Department, Commerce, Agriculture, ECA, and the Bureau of the Budget.
8. Ibid.

9. Ibid., p. 2103. Washington was concerned that a weakened India would create an ideal situation for subversive communist activities.

10. *New York Times*, 27 January 1951. Not all the press was favorable to Nehru's request. In a letter to Nehru, his sister wrote: 'The hymn of hate against India continues at a high pitch and a large section of the press is devoted to arguments of rejecting India's request for food grains.' Nehru was dismissive of all the negativity and called it 'hysterical'. See 'Letter from Vijayalakshmi Pandit,' 13 February 1951, Gopal, *Selected Works of Jawaharlal Nehru*, vol. 15, part 2, p. 533, ftn 2.

11. *New York Times*, 27 January 1951.

12. Ibid. In January 1951 some members of Congress had expressed their displeasure at giving aid to India. Quoted in McMahon, *The Cold War on the Periphery*, p. 87.

13. 'Memorandum of Conversation by the Secretary of State: Meeting with the President,' 1 February 1951, *FRUS*, vol. VI, part 2, p. 2106.

14. Acheson gave Truman a detailed memo outlining a proposal to provide 2 million tons of food grains at a cost of $180 million. See 'Memorandum by the Secretary of State to the President: Memorandum for the President,' 2 February 1951, *FRUS*, vol. VI, part 2, pp. 2109–10.

15. 'Special Message to the Congress on the Famine in India,' 12 February 1951, John T. Woolley and Gerhard Peters, *The American Presidency Project* [online] (Santa Barbara, CA: University of California), http://www.trumanlibrary.org/publicpapers/index. php?pid=241, last accessed 1 June 2013.

16. McMahon, *The Cold War on the Periphery*, p. 96. In addition, the comments of Bharatan Kumarappa, an Indian diplomat at the UN, fueled more congressional opposition. In a speech in March he 'claimed that India's chief enemy in the Far East is not Communism but Western imperialism.' The GOI quickly apologized, but the damage was already done. Ibid.

17. 'The Ambassador in India (Henderson) to the Secretary of State,' 24 March 1951, *FRUS*, vol. VI, part 2, p. 2130.

18. Ibid.

19. 'Report on the meeting between Director General Chen Jiakang and Indian Counselor, Kaul,' 26 March 1951. This document was released to the authors by the Chinese Foreign Ministry. This is Archive Document no. 105–00010–04(1); there are twelve pages in this file. Author's note: Chen Jaikang is the Pinyin spelling for the General. In keeping with how some Chinese military figures were known readers will find both the Pinyin and Wade-Giles systems used in translations.

20. Ibid.

21. 'Discussion record of the Ministry of Foreign Affairs of the Central People's Government between Indian Counselor Kaul and Director General Chen,' 26 March 1951, at the Foreign Ministry Headquarters, Chinese Foreign Ministry Archives, Document no. 105–00010–04(1). This document was released to the authors.

22. Ibid. What is shown in these Chinese Foreign Ministry documents is that the Chinese wanted the Government of India's support regarding Tibet.

23. 'Telegram 163 from the Legation at Amman, March 26, from Assistant Secretary of State McGhee,' and 'Secretary of State to the Embassy in Egypt,' 28 March 1951, *FRUS*, vol. VI, part 2, p. 2132, ftn 1.

24. 'Henderson to the Secretary of State,' 22 April 1951, *FRUS*, vol. VI, part 2, pp. 2150–1; 'The Ambassador in India (Henderson) to the Secretary of State,' 1 May 1951, *FRUS*,

vol. VI, part 2, pp. 2152–3; and 'Memorandum of Conversation the Director of the Office of South Asian Affairs (Matthews),' 2 May 1951, *FRUS*, vol. VI, part 2, pp. 2153–4. Also see McMahon, *The Cold War on the Periphery*, pp. 98–9.

25. *New York Times*, 30 April 1951.
26. Quoted in 'Memorandum of Conversation by the Director of the Office of South Asian Affairs (Matthews),' 2 May 1951, *FRUS*, vol. VI, p. 2153, ftn 1.
27. Ibid. and 'The Ambassador in India (Henderson) to the Secretary of State,' 7 May 1951, *FRUS*, vol. VI, part 2, p. 2158. Henderson had spoken in an off-the-record conversation with Bajpai, who apprised him of Nehru's intended speech.
28. 'Psychological Strategy Board Memo,' 28 September 1951, PSB Files 'Torrential,' File 1, Box 14, Harry S. Truman Presidential Library.
29. Ibid. This definition is in an undated memo, attached to a 25 July 1951 memorandum for Mr Sherman, acting assistant director of Office of Coordination, PSB files, Box 14, Harry S. Truman Presidential Library.
30. 'Note by the Executive Secretary to the National Security Council on Scope and Pace of Covert Operations,' 23 October 1951, quoted in Dennis Merrill, ed., *A Documentary History of the Truman Presidency* (Bethesda, MA: University Publications of America, 1995–2003), vol. 23, p. 370. Also Michael Warner, ed., *The CIA Under Harry Truman* (Washington, DC: Center for the Study of Intelligence, 1994), pp. 437–9.
31. Merrill, vol. 23, p. 370.
32. Ibid.
33. 'National Overt Propaganda Policy Guidance,' 14 November 1951, PSB 'Torrential' File 1, Box 14, Harry S. Truman Presidential Library.
34. Ibid.
35. Merrill, vol. 23, p. 377.
36. Ibid., p. xxi.
37. 'Outgoing Telegram from Acheson, Department of State,' 14 June 1951, to 'Amembassy Moscow, Amembassy London,' 793B.00/6–1451, Box 4227, NARA.
38. Acheson had asked Henderson whether the aid grants 'reflected any change in degree of friendliness.' Henderson believed that Bajpai and other advisors had persuaded Nehru that India could not make any economic progress without US aid. See 'The Ambassador in India (Henderson) to the Secretary of State,' 7 June 1951, *FRUS*, vol. VI, part 2, p. 2167.
39. 'Telegram from New Delhi, Steere to Secretary of State,' 18 June 1951, 793B.00/6–1851, Box 4227, NARA.
40. The Washington meeting was recorded in 'Memorandum of Conversation at the Department of State, 2 July 1951, with Mr Burrows, Counselor British Embassy, Mr Belcher, First Secretary British Embassy, and Mr Merchant FE, Mr Kennedy SOA, Mr Meyers UNP, and Mr Perkins CA,' 793B.00/7–25, Box 4228, NARA.
41. Ibid. The British were anxious to know if the US was going to 'issue a statement' on Tibet or support them in another UN bid. It was made very plain to Merchant that 'the Indians might help if their cooperation was enlisted and they might definitely hinder our efforts if it was not'. Ibid.
42. Ibid.
43. 'Memorandum by the Central Intelligence Agency, National Intelligence Estimate,' 4 September 1951, *FRUS*, vol. VI, part 2, p. 2174.
44. 'Paper Prepared in the Bureau of Near Eastern, South Asian, and African Affairs: Means

to Combat India's Policy of Neutralism,' 30 August 1951, *FRUS*, vol. VI, part 2, p. 2172. Nehru had sent his sister to discuss the negotiations over the Japanese peace treaty. 'Many of these meetings,' wrote Madame Pandit, 'took place in the early morning at Dulles' home where he paced back and forth as he spoke hoping that India would side with America …' On the morning that Dulles was given India's final decision, she wrote: 'He walked up and down the room with bent head and his hands behind his back … then he swung around and said, 'I cannot accept this. Does your Prime Minister realize that I have prayed at every stage of this treaty?' See Pandit, *Scope of Happiness*, p. 255.

45. 'Memorandum by the Central Intelligence Agency, National Intelligence Estimate,' 4 September 1951, *FRUS*, vol. VI, part 2, p. 2175.

46. Ibid.

47. Available in full at http://www.claudearpi.net/maintenance/uploaded_pics/1951Agreem entonMeasuresforthePeacefulLiberationofTibet.pdf, last accessed June 2013.

48. McMahon, *The Cold War on the Periphery*, p. 111.

49. Ibid., p. 118.

50. The new ambassador, his wife and children 'adopted Indian dress and ate Indian food.' The children rode their bicycles to Indian schools and the family 'patronized Indian dance and music.' They served traditional 'curry and rice' at their ambassadorial dinners. Pandit, *Scope of Happiness*, p. 261; Chester Bowles, *Ambassador's Report* (New York: Harper, 1954), p. 11.

51. 'The Ambassador in India (Bowles) to the Secretary of State', 15 November 1951, *FRUS*, vol. VII, Part 2, pp. 1848 9.

52. Ibid., p. 1849. Bowles believed that overt aid at this time would be viewed by the Communist Chinese as an American intervention in Tibet and would renew Chinese propaganda that the US was involved in Tibetan affairs. In addition, the ambassador knew that it would be 'highly unlikely' that Nehru would permit the US to transit through India, as this would negatively impact India's relations with China. Ibid.

53. Ibid.

54. 'Report of the Indian Agent at Lhasa, 16 November–15 December 1951, in Despatch from AMEMBASSY London to Department of State,' 6 February 1952, 793B.00/ 2–652, NARA.

55. Goldstein, *The Calm Before the Storm*, p. 179.

56. *The People's Daily*, 28 May 1951 quoted in Goldstein, *The Calm Before the Storm*, p. 180.

57. Ibid.

17. FORMOSA: THE UNSINKABLE AIRCRAFT CARRIER

1. 'Memorandum of Conversation by the Ambassador at Large (Jessup),' 26 June 1950, *FRUS*, vol. VII, p. 180.

2. Ibid.

3. Ibid., pp. 180–1. In effect the 7th Fleet was sent to neutralize the Taiwan Strait.

4. 'Statement Issued by the President,' 27 June 1950, *FRUS*, vol. VII, pp. 202–3. This was first distributed to the participants after a top secret meeting in the White House cabinet room that morning.

5. Ibid.

6. Ross Koen, *The China Lobby in American Politics*, p. 83.

7. Nancy Bernkopf Tucker, *Patterns in the Dust*, p. 196. Chiang and his wife were said to have

been 'fervently praying they could hold Taiwan until the advent of a third world war, an American rescue, or a sheer miracle.' See Laura Tyson Li, *Madame Chiang Kai-shek: China's Eternal First Lady*, p. 325.

8. Tucker, p. 199.

9. 'Memorandum by the Joint Chiefs of Staff to the Secretary of Defense (Johnson),' 27 July 1950, *FRUS*, vol. VI, pp. 391–4. The NSC discussed the JCS memo with President Truman presiding. The president 'approved in principle' the JCS memo, subject to agreement of the secretaries of defense and state. See *FRUS*, vol. VI, p. 394, ftn 6. (General Douglas MacArthur would lead the United Nations command in Korea until being removed by Truman in April 1951.)

10. Ibid.

11. Ibid. Also see 'Telegram from the Secretary of State to the US Embassy in China,' 14 August 1950, *FRUS*, vol. VI, pp. 434–5; and Garver, *The Sino-American Alliance, Nationalist China and American Cold War Strategy in Asia*, pp. 36–7.

12. 'Memorandum by the Joint Chiefs of Staff to the Secretary of Defense (Johnson),' 27 July 1950, *FRUS*, vol. VI, pp. 391–4 and also 'The Secretary of State to the Secretary of Defense (Johnson), 31 July 1950, FRUS, vol. VI, pp. 404–5. And just as importantly, they did not want to place the United States in a greater international political disadvantage on the sensitive subject of Formosa.

13. 'Report by the Departments of State and Defence on Immediate United States Courses of Action with Respect to Formosa in Memorandum by the Executive Secretary (Lay) to the National Security Council,' 3 August 1950, *FRUS 1950*, vol. VI, p. 414, ftn 4. The exact amount of aid was $14,344,599 and it was authorized in a letter from President Truman to Mr Acheson, 25 August 1950. Funds were made available from the 'Mutual Defence Assistance Act'. See *FRUS*, vol. VI, p. 414, ftn 4.

14. 'Paper Prepared by Mr John Foster Dulles, Consultant to the Secretary of State,' 30 November 1950, *FRUS*, vol. VI, pp. 162–3.

15. Ibid., p. 163.

16. Richard J. Aldrich, *The Hidden Hand: Britain, America and Cold War Secret Intelligence* (New York: Overlook Press, 2001), pp. 295–6. Aldrich noted that 'Pakistan, India, Burma, Thailand, Laos, Taiwan, Hong Kong, Japan and Korea all served as springboards for insurgency against Beijing.' The attacks 'were supported by the CIA, but were pressed home with even more vigour by Taiwan's secret agencies, still smarting from their defeats on the mainland.'

17. http://www.air-america.org/, last accessed June 2013; and also William M. Leary, *Perilous Missions: Civil Air Transport and CIA Covert Operations in Asia* (Washington, DC: Smithsonian Institution Press, 2002), p. x. This quote is in the preface to this new edition of Leary's book. President Ronald Reagan gave a memorial dedication on 5 May 1987 at the University of Texas at Dallas. See http://www.air-america.org/About/Memorial_Plaque.shtml, last accessed June 2013.

18. Tom Schuster, 'The CIA's War with Red China and other Asian Lands,' in *Man's* magazine, September 1972. CAT was known as the 'world's most shot at airline,' ibid. This romantic image of the airline was described by former CIA operative Bill Wells, who worked in Taiwan, and also by Roger McCarthy, who trained the Tibetans at Camp Hale, Colorado. Interview with William Wells, Bethesda, Maryland, July 2006; telephone interview with Roger McCarthy, October 2005.

19. At this time, the Nationalists owned part of CAT airline.

20. For example, the Nationalists helped evacuate more than 100,000 people from Mukden in Manchuria and brought in supplies and carried out the wounded during the epic battle of Hsuchow.
21. 'The Under Secretary of State (Webb) to the Director of the Office of Far Eastern Affairs (Butterworth),' 10 May 1949, *FRUS*, vol. IX, p. 517. In a meeting on 11 May 1949 with Dean Rusk, the assistant secretary of state, and Philip Sprouse, the head of the Division of Chinese Affairs, Chennault got directly to the point by beginning the discussion with his suggestion that his aircraft could assist in a program to prevent communism spreading throughout Indochina. See 'Transcript of Conversation with Maj. Gen. Claire Lee Chennault, Dean Rusk, Assistant Secretary of State, Philip D. Sprouse, Division of Chinese Affairs,' 11 May 1949, *FRUS*, vol. IX, p. 520.
22. William M. Leary, *Perilous Missions; Civil Air Transport and CIA Covert Operations in Asia* (Tuscaloosa: University of Alabama Press, 1984, first edn), p. 105.
23. Ibid.
24. 'Memorandum by the Special Assistant to the Secretary of Defence for Foreign Military Affairs and Assistance (Burns) to the Assistant Secretary of State for Far Eastern Affairs (Rusk),' 29 May 1950, *FRUS*, vol. VI, pp. 346–7.
25. Leary, *Perilous Missions*, pp. 105–6.
26. Ibid. The agreement was signed between CAT and Richard Dunn, who was a Washington banker representing the CIA. The CIA had the option to purchase the airline outright.
27. Ibid., p. 133.
28. 'Memorandum Prepared in the Department of State: Report on the Effect Within China and other Eastern Countries of United States Backing Chiang Kai-shek,' 9 February 1951, *FRUS*, vol. VII, pp. 1574–8.
29. Ibid.
30. Ibid.
31. 'Memorandum by the Executive Secretary of the National Security Council (Lay) to the National Security Council,' 21 March 21 1951, and 'Study Submitted by the Joint Chiefs of Staff: Courses of Action Relative to Communist China and Korea—Anti Communist Chinese,' 14 March 1951 in *FRUS*, vol. VII, pp. 1598–1605. The secretary of defense had requested the study be sent to the NSC, and a handwritten notation indicated that Acheson had seen the proposal. See p. 1598, ftn 1. On 17 May 1951 President Truman approved NSC 48/5, 'A Report to the National Security Council on United States Objectives, Policies and Courses of Action in Asia,' Editorial note in *FRUS 1951*, vol. VII, p. 1671.
32. Ibid.
33. Interview with Ambassador James Lilley, Washington, DC, January 2007; and also Ambassador James Lilley with Jeffrey Lilley, *China Hands: Nine Decades of Adventure, Espionage, and Diplomacy in Asia* (New York: Public Affairs, 2004), ch. 6.
34. Ibid. The 'third force' was an important but highly compartmentalized part of the intelligence effort. The Nationalists were often not informed. Those involved were flown for training on Saipan to the same facilities that Tibetan Khampa resistance fighters would use for their training in 1956.
35. Joseph Burkholder Smith quoted in Leary, p. 133. Smith was in Truman's Office of Policy Coordination (OPC). The OPC took direction by 1951 from the CIA, and this division expanded rapidly after the start of the Korean War. Also see Joseph Burkholder Smith,

Portrait of a Cold Warrior: Second Thoughts of a CIA Agent (New York: Random House, 1981), p. 77.

36. Leary, p. 133. Western Enterprises offered the CIA plausible deniability for these paramilitary and guerrilla activities.

37. Leary, p. 136; Kenneth Conboy and James Morrison, *The CIA's Secret War in Tibet* (Lawrence: University Press of Kansas, 2002), pp. 37–8; Frank Holober, *Raiders of the China Coast: CIA Covert Operations during the Korean War* (Annapolis: Naval Institute Press, 1999), p. 8.

38. Holober, *Raiders of the China Coast*, p. 2.

39. Ibid., p. 3.

40. Ibid., pp. 7 and 12. Madame Chiang was her 'husband's chief adviser on political and diplomatic relations with the US' and 'unofficially' she was the liaison 'between US intelligence service and her husband on intelligence and paramilitary operations.' See Laura Tyson Li, *Madame Chiang Kai-Shek*, p. 331.

41. Frank Holober, *Raiders of the China Coast*, p. 12.

42. Leary, p. 136; Kenneth Conboy and James Morrison, *The CIA's Secret War in Tibet*, pp. 37–8.

43. Richard J. Aldrich, Gary D. Rawnsley, and Ming-Yeh T. Rawnsley, eds., *The Clandestine Cold War in Asia, 1945–65: Western Intelligence, Propaganda and Special Operations* (London: Frank Cass, 2000), p. 296.

44. Discussion with Ray Cline, June 1988, Arlington, Virginia.

45. 'Credibility of K. M. Panikkar, Indian Ambassador to Communist China, Secret Memorandum,' 12 October 1950, 7pp, Digital National Security Archive.

46. Ibid.

47. McMahon, *The Cold War on the Periphery*, pp. 122–3.

48. Robert McMahon, 'U.S. Policy toward South Asia and Tibet during the Early Cold War,' *Journal of Cold War Studies*, vol. 8, no 3 (Summer 2006), pp. 136–7.

49. Quoted in the 'Address at the Annual Convention of the National Junior Chamber of Commerce,' Minneapolis, MN, 10 June 1953, http://www.presidency.ucsb.edu/ws/index.php?pid=9871, last accessed 1 June 2013.

18. THE EISENHOWER ERA

1. Edward T. Folliard, 'Ike Takes Helm in a Time of Tempest: Says "We Are Linked to All Free Peoples,"' *Washington Post*, 21 January 1953, p. A01.

2. Ibid.; John D. Morris, 'Eisenhower Takes Oath on 2 Bibles; Washington's and His Own Are Used in Solemn Moment of Inaugural Ceremony,' *New York Times*, 20 January 1953, p. 19.

3. 'State of the Union Message by President Eisenhower,' 2 February 1953, in Robert L. Branyan and Lawrence H. Larsen, *The Eisenhower Administration: A Documentary History 1953–1961* (New York: Random House, 1971), vol. I, pp. 32–8.

4. Speech by General Eisenhower, New York City, 25 August 1952, in Branyan and Larsen, vol. 1, p. 91.

5. 'State of the Union Message by President Eisenhower', 2 February 1953, in Branyan and Larsen, vol. 1, p. 94.

6. Ibid., p. 95.

7. Fred I. Greenstein and Richard H. Immerman, 'Effective National Security: Recovering the Eisenhower Legacy,' *Political Science Quarterly*, vol. 115, no. 3, p. 338.

8. Ibid., p. 443.

9. Ibid., p. 442.

10. Dwight D. Eisenhower, *Mandate for Change: 1953–1956* (London: William Heinemann, 1963), p. 168.

11. Ibid.

12. 'NSC 5409: United States Policy Towards South Asia,' 19 February 1954, *FRUS*, vol. XI, part 2, pp. 1089–93.

13. Ibid., p. 1093.

14. Ibid., p. 1094.

15. Dennis Kux, *Estranged Democracies: India and the United States, 1941–1991* (London: Sage Publishers, 1994), p. 131.

16. Ibid., p. 131. Kux was a former foreign service, South Asia specialist and former ambassador to the Ivory Coast.

19. PAKISTAN: A NEW AMERICAN ALLY

1. 'Memorandum of Conversation by Peter Delaney, Office of South Asian Affairs,' 28 January 1953, *FRUS 1952–54. Africa and South Asia*, vol. XI, part 2, p. 1822. On 17 September a loan of $15 million had been given to Pakistan for the purchase of wheat. The foreign minister expected the wheat shortage to be near 1.5 million tons, which he attributed to the GOI's reduced water flow needed for irrigation. Ibid. Originally $10 million in US aid was given to Pakistan in February 1952.

2. H. W. Brands, *The Specter of Neutralism: The United States and the Emergence of the Third World, 1947–1960* (New York: Columbia University Press, 1989), p. 83. Also 'Memorandum by the Secretary of State to the President,' 30 April 1953, *FRUS 1952–54. Africa and South Asia*, vol. XI, part 2, p. 1827. John Foster Dulles was in Pakistan as part of a Middle East tour 22–25 May 1953. He traveled throughout the region with Harold Stassen, the mutual security administrator, 9–29 May 1953.

3. 'The Secretary of State to the Department of State,' 26 May 1953, *FRUS 1952–54. The Near and Middle East*, vol. IX, part 1, p. 147. He wrote: 'I believe Pakistan would be cooperative member of any defense scheme that may emerge in Middle East and that we need not await formal defense arrangements as condition to some military assistance to Pakistan.' Ibid.

4. In the summer of 1956 Dulles called neutralism 'immoral' in a speech in Ames, Iowa. Quoted in Brands, *Specter of Neutralism*, p. 273, and also quoted in *Time* magazine, October 1960.

5. 'Minutes of a United States–United Kingdom Foreign Ministers Meeting, Department of State, Washington,' 31 January 1956, *FRUS 1952–54. East Asian Security; Cambodia; Laos*, vol. XXI, pp. 170–1.

6. *Life* magazine, 19 May 1952.

7. 'Memo of Conversation by the Secretary of State,' 22 May 1953, *FRUS 1952–54. The Near and Middle East*, vol. IX, part 1, pp. 119–21. And Gopal, *Jawaharlal Nehru, A Biography*, vol. II, p. 184.

8. 'Memo of Conversation by the Secretary of State,' 22 May 1953, *FRUS 1952–54. The Near and Middle East*, vol. IX, part 1, p. 121. Dulles also discussed Egypt, Africa, and Kashmir in this meeting.

9. 'Letter to K. P. S. Menon,' 13 October 1953, in Ravinder Kumar and H. Y. Sharada Prasad,

eds., *Selected Works of Jawaharlal Nehru* (New Delhi: Jawaharlal Nehru Memorial Fund, 1998–2001), vol. 24, pp. 602–3.

10. Quoted in 'Minutes of talks with Mao-Tse-tung, Beijing,' 23 October 1954, in Kumar and Prasad, *Selected Works of Jawaharlal Nehru*, vol. 27, p. 34.

11. At this time V. P. Menon was India's ambassador in Moscow. In a private meeting with Chairman Mao in Beijing in October 1954, Nehru is quoted in 'Minutes of talks with Mao-Tse-tung, Beijing,' 23 October 1954, in Kumar and Prasad, *Selected Works of Jawaharlal Nehru*, vol. 27, p. 34.

12. 'Memorandum of Discussion at the 147th Meeting of the National Security Council,' 1 June 1953, *FRUS 1952–54. The Near and Middle East*, vol. IX, part 1, pp. 382–3. But Dulles found Nehru 'very realistic on matters directly affecting India, such as the Kashmir dispute.' Ibid.

13. Ibid., pp. 379–85.

14. Ibid., p. 384. Dulles said that the 'old MEDO concept was certainly finished.' The Middle East Defense Organization was proposed by Paul Nitze in 1952, but was not endorsed by Egypt. It was to be a loosely structured defense pact. Dulles' proposed 'northern tier of nations' became part of the administration's policy in the Middle East and was adopted in NSC 155. Iran was considered too weak to be an effective partner. See 'Memorandum of Discussion at the 153rd Meeting of the National Security Council,' 9 July 1953, *FRUS 1952–54. The Near and Middle East,* vol. IX, part 1, p. 394.

15. McMahon, *The Cold War on the Periphery*, p. 165. McMahon wrote: 'In cooperation with Turkey, US military strategists calculated, Pakistan might help retard a Soviet advance toward the Persian Gulf oil fields and towards important Western-controlled military installations, thus buying time for the United States and Great Britain to launch a full-scale air assault from their Middle Eastern bases against vulnerable Soviet targets, especially the crucial oil fields of the Caucasus region.' Ibid., pp. 165–6.

16. Andrew J. Rotter, *Comrades at Odds: The United States and India, 1947–1965* (Ithaca: Cornell University Press, 2000), p. 59.

17. Ibid.

18. Ibid; also, M. S. Rajan, *India in World Affairs: 1954–56* (New York: Asia Publishing House, 1965), p. 262. The American correspondent, John P. Callahan, received a press release from the Pakistani government. The United States at the time denied the report.

19. *New York Times*, 'US–Pakistan Talk On Arms Awaited,' 2 November 1953. The events leading up to the signing of a defense agreement with Pakistan in February 1954 was played out, for the most part, through 'official leaks' to the media. Both countries would deliberately leak bits of their meetings and arrangements to the press. The *New York Times* covered this extensively in November and December; Karachi and Delhi ran pieces almost daily. See James W. Spain, 'Military Assistance for Pakistan,' *American Political Science Review*, vol. 48, no. 3 (September 1954), pp. 738–51.

20. *New York Times*, 17 November 1953. The newspaper reported that 'while no decision had been made, what the United States had in mind did not involve bases or the means of attacking another country.' Ibid. Washington, it seems, was very careful about revealing the details of their intentions with Pakistan. In fact the British had not been informed until mid-October 1953. Washington knew that the UK government believed that a US–Pakistani defense agreement at this juncture would derail a Kashmir solution between India and Pakistan. McMahon, *The Cold War on the Periphery*, p. 167.

21. *Time* magazine, 'Leaping to Conclusions,' 30 November 1953; *New York Times*, 19 November 1953.

22. *New York Times*, 17 November 1953; *Time* magazine, 30 November 1953.

23. *New York Times*, 26 November 1953.

24. 'Letter to Mahomed Ali,' 10 November 1953, in Gopal, *Jawaharlal Nehru, A Biography*, vol. II, pp. 184–5.

25. Ibid.

26. *New York Times*, 22 November 1953. The Pakistani governor general was not persuaded, nor was he cowed by Nehru, and lodged an official protest over Nehru's outbursts in New Delhi.

27. Ibid. Also see 'Memorandum of Conversation by the Ambassador in Pakistan (Hildreth),' 7 December 1953, *FRUS 1952–54. Africa and South Asia*, vol. XI, part 2, pp. 182–3.

28. 'Letter to K. M. Panikkar,' 12 November 1953, quoted in Gopal, *Jawaharlal Nehru, A Biography*, vol. II, p. 185. Nehru wrote that 'Pakistan becomes practically a colony of the United States.'

29. McMahon, *The Cold War on the Periphery*, p. 168; and 'Memorandum of Conversation by the Ambassador in Pakistan (Hildreth),' 7 December 1953, *FRUS 1952–54. Africa and South Asia*, vol. XI, part 2, pp. 1831–2; and 'The Ambassador in Pakistan (Hildreth) to the Department of State,' 8 December 1953, *FRUS*, vol. XI, part 2, pp. 1833–5. The governor general reassured Nixon that Turkey was eager to enter into a military agreement with Pakistan, but military aid should be given to Pakistan first without delay. The Pakistanis would then approach Turkey.

30. 'The Ambassador in Pakistan (Hildreth) to the Department of State,' 8 December 1953, *FRUS 1952–54. Africa and South Asia*, vol. XI, part 2, p. 1832. The Pakistani governor general insisted that if Washington did not give military assistance, the effects would be 'disastrous.' Ibid., p. 1834.

31. Richard Nixon, *The Memoirs of Richard Nixon* (New York: Grosset & Dunlap, 1978), p. 133. Khan later became president of Pakistan. As Nixon wrote at that time, 'Khan was very pro-American and concerned about the Communist threat.' Ibid.

32. *New York Times*, 3 January 1954.

33. Ibid. Knowland became a very outspoken critic of India's non-alignment stance during 1954. He advocated the idea of collective security agreements as a way to stand against communism.

34. 'Memorandum by the Assistant Secretary of State for Near Eastern, South Asian, and African Affairs (Byroade) to the Assistant Secretary of Defense (Nash),' 15 October 1953, *FRUS 1952–54. The Near and Middle East*, vol. IX, part 1, p. 421.

35. Nixon, *The Memoirs of Richard Nixon*, p. 131.

36. Ibid., p. 132.

37. Ibid.

38. Kux, *Estranged Democracies*, p. 109.

39. Ibid.

40. "Special Estimate: The Probable Repercussions of a US Decision to Grant or Deny Military Aid to Pakistan," January 15, 1954, *FRUS, 1952–54, Africa and South Asia*, Vol. XI, part II, pp. 1839–1845. The Pentagon's senior analysts believed that this would 'tighten' US–Pakistani ties and 'pave the way for regional defense arrangements' and 'possibly for the later acquisition of base rights.' See McMahon, *The Cold War on the Periphery*, p. 169.

41. 'Special Estimate: The Probable Repercussions of a US Decision to Grant or Deny Military Aid to Pakistan,' 15 January 1954, *FRUS 1952–54, Africa and South Asia*, vol. XI, part 2, pp. 1839–45.

42. 'The Acting Secretary of State to the Embassy in India,' 18 February 1954, *FRUS 1952–54, Africa and South Asia*, vol. XI, part 2, pp. 1735–6.

43. Ibid. The president also offered India military assistance. Ibid., p. 1736.

44. 'The Secretary of State to the Embassy in India,' 20 February 1954, *FRUS 1952–54, Africa and South Asia*, vol. XI, part 2, p. 1737. Former Secretary of State Henry Kissinger wrote later that 'Pakistan's motive for obtaining US arms was not security against a Communist attack but protection against India.' Henry Kissinger, *American Foreign Policy; Three Essays* (London: Weidenfeld and Nicolson, 1969), p. 66.

45. John T. Woolley and Gerhard Peters, *The American Presidency Project* [online], Santa Barbara, CA: University of California (hosted), Gerhard Peters (database), available at http://www.presidency.ucsb.edu/ws/?pid=10171, last accessed 1 June 2013.

46. Nehru had notified UN Secretary General Hammarskjöld that he wanted the American team members removed, and in the end it was agreed that they would not be replaced as observers when their term expired. See Gopal, *Jawaharlal Nehru, A Biography*, vol. II, p. 189.

47. 'Memorandum from USIA Leonard Ware to OCB Mr Max Bishop,' undated memo, File Folder OCB 091.4 Asia (File #1 920), Box 64, OCB Central Files, Dwight D. Eisenhower Library. In a report dated 2 September 1954 the State Department wrote to USIS regarding their operating program in India: 'Military aid to Pakistan can best be explained not in terms of warding off the Communist threat to South Asia but in terms of strengthening the ability of the countries of the Middle East to defend themselves against possible Communist aggression.' See 'Comments on evaluation of US operating programs in India, White House Office National Security Council Staff Papers, File Folder OCB India File 1(4), Box 37, OCB Central Files, Dwight D. Eisenhower Library (hereafter DDE Library). The Middle East was underlined in the report.

48. Ibid. Overall, USIS was trying to change India's view of the United States. In a memo dated 19 October 1954 it was noted that unfortunately 'Nehru's previous visit to the United States led him to believe that we were a nation of selfish materialists, and not to be trusted leadership in world affairs.' See 'Memorandum for OCB Working Group on 5409 in White House Office National Security Council Staff Papers,' File Folder OCB 091 India, File 1(6), Box 37, OCB Central Files, DDE Library.

49. 'Letter to Chief Ministers,' 26 April 1954, in Kumar and Prasad, *Selected Works of Jawaharlal Nehru*, vol. 25, p. 557.

50. Ibid., p. 560.

51. Note to Secretary General, 4 March 1954, in Kumar and Prasad, *Selected Works of Jawaharlal Nehru*, vol. 25, p. 489. Nehru wrote that large sums of American dollars were being spent on various programs; the press, he felt, was affected and also the US government was helping some of India's smaller political parties. Ibid., p. 490.

52. Ibid., p. 490. Nehru felt that the Americans involved in these activities in India were 'lavish with their money and with entertainment.' He did not like that 'large numbers' of Indian officers and citizens were being invited to events where they were entertained with 'alcoholic drinks in large quantities.' Ibid.

53. McMahon, *The Cold War on the Periphery*, p. 175. McMahon wrote: 'One searches through the voluminous American planning documents in vain for a more concrete explanation of the role that Pakistan was expected to play in the containment of Soviet influence and power, in war or in peace.' Ibid. Further, 'the notion that Pakistan, in conjunction with other "northern tier" states, could mobilize sufficient forces to help deter or retard a Soviet military sweep into the Middle East was almost farcical.' Ibid., p. 338.

54. Stanley Wolpert, *Roots of Confrontation in South Asia* (New York: Oxford University Press, 1982), p. 142. Wolpert wrote that the 'US military alliance with Pakistan first antagonized India, rapidly escalating the South Asian arms race, soon turned New Delhi toward Moscow in search of military supplies and support, and ultimately alienated Pakistan as well.' Ibid.

55. 'Letter to Chief Ministers,' 26 April 1954, in Kumar and Prasad, *Selected Works of Jawaharlal Nehru*, vol. 25, pp. 559–60.

56. There are some historians who maintain that India initiated the Panchsheel Agreement because of the US–Pakistan treaty. In fact a member of Nehru's parliament, Dr Lanka Sundaram, made this claim to him. In a parliamentary debate on 24 December 1953 Nehru responded to this claim and said: 'As a matter of fact this question of our talks in Peking has been under correspondence for the last many, many months and ultimately, I should think, about three months back, we suggested to the Chinese Government that we would like to have some talks with them …' See Gopal, *Jawaharlal Nehru, A Biography*, vol. II, p. 577.

20. THE PANCHSHEEL AGREEMENT: AN INDO–CHINESE CONDOMINIUM

1. 'Toast by the Indian Ambassador to Beijing, Raghavan, to Zhou En Lai upon the signing of the Panch Sheel Agreement,' quoted by Indian diplomat T. N. Kaul, who was present, in T. N. Kaul, *A Diplomat's Diary: China, India and the USA* (New Delhi: Macmillan, 2000), p. 64.

2. This conversation took place on 23 June 1952. Kaul referred to conversations on Tibet between Panikkar and Chou En-lai earlier in June and in February 1952. See 'Discussion record between PRC Vice Foreign Minister Zhang Hanfu and Indian representatives on Tibetan issues,' 23 June 1952 in Chinese Foreign Ministry Files, 105–00025–03, p. 29. A version of this also appears in Kumar and Prasad, *Selected Works of Jawaharlal Nehru*, vol. 24, p. 595, ftn 2.

3. 'Cable to Indian Mission, Lhasa,' 6 September 1952, in Gopal, *Selected Works of Jawaharlal Nehru*, vol. 19, pp. 651–2, ftn 2.

4. Ibid.

5. Ibid

6. Ibid. There was another dimension here that was discussed in Chapter 3. Through recently declassified CIA documents it is now known that in fact during this period the Indian prime minister had his intelligence officers approach the Dalai Lama's brother, Gyalo, in order to establish covert operations in Tibet to gather information about the PLA and specifically their activities on the Tibet–Indian border.

7. Cable to K. M. Panikkar, 18 June 1952, in Gopal, *Selected Works of Jawaharlal Nehru*, vol. 17, pp. 474–5. Nehru was concerned about India's northern and north-eastern borders or 'frontiers' with China. Some of these areas were remote and inhabited by tribal peoples.

8. Ibid., and also see 'The North Eastern Frontier Situation, Note to the Secretary General and Foreign Secretary,' 5 March 1953, in Gopal, *Selected Works of Jawaharlal Nehru*, vol. 21, p. 558. Nehru wrote that Panikkar had assured him that the Chinese understood that India's border with Tibet was the McMahon line. Ibid.

9. India and Nepal had signed a treaty in July 1950 acknowledging their special relationship and the friendly relations that had existed between the two nations. It was agreed that if

either country's security were threatened they would notify the other. Nehru had signed a 'Treaty of Perpetual Peace and Friendship' with Bhutan in 1949, and Sikkim was an Indian protectorate.

10. 'Cable to K. M. Panikkar,' 12 April 1952, in Gopal, *Selected Works of Jawaharlal Nehru*, vol. 18, pp. 471–2. Nehru had cabled Panikkar and wrote: 'We are surprised to learn of Chou En Lai's apparent reluctance to discuss [the] general problem of our interests in Tibet. Chou En Lai's present excuse that the Chinese have been in Tibet only for a short time and have not yet studied [the] problem thoroughly does not carry conviction.' Ibid. In the course of conversation with Chou, Panikkar was told that the PRC wanted to build a road from India to Lhasa. Ibid.

11. Ibid. Also see 'Note to Foreign Secretary and K. M. Panikkar,' 29 July 1952 in Gopal, *Selected Works of Jawaharlal Nehru*, vol. 19, p. 651. Panikkar suggested at this time that they should not raise any further questions over the Indian frontier with the Chinese.

12. See 'Remarks at a Press Conference,' New Delhi, 21 June 1952, in Gopal, *Selected Works of Jawaharlal Nehru*, vol. 18, p. 476.

13. 'Letter to Chief Ministers,' 2 August 1952, in Gopal, *Selected Works of Jawaharlal Nehru*, vol. 19, p. 695.

14. 'North Eastern Frontier Situation, Note to the Secretary General and Foreign Secretary, Ministry of External Affairs,' 5 March 1953, in Gopal, *Selected Works of Jawaharlal Nehru*, vol. 21, pp. 555–7.

15. 'Message to Chou En-Lai, sent to N. Raghavan to Convey to the Chinese Premier,' 1 September 1953, in Kumar and Prasad, *Selected Works of Jawaharlal Nehru*, vol. 23, pp. 485–6. The Chinese government had expressed their interest in resolving outstanding matters on 14 June 1952, but discussions had been at a standstill. Nehru wrote: 'The Government of India feels that it would be advantageous to both our countries to deal with all remaining problems together.' Ibid.

16. 'Message to Chou En-Lai,' in Kumar and Prasad, *Selected Works of Jawaharlal Nehru*, vol. 23, p. 485.

17. 'Discussion between Premier Zhou and Raghavan Regarding Sino-Indian Negotiation Issues,' 21 December 1953, no. 105–00032–20, Chinese Ministry of Foreign Affairs.

18. Ibid.

19. Ibid.

20. 'Ministry of Foreign Affairs: Various Problems Concerning Sino-Indian Relations in Tibet,' 21 October 1953, Document no. 105–00032025, Chinese Foreign Ministry, Memo written by Zhang Jingwu of the Ministry of Foreign Affairs. While the Chinese wanted to resolve the Tibet issue quickly, their strategy regarding Sino-Indian borders was quite the opposite. The Chinese maintained that India 'occupied' Tawang (located in present-day Arunachal Pradesh) and thought it 'beneficial' for them 'to drag on these issues for the time being' while still stating that this was Chinese territory. But by the end of 1953, the PRC felt it was more important to resolve the Tibetan issue and then push their claims on border issues. Ibid.

21. See 'Telegram from the Ministry of Foreign Affairs to Tibetan Regional Representative Zhang Jingwu,' 14 December 1953, Document no. 105–00032–25, Chinese Foreign Ministry Archives.

22. Declassified report, 'The Proper approaches of local Tibetan government towards issues such as India's establishment of its consulate general in Lhasa,' 14 November 1952, Document no. 105–00025–06(1), Chinese Foreign Ministry Archives.

23. 'Report to the Ministry: Kashag's Reply on Issues Regarding Unified Actions Towards the Indian Consulate,' 7 November 1952, Document no. 105–00025–06(1), Chinese Foreign Ministry Archives.

24. 'Report to Zhang and Yang Gongsu: Issues Regarding Tibetan Region's Unified Action towards Indian Consulate and the Treatment of its Foreign Bureau, Etc.,' 25 November 1952, Document no. 105–00025–06(1), Chinese Foreign Ministry Archives.

25. Ibid.

26. 'Letter to Prime Minister Nehru from Chou En-lai,' 15 October 1953, in 'Letter Presented to the Indian Ambassador Raghaven by Vice Foreign Minister Zhang Hanfu Regarding Premier's Chou's response to Three Memoranda from India Concerning Tibetan Problems,' Document no. 105–00032–08, Chinese Foreign Ministry Archives; and also 'Cable to Chou En-lai from Nehru,' 22 October 1953, in Kumar and Prasad, *Selected Works of Jawaharlal Nehru*, vol. 24, pp. 595–6.

27. Kaul, *A Diplomat's Diary: China, India and the USA*, p. 61.

28. 'The Beijing Conference, Note to the Secretary General,' 3 December 1953, in Kumar and Prasad, *Selected Works of Jawaharlal Nehru*, vol. 24, p. 598, ftn 2.

29. 'Incoming Telegram from London to the Secretary of State,' 4 February 1954, 793B.00/2–454, NARA. This document was released through our Freedom of Information request. Parts had been previously redacted.

30. Ibid.

31. 'Telegram from the American Embassy in London to the Department of State, Washington,' 30 March 1954, 793B.00/3–3054, NARA. US officials in London told Washington that 'The embassy would again like to emphasize that all information concerning Tibet received through this channel should be treated as 'US Eyes Only' in view of Indian sensitivity to information of this type being passed on by the British.' This telegram was declassified through our FOIA request.

32. 'Telegram from the American Embassy in London to the Department of State, Washington,' 30 March 1954, 793B.00/3–3054, NARA.

33. Ibid.

34. The negotiations concluded with the signing of an 'Agreement of Trade and Intercourse between the Tibet region of China and India' which became known as the Panchsheel Agreement. (In Sanskrit *panch* means five and *shila* is a rock.) The five tenets of the agreement were: mutual respect for each other's territorial integrity and sovereignty; mutual non-aggression; mutual non-interference in each other's internal affairs; equality and mutual benefit; and peaceful co-existence. The GOI ended its treaty relations with Tibet, 'unilaterally renounced its rights and obligations and offered them to the Chinese government.' The Indian government kept the three trade agencies in Yatung, Gyantse, and Gartok. But in return they gave the Chinese three new trade marts. The GOI agreed to: withdraw its military escorts in Yatung and Gyantse; to hand over their postal, telegraph, and public telephone services and equipment for a fee; and give Beijing 'at a reasonable price' twelve Indian rest houses. There was no discussion of the McMahon line boundaries.

35. See 'Telegram from American Consul in Calcutta to the Department of State,' 29 July 1954, 793B.00/7–2954, NARA.

36. Gopal, *Jawaharlal Nehru, A Biography*, vol. II, p. 180. Nehru told the Indian parliament regarding Tibet and the Panchsheel that 'it is recognition of the existing situation there. In fact, that situation had been recognized by us two or three years ago.' Ibid., p. 181.

37. Ibid., p. 181.

38. Ibid., p. 181. See Arpi, *Born in Sin: The Panchsheel Agreement and the Sacrifice of Tibet* (New Delhi: Mittal Publications, 2004), p. 121. In September 1955 Chinese soldiers came 10 miles onto India soil and by September 1957 the Chinese had built the Aksai Chin Road through Ladakh.

39. 'Reply to a Debate on the International Situation and the Policy of the Government of India, Lok Sabha,' 30 September 1954, in Kumar and Prasad, *Selected Works of Jawaharlal Nehru*, vol. 26, p. 336.

40. Ibid. Nehru told members to look at the history between China and Tibet and the history of the British in Tibet for an understanding of his position. He said, 'we have to see all these things in some larger context of policy.' Ibid., pp. 336–7.

41. Hugh E. Richardson, *Tibet and its History* (London: Shambhala, 1984), p. 197. Throughout the document Tibet was always referred to as the 'Tibet region of China.' Also see R. K. Jain, ed., *China South Asian Relations 1947–1980* (Brighton: Harvester Press, 1981), pp. 61–6.

42. Richardson, p. 197.

43. B. N. Mullik, *My Years with Nehru: The Chinese Betrayal* (New Delhi: Allied Publishers, 1971), pp. 85 and 181.

44. Ibid.

45. Christopher Andrew, *The Defense of the Realm; The Authorized History of MI5* (New York: Alfred A. Knopf, 2011).

21. NEHRU'S BID FOR GLOBAL PROMINENCE

1. The Colombo conference was held in Ceylon from 28 April to 2 May. The prime ministers of Burma, Ceylon, India, Indonesia, and Pakistan attended the conference. It was a forum to discuss issues of mutual concern to the nations in the region. The Geneva conference began on 26 April 1954.

2. Brands, *India and the United States*, p. 78. Dulles thought him a 'very adroit and unscrupulous man who liked to have his finger in every pie.' Telephone conversations between President Eisenhower and John Foster Dulles, 15 March 1055, Dulles Papers, ftn 2 in 'Eisenhower, Dwight D. Personal and confidential to John Foster Dulles, 23 March 1955' in *The Papers of Dwight David Eisenhower*, ed. L. Galambos and D. van Ee, doc. 1360. World Wide Web facsimile by the Dwight D. Eisenhower Memorial Commission of the print edition (Baltimore, MD: Johns Hopkins University Press, 1996), http://www.eisenhowermemorial.org/presidential-papers/first-term/documents/1360.cfm. Also see Janaki Ram, *V. K. Krishna Menon: A Personal Memoir* (Oxford: Oxford University Press, 1997), p. 103.

3. George C. Herring, '"A Good Stout Effort": John Foster Dulles and the Indochina Effort,' in Richard H. Immerman, ed., *John Foster Dulles and the Diplomacy of the Cold War* (Princeton: Princeton University Press, 1992), p. 219. Herring wrote that Dulles was 'roundly criticized for the general rudeness of his demeanour and his apparent willingness to wreck the conference. As much as any other single individual, he has been held responsible for the failure of the conference to negotiate a lasting settlement of the Indochina problem.' Ibid. Janaki Ram, Menon's grandniece, wrote in her account of the event: 'Whenever difficulties developed with China because Washington did not recognize Beijing, Menon

acted as mediator, thereby preventing any irretrievable situations from developing or the talks from breaking down as they so often threatened to.' Janaki Ram, *V. K. Krishna Menon*, p. 104.

4. Ibid. George C. Herring, 'A Good Stout Effort,' p. 219; Townsend Hoopes, *The Devil and John Foster Dulles* (Boston: Little Brown, 1973), p. 222.

5. President Eisenhower and Dulles met with Menon in 1955 at the White House. Eisenhower did not like the Indian diplomat and considered him 'a master at twisting words,' a man who thought he was 'intellectually superior' to others. Eisenhower thought that Menon 'coyly' covered his conceived intellectual superiority by 'a cloak of excessive humility and modesty.' Robert H Ferrell, ed., *The Eisenhower Diaries* (New York: W.W. Norton, 1981), p. 300.

6. Chen Jian, 'China and the Indochina Settlement at the Geneva Conference of 1954,' in Mark Atwood Lawrence and Fredrik Logevall, eds., *The First Vietnam War: Colonial Conflict and Cold War Crisis* (Cambridge, MA: Harvard University Press, 2007), p. 242. See Chen Jian, *China's Road to the Korean War* (New York: Columbia University Press, 1994), p. 221.

7. Chen Jian, 'China and the Indochina Settlement,' pp. 240–62.

8. Ibid., pp. 240–62.

9. Ibid., p. 240. Zhou had prepared well for his first conference, reading 'a large amount of documents, telegrams, materials and intelligence reports, as well as all the exchanges between the US and the Soviet governments.' Ibid., p. 242.

10. Ibid., p. 241.

11. Ibid.

12. 'Statement in Parliament,' 18 May 1954, in Gopal, *Jawaharlal Nehru, A Biography*, vol. II, p. 422.

13. Ibid.

14. Speech of John Foster Dulles, 'The Threat of a Red Asia,' *FRUS 1952–54*, vol. XII, part 1, Editorial note, p. 400. The United States was hopeful that this collective security arrangement would be enough to deter the Chinese from entering into the war in Indochina and also would 'moderate communist demands at Geneva and bolster the French to resist, thus making outside intervention unnecessary.' Ibid.

15. The Secretary of State began a round of talks with representatives of other nations to explain the term 'united front,' as listed above. Dulles was hopeful of having a coalition together before going to the Geneva talks. See 'Memorandum of Conversation by the Officer in Charge of Philippines Affairs (Bell),' 5 April 1954, *FRUS*, vol. XII, part 1, p. 404.

16. George C. Herring, 'A Good Stout Effort,' p. 211.

17. Gopal, *Jawaharlal Nehru, A Biography*, vol. II, p. 192.

18. Kux, *Estranged Democracies: India and the United States, 1941–1991*, p. 121.

19. Gopal, *Jawaharlal Nehru, A Biography*, vol. II, p. 193.

20. 'Cable to V. K. Krishna Menon,' 21 June 1954, in Kumar and Prasad, Gopal, *Selected Works of Jawaharlal Nehru*, vol. 26, p. 352. Nehru cabled Menon and said, 'I have appreciated your magnificent work at Geneva which undoubtedly has helped in the measure of success that has been achieved thus far.' Ibid.

21. 'Conversation with Zhou En-Lai,' 25 June 1954, in Kumar and Prasad, *Selected Works of Jawaharlal Nehru, FRUS 1952–54. East Asia and the Pacific*, vol. 26, p. 373. In this vol-

ume there are complete records of five conversations that Nehru had with Chou 25–27 June. See pp. 366–406.

22. Ibid., p. 380.
23. Ibid. Nehru referred to the South-East Asia Treaty Organization that was being proposed by the United States.
24. Chen Jian, 'China and the Indochina Settlement,' p. 254.
25. 'Conversation with Chou En-Lai,' in Gopal, *Jawaharlal Nehru, A Biography*, vol. II, p. 395.
26. Ibid., p. 195.
27. 'Joint Statement issued after the talks between Nehru and Chou En-Lai, New Delhi,' 28 June 1954; 'Panchsheel, A Model Code for Bilateral Relations,' in Kumar and Prasad, *Selected Works of Jawaharlal Nehru*, vol. 26, pp. 410–12. The next day Chou signed an agreement based on these principles with the prime minister of Burma. Ibid., p. 412.
28. Ibid., pp. 417–19
29. 'The Ambassador in India (Allen) to the Department of State,' 28 July 1954, *FRUS 1952–54. East Asia and the Pacific*, vol. XII, part 1, pp. 678–9.
30. Ibid.
31. Gopal, *Jawaharlal Nehru, A Biography*, vol. II, p. 226.
32. 'Summary of Talks with Mao Tse-tung, Beijing,' 19 October 1954, in Kumar and Prasad, *Selected Works of Jawaharlal Nehru*, vol. 27, p. 7.
33. 'Minutes of talks with Chou En-lai, Beijing,' 20 October 1954, in Kumar and Prasad, *Selected Works of Jawaharlal Nehru*, vol. 27, pp. 11–20.
34. 'Statement in the Lok Sabha,' 22 November 1954, in Kumar and Prasad, *Selected Works of Jawaharlal Nehru*, vol. 27, pp. 90–3.
35. Gopal, *Jawaharlal Nehru, A Biography*, vol. II, pp. 166–95; Kux, *Estranged Democracies*, p. 123. In a speech before the Indian parliament on the eve of his trip, Nehru spoke of India's potential for becoming a 'fourth great country.' See 'Press Conference at Government House,' 15 October 1954, in Kumar and Prasad, *Selected Works of Jawaharlal Nehru*, vol. 27, p. 3, ftn 4.
36. 'Editorial note,' in Kumar and Prasad, *Selected Works of Jawaharlal Nehru*, vol. 28. The editors called the conference 'an initiative of truly global significance.' Ibid.
37. Nehru had stated at Bandung that he did not belong to one bloc or another. Kumar and Prasad, *Selected Works of Jawaharlal Nehru*, vol. 28, p. 243. Along with Nehru, Tito of Yugoslavia and Nasser of Egypt gave the non-aligned movement momentum.
38. Ibid., p. 132.
39. Ibid.
40. 'Letter to Lady Mountbatten,' in Kumar and Prasad, *Selected Works of Jawaharlal Nehru*, vol. 28, p. 141.
41. H. W. Brands, *The Specter of Neutralism*, p. 113.
42. Ibid.
43. Interview with Winston Lord, Washington, DC, 10 March 2008. It should be added that Winston Lord met Mao in 1971, five years before his death at the age of eighty-two.
44. *Life* magazine, 2 May 1955, p. 29.
45. Ibid. *Life* had numerous pictures of the event and the attendees. One of the pictures showed Nehru having a 'temper tantrum' when he found that the front door to the conference building was 'not reserved for the delegates' car.' Ibid., p. 35.
46. Ibid. And also see Brands, *The Specter of Neutralism*, p. 111. Ultimately the Bandung conference brought some benefit for Washington as the Chinese agreed to talks on the Taiwan Straits.

47. Stanley Wolpert, *Roots of Confrontation in South Asia* (New York: Oxford University Press, 1982), p. 142.

48. Ibid. Wolpert wrote that India purchased MIGs and Russian steel plants opened in India in the new era of Indo–Soviet cooperation. 'Were it not for stimulus provided by Dulles' "containment" chains of alliances stretching from Turkey to Pakistan—with links missing across Afghanistan and India—it would have been hard to imagine Russia investing so heavily in Indian development.' Ibid., pp. 142–3.

49. *New York Times*, 7 June 1955.

50. Ibid.

51. *New York Times*, 6 June 1955.

52. *Life* magazine, 20 June 1955, p. 41.

53. *New York Times*, 23 June 1955. Also see 'Talks with N. A. Bulganin,' 8 June 1955, in H. Y. Sharada Prasad and A. K. Damodaran, eds., *Selected Works of Jawaharlal Nehru* (New Delhi: Jawaharlal Nehru Memorial Fund, 2001–3), vol. 29, pp. 207–10. The full transcripts of all of Nehru's talks in Moscow are in this volume, pp. 201–31.

54. 'Speech at a public meeting at Dynamo Stadium, Moscow,' 21 June 1955, in Prasad and Damodaran, *Selected Works of Jawaharlal Nehru*, vol. 29, p. 225, ftn 2. This was the first time since 1917 that the leader of a non-communist nation was allowed to address an audience in Moscow.

55. Ibid.

56. 'Memorandum of Discussion at the 266th Meeting of the National Security Council, Washington,' 15 November 1955, *FRUS 1955–57. Foreign Aid and Economic Defense Policy*, vol. X, p. 28.

57. Ibid., p. 28. The Soviets promoted a program of economic assistance and development to underdeveloped nations, including the building of 'industrial plants and other installations.' Ibid., p. 29. Also see 'Memorandum of Discussion at the 267th Meeting of the National Security Council, Camp David, Maryland,' 21 November 1955, *FRUS 1955–57. Foreign Aid and Economic Defense Policy*, vol. X, p. 32.

58. 'Telegram from the Embassy in India to the Department of State,' 25 November 1955, *FRUS 1955–1957 South Asia*, vol. VIII, p. 298.

59. Ibid., p. 299.

60. 'Memorandum of Discussion at the 273rd Meeting of the National Security Council, Washington,' 18 January 1956, *FRUS 1955–57. Foreign Aid and Economic Defense Policy*, vol. X, pp. 64–7.

22. NSC DIRECTIVE 5412: STRUCTURING CIA OPERATIONS

1. Christopher Andrew, *For the President's Eyes Only: Secret Intelligence and the American Presidency from Washington to Bush* (London: HarperCollins, 1995), p. 3.

2. Ibid.

3. Ibid., pp. 3–4. The president was particularly aware of the use of 'signals intelligence' and 'imagery' intelligence. The use of spy planes and satellites were revolutionized by Eisenhower during the 1950s and greatly impacted the Cold War. Ibid.

4. 'Note on US Covert Action Programs,' editorial brief, *FRUS 1964–68*, vol. XII, pp. xxxi–v.

5. 'National Security Council Directive on Covert Operations,' attachment to 'Note by the Executive Secretary to the National Security Council on Covert Operations,' File Folder

OCB 091 Indo-China, File 1(1), Box 37, OCB Central Files, White House Office National Security Council Staff Paper, 1948–61, DDE Library.

6. Ibid.

7. William M. Leary, ed., *The Central Intelligence Agency: History and Documents* (Tuscaloosa: University of Alabama Press, 1984), p. 63.

8. Ibid., pp. 63–4.

9. Stephen E. Ambrose, *Eisenhower, Soldier and President* (New York: Simon & Schuster Paperbacks, 1990), p. 377. Eisenhower said that his 'Old Guard', the joint chiefs of staff, the National Security Council, and often the secretary of state urged him to be more aggressive; they wanted an atomic strike against China. Ibid.

10. 'Secret Memo from Dwight D Eisenhower to James Harold Doolittle,' 26 July 1954, "The Papers of Dwight David Eisenhower, Volume XV—The Presidency: The Middle Way Part V: Maintaining "a united Defense"; April 1954 to August 1954, Chapter 11: "The men in the Kremlin are not to be trusted," http://eisenhower.press.jhu.edu/, last accessed June 2013. Also see ftn 2 in *The Papers of Dwight David Eisenhower*; Interview with editor, Daun van Ee, Library of Congress, Washington, DC, 10 December 2007; and Ambrose, *Eisenhower, President and Soldier*, p. 377. Historian Athan Theoharis pointed out that the president authorized NSC 5412 'to ensure that the CIA would operate as a presidential agency, that its formulations and execution of covert operations would be responsive only to the president's objectives.' Theoharis worried that decisions taken by the '5412 Group' were an unacceptable departure from the values to which the nation was committed. Thomas Parrott, secretary of the 5412 Committee, saw this matter differently. In our discussion he said: 'Some thought that all views weren't taken into account and that this was terrible, but I thought it was a very impartial group.' Parrott added that while Allen Dulles certainly had his own ideas, he was 'very careful not to push them' and solicited opinions from the others in the committee. The committee, in Parrott's opinion, did take all the available information and factors into consideration before making decisions. Interview with Thomas Parrott, Washington, DC, December 2004. Historian Stephen Knott agreed with Parrott's assessment. Knott wrote that during the Cold War, in his opinion, there was in fact no conspiracy, rather 'America's Cold War legislators let the executive branch do its job.' See Athan Theoharis, 'New Agency: The Origins and Expansion of CIA Covert Operations' in Athan Theoharri et al., *Understanding our Government: The Central Intelligence Agency, Security Under Security* (Connecticut: Greenwood Press, 2005), pp. 162–7. And also Stephen F. Knott, *Secret and Sanctioned: Covert Operations and the Presidency* (Oxford: Oxford University Press, 1996), p. 163.

11. 'Secret Memo from Dwight D. Eisenhower to James Harold Doolittle,' 26 July 1954, "The Papers of Dwight David Eisenhower, Volume XV—The Presidency: The Middle Way Part V: Maintaining "a united Defense"; April 1954 to August 1954, Chapter 11: "The men in the Kremlin are not to be trusted," http://eisenhower.press.jhu.edu/, last accessed June 2013.

12. Ibid. There is some debate among scholars about the broader impact of NSC 5412 and the recommendations of the Doolitte Committee. This merits a comment. NSC 5412 was authorized 'secretly and unilaterally' without public or Congressional debate.

13. 'Secret Memo from Dwight D. Eisenhower to James Harold Doolittle,' 26 July 1954, "The Papers of Dwight David Eisenhower, Volume XV—The Presidency: The Middle Way Part V: Maintaining "a united Defense"; April 1954 to August 1954, Chapter 11:

"The men in the Kremlin are not to be trusted," http://eisenhower.press.jhu.edu/, last accessed June 2013.

14. Ibid. Also see Michael Leary, ed., *The Central Intelligence Agency: History and Documents*, p. 144.

15. Editorial brief, *FRUS 1964–68*, vol. XII, pp. xxxi-v.

16. John Prados, *Presidents' Secret Wars, CIA and Pentagon Covert Operations from World War II through Iranscam* (New York: William Morrow, 1986), p. 112. Prados wrote that while the president was not in attendance at the meetings, in order to preserve his deniability, he was in constant contact with its members. Ibid.

17. Ibid.

18. Interview with Thomas Parrott, Washington, DC, December 2004.

19. Ibid.

20. Ibid. Parrott was not simply the secretary for the 5412 Group, he also read all the incoming intelligence on various operations, including Tibet, and reported this to the committee when they met.

21. 'Memorandum for the Special Assistant to the President for National Security Affairs,' *Historical Background of Functioning of the NSC 5412/2 Special Group and its Predecessors*, 19 January 1959, NSC Series, Policy Papers Subseries, Box 10, NSC 5412-Covert Operations, DDE Library; Douglas Keane and Michael Warner, eds., *Foreign Relations, 1950–1955: The Intelligence Community* (Washington, DC: United States Government Printing Office, 2007), p. 748.

22. Gordon Gray quoted in Stephen E. Ambrose, *Ike's Spies: Eisenhower and the Espionage Establishment* (New York: Doubleday, 1981), p. 240.

23. 'Memorandum for the Special Assistant to the President for National Security Affairs,' *Historical Background of Functioning of the NSC 5412/2 Special Group and its Predecessors*, 19 January 1959, NSC Series, Policy Papers Subseries, Box 10, NSC 5412-Covert Operations, DDE Library.

24. Ibid.

25. Interview with Thomas Parrott, Washington, DC, December 2004.

26. Ibid.

27. Ibid. Fitzgerald ran the Tibetan operation and died while playing tennis at his home in Virginia on 23 July 1967. The details of Fitzgerald's death were provided to me in the interview referenced above.

28. For example in interviews with Bill Turner, Chevy Chase, Maryland, March 2005; and Ken Millian, Washington, DC, April 2005.

29. Thomas Parrott, interview. John Foster Dulles, known as Foster Dulles, was Eisenhower's secretary of state. His brother, Allen Dulles, was the director of the CIA. He was commonly referred to as DCI Dulles or just the DCI.

30. Ibid.

31. Ibid.

32. Interview with James R. Schlesinger, Mitre Corporation, McLean, Virginia, 24 January 2008.

33. Parrott emphasized this in our interview. Parrott noted that the President worked closely with Allen Dulles on covert operations and added firmly that 'Allen Dulles did not make decisions alone—the CIA was not some sort of rogue element.' Interview, December 2004. This issue was also discussed in a meeting with Daun van Ee at the Library of Con-

gress, 12 December 2007. Mr van Ee, who has spent twenty-seven years organizing Dwight D. Eisenhower's papers for Johns Hopkins University, agreed with Parrott's recollections. Eisenhower's involvement in the 5412 Group is also discussed in Prados, *The President's Secret War*, p. 112.

34. Interview with Professor Christopher Andrew, Cambridge, June 2012.
35. Fred I. Greenstein, *The Hidden-Hand Presidency: Eisenhower as a Leader* (New York: Basic Books, 1982), p. 234; and also see Andrew, *For the President's Eyes Only*, p. 202.
36. Interview with General Goodpaster conducted by Stefan Halper and Lezlee Brown Halper in Washington, DC, on 16 May 2000. Goodpaster was Eisenhower's confidant and trusted friend.
37. Ibid.
38. Ibid.

23. MOBILIZING RELIGION

1. Blanche Wiesen Cook, *The Declassified Eisenhower* (New York: Penguin Books, 1984), p. xi.
2. Ibid.
3. President Eisenhower's 8 October 1952 speech, quoted in Wiesen Cook, p. 121. Also see Shawn J. Parry Giles, *The Rhetorical Presidency, Propaganda, and the Cold War, 1945–1955* (Westport: Praeger, 2002), p. 130; Rhodri Jeffery-Jones, *The CIA and American Democracy* (New Haven, CT: Yale University Press, 1989), p. 85.
4. Cook, pp. xi and 121.
5. Ibid., p. 121. The relationship between *Time–Life* and the Eisenhower administration is discussed more fully in Chapter 4. C. D. Jackson had been the chief creator of Radio Free Europe and Radio Liberty.
6. Jackson quoted in Cook, p. 177.
7. Quoted in John Lewis Gaddis, *Strategies of Containment: A Critical Appraisal of Postwar American Security Policy* (Oxford University Press: London, 1982), p. 155.
8. Gregory Mitrovich, *Undermining the Kremlin: America's Strategy to Subvert the Soviet Bloc, 1947–1956* (Ithaca: Cornell University Press, 2000), p. 10.
9. Stephen Whitfield, *The Culture of the Cold War* (Baltimore: Johns Hopkins University Press, 1991), ch. 4, pp. 77–101.
10. Merlin Gustafson 'The Religious Role of the President,' *Midwest Journal of Political Science*, vol. 14, no. 4 (Nov. 1970), pp. 709–10.
11. Whitfield, p. 79.
12. Ibid. Graham created his Evangelistic Association in 1950 with just one secretary in a one-room office; by 1958 he had a four-storey building with a staff of 200.
13. Whitfield, p. 83.
14. Ibid.
15. Ibid., p. 87.
16. 'First Inaugural Address of President Eisenhower,' 20 January 1953, in *The Eisenhower Administration: A Documentary History, 1953–1961*, pp. 26–7.
17. The phrase 'little Moscovites who were solemnly pledging to their hammer and sickle flag' is attributed to Rev. George M. Docherty, the pastor of the First Presbyterian Church in Washington, which Eisenhower attended. http://www.eisenhower.archives.gov/Research/Subject_Guides/PDFs/Eisenhower_and_religion.pdf, last accessed 1 June 2013; Whitfield, p. 89.

18. Dwight D. Eisenhower, 'Remarks Upon Lighting the National Christmas Tree,' 24 December 1953 at http://www.presidency.ucsb.edu/ws/?pid=9791, last accessed 1 June 2013.

19. Thomas C. Sorenson, *The Word War, The Story of American Propaganda* (New York: Harper & Row, 1968), p. 49. Sorenson was an employee during this period.

20. 'Remarks to the Staff of the United States Information Agency,' 10 November 1953, *The American Presidency Project* at http://www.presidency.ucsb.edu/ws/?pid=9758, last accessed 1 June 2013.

21. Shawn J. Parry-Giles, *The Rhetorical Presidency, Propaganda, and the Cold War*, p. 130.

22. Jonathan Fox, 'Religion as an Overlooked Element of International Relations,' *International Studies Review*, vol. 3, no. 3 (Autumn 2001), p. 53. Fox's article specifically examines why policy-makers and academics often overlook religion and how religion influences international politics. The administration's interest in using religion is reflected in an OCB proposal dated 13 July 1956. It was noted that 'inadequate consideration has been given to the role of religion and religious organization in international relations.' See 'Proposals Regarding US Relations with Theravada Buddhist Countries,' 13 July 1956, Attachment to 'Memorandum for Committee on Buddhism,' 15 August 1956, DDE Library.

23. 'Memo to Dr Lilly from R. Hirsch', 20 May 1954, OCB Central Files, Box 2, OCB 000.3 File-1(1) Feb-54–Jan 57, DDE Library. According to the memo this idea was discussed during the Truman administration in September 1951.

24. Ibid.

25. 'Letter from the Office of the Vice President, Secret, to The Honorable Walter B. Smith,' 10 September 1954, OCB Central Files, Box 2, 000.3 File 1(1), Feb. 54–Jan. 57, DDE Library. Dr Charles Lowry was the chairman of the Foundation for Religious Activism in the Social and Civil Order. Nixon had made a lengthy tour of the Far East and Asia the previous year. See Chapter 6 for details on his trip.

26. Ibid. The proposal from Dr Lowry was attached to Nixon's letter.

27. Ibid.

28. *Life* magazine, 7 March 1955. The headline read: 'Millions of Asians Follow a Gentle Sage who found the way to Enlightenment.' The article began: 'From the island of Ceylon to the islands of Japan, and throughout large sections of the Asian mainland, hundreds of millions of people—perhaps as many as 500 million—believe in a gentle and peaceable religion called Buddhism.' Ibid., p. 79. Tibet and the Dalai Lama were discussed in *Life*'s report.

29. Ibid.

30. Ibid., p. 102.

31. Ibid.

32. 'Office Memorandum from Mr Elmer B. Staats to Kenneth P. Landon RE: Outline Plan Regarding Buddhist Organizations in Ceylon, Burma, Thailand, Laos and Cambodia,' 13 December 1956, OCB 000.3, DDE Library.

33. Ibid.

34. 'United States Information Agency Memorandum to Mr Elmer B. Staats, Executive Officer, Operations Coordinating Board,' 22 May 1956, OCB Central Files, Box 2, OCB 000.3, Feb. 1954–Jan. 1957, DDE Library. The USIA viewed this celebration as 'an extraordinarily important event in the religious calendar of millions of our friends and potential allies throughout Asia.' The agency remarked that 'no similar occasion of this sort will again present itself at which we may show our respect for the Buddhist religion.' Ibid.

35. Ibid.
36. 'Memorandum to Operations Coordinating Board, Mr Landon,' 27 August 1956, OCB Central Files, Box 2, OCB 000.3, File 1(4), Feb. 54–Jan. 57, DDE Library.
37. Ibid., p. 2.
38. 'Study of Religious Factor Overseas,' OCB Central Files, Box 2, OCB 000.3, File 1(1), Feb. 54–Jan. 57. In Ceylon the United National Party was defeated and driven from office by a coalition called the People's United Front. This coalition was strongly backed by Ceylonese Buddhists who promised to make Sinhalese the national language and address past Buddhist grievances. See Robert N Kearny, 'Sinhalese Nationalism and Social Conflict in Ceylon,' *Pacific Affairs*, vol. 37, no. 2 (Summer 1964), pp. 125–36.
39. 'Memorandum to Operations Coordinating Board, Mr Landon,' 27 August 1956, OCB Central Files, Box 2, OCB 000.3, File 1(4), Feb. 54–Jan. 57, DDE Library.
40. 'Memorandum of Meeting: Committee on Buddhism, Operations Coordinating Board,' 29 June 1956, OCB Central Files, Box 2, OCB 000.3, File 1(3), DDE Library.
41. Ibid.
42. 'Memorandum from James Meader to H. S. Hudson,' 11 July 1956, OCB 000.3, File 1(4), Feb. 54–Jan. 57, Annex B, Discussion of Government Broadcasts on Buddhist Themes, DDE Library.
43. 'Proposals Regarding US Relations with Theravada Buddhist Countries,' 13 July 1956, DDE Library.
44. 'Operations Coordinating Board, Memorandum from Committee on Buddhism,' 15 August 1956, OCB Central Files, OCB 000.3, File 1(4), Feb. 54–Jan. 57, DDE Library.
45. *Life* magazine, 23 December 1957, p. 100.
46. 'Operations Coordinating Board, Memorandum from Committee on Buddhism,' 15 August 1956, OCB Central Files, OCB 000.3, File 1(4), Feb. 54–Jan. 57, DDE Library.
47. 'Proposals Regarding US Relations with Theravada Buddhist Countries,' 13 July 1956, DDE Library.
48. Ibid., p. 2.
49. *Executive Sessions of the Senate Foreign Relations Committee* (Historical Series), vol. XI, Eighty-Sixth Congress First Session, 1959 (Washington, DC: Government Printing Office, 1960), p. 316. This was Allen Dulles' response to Senator Fulbright's query in April 1959 about the relationship between Tibetan Buddhism and Buddhism practiced in Burma and Thailand.
50. Ibid.

24. MEANWHILE, A WORLD AWAY…

1. Dalai Lama, *My Land and My People: Memoirs of the Dalai Lama in Tibet* (New York: McGraw Hill, 1962), pp. 140–1.
2. Ibid.
3. Shakya, *Dragon in the Land of Snows*, p. 209. In time some of Kham had been incorporated into Sikang and much of Amdo into Qinghai.
4. Shakya, p. 121.
5. Dalai Lama, *My Land and My People*, pp. 118–20.
6. Shakya, pp. 124–5.
7. Ibid. PCART was presented as a way for the Tibetans to have a greater input to the new democratic reforms being implemented in Tibet. In the previous years, reforms had been

done through the Tibet Military Commission and most Tibetans were hostile to this institution which often was in direct confrontation to the government of the Dalai Lama. Ibid. p. 125

8. Conboy and Morrison, *The CIA's Secret War in Tibet*, p. 27. The PRC inaugurated PCART in Lhasa in April 1956 with a large celebration. There were Tibetans on PCART, but their votes were controlled by Beijing.

9. Dalai Lama, *Freedom in Exile*, p. 104.

10. Ibid.

11. Ibid., p. 104.

12. Ibid.

13. Gompo Tashi Andrugtsang, *Four Rivers, Six Ranges: Reminiscences of the Resistance Movement in Tibet* (Dharamsala, India: Information and Publicity Office of the Dalai Lama, 1973), p. 38.

14. Shakya, p. 139.

15. Ibid., p. 104.

16. Andrugtsang, *Four Rivers, Six Ranges*, p. 47.

17. Conboy and Morrison, p. 26. This aircraft was almost an exact Soviet copy of the American B-29 bomber used in bombing Japan in WWII. Ten airplanes had been given to Mao as a birthday present by Stalin in 1953. Ibid. p. 264, ftn 23.

18. John Kenneth Knaus, *Orphans of the Cold War: America and the Tibetan Struggle for Survival* (New York: Public Affairs, 2000), p. 129.

19. Ibid.

20. Shakya, p. 141.

21. Shakya, pp. 148–9; Dalai Lama, *My Land and My People*, p. 141.

22. See Shakya, p. 149 and Dalai Lama, *My Land and My People*, p. 138.

23. Dalai Lama, *My Land and My People*, p. 140.

24. Ibid., p. 141.

25. Dalai Lama, *Freedom in Exile*, p. 113; and also 'Mao's speech at the Second Plenary Session of the Eighth Central Committee of the Communist Party of China,' 15 November 1956, in *Selected Works of Mao Tse-tung* (Oxford: Pergamon Press, 1977), vol. V, p. 346; Dalai Lama, *My Land and My People*, pp. 141–2; Roger E. McCarthy, *Tears of the Lotus: Accounts of Tibetan Resistance to the Chinese Invasion, 1950–1952* (London: McFarland, 1997), p. 67.

26. Dalai Lama, *Freedom in Exile*, p. 113. The Dalai Lama knew this was a warning meant for him and that 'no other country would be allowed to interfere in Tibet.' Ibid.

27. 'Speech at the Second Plenary Session' in *Selected Works of Mao Tse-Tung*, vol. V, p. 346.

28. Ibid.

29. Ibid., p. 346.

30. Ibid. He had told his troops in Tibet to prepare for this by building 'fortifications' and storing food and water. Mao now used the word 'disturbance' to describe both the revolt in Hungary and the uprising in Tibet.

31. Dalai Lama, *Freedom in Exile*, pp. 114–15. His Holiness was greeted by the Indian Political Officer Mr Apa B. Pant, who was previously at the Indian consulate in Lhasa. He was taken to a small village on the edge of Lake Tsongo, where he met with his two brothers, Gyalo Thondup and Thubten Norbu. Sikkim was a kingdom that became a protectorate of India in 1947 and then a full state in 1973.

32. *My Land and My People*, p. 145.

33. Ibid.
34. Ibid. and also *Freedom in Exile*, pp. 114–15.
35. Dalai Lama, *Freedom in Exile*, p. 117. And also see 'Talks with Dalai Lama: Nehru's jotting of his talks with the Dalai Lama on 26 and 28 November 1956' in H. Y. Sharada Prasad, A. K. Damodaran, and Mushirul Hasam, eds., *Selected Works of Jawaharlal Nehru* (New Delhi: Jawaharlal Nehru Memorial Fund, 2003–5), vol. 35, pp. 520–1.
36. Dalai Lama, *Freedom in Exile*, p. 117.
37. Dalai Lama, *My Land and My People*, p. 147. The Dalai Lama also felt helpless as all peaceful resolutions thus far had failed and he would not resort to violence though many Tibetan favored this alternative. He told Nehru that he thought the Chinese to be ruthless and intent upon destroying Tibetan 'religion and customs.' Ibid.
38. 'Talks with Dalai Lama: Nehru's jotting of his talks with the Dalai Lama on 26 and 28 November 1956,' in Prasad, et al., *Selected Works of Jawaharlal Nehru*, vol. 35, p. 520.
39. Ibid., p. 520 and also see Dalai Lama, *My Land and My People*, p. 148.
40. H. Y. Sharada Prasad, et al., vol. 35, p. 521.
41. Dalai Lama, *My Land and My People*, p. 133; Prasad, et al., vol. 35, p. 520.
42. 'Welcoming Chou En-Lai,' Nehru's speech when receiving the Chinese prime minister at Palam Airport, New Delhi, 28 November 1956, in H. Y. Sharada Prasad, et al., vol. 35, p. 522; and 'Significance of Panshcheel: Speech at a banquet given in honour of Chou En-Lai,' 29 November 1956, in Prasad, et al., *Selected Works of Jawaharlal Nehru*, vol. 35, p. 523.
43. Ibid.
44. 'Relevance of Buddha: Speech on the occasion of Buddha Jayanti celebrations,' 24 November 1956, in Prasad, et al., *Selected Works of Jawaharlal Nehru*, vol. 35, pp. 523 and 617.
45. Dalai Lama, *My Land and My People*, pp. 133–4 and *Freedom in Exile*, pp. 128–9.
46. Dalai Lama, *Freedom in Exile*, p. 130.
47. *Freedom in Exile*, pp. 118.
48. Dalai Lama, *Freedom in Exile*, p. 130 and also Dalai Lama, *My Land and My People*, p. 134; Shakya, *Dragon in the Land of Snows*, p. 154.
49. 'Talks with Chou En-lai' in Prasad, et al., *Selected Works of Jawaharlal Nehru*, vol. 35, p. 583.
50. Ibid.
51. Ibid.
52. Ibid.
53. Ibid.
54. Ibid.
55. Ibid.
56. 'Talks with Chou En-lai,' in Prasad, et al., *Selected Works of Jawaharlal Nehru*, vol. 35, p. 598.
57. Ibid. Nehru was disingenuous here as his Indian Intelligence Service was working with Gyalo Thondup and he was aware of all Tibetan activities in Kalimpong at this time. See Chapter 3 for a fuller discussion of this.
58. Ibid., pp. 603–5.
59. 'Talks with Chou En-lai,' in Prasad, et al., *Selected Works of Jawaharlal Nehru*, vol. 35, p. 603 and ftn 1. Also see Dalai Lama, *My Land and My People*, p. 136.
60. Dalai Lama, *My Land and My People*, p. 151.
61. Ibid., p. 152.
62. Dalai Lama, *Freedom in Exile*, pp. 120–1.

25. THE ENIGMATIC GYALO THONDUP

1. Goldstein, *The Calm Before the Storm*, p. 235. Goldstein notes that sending your child to study in China in this period was 'unheard of in the aristocracy.' Children who were educated outside Tibet went to India, but Gyalo was keen to go to Nanking and his father thought it would be good experience for him. Ibid.
2. Goldstein, *The Calm Before the Storm*, p. 237.
3. Conboy and Morrison, *The CIA's Secret War in Tibet*, p. 30.
4. Goldstein, p. 238.
5. Conboy and Morrison, p. 31; Goldstein, p. 239.
6. Goldstein, p. 238. The US government supplied financial assistance to Taktser but refused to provide Gyalo in Taiwan with any financial aid. This was made adamantly clear in Department memos. See 'Amconsul Calcutta to American Embassy New Delhi,' 23 August 1951, 793B.00/8–1351, NARA; 'Telegram from Calcutta (Soulen) to Secretary of State,' 12 September 1951, no. 159, 793B.11/1–1251, NARA. Gyalo again requested funds but US officials refused to exchange rupees for dollars. When the telegram was sent to the Office of Chinese Affairs, Anderson and Soulen had written: 'Dept and Hong Kong might consider advisability authorizing Calcutta forward Indian rupees now our possession by pouch to Hong Kong for delivery to Gyalo.' Anderson wrote in the margin a bold NO. Ibid.
7. 'Telegram from Calcutta (Soulen) to the Secretary of State,' 12 September 1951, 793B.11/9–1251, NARA. Gyalo had telegraphed the American consulate in Calcutta to question whether they had received any funds for him from Lhasa. However, he had sent the telegram by ordinary telegraphic services and Soulen was peeved. He wrote to the consulate in Hong Kong: 'Hong Kong please urgently request Gyalo route all communications re matter thru you and under no circumstances send further communications direct CONGEN Calcutta by ordinary tel.' Ibid.
8. Goldstein, p. 239.
9. 'Office Memorandum from Bureau of Far Eastern Affairs (Mr Allison and Mr Johnson) to Chinese Affairs, Mr Perkins,' 11 January 1952, 793B.00/1–1152, NARA. John Allison was the assistant secretary of state for Far Eastern Affairs, succeeding Dean Rusk. Gyalo received visas from the Indian embassy in Washington for himself, his wife and child—all duly noted in both Washington and Calcutta by American officials—and then left the United States for the long journey to Lhasa. It was noted that 'nothing be done by the US government to assist Gyalo in making arrangements to enter India.' The movements of the Dalai Lama's mother and sister were in Calcutta's telegram to the secretary of state, 5 January 1952. See 'Calcutta [Gibson and Wilson] to Secretary of State,' no. 311, 5 January 1952, 793B.00/1–552, NARA.
10. Goldstein, *The Calm Before the Storm*, pp. 373–5.
11. 'Conversation with the Dalai Lama's Brother, Gyalo Thondup and Wife, Amconsul, Calcutta India to the Department of State,' 22 July 1952. Mrs Thondup spoke to Wilson on 8 July while her husband was recovering. Released to the authors on a FOIA request, 793B.11/2–2252, NARA. It was reported by Sinha, the Indian Political Agent in Lhasa, that Gyalo was embarrassed about his presence in Lhasa. See 'The Officer in Charge, Indian Mission, Lhasa to the Political Officer in Sikkim, Monthly Report for period ending 15 June 1952 sent to the Department of State from the American Embassy in London,' Despatch 6165, 27 June 1952, 793B.00/9–352, NARA. Released to author on FOIA request.

12. Ibid. Gyalo was not present at the meeting as he was in hospital recovering from typhoid fever.
13. Ibid.
14. Ibid.
15. Ibid.
16. Ibid.
17. 'American Consul, Calcutta to the Department of State, Memorandum of Conversation,' 22 July 1952, 793B.11/7–2252, NARA.
18. 'Telegram from AmCon Gen, Calcutta to the Department of State,' 6 September 1952, Despatch no. 215, 793B.11/9–1852, NARA. This was discussed with Gary Soulen in September 1952.
19. Ibid. The Thondups told Soulen that they did not have any Communist sympathies but needed the income. In his report Soulen noted: 'This was another incident in which Gyalo mentioned friends, who would appear to me to be absolutely untrustworthy, especially from the standpoint of their learning of US interests in Tibet.' Ibid. In a memo from Calcutta to the Secretary of State, dated 12 September 1951, Gary Soulen suggested that Gyalo might be discreetly questioned about 'sympathies' in view of the present political situation in Tibet. See 'Telegram from Calcutta to Secretary of State,' 12 September 1951, no. 159, 793B.11/9–1251, NARA.
20. 'Outgoing Airgram from the Department of State, to the Amembassy, New Delhi,' 18 June 1952, 793B.11/6–1852, NARA. Declassified memo released to writer under FOIA, September 2008. Mrs Thondup had mailed a letter that her husband had brought out of Tibet to Washington. The State Department was concerned over her lack of judgment. Acheson wrote to the American embassy in Delhi that 'It is suggested that Mrs Thondup be cautioned discreetly against endangering her husband's security by messaging messages from him to the public mail service.' Ibid.
21. 'The Consul at Calcutta (Soulen) to the Department of State,' 10 September 1952, *FRUS*, vol. XIV, p. 96 ftn. In a memo of August 1952 the State Department commented that 'it may be possible in the future to use Gyalo's background information, with his consent and without attribution, in developing material for VOA programs.' 'Department of State to the American Embassy in New Delhi,' 6 August 1952, 793B.11/8–652, NARA.
22. 'Foreign Service Despatch, From AMEMBASSY, London to the Department of State,' 3 September 1952, 793B.00 /9–352, NARA. Declassified to writers. This report is for the period of 16 April–16 May 1952. The reports were sent from the officer in charge in Lhasa to the political officer in Gangtok, Sikkim and then to London where an American embassy official was allowed to see the report.
23. 'Telegram from AmCon Gen, Calcutta to the Department of State,' 6 September 1952, Despatch no. 215, 793B.11/9–1852, NARA. This sixteen-page document was released to the writers in September 2008 under a FOIA request allowing for a more complete description and understanding of the events of the period. Until this time there had been one short paragraph on these meetings.
24. Ibid.
25. 'Discussions with the Dalai Lama's Brother, Gyalo Thondup, in Darjeeling, India,' 6 September 1952, Despatch 215, 793B.11/9–1852, NARA. Declassified to writer.
26. Ibid., p. 10. Gyalo intended for his organization to be headquartered either in Darjeeling or Kalimpong and that they would produce anti-communist literature to smuggle into Tibet.

27. Ibid.

28. Ibid. Revealing his sympathies, here Soulen went beyond the confines of his diplomatic role to provide advice on intelligence methods

29. 'Notes of Conversation with Gyalo Thondup, in Darjeeling, India,' 6 September 1952, Despatch 215, 793B.11/9–1852, NARA. This was reported to Soulen in a second meeting that day. Gyalo discreetly met the vice consul at his hotel. The GOI were keen for intelligence. The director of Indian Intelligence, B. N. Mullik, wrote in his memoirs that he was aware the PRC would try to extend their 'sphere of influence.' To that end, 'it was necessary for us to develop our own administration in these areas as rapidly as possible so that when the Chinese threat appeared they would find a fully developed administration able to take care of itself.' B. N. Mullik, *My Years with Nehru: The Chinese Betrayal* (New Delhi: Allied Publishers, 1971), p. 179.

30. 'Notes of Conversation with Gyalo Thondup, in Darjeeling, India,' 6 September 1952, Despatch 215, 793B.11/9–1852, NARA, p. 2; also see 'Telegram from AmConGen Calcutta to the Department of State,' 18 September 1952, Despatch 215, 793B.11/9–1852, p. 11, NARA. Kumar wanted Gyalo to arrange to 'send three people each month into Tibet for espionage work and said that he would pay all of their expenses.' Ibid.

31. 'Notes of Conversation with Gyalo Thondup, in Darjeeling, India', 6 September 1952, Despatch 215, 793B.11/9–1852, NARA. Gyalo's conversation with Soulen is consistent with the recollection of the Indian Intelligence chief. Mullik, *My Years with Nehru: The Chinese Betrayal*, pp. 85 and 181.

32. 'Notes of Conversation with Gyalo Thondup, in Darjeeling, India,' 6 September 1952, Despatch 215, 793B.11/9–1852, NARA. Soulen told Gyalo he was 'extremely interested in his ideas' but could not supply arms.

33. Ibid. Soulen wrote in his report: 'I have also advised them against making any statements or voicing any opinions which could in any way be construed as linking themselves and the Tibetan people with the United States or with US officials.' Thus, while Soulen advised Gyalo on codes and operations, he again made it clear that the Tibetan should not associate himself or others with the United States government. 'Discussions with the Dalai Lama's Brother, Gyalo Thondup, in Darjeeling India,' 6 September 1952, 793B.11/9–1852, NARA.

34. Ibid. Gyalo requested that the US government provide him with a wireless set, but Soulen wrote that 'in the hands of these people, for the purpose outlined, would certainly do more harm than good.' Ibid.

35. 'Conversations with Gyalo Thondup, Brother of the Dalai Lama, and Tsepon Shakabpa, Former Foreign Secretary of Tibet, Memo from the Amconsul, Calcutta to the Department of State Washington,' 7 October 1952. The conversation took place on 5 October.

36. 'Discussions with the Dalai Lama's Brother, Gyalo Thondup in Darjeeling India,' 6 September 1952, 793B.11/9–1852, NARA. Washington did transmit an oral reply to Gyalo 'expressing US sympathies for Tibetans' but pointed out the necessity for GOI cooperation. See 'Memorandum of Conversation from Amconsul Calcutta to the State Department,' 8 January 1954, Despatch 373, NARA. Declassified to the authors.

37. Ibid. Not only would it be difficult logistically, but the Dalai Lama felt he could not leave his country and people at this time.

38. Ibid.

39. 'Memorandum of Conversation from Amconsul Calcutta to the State Department,' 8 January 1954, Despatch 373, NARA. Declassified to the authors.

40. Ibid.
41. Ibid.
42. 'Telegram from CONGEN Calcutta to Secretary of State,' 4 December 1952, 793B.11/12–452; and 'Calcutta to Secretary of State,' 24 December 1952, no. 206, 793B/12–2452, NARA. Marginalia stated 'Noted.' Also see 'Memo from Calcutta to the Secretary of State,' Declassified Telegram no. 194, 4 December 1952, 793B.11/12–452. Declassified to these writers.
43. Ibid.
44. Ibid.
45. 'Telegram from the Department of State to the Amembassy, New Delhi,' 22 December 1952, 793B.00/12–1752, NARA.
46. 'Memorandum of Conversation from Amconsul Calcutta to the State Department,' 8 January 1954, Despatch 373, NARA.
47. Ibid.
48. 'Memorandum of Conversation from Amconsul Calcutta to the State Department,' 11 January 1954, Despatch 373, 793B.00/1–1154, Enclosure 1, NARA. Declassified to the writers.
49. Ibid. The conversation took place on 7 January 1954. Soulen noted in his report that 'The GOI raised serious objections to the transmittal of any messages to Gyalo and the project was shelved.' Ibid.
50. 'Amconsul Calcutta to the Department of State,' 24 February 1953, 793B.1.1/2–2453, NARA. Declassified to the writers. In this memorandum of conversation it is noted that the Indian government had recently ruled that no foreigners or foreign expeditions could enter a security zone along the Indian Tibetan border.
51. 'Memorandum of Conversation from Amconsul Calcutta to the State Department,' 8 January 1954, Despatch 373, NARA. Gary Soulen wrote the memo on his conversation with the Thondups.
52. Ibid.
53. Ibid.
54. Ibid.
55. Ibid. After Kapur's warnings, Gyalo led a rather quiet life, seldomly going out except to play tennis. He continued though to meet with Tibetan friends. Ibid., p. 3. Kapur was a very experienced diplomat and Soulen believed because of his high status that he was most probably acting under direct orders from the Government of India. Ibid.
56. Ibid. Soulen was not surprised that Gyalo was at a loss to understand the GOI's policy toward Tibet. Gyalo told Soulen that sometimes the Indian government 'takes actions which are favourable to the Tibetans but at the same time it takes other actions which are distinctly against the interests of Tibet.' Ibid.
57. Ibid. Soulen reflected that Gyalo's new-found confidence could be a 'reflection of actual confidence that with continuing Indian intelligence agencies' interest in him and his friends, he no longer has that feeling of insecurity which dominated his thinking a year or so ago.' Ibid., p. 6.
58. Ibid.
59. Ibid. Gyalo had however received an 'innocuous reply,' orally, to his request for US assistance with his resistance plan.
60. Ibid.
61. Ibid.

62. Ibid.
63. Ibid.
64. Ibid.
65. Ibid.
66. Ibid. Soulen wrote 'It [the consulate] would be careful not to give unfounded hope but would endeavour to re-instil confidence in US objectives and US officials.' Ibid. In addition Soulen recommended that Gyalo receive a response to his seventeen-month old letter, which might improve relations between him and US field officers. Soulen wanted to reiterate to Gyalo that in order for any resistance operation to be a success, it would need 'at least GOI condemnation and for that reason the Embassy had used it good office to sound out the GOI in December 1952.' Ibid.
67. Mullik, p. 181; Goldstein, *History of Modern Tibet*, vol. II, p. 470. Mullik wrote that the Tibetans 'felt that they had been let down badly by India, though they had reposed their trust in her …' Mullik, p. 181. As Indian Intelligence chief, Mullik made a trip to Kalimpong and Darjeeling. But according to Mullik, Nehru intended to look the other way and 'would not take any notice' of Tibetan resistance activities on Indian soil unless they comprised themselves too openly. According to Mullik, Nehru suggested however that 'the best form of resistance would be through non-violence …' Ibid., p. 85.
68. Goldstein, vol. II, p. 471.
69. Goldstein, vol. II, p. 473. Goldstein wrote that the GOI was 'regularly providing funds to Jenkhentsisum by late 1955.' This information was obtained from the diary of Tsepon Shakabpa. See Goldstein, vol. II, p, 477, ftn 29. Gyalo discussed his idea to set up a secret organization with Gary Soulen in September 1952. 'Telegram from AmCon Gen, Calcutta to the Department of State,' 6 September 1952, Despatch no. 215, 793B.11/9–1852, NARA.
70. 'AMCONGEN, Calcutta to the Department of State,' 27 September 1954, 793B.00/9–2754, NARA.
71. Knaus, p. 129.
72. Ibid., p. 130.
73. *New York Times*, 28 November 1956.
74. Intelligence Report, no. 7342, Copy 13, NND760175, prepared on 1 November 1956, Office of Intelligence Research.
75. Knaus, p. 135.
76. Ibid., p. 138.
77. Conboy and Morrison, p. 33.
78. George Patterson interview, June 2006.
79. Ibid.
80. Conboy and Morrison, p. 37.

26. WASHINGTON'S CLANDESTINE PROGRAM IN TIBET

1. Secretary John Foster Dulles, '*Face the Nation*,' 21 October 1956, quoted in *The Eisenhower Administration, 1953–1961, A Documentary History*, pp. 665–71.
2. Ibid. On 4 July 1821, Adams gave an address to Congress saying the USA 'goes not abroad, in search of monsters to destroy. She is the well-wisher to the freedom and independence of all. She is the champion and vindicator only of her own.'
3. Ibid.

4. Blanche Wiesen Cook, *The Declassified Eisenhower*, pp. 198–202. According to Cook, Radio Free Europe had been blanketing the region for seven years and the US government, in fact, intensified the broadcasts as the situation in Poland and Hungary became more volatile.

5. 'Statement by President Eisenhower on Hungarian Refugees,' 8 November 1956, quoted in *The Eisenhower Administration, 1953–1961, A Documentary History*, pp. 679–80.

6. John Prados, *The President's Secret Wars: CIA and Pentagon Covert Operations from World War II Through Iranscam* (New York: William Morrow, 1986), p. 124.

7. Stephen E. Ambrose, *Eisenhower, Soldier and President* (New York: Simon & Schuster Paperbacks, 1990), p. 423.

8. Ibid.

9. Ibid., pp. 422–3. Ambrose noted that, while the US had anticipated a revolt and had 'indeed encouraged it,' there was no plan in place when it happened and that, moreover, Washington was not prepared to do anything about the situation. As the Hungarian crisis unfolded, Eisenhower was dealing with the Suez Canal crisis, a presidential election, and the illness of his secretary of state Dulles—all in one week.

10. James Reston, *New York Times*, 25 October 1956.

11. Interview with Thomas Parrott, December 2004.

12. Dwight D Eisenhower, *The White House Years 1956–1961, Waging Peace* (New York: Doubleday, 1965), p. 95.

13. 'Talks at a Conference of Secretaries of Provincial, Municipal and Autonomous Region Party Committees,' 18 January 1957, in *Selected Works of Mao Tse-tung*, vol. V, p. 358. There had been a small demonstration in a school in Shihchiachuang, but the 'ultra-reactionaries' had been put down. Mao thought the Hungarian revolt had a positive impact because 'these ants in China were thus lured out of their holes.' Also see 'Talks at a Conference of Secretaries of Provincial, Municipal and Autonomous Region Party Committees,' 18 January 1957, in *Selected Works of Mao Tse-tung*, vol. V, p. 350.

14. 'Mao's speech at Conference,' 27 January 1956, *Selected Works of Mao Tse-tung*, vol. V, p. 363.

15. 'On the Correct Handling of Contradictions Among the People,' 27 February 1957, in *Selected Works of Mao Tse-tung*, vol. V, p. 373.

16. Ibid., p. 391. The speech was given during Mao's period of democratic reform, known as the Cultural Revolution, which began in 1956.

17. Ibid., p. 399.

18. Andrugtsang, *Four Rivers, Six Ranges*, p. 42.

19. Andrugtsang, p. 52.

20. Ibid., p. 53. A number of silver and gold lamps and other items were made and given to monasteries.

21. Carole McGranahan, 'The CIA and the Chushi Gangdrug Resistance, 1956–1974,' *Journal of Cold War Studies*, vol. 8, no. 3 (Summer 2006), p. 109. The Tibetan name was *chu bzhi gangs drug dmag*; the four rivers in Tibet are the Mekong, Salween, Yangtze, and Yalung.

22. Andrugtsang, p. 58.

23. Ibid.

24. Andrugtsang, pp. 62–3. The army was also called the National Volunteer Defense Army (NDVA).

25. McGranahan, p. 110.

26. Ibid.

27. There were twenty-seven men in all, some still teenagers, who had met with the Dalai Lama while he attended the Buddhist festivities in India. The men pleaded for Lhasa's help against the Chinese in eastern Tibet, but His Holiness 'counseled patience.' They later visited the religious city of Bodh Gaya, where their pictures were taken by the Dalai Lama's brother, Thubten Norbu. It was from these pictures that the men were eventually chosen to be the first group of Khampas trained by the US. See Shakya, *Dragon in the Land of Snows*, p. 172; Conby and Morrison, p. 36. The Mariana Islands are in the Western Pacific Ocean, north of New Guinea and south of Japan.

28. A *longhi* is a cotton piece of fabric which when wrapped looks like a skirt and is often worn by male Indian workers.

29. James Rhinehart, 'Covert Action in High Altitudes,' *Studies in Intelligence* (Washington, DC: Central Intelligence Agency), Spring 1976. Only a very small portion of this study is available in the public domain as most of it is still classified.

30. This is a first-person account by Athar Norbu, one of the Tibetan resistance fighters chosen by the Dalai Lama's brother, Gyalo Thondup, to train at the CIA installation in Saipan. Quoted in Mikel Dunham, *Buddha's Warriors* (New York: Jeremy P. Tarcher/Penguin, 2004), pp. 197–200.

31. Kurmitola is today home to the Hazrat Shahjalal international airport, the largest in Bangladesh. During WWII the British used Kurmitola, operating planes that flew to Burma and other areas.

32. Conboy and Morrison, p. 46.

33. William M. Leary, 'Secret Mission to Tibet,' *Air and Space* (December 1997/January 1998), p. 64.

34. Roger McCarthy interview, February 2006, and also Leary, p. 64. They were also trained to mark the terrain for future CIA airdrops.

35. Roger E. McCarthy, *Tear of the Lotus* (London: McFarland & Company, 1997), p. 139. Also see Leary, p. 64.

36. Roger McCarthy interview, February 2006; James Lilley interview; Robert Ford interview. Ford, the former British radio operator in Chamdo, talked to the authors at length about the difficulties of scheduling meetings or radio transmissions with the Tibetans with no idea of the 24-hour clock. And also see Conboy and Morrison, p. 48.

37. Roger McCarthy interview, February 2006, and Conboy and Morrison, p. 48.

38. Roger McCarthy interview, February 2006.

39. Ibid.

40. Conboy and Morrison, p. 56.

41. Ibid., p. 57.

42. Ibid., p. 59.

43. Interview with Roger McCarthy, February 2006.

44. The flight crew was Polish and was picked up in Wiesbaden, Germany under the code name 'Ostiary.' Roger McCarthy interview; Leary, p. 64; and also Dr Joe Leeker, 'Missions to Tibet,' *The History of Air America* at http://www.utdallas.edu/library/collections/speccoll/Leeker/history/index.html

45. Leary, p. 64; Roger McCarthy interview; and Conboy and Morrison, pp. 59–64

46. Interview with Roger McCarthy, February 2006.

47. Leary, p. 65.

48. Lawrence Ropka, quoted in Leary, p. 65. In dead reckoning, the pilot must use a compass and a clock. Ropka said that the maps they used were outdated or poorly put together; and that 'you would marry one chart with another, as was the custom at the time … it was always intriguing because the mountain ridges and rivers on one chart wouldn't match the mountain ridges and rivers on another.' This of course did not instill a lot of confidence in the validity of the charts. Ibid.
49. Conboy and Morrison, p. 63.
50. Ibid., p. 64.
51. Ibid.
52. Ibid., p. 66.
53. Knaus, p. 147; Conboy and Morrison, p. 68.
54. Conboy and Morrison, p. 68.
55. Ibid., p. 69; Knaus, pp. 147–8.
56. Conboy and Morrison, p. 69; Knaus, p. 148.
57. Conboy and Morrison, p. 65.
58. Knaus, p. 148. Dick, the Tibetan who hyperventilated on the plane, was eventually dropped into eastern Tibet but was killed.
59. Leary, p. 65.
60. Leary, p. 66.
61. Ibid. Most often the planes would have to stop in East Pakistan (Kermitola) for refueling.
62. Conboy and Morrison, p. 79.

27. THE SOUTH ASIAN RUBIK'S CUBE

1. H.W. Brands, *India and the United States*, p. 90.
2. Dulles met with Nehru at the prime minister's residence in Delhi on 9 and 11 March 1956 on his way to the 1956 Colombo conference in Ceylon. In these talks the issue of purchasing military planes was discussed. Dulles wrote in his memo to the president that 'Nehru led up this subject with obvious caution and gave quite a story as to the background, trying to make it appear as innocent as possible.' See 'Telegram from the Secretary of State to the Department of State: Letter to the President,' 11 March 1956, *FRUS 1955–57. South Asia*, vol. VIII, pp. 308–9; and H. W. Brands, *India and the United States*, pp. 86–7.
3. Ibid., *FRUS*, vol. VIII, p. 309.
4. Ibid., p. 310; Kux, *Estranged Democracies*, p. 128.
5. 'Telegram from the Secretary of State to the Department of State: Letter to the President,' 11 March 1956, *FRUS*, vol. VIII, p. 310.
6. H. W. Brands, *India and the United States*, p. 87; and also 'A Feasible Program of US Economic Assistance for India,' 13 March 1956, *FRUS*, vol. VIII, pp. 311–12. The British were prepared to take a financial loss and sell planes that were intended for the Royal Air Force. Ibid.
7. 'Telegram from the Secretary of State to the Department of State: Letter to the President,' 11 March 1956, *FRUS*, vol. VIII, p. 309.
8. Ibid.
9. Ibid.
10. McMahon, *The Cold War on the Periphery*, p. 226.

11. Kux, *Estranged Democracies*, p. 129. The speech was given on 9 June 1956.

12. Quoted in 'Nehru's letter to G. L. Meta,' 19 August 1956, Prasad, et al., *Selected Works of Jawaharlal Nehru*, vol. 34, p. 317, ftn 3.

13. 'A Feasible Program of US Economic Assistance for India,' 13 March 1956, *FRUS*, vol. VIII, pp. 311–12.

14. The president's invitation to visit Washington was originally for June 1956, but Eisenhower had an attack of ileitis on 7 June and the visit had to be postponed. This suited Nehru, because a delay would enable him to include Menon. Confidently Eisenhower expressed his displeasure, saying that Menon would 'louse it up terribly' and ultimately the GOI was told the 'addition of Menon would complicate the visit.' See 'Telegram from the Embassy in India to the Department of State,' 7 December 1956, *FRUS*, vol. VIII, p. 319, ftn 2.

15. One of the briefing papers the President was given was entitled 'US Objectives of the Nehru Visit.' Some of the objectives Washington hoped to obtain were 'increasing Nehru's understanding of US foreign policy; to bring out the broad and significant areas of agreement; and to give a sympathetic hearing to the Prime Minister's views and make him feel has been consulted on the problems discussed.' In 'Nehru Visit-December 16–20, 1956: Objectives,' Ann Whitman Files, Box 31, DDE Library.

16. 'Personal Requirement Suggestions: Visit of Prime Minister Nehru of India,' Box 31, Ann Whitman Files, DDE Library. Nehru's favorite cigarettes were English brands such as 555 and Black and White. If these were not available, the State Department would provide either Virginia Rounds or Benson and Hedges, as these were considered other acceptable brands. Ibid.

17. Ibid. The restrictions on beef and pork were due to the religious observances of the many Indians who would be present at the functions. However, it was noted that in a private lunch or dinner Nehru 'might well enjoy filet mignon or something of that type.' Ibid.

18. Ibid.

19. Ibid.

20. Ibid.

21. Ibid.

22. 'Memorandum of Conversations with Prime Minister Nehru of India,' 17–18 December 1956, Box 31, Ann Whitman Files, Box 31, DDE Library, p. 4.

23. Ibid.

24. 'Telegram from the Embassy in India to the Department of State,' 7 December 1956, *FRUS*, vol. VIII, p. 325.

25. Quoted in 'Letter from Nehru to Menon,' 6 May 1956, in Gopal, *Jawaharlal Nehru, A Biography*, vol. III, p. 34.

26. 'Memorandum of Conversations with Prime Minister Nehru of India,' 17–18 December 1956, Box 31, Ann Whitman Files, DDE Library.

27. Prasad, et al., *Selected Works of Jawaharlal Nehru*, vol. 35, p. 537, ftn 5.

28. 'Memorandum of a Conversation between President Eisenhower and Prime Minister Nehru, The White House, Washington,' 10.25 a.m. 19 December 1956, *FRUS*, vol. VIII, p. 331, ftn 1. The president spoke to Nehru both at the White House on 19 December and at his farm on 17 and 18 December. See Prasad, et al., *Selected Works of Jawaharlal Nehru*, vol. 35, p. 537, ftn 5.

29. Prasad, et al., *Selected Works of Jawaharlal Nehru*, vol. 35, p. 543.

30. Ibid.

31. 'NSC 5701 Statement of Policy on US Policy Toward South Asia,' 10 January 1957, *FRUS*, vol. VIII, pp. 29–30.
32. Ibid., p. 35.
33. Ibid., p. 30.
34. Ibid., pp. 35–6.
35. Ibid., p. 36.
36. Ibid., p. 36.
37. This comment was expressed by the President to Ambassador Bunker in India and recorded in a letter. See 'Letter from the Ambassador in India (Bunker) to Frederic P. Bartlett at London,' 27 June 1955, *FRUS*, vol. VIII, p. 348. Ellsworth Bunker had met with the president for eleven minutes on 5 June. Bunker was considered a very effective US ambassador to India, earning the respect of Nehru, and helped to ease tensions between the two countries. Bartlett was a former chargé to India.
38. 'Study Prepared in the Embassy of India,' 8 November 1957, *FRUS*, vol. VIII, p. 397.
39. 'Letter from the Ambassador in India (Bunker) to Frederic P. Bartlett at London,' 27 June 1955, *FRUS*, vol. VIII, p. 348; and also Kux, *Estranged Democracies*, p. 150.
40. 'Statement of Policy on US Policy Toward South Asia,' 10 January 1957, *FRUS*, vol. VIII, p. 32. The administration felt that 'Pakistan after nine years of independent existence still lack[ed] many of the basic ingredients of internal stability.' Ibid.
41. 'Memorandum of Discussion at the 308th Meeting of the National Security Council, Washington,' 3 January 1957, *FRUS*, vol. VIII, pp. 18–19.
42. Ibid. Even though the president acknowledged that providing military assistance to Pakistan had been a mistake, by 1959 the US had established a military facility in Peshawar, near the Khyber Pass, and in Afghanistan, providing intelligence on Soviet activities. This was an important asset for the US government, and so Washington continued to supply Pakistan with military aid. See Kux, *Estranged Democracies*, p. 160
43. McMahon, *Cold War on the Periphery*, p. 179.
44. 'Attachment to Memorandum for Members of South Asia Working Group from the Operations Coordinating Board,' 27 February 1957, OCB 091 India, File 2(2), Box 37, OCB Central Files, DDE Library.
45. The Chinese call Arunachal Pradesh 'southern Tibet.'
46. 'Extract of Indian note to China,' 21 August 1958, in R. K. Jain, ed., *China South Asian Relations 1947–1980*, pp. 100–1.
47. 'Chou En-lai reply to Nehru's letter of 14 December 1958,' 23 January 1959, in Jain, ed., *China South Asian Relations 1947–1980*, pp. 105–10. The conditions, Chou wrote in 1954, were 'not ripe' for settlement and the MacMahon line, on which India based its borders, was just 'a product of the British policy of aggression against the Tibet Region of China...' Ibid., p. 106.
48. 'The Sino–India Border Dispute: Section 1:1950–59,' DD/I Staff Study, CIA/RSS, Reference title Polo XVI, 2 March 1963, Declassified May 2007, p. ii.
49. Quoted at http://claudearpi.blogspot.co.uk/2011/02/on-aksai-chin-road.html, last accessed June 2013.
50. 'The Sino-India Border Dispute: Section 1:1950–59,' DD/I Staff Study, CIA/RSS, Reference title Polo XVI, 2 March 1963, Declassified May 2007, p. 2.
51. Ibid., p. 2.
52. Ibid., p. iii.
53. Gopal, *Jawaharlal Nehru, A Biography*, vol. III, p. 39.

54. Ibid.
55. 'Extract of Chinese Note to India,' 10 July 1958, in R. K. Jain, pp. 97–8.
56. 'Extract of Indian note to China', 2 August 1958, in R. K. Jain, pp. 99–100. Nehru effectively validated China's claim by using the phrase 'China's Tibet region.'
57. Ibid.
58. In January 1958 the Dalai Lama had sent a personal invitation to Nehru to visit him; the Chinese later refused to let the prime minister visit. Nehru visited Bhutan and passed through Yatung and was able to see the Tibetan situation first-hand. See Gopal, *Jawaharlal Nehru, A Biography*, vol. III, pp. 79–81 and p. 81, ftn 39.
59. Ibid.

28. THE DALAI LAMA LEAVES TIBET

1. Dalai Lama, *My Land and My People*, p. 161.
2. Ibid., p. 163.
3. Ibid.
4. Ibid., pp. 164–66.
5. Usually His Holiness had an escort of at least twenty-five armed guards and more armed guards were posted on any route that he took. Ibid., p. 167.
6. *My Land and My People*, p. 167–8.
7. Shakya, *Dragon in the Land of Snows*, p. 191. Mrs Yuthok quoted in Dorje Yudon Yuthok, ed. Michael Harlin, *The House of the Turquoise Roof* (Ithaca: Snow Lion Publications, 1990).
8. Dalai Lama, *My Land and My People*, p. 170.
9. Shakya, p. 196.
10. *My Land and My People*, pp. 174–75; *Freedom in Exile*, p. 136.
11. *My Land and My People*, p. 194.
12. Ibid., p. 195.
13. Ibid., p. 197.
14. Ibid.
15. Ibid., pp. 197–99.
16. Ibid.
17. Dalai Lama, *Freedom in Exile*, pp. 139–140.
18. Dalai Lama, *My Land and My People*, p. 205; Shakya, p. 205; *Freedom in Exile*, p. 140.
19. Conboy and Morrison, p. 91. According to the authors, the Dalai Lama was told about CIA drops and their radio with which they were able to contact the Americans on Okinawa. Ibid.
20. Ibid.
21. *My Land and My People*, p. 210.
22. *Freedom in Exile*, p. 141.
23. Ibid., Shakya, p. 205.
24. *My Land and My People*, p. 141.
25. Ibid.
26. Conboy and Morrison, pp. 92–3. It appears that CIA Director Allen Dulles was aware that Nehru would grant asylum to the Dalai Lama, as this was relayed to officials at the NSC meeting on 26 March 1959. At this meeting Dulles also discussed the events in

Lhasa and the Dalai Lama's flight in detail. See 'US Response to the Rebellion in Tibet,' Editorial note 367, *FRUS 1958–60*, vol. XIX, China, p. 751.

27. *My Land and My People*, p. 213.
28. Ibid.
29. Ibid., p. 216.
30. Allen Dulles speaking before the Senate Foreign Relations Committee. This was a closed-door briefing on Tibet, chaired by J. William Fulbright. *Executive Sessions of the Senate Foreign Relations Committee* (Historical Series), vol. XI, Eighty-Sixth Congress, First Session, 29 April 1959, p. 311, DDE Library.
31. 'Letter and Message from Allen Dulles to A. Goodpaster', 2 April 1959, White House Office, Office of the Staff Secretary Record, 1952–1961, Subject Series, Alpha Subseries, Box 15, Intelligence Matters (9), DDE Library.
32. 'Briefing by Allen Dulles to the Senate Foreign Relations Committee,' in *Executive Sessions of the Senate Foreign Relations Committee*, p. 347.
33. Ibid., pp. 309–10. When Dulles discussed the 'dramatic escape' of the Dalai Lama, it is noted 'Discussion Off The Record.'
34. Ibid., pp. 310–11.
35. Ibid.
36. Ibid., p. 313. While this was not exactly the full truth on the brothers' activities, it provides another insight into how Allen Dulles and the President strove to keep covert activity closely held. Interestingly, this question came from Senator Mansfield, who had tried in 1955, like Senator McCarthy a year earlier, to establish Congressional oversight of CIA activities. Specifically, Mansfield wanted to create a 'Joint Committee on CIA oversight,' a resolution that Eisenhower vowed would be 'passed over my dead body.' See Ambrose, *Ike's Spies*, p. 187.
37. 'Briefing by Allen Dulles to the Senate Foreign Relations Committee,' p. 314.
38. Ibid., p. 315. Also see '403rd Meeting of the National Security Council,' 23 April 1959, Editorial note 371, *FRUS 1958–60*, XIX China, p. 755. Dulles said in his briefing that the Chinese had put on a very effective military showing and were using Korean War veterans to fight the resistance in Tibet.
39. 'Briefing by Allen Dulles to the Senate Foreign Relations Committee,' p. 315.
40. Ambassador James Lilly (interview March 2006).
41. Interview with Thomas Parrott, December 2004.
42. Ibid.
43. 'Briefing by Allen Dulles to the Senate Foreign Relations Committee,' p. 315. The words after this are redacted.
44. Ibid.
45. Ibid., p. 316. While Fulbright seemed brusque in this meeting, according to Ken Knaus, he agreed to endorse further funding for the Tibetan resistance after Knaus showed him a very dramatic film of the Dalai Lama's escape and a Tibetan ceremony. Interview with Ken Knaus, December 2004. Fulbright did establish an educational fund, and every year since 1988 the United States Fulbright Program has brought approximately fifteen Tibetan students to study at university level in the United States. See http://www.tibetfund.org/annual_reports/2003report/pg3.html, last accessed 1 June 2013.
46. 'Briefing by Allen Dulles to the Senate Foreign Relations Committee,' in *Executive Sessions of the Senate Foreign Relations Committee*, (Historical Series), vol. XI, Eighty-Sixth Congress, First Session, 29 April 1959, DDE Library, p. 316.

47. 'Briefing by Allen Dulles to the Senate Foreign Relations Committee,' p. 316.

48. Ibid.

49. Ibid.

50. Ibid., p. 317. Also see David M. Barrett, *The CIA and Congress* (Lawrence, Kansas: University of Kansas Press, 2005), pp. 347–50.

51. 'Briefing by Allen Dulles to the Senate Foreign Relations Committee,' p. 317.

52. 'Memorandum for Mr Karl Marr,' *OCB Luncheon Discussions: Exploitation of Tibetan Revolt, 31 March 1959*, 1 April 1959, p. 1, DDE Library.

53. Ibid., p. 2.

54. '403rd Meeting of the National Security Council,' 23 April 1959, Editorial note in *FRUS*, vol. XIX, pp. 755–6. McElroy was the Secretary of Defense from 9 October 1957 until 1 December 1959.

55. Ibid.

56. Ibid., p. 755.

57. 'CIA Report, RE: Desire of Dalai Lama to Continue Struggle for Freedom and Independence of Tibet,' Central Intelligence Agency Report, 23 April 1959, p. 1. Ann Whitman, International Series, Box 48, DDE Library.

58. P. N. Menon was married to Malini, the first daughter of K. P. S. Menon, the Indian minister of Foreign Affairs.

59. 'CIA Report, RE: Desire of Dalai Lama to Continue Struggle for Freedom and Independence of Tibet,' Central Intelligence Agency Report, 23 April 1959, p. 1. Ann Whitman, International Series, Box 48, DDE Library.

60. Ibid., p. 3.

61. http://www.claudearpi.net/maintenance/uploaded_pics/Tezpur.pdf, last accessed June 2013.

62. *Freedom in Exile*, p. 145.

63. Ibid., p. 4 and also *Freedom in Exile*, p. 146.

64. *Freedom in Exile*, p. 161.

65. Ibid.

29. TIBET AT THE UNITED NATIONS

1. 'Memorandum for the President, Subject: Message from the Dalai Lama,' 2 May 1959, Ann Whitman, International Series, Box 48, DDE Library.

2. Ibid.; and also see 'Memorandum from Acting Secretary of State Dillon to President Eisenhower,' 30 April 1959, *FRUS*, vol. XIX, China, p. 763. The president was briefed on 2 May 2.

3. 'Memorandum for the President, Subject: Message from the Dalai Lama,' 2 May 1959, Ann Whitman, International Series, Box 48, DDE Library, p. 2; and also see 'Memorandum from Acting Secretary of State Dillon to President Eisenhower,' 30 April 1959, *FRUS*, vol. XIX, China, p. 764.

4. 'Revision of Attachment to FE no. 675, Desire of Dalai Lama to Continue Struggle for Freedom and Independence of Tibet,' Ann Whitman File, International Series, Box 48, Tibet, DDE Library. Emphasis added.

5. 'Memorandum from the Assistant Secretary of State for Far Eastern Affairs (Parsons) to Secretary of State Herter,' 14 October 1959, *FRUS 1958–60*, Note 394, vol. XIX, pp. 792–3. Emphasis added.

6. Ibid. 'Memorandum for the Record, Goodpaster conversation with the President,' 20 June 1959, Ann Whitman International Series, Box 48, Tibet, DDE Library.

7. Ibid.

8. Ibid.

9. Ibid. Also see 'Memorandum from the Assistant Secretary of State for Far Eastern Affairs (Parsons) to Secretary of State Herter,' 14 October 1959, *FRUS 1958–60*, Note 394, vol. XIX, pp. 792–3.

10. 'Memorandum for the Record, Goodpaster conversation with the President,' 20 June 1959, Ann Whitman International Series, Box 48, Tibet, DDE Library.

11. 'Memorandum from acting Secretary of State Dillon to President Eisenhower,' 16 June 1959, *FRUS 1958–60*, vol. XIX, China, p. 773, ftn 2; and also Memo of 6 July, Declassified, MR 94–168–3, Ann Whitman International Series, Box 48, Tibet, DDE Library.

12. Editorial note, no. 382, *FRUS 1958–60*, vol. XIX, China, pp. 773–4.

13. Ibid., p. 774.

14. Ibid.

15. 'Memorandum from the Assistant Secretary of State for Far Eastern Affairs (Parsons) and the Acting Assistant Secretary for International Organization Affairs (Walmsley) to Secretary of State Herter,' 5 August 1959, *FRUS 1958–60*, vol. XIX, China, p. 774.

16. Ibid., p. 775.

17. Ibid., p. 775.

18. 'Telegram from the Embassy in India to the Department of State,' 4 September 1959, *FRUS 1958–60*, vol. XIX, China, p. 778.

19. Ibid.

20. Ibid.

21. 'Telegram from the Embassy in India to the Department of State,' 5 September 1959, *FRUS 1958–60*, vol. XIX, China, p. 780.

22. Ibid. Brown pushed further and asked that even if India could not sponsor Tibet's case, would their delegation support a constructive action that might be taken by the UN. He said it would depend on the action proposed and then said 'you never know what Krishna Menon will do.' Menon was to be the head of the delegation.

23. 'Telegram from the Department of State to the Embassy in India,' 9 September 1959, *FRUS 1958–60*, vol. XIX, China, pp. 782–3.

24. '418th Meeting of the National Security Council,' 10 September 1959, *FRUS 1958–60*, vol. XIX, China, Editorial note, no. 388, pp. 784–5.

25. 'Telegram from the Delegation to the UN General Assembly to the Department of State,' 18 September 1959, *FRUS 1958–60*, vol. XIX, China, pp. 785–6.

26. Ibid. Oman had an uprising in 1957–9 where the British intervened. They eventually won their independence

27. Ibid., p. 786. Selwyn Lloyd described Nehru as depressed about this futile action in the United Nations. Ibid.

28. Ibid., p. 786.

29. Ibid., p. 787.

30. Ibid.

31. Clearly international law was an important dimension of Tibet's struggle. The hope held by many in Washington was that a successful UN resolution challenging Chinese human rights violations in Tibet would open the way for further discussion and, eventually, a compromise leading to China's agreement on suzerain status for Tibet or US recognition

of the Tibetan government. Gaining these objectives could not occur without US lead-ership, however, and the State Department believed that US support for these goals would serve neither US nor Tibetan interests.

32. 'Telegram from the Delegation to the UN General Assembly to the Department of State,' 8 October 1959, *FRUS 1958–60*, vol. XIX, China, pp. 790–1.

33. Ibid., p. 791.

34. 'Memorandum from the Assistant Secretary of State for Far Eastern Affairs, Parsons, to Secretary of State Herter,' 14 October 1959, *FRUS 1958–60*, vol. XIX, China, p. 793.

35. Ibid.

36. Ibid., p. 793.

37. Ibid.

38. 'Telegram from the Delegation to the UN General Assembly to the Department of State,' 23 October 1959, *FRUS 1958–60*, vol. XIX, p. 796.

39. Ibid.

40. Ibid.

41. 'Memorandum of Conversation (Mr Murphy, Under Secretary for Political Affairs), Wash-ington,' 29 October 1956, *FRUS 1958–60*, vol. XIX, pp. 797–800.

42. Ibid., p. 798.

43. Ibid. A United Nations resolution was passed on 21 October addressing the issue of human rights in Tibet.

44. Interview with Thomas Parrott, December 2005.

45. 'Telegram from the Embassy in India to the Department of State,' 23 November 1959, *FRUS 1958–60*, vol. XIX, pp. 804–5.

46. 'Memorandum for the President The White House, from the Secretary of State, Chris-tian A. Herter,' 7 April 1960, Dulles–Herter Series, Box 12, Folder: Herter, Christian, April 1960 (2), DDE Library. Declassified in 2007.

47. Ibid.

48. Ibid.

49. Ibid.

50. Ibid.

51. 'Memorandum for the Record by the President's Special Assistant for National Security Affairs (Gray),' 4 February 1960, *FRUS 1958–60*, vol. XIX, p. 808.

52. 'Memorandum for the Record, Discussion with the President on Tibet (Gray), 4 Febru-ary 1960, Special Assistants Series, Presidential Subseries, Box 4, 1960—Meetings with the President—Volume 1(7), DDE Library.

53. Ibid., p. 2.

30. THE DALAI LAMA, NEHRU, AND THE CHINESE: A DIFFICULT MIX

1. Note to Nehru, quoted in 'The Sino–Indian Border Dispute,' Section 1:1950–59, DD/I Staff Study, 2 March 1963, CIA/RSS Reference Title Polo XVI, Approved for Release May 2007, p. 8, at http://www.foia.cia.gov/sites/default/files/document_conversions/14/polo-07.pdf, last accessed 1 June 2013.

2. Nehru to Chou En-lai, quoted in 'The Sino–Indian Border Dispute', p. 9.

3. Nehru's letter of 14 December 1958 and Chou's letter of 23 January 1959, in 'The Sino–Indian Border Dispute,' p. 9.

4. Ibid.

5. Ibid.
6. 'The Sino–Indian Border Dispute,' p. i.
7. Avedon, p. 118; Leary, p. 67.
8. Gendun quoted in Avedon, p. 116.
9. Ibid.
10. Ibid.
11. Ibid.
12. Ibid.
13. Avedon, p. 120. In the morning the men were taught to use a 'twenty-six letter, ten number code' for use in their 'wireless transmissions.' The CIA had special radios manufactured for the Tibetans which were no larger than a hand but 'powerful enough to clearly transmit over vast distances.' They were also taught how to parachute out of a plane, rock climbing, and were 'introduced to the fine arts of espionage.' Ibid.
14. Avedon, p. 120; Leary, p. 68.
15. Ibid., p. 121. In Tibet the trained guerrillas would establish resistance cells and would report on the movement of Chinese troops. Ibid. The training of Tibetans at Camp Hale ended in 1965, five years after the new base at Mustang in Nepal.
16. Carole McGranahan, 'Tibet's Cold War: The CIA and the Chushi Gangdrug Resistance, 1956–1974,' *Journal of Cold War Studies*, vol. 8, no. 3 (Summer 2006), p. 119.
17. Roger E. McCarthy, *Tears of the Lotus*, p. 231.
18. Ibid.
19. Ibid., p. 231.
20. McGranahan, p. 120.
21. Interview with Ambassador Lilly, March 2005.
22. Editorial note 337, *FRUS 1964–68*, vol. XXX, p. 713. This training was at Camp Hale and 1964 was the last year of the operation in Colorado before it closed in 1965. See 'Memorandum for the 303 Committee,' 26 January 1968, *FRUS 1964–68*, vol. XXX, pp. 739 and 741.
23. Ibid., p. 723.
24. Ibid.; and also see 'Questions Pertaining to Tibet,' *FRUS 1969–76*, vol. XVII, pp. 1138–9.
25. This was memorialized in the Tashkent Declaration of 10 January 1966.
26. Kristin L. Ahlberg, *Transplanting the Great Society: Lyndon Johnson and Food for Peace* (Columbia, MO: University of Missouri Press, 2008), p. 121.
27. Ibid.
28. Lyndon B. Johnson, 'Address at Johns Hopkins University: Peace Without Conquest,' 7 April 1965. Online by Gerhard Peters and John T. Woolley, *The American Presidency Project*, http://www.presidency.ucsb.edu/ws/?pid=26877, last accessed 1 June 2013.
29. See 'Memorandum from the President's Assistant for National Security Affairs (Kissinger) to President Nixon,' 23 March 1970, *FRUS 1969–76*, vol. XVII, p. 1140.
30. Editorial Note, 274: 'Questions Pertaining to Tibet,' *FRUS 1969–76*, vol. XVII, p. 1140.
31. 'Memorandum Prepared for the 40 Committee,' 11 January 1971, *FRUS 1969–76*, vol. XVII, p. 1146, ftn 1. Henry Kissinger attended this meeting and he asked if everyone agreed with the reduction in financial assistance. The minutes indicate 'All Agreed.' See 'Memorandum from the President's Assistant for National Security Affairs (Kissinger) to President Nixon, 23 March 1970, *FRUS 1969–76*, vol. XVII, p. 1140.

32. Huang Hua translated for Edgar Snow when he interviewed Mao Tse-tung in Yan'an in 1936. In 1971 he was ambassador to Canada and later became China's foreign minister.

33. Ji Chaozhu was a high-level interpreter who later served in Washington and as ambassador to the United Kingdom.

34. Zhang Wenjin was later an ambassador to the US.

35. 'Getting to Beijing: Henry Kissinger's Secret 1971 Trip,' US–China Institute, University of Southern California. Declassified and released 07/21/2011.

36. 'Memorandum of Conversation, Kissinger and Zhou,' 9 July 1971, 4:35–11:20 PM, Top Secret/Sensitive/Exclusively Eyes Only, with cover memo by Lord, 29 July 1971, Box 1033, NSC Files, Miscellaneous Memoranda Relating to HAK Trip to PRC, July 1971, Document 34, http://www.gwu.edu/~nsarchiv/NSAEBB/NSAEBB66/ch-34.pdf, p. 1. Among the Chinese participants were Yeh Chien-ying, vice chairman, Military Affairs Commission. Americans present included Kissinger, NSC staff member John Holdridge, NSC staff member Winston Lord, and NSC staff member Richard Smyser.

37. Ibid., p. 4.

38. Ibid.

39. Ibid., p. 9.

40. Included among Kissinger's small traveling staff was Marine Col. Bud McFarlane, who relayed to the authors in Beijing in 2009 that in three days of top secret talks with senior PLA officers, held in the basement of the Great Hall of the People during that 1971 trip, he detailed the Red Army 'Order of battle': the troops, armaments, and capabilities of the Soviet divisions on China's northern border. The Chinese were impressed with the specificity of McFarlane's briefing and it was later confirmed to have been an important step towards the new US–China relationship.

41. Ibid., p. 10.

42. The Diaoyutai State Guesthouse was built on the site of an 800-year-old garden in Beijing, dating to the Jin dynasty

43. Ibid, p. 6.

44. 'Getting to Beijing: Henry Kissinger's Secret 1971 Trip,' US–China Institute, University of Southern California. Memorandum from Henry Kissinger to the President, 14 July 1971. Declassified and released 07/21/2011.

45. 'My Talks with Chou En-Lai,' 14 July 1971, memo, Kissinger to President, Box 1033, NSC Files, Miscellanous Memoranda Relating to HAK Trip to PRC, July 1971, p. 7. http://www.gwu.edu/~nsarchiv/NSAEBB/NSAEBB66/ch-40.pdf, last accessed 1 June 2013. Chou was just as enthusiastic about the course of events and said to Kissinger that Nixon's agreement to meet Mao 'would shake the world.' Ibid., p. 13.

46. Ibid., p. 26.

47. 'Briefing of the White House Staff on the July 15 Announcement of the President's Trip to Peking,' Secret, Memorandum for the Record, 19 July 1971, Kissinger Transcripts, Item no. KT00309, Digital National Security Archives, p. 5.

48. Ibid.

49. Mao had been ill before the arrival of the Americans and Winston Lord, the note-taker in the historic meeting, remembered Mao, elderly and infirm, reclining in a lounge chair and speaking with difficulty.

50. John Holdridge died in July 2001.

51. Meeting with Peter Rodman, April 2007.

52. White House Memorandum, Top Secret/NODIS/XGDS, Thursday 4 December 1975, Great Hall of the People, Peking. Digital National Security Archives, file no. 00328.

53. Ibid., p. 14.

54. Ibid., p. 9. [Meetings took place on 27 November 1975.]

55. Ibid. He is referring to the Office of Tibet in New York which opened in 1964.

56. Ibid., p. 9

58. Ibid., p. 9. Teng went on to say that it would have been easier if the US had refused the Tibetans visas, to which Ford responded that 'it was done privately.' Ibid.

59. *New York Times*, 15 October 1975.

60. Ibid.

61. Telecon, Mr Habib/The Secretary, 13 October 1975, Kissinger Telephone Conversations: 'Policy Toward Tibet,' Item no. KA14201, Digital National Security Archives, p. 1.

62. Ibid., p. 1.

63. Ibid.

64. Ibid.

65. Ibid.

31. CONCLUSION

1. B. N. Mullik, *My Years with Nehru: The Chinese Betrayal*, pp. 85 and 181.

2. R. Satakopan, 'Nehru will Try to Help Tibetans,' *Modesto Bee and News Herald* (Modesto, California), 31 March 1959, p. 1.

3. See Chapter 10, footnote 451 statement by the State Department legal advisor, Conrad Snow.

4. Beijing's use of maps to support territorial claims has, more recently, been seen in the South China Sea in the 2010–13 period. Beijing claims 80% of the South China Sea, or 3.5 million square miles of ocean, islands, and outcroppings based upon a so-called 'Nine-Dash Line Map' issued by Chiang Kai-shek in 1947. China also claims the Senkakus and other islands in the East China Sea (oil reserves were discovered near the islands in 1968) as traditional and historical territories detailed by a Ming dynasty imperial map.

5. See Professor Mohan Malik, *China's History Card* (Honolulu, HI: Asia–Pacific Center for Security Studies, 2012).

6. See Chapter 30.

7. Discussion at Gyalo Thondup's home with Lezlee Brown Halper, Kalimpong, India, December 2013.

8. Ibid.

9. Authors' interview with Thomas Parrott, Executive Secretary NSC 5412 Group, April 2004.

10. See Kenneth Knaus, *Beyond Shangri-La: America and Tibet's Move into the Twenty-First Century* (Durham, NC: Duke University Press, 2012).

11. Peter Bishop, *The Myth of Shangri-La*.

12. Ibid.

13. Ibid., p. 25.

14. See Matt Spetalnick, 'Obama meets Dalai Lama, angering China,' Washington: Reuters, 18 February 2010.

32. POSTSCRIPT

1. *New York Times*, 4 September 1979. The toned-down version appeared 12 September 1979.
2. HR 3590 was one of fourteen measures concerning conditions in and policy toward Tibet introduced in the US Congress in 1987–8.
3. Mayank.Chhaya, *Dalai Lama: Man, Monk, Mystic*, (New York: Doubleday, 2007).
4. Stefan Halper interview with Senator George Mitchell in Washington, DC, September 2007.
5. Stefan Halper interview with Senator Jesse Helms in Washington, DC, September 2007.
6. Todd Stein, 'Ideas, Advocacy and Dialog on Tibet,' *Wikileaks Documents Open Window on Early US Tibet Policy, and its Mistakes*, International Campaign for Tibet, 2011.
7. Author's conversation with former Secretary of Defense James R. Schlesinger at the Mitre Corporation, April 2008.
8. The new system provides radio and television broadcasts in 56 languages, 24 hours a day, seven days a week.
9. The more things change, the more they remain the same.
10. The conversation took place at the offices of the National Interest in Washington, March 2008. The PLA general has requested his name not to be used.

BIBLIOGRAPHY

Manuscripts and Archival Collections

Archives of the Ministry of Foreign Affairs, Beijing, China

Records of Ministry of Foreign Affairs of the People's Republic of China

British Library, London, UK

Frank Ludlow Papers, India Records Office
A. J. Hopkinson Papers, India Records Office
India Office Records and Archives: Files of the Political and Secret
Office of the Government of India

Dwight D. Eisenhower Library, Abilene, Kansas

Henry A. Bryoade Papers
Robert Cutler Papers
John Foster Dulles Papers
Dwight D. Eisenhower Papers
C. D. Jackson Papers
Ann Whitman Files

Library of Congress, Washington, DC

Loy W. Henderson Papers
Clare Booth Luce Papers
Henry Robinson Luce Papers

National Archives and Records Administration (NARA), College Park, Maryland

Records of the Department of State
Records of the Central Intelligence Agency
Records of the National Security Council
Records of the Office of the Secretary of Defense
Records of the Office of Strategic Services Records (OSS)

BIBLIOGRAPHY

The National Archives, Kew, UK

Records of the Foreign Office

Harry S. Truman Library, Independence, Missouri

Dean Acheson Papers
Henry F. Grady Papers
Gordon Gray Papers
George C. McGhee Papers
Harry S. Truman Papers

Published Government Documents and Documentary Collections

Ashton, S. R. and G. Bennett, eds., *Foreign & Commonwealth Office: Documents of British Policy Overseas*, vol. VIII. London: Whitehall History Publishing, 1997.

Congressional Record: Major Speeches and Debates of Senator Joe McCarthy delivered in the Untied States Senate 1950–1951. New York: Gordon Press, 1975.

Executive Sessions of the Senate Foreign Relations Committee (Historical Series) vol. XI, Eighty-Sixth Congress First Session, 1959. Washington: Government Printing Office, 1960.

Foreign Relations of the United States (FRUS). Washington: Government Printing Office, and http://digicoll.library.wisc.edu/cgi-bin/FRUS/FRUS-idx?type=browse&scope=FRUS. FRUS1.

Gopal S., ed., *Selected Works of Jawaharlal Nehru, vols. 1–21.* New Delhi: Jawaharlal Nehru Memorial Fund, 1984–1997.

Kumar, Ravinder and H. Y. Sharada Prasad, eds. *Selected Works of Jawaharlal Nehru, vols. 22–28.* New Delhi: Jawaharlal Nehru Memorial Fund, 1998–2001.

Prasad, H. Y. Sharada and A. K. Damodaran, eds., *Selected Works of Jawaharlal Nehru, vols. 29–32.* New Delhi: Jawaharlal Nehru Memorial Fund, 2001–3.

Prasad, H. Y. Sharada, A. K. Damodaran and Mushirul Hasan, eds., *Selected Works of Jawaharlal Nehru, vols. 33–35.* New Delhi: Jawaharlal Nehru Memorial Fund, 2003–5.

Presidential Documents Series: Official Conversations and Meetings of Dean, Acheson, 1949–1953. Microfilm. Frederick, Maryland: University Publications of America, 1980.

Public Papers of the Presidents of the United States, Harry S. Truman, January 1 to December 31, 1950. Washington: Government Printing Office, 1965.

Public Papers of the Presidents of the United States: Harry S. Truman 1951. Washington: Government Printing Office, 1965.

Selected Works of Mao Tse-tung, vol. V. Oxford: Pergamon Press, 1977.

'Sino–Indian Border Dispute,' Section 1:1950–59, DD/I Staff Study, 2 March 1963, CIA/RSS Reference Title Polo XVI, Approved for Release May 2007, at http://www.foia.cia.gov/sites/default/files/document_conversions/14/polo-07.pdf, last accessed 1 June 2013.

Tracking the Dragon: National Intelligence Estimates on China During the Era of Mao, 1948–1976. Pittsburgh, PA: Government Printing Office, 2004.

Interviews

Professor Christopher Andrew, Fellow and former President, Corpus Christi College, Cambridge

BIBLIOGRAPHY

Dolma Choephel, Secretary of the Tibetan Youth Congress, Tibetan government-in-exile, Dharamsala, India.

Tsering Dhundup, Secretary of the Department of Home, Tibetan government-in-exile, Dharamsala, India.

Nicolas Dujmovic, CIA historian and intelligence analyst.

Mikel Dunham, author of *Buddha's Warriors*.

Stanton Evans, historian and author of *Blacklisted by History: The Untold Story of Senator Joe McCarthy*.

Robert Ford, radio operator in Tibet and captured by the PLA in 1950, author of *Wind Between the Worlds*.

Bill Gibson, CIA operative in India in the 1950s, and field officer in the Tibet/India theater.

General Andrew Goodpaster, executive assistant and confidant to President Eisenhower and privy to covert operation plans in Tibet.

Keyong He, Professor and Director of the Central University of Nationalities, Beijing.

Bi Hua, Professor and Vice Director at the China Tibetology Research Center, Beijing.

Kenneth Knaus, former CIA operative in India, instructor to the Tibetan resistance fighters and author of *Orphans of the Cold War*.

Thomas Laird, journalist, Tibetan activist and author of *Into Tibet* and *The Story of Tibet: Conversations with the Dalai Lama*.

Ambassador James Lilly, senior American Sinologist, career CIA official, former ambassador to South Korea (1986–9) and to the People's Republic of China (1989–91), and author of *China Hands*.

Winston Lord, Member of the US National Security Council and aid to Henry Kissinger. He accompanied him on the secret trip to China in 1971, and was President Nixon's translator on the 1972 trip where he played a key role in opening up relations with Beijing in 1972. He was a member of the US National Security Council and an aid to Henry Kissinger, accompanying him on the secret trip to China in 1971, and President Nixon's translator on his 1972 trip.

Roger McCarthy, CIA operative and head of the US training program for Tibetan resistance fighters both in Saipan and in Colorado.

Robert McFarlane, military assistant to Henry Kissinger, accompanying him on trips to China. Formerly, he was the National Security advisor to Ronald Reagan.

Ken Millian, CIA operative under cover as American vice consul in Calcutta, involved in the Tibetan operation.

Chris Mullin, Member of Parliament, friend of the Dalai Lama and former journalist.

Ven Thupten Ngodup, the medium of Tibet's state Oracle, Nechung monastery, Tibetan government-in-exile, Dharamsala, India.

Thomas Parrott, secretary to the 5412 Group under President Dwight Eisenhower.

George Patterson, former Scottish missionary, Tibetan activist, author and friend of the Dalai Lama.

Hayden Peake, Curator of the CIA Historical Intelligence Collection.

Thubten Phuntrog, Professor at the Department of Tibetan Studies Central University for Nationalities, Beijing.

William (Bill) D. Roosevelt, Franklin D. Roosevelt's grandson, White House resident and policy analyst.

Samdhong Rinpoche, Prime Minister, Tibetan government-in-exile, Dharamsala, India.

BIBLIOGRAPHY

Thubten Samphel, Secretary of the Department of Information and International Relations, Tibetan government-in-exile, Dharamsala, India.

Tsering Shakya, Tibetan historian and author of *Dragon in the Land of Snows.*

James R. Schlesinger, former Director of the CIA and Secretary of Defense under Presidents Nixon and Ford.

Evan Thomas, journalist and author of *The Very Best Men: The Early Years of the CIA.*

Tsering Thar, Professor and Vice Director of the Department of Tibetan Studies at the Central University for Minorities, Beijing.

John Turner, senior CIA officer in Calcutta and involved in the Tibetan operations.

Daun van Ee, historian and librarian at the Library of Congress, Phuntsog Wangyal, Tibet Foundation, London.

William Wells, former CIA operative in China in the 1940s.

Lian Xiangmin, Professor at the China Tibetology Research Center, Beijing.

Hu Yan, Professor and Director of Ethno-Religion at the Social Development Institute, Party School of the Central Committee of CPC.

Karma Gelek Yuthok, Secretary of the Department of Education, Tibetan government-in-exile, Dharamsala, India.

Lobsang Nyandak Zayul, Minister of Finance and Health, Tibetan government-in-exile, Dharamsala, India.

Books and Articles

Acheson, Dean. *Present at the Creation.* New York: W. W. Norton and Company, 1969.

Ahlberg, Kristin L. *Transplanting the Great Society: Lyndon Johnson and Food for Peace.* Columbia, MO: University of Missouri Press, 2008.

Aldrich, Richard J. *The Hidden Hand: Britain, American and Cold War Secret Intelligence.* New York: Overlook Press, 2001.

———, Gary D. Rawnsley and Ming-Yeh T. Rawnsley, eds. *The Clandestine Cold War in Asia, 1945–65: Western Intelligence, Propaganda and Special Operations.* London: Frank Cass, 2000.

Ambrose, Stephen E. *Eisenhower: Soldier and President.* New York: Simon & Schuster, 1990.

———, *The Victors, Eisenhower and his Boys: The Men of World War II.* New York: Simon & Schuster, 1998.

———, with Richard H. Immerman. *Ike's Spies: Eisenhower and the Espionage Establishment.* New York: Doubleday & Company, Inc, 1981.

Anderson, Benedict, *Imagined Communities.* London: Verso, 1983.

Anderson, Jack. *Confessions of a Muckraker.* New York: Random House, 1979.

Anderson, Jack with Ronald W. May. *McCarthy The Man, The Senator, The 'ISM'.* London: Victor Gollancz Ltd, 1953.

Andrew, Christopher. *For the President's Eyes Only: Secret Intelligence and the American Presidency from Washington to Bush.* London: HarperCollins, 1995.

Andrugtsang, Gompo Tashi. *Four Rivers, Six Ranges.* Dharamsala, India: Information and Publicity Office of the Dalai Lama, 1973.

Arpi, Claude. *The Fate of Tibet.* New Delhi: HarAnand Publishers, 1999.

———, Born in Sin: *The Panchsheel Agreement.* New Delhi: Mittal Press, 2004.

Avedon, John F. *In Exile of the Land of Snows.* New York: Knopf, 1984.

Barrett, David M. *The CIA and Congress: The Untold Story From Truman to Kennedy.* Lawrence, Kansas: University Press of Kansas, 2005.

Beisner, Robert, L. *Dean Acheson: A Life in the Cold War*. Oxford: Oxford University Press, 2006.

Bell, Charles. *Portrait of a Dalai Lama*. London: Rupert Hart-Davis, 1957.

Bishop, Peter. *The Myth of Shangri-La: Tibet, Travel Writing and the Western Creation of Sacred Landscape*. Berkeley: University of California Press, 1989.

Bowles, Chester. *Ambassador's Report*. London: Victor Gollancz Ltd, 1954.

Brands, H. W. *Inside the Cold War, Loy Henderson and the Rise of the American Empire 1918–1961*. New York: Columbia University Press, 1991.

———, *India and the United States: The Cold Peace*. Boston: Twayne Publishers, 1990.

———, *The Specter of Neutralism: The United States and the Emergence of the Third World*. New York: Columbia University Press, 1989.

Branyan, Robert L. and Lawrence H. Larsen, eds. *The Eisenhower Administration, A Documentary History 1953–1961*. New York: Random House, 1971.

Brendon, Piers. *Ike*. New York: Harper and Row, 1986.

Bull, Geoffrey T. *When Iron Gates Yield*. Chicago: Moody Press, 1955.

Chhaya, Mayank. *Dalai Lama: Man, Monk, Mystic*. New York: Doubleday, 2007.

Conboy, Kenneth, and James Morrison. *The CIA's Secret War in Tibet*. Lawrence: University Press of Kansas, 2002.

Cook, Blanche Wiesen. *The Declassified Eisenhower*. New York: Doubleday and Company, 1981.

Craig, Mary. *Kundun. A Biography of the Family of the Dalai Lama of Tibet*. Washington, DC: Counterpoint, 1997.

Crockatt, Richard. *The Fifty Years War: The United States and the Soviet Union in World Politics, 1941–1991*. London: Routledge, 1995.

Cutler, Robert. 'The Development of the National Security Council.' *Foreign Affairs*, vol. 34, April 1956.

Dalai Lama. *Freedom in Exile: The Autobiography of the Dalai Lama*. New York: HarperCollins, 1990.

———, *My Land and My People: Memoirs of the Dalai Lama of Tibet*. New York: McGraw Hill, 1962.

Dodin, Thierry, and Heinz Rather, eds. *Imaging Tibet: Perceptions, Projections and Fantasies*. Boston: Wisdom Publications, 2001.

Dulles, Allen. *The Craft of Intelligence*. New York: Harper and Row, 1963.

———, *The Secret Surrender*. New York: Harper and Row, 1966.

Dunham, Mikel. *Buddha's Warriors*. New York: Penguin, 2004.

Eisenhower, Dwight D. *Mandate for Change: The White House Years, 1953–1956*. New York: Doubleday, 1963.

———, *The White House Years 1956–1961 Waging Peace*. New York: Doubleday, 1965.

Ellsberg, Daniel, *Secrets: A Memoir of Vietnam and the Pentagon Papers*. New York: Viking Penguin, 2002.

Ferrell, Robert H., ed. *Dear Bess, The Letters from Harry to Bess Truman, 1910–1959*. New York: W. W. Norton & Company, 1983.

———, *The Eisenhower Diaries*. New York: W. W. Norton & Company, 1981.

Ford, Corey. *Donovan of the OSS*. London: Robert Hale & Company, 1971.

Ford, Robert. *Wind Between the Worlds*. New York: David McKay, 1957.

Fox, Jonathan. 'Religion as an Overlooked Element of International Relations.' *International Studies Review*, vol. 3, no. 3, Autumn 2001.

BIBLIOGRAPHY

French, Patrick. *Younghusband: The Last Great Imperial Adventurer*. London: HarperCollins, 1994.

Gaddis, John Lewis. *Strategies of Containment: A Critical Appraisal of Postwar American Security Policy*. Oxford: Oxford University Press, 1982.

———, *The United States and the End of the Cold War*. Oxford: Oxford University Press, 1992.

———, *The United States and the Origins of the Cold War, 1941–1947*. New York: Columbia University Press, 1972.

Garver, John W. *The Sino-American Alliance: Nationalist China and American Cold War Strategy in Asia*. New York: M. E. Sharpe, 1997.

George, T. J. S. *Krishna Menon: A Biography*. Edinburgh: J. & J. Gray, 1964.

Giles, Shawn J. Parry. *The Rhetorical Presidency, Propaganda and the Cold War: 1945–1955*. Westport, Connecticut: Praeger, 2002.

Goldstein, Melvyn C. *A History of Modern Tibet, Volume 1, The Demise of the Lamaist State, 1913–1951*. Berkeley, California: University of California Press, 1989.

———, *A History of Modern Tibet, Volume 2, The Calm Before the Storm, 1951–1955*. Berkeley, California: University of California Press, 2007.

———, *The Snow Lion and the Dragon*. Berkeley, California: University of California Press, 1997.

———, 'The United States, Tibet and the Cold War.' *Journal of Cold War Studies*, vol. 8, no. 3, Summer 2006.

Goncharov, Sergei, John W. Lewis, and Kitai Xue. *Uncertain Partners: Stalin, Mao and the Korean War*. Stanford, California: Stanford University Press, 1993.

Gopal, Sarvepalli. *Jawaharlal Nehru, A Biography, Volume II: 1947–1956*. London: Jonathan Cape Ltd., 1979.

———, *Jawaharlal Nehru, A Biography, Volume III: 1956–1964*. London: Jonathan Cape Ltd, 1984.

Gould, B. J. *The Jewel in the Lotus*. London: Chatto and Windus, 1957.

Greenstein, Fred I. and Richard H. Immerman. 'Effective National Security: Recovering the Eisenhower Legacy.' *Political Science Quarterly*, vol. 115, no. 3.

Griffith, Robert. *The Politics of Fear: Joseph R. McCarthy and the Senate*. New York: Hayden Press, 1970.

Grunfeld, Tom A. *The Making of Modern Tibet*. New York: M. E. Sharpe, 1996.

Gupta, Akhil and James Ferguson, eds. *Culture, Power and Place*. Durham: Duke University Press, 2001.

Guptal, Karunakar. *Sino-Indian Relations, 1948–52: The Role of K. M. Panikkar*. New Delhi: T. K. Mukherjee, 1987.

Gustafson, Merlin. 'The Religious Role of the President.' *Midwest Journal of Political Science*, vol. 14, no. 4, November 1970.

Guthrie, Anne. *Madame Ambassador: The Life of Vijaya Lakshmi Pandit*. London: Macmillan, 1963.

Harrer, Heinrich. *Seven Years in Tibet*. New York: E. P. Dutton, 1954.

Herzstein, Robert, E. *Henry R. Luce, Time, and the American Crusade*. Cambridge: Cambridge University Press, 2005.

Hillman, William. *Mr President: Personal diaries, private letters, papers and revealing interviews of Harry S. Truman*. London: Hutchinson, 1952.

Hilton, James. *Lost Horizon*. New York: William Morrow, 1961.

BIBLIOGRAPHY

Holober, Frank. *Raiders of the China Coast: CIA Covert Operations during the Korean War.* Annapolis: Naval Institute Press, 1999.

Hoopes, Townsend. *The Devil and John Foster Dulles.* Boston: Little Brown, 1973.

Hopkirk, Peter. *The Great Game.* New York: Kodansha International, 1992.

———, *Trespassers on the Roof of the World.* London: John Murray, 1982.

Immerman, Richard H., ed. *John Foster Dulles and the Diplomacy of the Cold War.* Princeton: Princeton University Press, 1992.

Jain, Girlal. *Panchsheela and After: A Re-appraisal of Sino-Indian Relations in the Context of the Tibetan Insurrection.* New York: Asia Publishing House, 1960.

Jain, R. K., ed. *China South Asian Relations 1947–1980.* Brighton: Harvester Press, 1981.

Jeffrey-Jones, Rhodri. *The CIA and American Democracy.* New Haven, CT: Yale University Press, 1989.

Jian, Chen. *China's Road to the Korean War.* New York: Columbia University Press, 1994.

Jiang, Arnold Xiangze. *The United States and China.* Chicago: University of Chicago Press, 1988.

Kahn, E. J. Jr. *The China Hands: America's Foreign Service Officers and What Befell Them.* New York: Viking Press, 1972.

Kaul, T. N. *A Diplomat's Diary: 1947–1999, China, India and the United States.* New Delhi: Macmillan. 2000.

———, *Diplomacy in Peace and War: Recollections and Reflections.* Bombay: Vikas Publishing House, 1979.

Keane, Douglas and Michael Warner, eds. *Foreign Relations, 1950–1955: The Intelligence Community.* Washington, DC: United States Government Printing Office, 2007.

Kearny, Robert N. 'Sinhalese Nationalism and Social Conflict in Ceylon.' *Pacific Affairs,* vol. 37, no. 2, Summer 1964.

Kennan, F. George. *George F. Kennan: Memoirs 1925–1950.* London: Hutchinson, 1968.

Kissinger, Henry. *Diplomacy.* New York: Simon & Schuster, 1994.

———, *American Foreign Policy; Three Essays.* London: Weidenfeld & Nicolson, 1969.

Knaus, John Kenneth. *Orphans of the Cold War.* New York: Public Affairs, 1999.

———, *Beyond Shangri-La: America and Tibet's Move into the Twenty-First Century.* Durham, NC: Duke University Press, 2012.

Knott, Stephen F. *Secret and Sanctioned: Covert Operations and the Presidency.* Oxford: Oxford University Press, 1996.

Koen, Ross Y. *The China Lobby in American Politics.* New York: Octagon Books, 1974.

Kux, Dennis. *Estranged Democracies: India and the United States, 1941–1991.* London: Sage Publishers, 1994.

Laird, Thomas. *Into Tibet: The CIA's First Atomic Spy and his Secret Expedition to Lhasa.* New York: Grove Press, 2002.

———, *The Story of Tibet: Conversations with the Dalai Lama.* New York: Grove Press, 2006.

Lamb Alistar. *Tibet, China and India, 1914–1950.* Hertingfordbury, UK: Roxford Books, 1989.

Lauren, Paul Gordon, ed. *The China Hand's Legacy: Ethics and Diplomacy.* Boulder, Colorado: Westview Press, 1987.

Lawrence, Mark Atwood and Fredrik Logevall, eds. *The First Vietnam War: Colonial Conflict and Cold War Crisis.* Cambridge, Mass: Harvard University Press, 2007.

Leary, William M. *Perilous Missions: Civil Air Transport and CIA Covert Operations in Asia.* Tuscaloosa, Alabama: University of Alabama Press, 1984.

————, ed. *The Central Intelligence Agency: History and Documents*. Tuscaloosa, Alabama: University of Alabama Press, 1984.

————, 'Secret Mission to Tibet.' *Air and Space*, December 1997/January 1998.

Li, Hongshan and Zhaohui Hong, eds. *Image, Perception, and the Making of US–China Relations*. Lanham, Maryland: University Press of America, 1998.

Li, Laura Tyson. *Madame Chiang Kai-shek*. New York: Grove Press, 2006.

Lilley, James. *China Hands: Nine Decades of Adventure, Espionage, and Diplomacy in Asia*. New York: Public Affairs, 2004.

Lopez, Donald S. Jr. *Prisoners of Shangri-La: Tibetan Buddhism and the West*. Chicago: University of Chicago Press, 1998.

Maraini, Fosco. *Secret Tibet*. New York: Viking Press, 1952.

Marchetti, Victor, and John D. Marks. *The CIA and the Cult of Intelligence*. New York: Alfred A. Knopf, 1974.

Maxwell, Neville. *India's China War*. New York: Pantheon Books, 1971.

McCarthy, Roger E. *Tears of the Lotus*. Jefferson, NC: McFarland and Company, 1997.

McCullough, David. *Truman*. New York: Simon & Schuster, 1992.

McGhee, Ambassador George. *Envoy to the Middle World*. New York: Harper and Row, 1969.

McGranahan, Carole. 'Arrested Histories: Between Empire and Exile in 20th Century Tibet.' PhD dissertation, University of Michigan, Ann Arbor, 2001.

————, 'Tibet's Cold War: The CIA and the Chushi Gangdrug Resistance, 1956–1974.' *Journal of Cold War Studies*, vol. 8, no. 3, Summer 2006, pp. 102–30.

McKay, Alex, ed. *Tibet and her Neighbours: A History*. London: Edition Hanshorg Mayer, 2003.

McMahon, Robert, J. *The Cold War on the Periphery: The United States, India and Pakistan*. New York: Columbia University Press, 1994.

————, 'US Policy toward South Asia and Tibet during the Early Cold War.' *Journal of Cold War Studies*, vol. 8, no. 3, Summer 2006.

Merrill, Dennis, ed. *The Documentary History of the Truman Presidency, The Central Intelligence Agency, Its Founding and the Dispute over Its Mission, 1945–1954*. Maryland: University Publications of America, 1998.

Millis, Walter, ed. *The Forrestal Diaries: The Inner History of the Cold War*. London: Cassell & Company, 1952.

Mitrovich, Gregory. *Undermining the Kremlin: America's Strategy to Subvert the Soviet Bloc, 1947–1956*. Ithaca: Cornell University Press, 2000.

Moraes, Frank. *Jawaharlal Nehru: A Biography*. New York: Macmillan, 1956.

————, *The Revolt in Tibet*. New York: Sterling Publishers, 1960.

Mullik, B. N. *The Chinese Betrayal, My Years with Nehru*. Bombay, India: Allied Publishers, 1971.

Mullin, Chris. 'Tibetan Conspiracy.' *Far Eastern Economic Review*, vol. 39, no. 36, 5 September 1975, pp. 30–4.

Neils, Patricia. *China Image: In the Life and Times of Henry Luce*. Savage, Maryland: Rowman and Littlefield, 1990.

Nixon, Edgar B., ed. *Franklin D. Roosevelt and Foreign Affairs*. 3 vols. Cambridge, Mass.: Belknap Press of Harvard University Press, 1969.

Nixon, Richard. *The Memoirs of Richard Nixon*. New York: Grosset and Dunlap, 1978.

Norbu, Dawa. *Red Star over Tibet*. London: Collins, 1974.

Norbu, Thubten J. *Tibet is My Country*. New York: Dutton, 1961.

BIBLIOGRAPHY

Otis, Graham L. Jr. and Meghan Robinson Wander, eds. *Franklin D. Roosevelt: His Life and Time*. Boston: G. K. Hall and Co., 1985.

Pandit, Vijaya Lakshmi. *The Scope of Happiness*. New York: Crown Publishers, 1979.

Panikkar, K. M. *In Two Chinas: Memoirs of a Diplomat*. London: Allen and Unwin, 1955.

Patterson, George N. *A Fool at Forty*. Waco, Texas: Word Books, 1970.

———, *God's Fool*. London: Faber and Faber, 1956.

———, *Journey with Loshay: A Tibetan Odyssey*. London: Long Riders' Guild Press, 2004.

———, *Requiem for Tibet*. London: Aurum Press, 1990.

———, *Patterson of Tibet*. San Diego: ProMotion Press, 1998.

———, *Tibet in Revolt*. London: Faber and Faber, 1960.

_———, *Tragic Destiny*. London: Faber and Faber, 1959.

Peissel, Michel. *Mustang, The Secret Kingdom*. New York: E. P. Dutton, 1967.

———, *The Secret War in Tibet*. Boston: Little, Brown and Company, 1972.

Powers, John. *History as Propaganda: Tibetan Exiles versus the People's Republic of China*. Oxford: Oxford University Press, 2004.

Prados, John. *Presidents' Secret Wars: CIA and Pentagon Covert Operations from World War II through the Persian Gulf*. Chicago: Ivan R. Dee, 1996.

———, *Safe for Democracy: The Secret Wars of the CIA*. Chicago: Ivan R. Dee, 2006.

Rajan, M. S. *India in World Affairs: 1954–56*. New York: Asia Publishing House, 1965.

Ram, Janaki. *V. K. Krishna Menon: A Personal Memoir*. Oxford: Oxford University Press, 1997.

Rhinehart, James. 'Covert Action in High Altitudes,' *Studies in Intelligence*. Langley, Virginia: Central Intelligence Agency, Spring 1976.

Richardson, Hugh E. *High Peaks, Pure Earth: Collected Writings on Tibetan History and Culture*. London: Serinda Publications, 1998

———, *Tibet and its History*. Boulder, Colorado: Shambhala Publications, 1984

———, 'Tibetan Précis.' Calcutta: Government of India Press, 1945.

Robbins, Christopher. *Air America*. London: Corgi/Transworld Publishers, 1988.

Rositzke, Harry. *CIA's Secret Operations*. New York: Reader's Digest Press, 1977.

Ross, Robert S. and Jiang Changbin, eds. *Re-examining the Cold War: US–China Diplomacy, 1954–1973*. Cambridge, Mass.: Harvard University Press, 2001.

Rotter, Andrew, J. *Comrades at Odds: The United States and India, 1947–1964*. Ithaca: Cornell University Press, 2000.

Schewe, Donald B., ed. *Franklin D. Roosevelt and Foreign Affairs, January 1937–August 1939*. 11 vols. New York: Garland, 1979–83.

Schrecker, Ellen. *The Age of McCarthyism: A Brief History with Documents*. Boston: Bedford/St Martins, 2002.

Schuster, Tom. 'The CIA's War with Red China and other Asian Lands.' *Man's* Magazine, September 1972.

Sen, Chanakya. *Tibet Disappears*. London: Asia Publishing House, 1960.

Shakabpa, Tsepon W. D. *Tibet, A Political History*. New York: Potala Publications, 1984.

———, *One Hundred Thousand Moons*. Leiden: Brill, 1976.

Shakya, Tsering. *Dragon in the Land of Snows: A History of Modern Tibet since 1947*. London: Pimlico, 1999.

Smith, Harris R. *OSS: The Secret History of America's First Central Intelligence Agency*. Berkeley, California: University of California Press, 1972.

BIBLIOGRAPHY

Smith, Joseph Burkholder. *Portrait of a Cold Warrior: Second Thoughts of a CIA Agent*. New York: Random House, 1981.

Smith, Warren W. *Tibetan Nation: A History of Tibetan Nationalism and Sino-Tibetan Relations*. Boulder, Colorado: Westview Press, 1996.

Snellgrove, David, and Hugh E. Richardson. *A Cultural History of Tibet*. London: George Weidenfeld & Nicolson, 1968.

Sorenson, Thomas C. *The Word War, The Story of American Propaganda*. New York: Harper and Row, 1968.

Swanberg, W. A. *Luce and his Empire*. New York: Charles Scribner, 1972.

Theoharis, Athan, Richard Immerman, Loch Johnson, Kathryn Olmsted, and John Prados, eds. *The Central Intelligence Agency: Security Under Scrutiny*. Westport, Connecticut: Greenwood Press, 2006.

Thomas, Evan. *The Very Best Men*. New York: Simon and Schuster, 1995.

Thomas, Lowell, Jr. *Out of This World*. New York: Greystone Press, 1950.

Tolstoy, Ilya. 'Across Tibet from India to China.' *National Geographic*, August 1946.

Tong, Hollington K., edited by Walter C. Mih. *Chiang Kai-shek's Teacher and Ambassador*. Bloomington, Indiana: Authorhouse, 2005.

Truman, Harry S. *Memoirs of Harry S. Truman. Volume One, 1945: Year of Decisions*. New York: Doubleday & Company, Inc., 1955.

————, *Memoirs of Harry S. Truman. Volume Two, 1946–1952: Years of Trial and Hope*. New York: Doubleday, 1955.

Tuchman, Barbara. *Stilwell and the American Experience in China*. New York: Macmillan, 1970.

Tucker, Nancy Bernkopf. *Patterns in the Dust*. New York: Columbia University Press, 1984.

Van Slyke, Lyman P. *The China White Paper*. Stanford: Stanford University Press, 1967.

Warner, Michael, ed. *CIA Cold War Records: The CIA Under Harry Truman*. Washington, DC: Government Printing Office, 1994.

Whitfield, Stephen. *The Culture of the Cold War*. Baltimore: Johns Hopkins University Press, 1991.

Wolpert, Stanley. *Roots of Confrontation in South Asia*. New York: Oxford University Press, 1982.

Younghusband, Sir Francis. *India and Tibet*. London: John Murray, 1910.

Yuthok, Dorje Yudon, ed. Michael Harlin. *House of the Turquoise Roof*. Ithaca: Snow Lion Publications, 1990.

Zhai, Qiang. *The Dragon, the Lion, and the Eagle: Chinese/British/American Relations, 1949–1958*. Kent, Ohio: Kent State University Press, 1994.

Zhang, Shuguang and Jian Chen, eds. *Chinese Communist Foreign Policy and the Cold War in Asia: New Documentary Evidence, 1944–1950*. Chicago: Imprint Publications, 1996.

Newspapers and Magazines

Life magazine
Newsweek magazine
New York Times
Time magazine
Washington Post

BIBLIOGRAPHY

Online Resources and Papers

Acheson, Dean. 'Congressional Testimony.' 1 June 1951 at http://www.trumanlibrary.org/whistlestop/study_collections/korea/large/koreapt4_4.htm, last accessed 1 June 2013.

Eisenhower, Dwight D. 'Address to the Annual Convention at the National Junior Chamber of Commerce, Minneapolis, Minnesota.' 10 June 1953 at http://www.eisenhowermemorial.org/speeches/19530610Address at the Annual Convention of the National Junior Chamber of Commerce.htm, last accessed 1 June 2013.

Eisenhower, Dwight D. 'Remarks to the Staff of the United States Information Agency.' 10 November 1953 at http://www.presidency.ucsb.edu/ws/?pid=9758, last accessed 1 June 2013.

Eisenhower, Dwight D. 'Remarks Upon Lighting the National Community Christmas Tree.' 24 December 1953 at http://www.presidency.ucsb.edu/ws/?pid=9791, last accessed 1 June 2013.

Eisenhower, Dwight D. 'Statement on Military Aid to Pakistan.' 25 February 1954 at http://www.presidency.ucsb.edu/ws/?pid=10171, last accessed 1 June 2013.

Herzstein, Robert. 'Alfred Kohlberg, Global Entrepreneur and Hyper-Nationalist.' A paper presented to a conference at the Historical Society, Chapel Hill, North Carolina, 3 June 2006.

'Introduction to Eisenhower and Religion at the Dwight D. Eisenhower Library.' http://www.eisenhower.archives.gov/Research/Subject_Guides/PDFs/Eisenhower_and_religion.pdf, last accessed 1 June 2013.

Leeker, Joe S. 'The History of Air America'. 15 August 2003 at http://www.utdallas.edu/library/collections/speccoll/Leeker/history/index.html, last accessed 1 June 2013.

Memorial Plaque, Air America. 30 May 1987 at http://www.air-america.org/About/Memorial_Plaque.shtml, last accessed 1 June 2013.

Nye, Joseph S. and Joanne J. Myers. 'Soft Power: The Means to Success in World Politics.' 13 April 2004 at http://www.cceia.org/resources/transcripts/4466.html, last accessed 1 June 2013.

'Panel of Consultants on covert activities of the Central Intelligence Agency.' 26 July 1954 at http://www.eisenhowermemorial.org/presidential-papers/first, term/documents/993.cfm, last accessed 1 June 2013.

The Tibet Fund: Fulbright Scholars. Annual Report 2003 at http://www.tibetfund.org/annual_reports/2003report/pg3.html, last accessed 1 June 2013.

Truman, Harry S. 'Radio and Television Address to the American People on the Situation in Korea.' 1 September 1950 at http://www.presidency.ucsb.edu/ws/?pid=13604, last accessed 1 June 2013.

Truman, Harry S. 'Special Message to the Congress on the Famine in India.' 12 February 1951 at http://www.presidency.ucsb.edu/ws/?pid=14011, last accessed 1 June 2013.

Truman, Harry S. 'The Truman Doctrine.' 12 March 1947 at http://avalon.law.yale.edu/20th_century/trudoc.asp, last accessed 1 June 2013.

Truman, Harry S. 'The President's News Conference.' 3 January 1950 at http://www.presidency.ucsb.edu/ws/?pid=13678, last accessed 1 June 2013.

INDEX

INDEX